THE FUTURE OF THE SOVIET PAST

THE FUTURE OF THE SOVIET PAST

The Politics of History in Putin's Russia

Edited by Anton Weiss-Wendt
and Nanci Adler

Indiana University Press

This book is a publication of

Indiana University Press
Office of Scholarly Publishing
Herman B Wells Library 350
1320 East 10th Street
Bloomington, Indiana 47405 USA

iupress.org

© 2021 by Indiana University Press

Manufactured in the United States of America

Cataloging information is available from the Library of Congress.

ISBN 978-0-253-05759-4 (hardback)
ISBN 978-0-253-05762-4 (paperback)
ISBN 978-0-253-05761-7 (ebook)

First printing 2021

For Arsenii Roginskii
in lasting memory

Contents

Part III: Remembering and Framing the Soviet Past beyond Russia's Borders

Acknowledgments

THIS VOLUME WAS inspired by a number of rich contributions to a 2016 international conference on "The Future of the Soviet Past," a concern one of the present editors had been pondering for over a decade. The event, accompanied by the opening of an exhibition, *The Gulag: What Grandfather Didn't Tell*, was generously supported by the Norwegian Foreign Ministry and organized by the Norwegian Holocaust Center in Oslo. The editors selected those presentations that stood out for their originality and recruited additional submissions from leading colleagues in the field. The editorial process has been long and rigorous, and in the course of writing, we witnessed, experienced, and subsequently incorporated many new, troubling manifestations of the current regime's history politics.

We thank the authors for their diligence; willingness to engage with our critical comments, patience, and conscientiousness; and, above all, the high quality of their work. We hope the provocative questions they raise on the fraught, politicized history and historicized politics of the Soviet experience will now—a generation after the system's collapse—advance the discussion.

The team at Indiana University Press, especially Jennika Baines, has been exceptional—substantively engaged and highly supportive of this project from early on. We would also like to express our gratitude to the external referees for their careful scrutiny and very helpful comments and suggestions.

Last, but perhaps most important of all, we are deeply indebted to Arsenii Roginskii for his moral fiber, erudition, and courage. The founder and decades-long chairman of Memorial, Roginskii prioritized the pursuit of historical accuracy above his personal safety. He was at the helm of most initiatives and debates in Russia regarding the remembrance and commemoration of victims of Stalinism. Roginskii—historian, former dissident, former Gulag prisoner, the son of a victim of the Stalinist terror, born in the camp "zone"—led Memorial in challenging, by scholarly and civil means, the arbitrary use of authority and demanded no less than an accounting of and accountability for past crimes. This book is dedicated to his legacy.

Nanci Adler and Anton Weiss-Wendt

THE FUTURE OF THE SOVIET PAST

Introduction

Revisiting the Future of the Soviet Past and the Memory of Stalinist Repression

Nanci Adler and Anton Weiss-Wendt

At the end of the Soviet era, it seemed inevitable that the nation's history of repression would be more fully acknowledged and redressed. By 2005, as the future of the Soviet past became increasingly unpredictable, this expectation proved inaccurate.[1] Since then, the trend to manage national and public memory by repressing, controlling, or even co-opting the memory of repression grew stronger. Such fashioning of a good future out of a "bad past" has been facilitated by the construction of a "usable past" for the national narrative.[2] This narrative is reinforced by a patriotism cultivated through museum exhibitions, publications, films, school curricula, and legislation. Included in this form of patriotism is the casual acceptance of repression, which has been successfully coupled with the valorization of Stalin and his role in the Second World War. Many of these trends are generated from the top down, but they have found broad public resonance and are also reinforced from the bottom up—with the support of the Orthodox Church and the emergent cult surrounding the Soviet (and Stalin's) victory in the Great Patriotic War. While there are countercurrents from parts of civil society, they have met considerable resistance. In the absence of judicial reckoning, a truth commission, or a host of other institutionalized approaches to confront a repressive past, the current regime appears to be trudging forward with no coherent vision or even particular impetus to move past its Soviet past. This is the backdrop that forms the current collection. In this introductory chapter, we outline some of the more prominent, sometimes contradictory trends that inform present remembrance of the Soviet past and the politics of history and raise a number of questions that receive a more comprehensive treatment in individual chapters.

Before turning to the volume's contents, in this chapter we seek to examine the efforts to repress the memory of repression, the unifying force of "triumph" in the national narrative, and the evolving authoritarian turn in historymaking. Although it is not our intention to conflate the Soviet past with the Stalinist past, our approach derives from the premise that a default political culture of authoritarianism both preceded Stalin and characterized his successor regimes. Hence, in this volume, the editors define Stalinism not so much as the personal evil of Stalin (the person) but rather as a larger phenomenon (the system). Thus framed, it might well be applied to the entire Soviet period—as it was by the nascent organization Memorial in the 1980s. Arguably its effects have persisted all the way into the present. We hope with these reflections to contribute to the debate on the long shadow of Stalinism.

Since coming to power in 1999, Vladimir Putin successfully wrestled control over state affairs. In the process of consolidating power, he curbed many elements of a democratic society that had been emerging since the late 1980s, including a pluralistic vision of the country's past. The post-1991 period offered no shortage of examples that attest to the enduring legacy of the Soviet past, including the fact that since 2014, references to all things Soviet have become ubiquitous. Sponsored and variously promoted by Putin's government, an emphasis on the positive aspects of the Soviet experience has become a staple of the new (old) Russian national narrative.

Some of the more recent events and debates related to history in Russia—complete with the attendant resurrection of Soviet-era symbols—offer insight into the main narrative on the past promoted by the present regime. This narrative has come to include the (unofficial) rehabilitation of Stalin. In February of 2015, for example, a monument to Stalin, Churchill, and Roosevelt attending the 1943 Tripartite Conference opened at Yalta, in Crimea. In his speech at the UN General Assembly that September, President Putin referred to the Yalta Agreement (sometimes referred to as the "Yalta betrayal" in early Western historiography) as a foundation for world peace and security.[3] Alongside Russian state officials attending the monument unveiling ceremony at Yalta was Alexander "the Surgeon" Zaldostanov, leader of the "patriotic" biker club Night Wolves (see chap. 2). In the run-up to the seventieth anniversary of May 9 (Victory Day), widely celebrated in Russia, Zaldostanov made headlines organizing a Night Wolves' bike ride through Belorussia and Poland all the way to Berlin.[4] Later that year, the Night Wolves ran a "patriotic" biker show in Sevastopol that was covered by major Russian television channels. Featuring an eclectic mix of Russian and Soviet paraphernalia, the show's grand finale reconstructed the Battle of Stalingrad with bikers dressed up as Red Army soldiers and German "fascists." Zaldostanov, who codirected the show, evoked the "great Stalin and the great Soviet people."[5] Stalingrad, a seminal battle and turning point in the war, was being instrumentalized to cultivate national pride in the Soviet past, which was conflated with pride in Stalin and vice versa.

The glorification of this past is becoming more pronounced. As if it were coordinated, shortly after the Sevastopol performance, a three-meter-tall statue of Stalin opened in the Mari El Republic—one of over forty such edifices built by local initiative across Russia in the past few years. If lucky, one can even catch a glimpse of Stalin and/or Putin emblazoned by some motorists on their (expensive foreign) cars in Moscow and other major cities. Following the 2014 publication of a calendar devoted to Stalin by the Russian Orthodox Church, Patriarch Kirill of Moscow suggested that the Russians should forget neither the mass terror of the 1930s nor all the good that Stalin had done for the country—a message supported by the Kremlin and receiving broad resonance among the populace.

Nearly thirty years—an entire generation—after the collapse of the Soviet Union, the history of the crimes of Stalin has been so successfully glossed over that nationwide polls show his popularity edging back toward its pre-de-Stalinization levels.[6] According to a 2015 poll (and many later surveys), 38 percent of the respondents agreed that the sacrifices of the Soviet people during the Stalin era were justified by the results that were achieved in such a short period.[7] Apparently industrialization and the wartime victory were more relevant to those polled than the millions of victims who can be traced back, in part, to the very same accomplishments. In 2016, 40 percent of the respondents believed Stalin should *not* be considered a state criminal and appraised the Stalin era as being more "good" than "bad."[8] Finally, in 2017, 46 percent of those polled viewed Stalin with respect and even enthusiasm.[9] Stalin's burgeoning popularity reflects the longing to restore the country's former prestige and the security of a more strictly, if forcibly, regulated society—a trend followed but also led by the present regime.

Such ambivalence is reflected at all levels. In August of 2015, Prime Minister Dmitrii Medvedev signed a bill memorializing the victims of Soviet political repression, followed by the opening of a new Gulag history museum sponsored by the Moscow city government later that year. In its permanent display and public programs, the museum focuses not on how many millions Stalin killed but rather on the individual fates of the victims.[10] Although its depiction of gross human rights violations within the Gulag is accurate, it avoids mentioning that the system of repression beyond the Gulag was the modus operandi of Soviet rule. Nor does its critical appraisal extend to the present regime and current human rights violations.

At the same time, even as the Russian Duma considered the draft proposal against the revival of Stalinism, the authorities cracked down on, among others, the anti-Stalinist organization Memorial—Russia's oldest and most respected human rights watchdog. In 2015, the label of "foreign agent" was slapped on the St. Petersburg branch of Memorial for being a recipient of foreign funds, and the following year the Ministry of Justice confiscated thirty-two thousand pages of documents from Memorial's Moscow headquarters.[11] The organization has been accused of "undermining Russia's constitutional foundations" and even of attempting to overthrow the government.[12] In this environment of mixed messages, despite formal measures that purport to criminalize pro-Stalin propaganda, the parallel process of rehabilitation of Stalin continues—on busses and monuments, in stores and textbooks, and in the public space.[13] The Communist Party capitalized on this trend by declaring 2016 the year of Stalin and the "Stalin Spring."[14] The initiative to better educate the populace on Stalin marked the eightieth anniversary of the 1936 Constitution (popularly known as the Stalin Constitution), which proclaimed the primacy of the Communist Party. Such select remembrance led one liberal politician to cynically comment at the time, "When they talk about the Stalin era, they imagine the holster at the side, but not the barrel to the back of their neck."[15]

Had Stalin and Stalinism been formally judged after the collapse of the Soviet Union, any related glorification or commercialization would have been proscribed. Such an opportunity presented itself at the 1992 trial to determine the constitutionality of the ban on the Communist Party (see chap. 3). Looking back, in a 1998 interview with one of this volume's editors, Sergei Kovalev, former dissident and human rights commissioner under Yeltsin, suggested this could have been a "Russian Nuremberg" on the crimes of Communism.[16] It never ended up getting beyond the issue at hand and decidedly did not address Stalin's crimes head on. Consequently, nearly thirty years later, Stalin, his era, and his symbols—not illegal or taboo—have been gradually appropriated by mass culture. Stalin has increasingly seeped into the public space: matreshka dolls with the image of Stalin have been a permanent feature of tourist bazaars; one can dine at restaurants named after Stalin (Novosibirsk, Nizhnii Novgorod), hire security services from Chekist (Tiumen), get pipelines repaired by Stalinism (Sochi), and pay Beria (Volgograd) to carry out soil works. A Soviet-era adage proclaimed that "Lenin is always with us." It alluded to the omnipresence of the leader of the Bolshevik Revolution in public and private spaces. Lenin—although still physically with us, as he lays embalmed in a mausoleum on Red Square—has now been more or less relegated, along with the Revolution, to the Communist past. Stalin has not; one might cogently argue that "Stalin is always with us."

The Repressed Memory of Repression

In 2009, Memorial presciently asserted that "de-Stalinization was Russia's acutest problem at the moment."[17] It is an even larger problem now, ten years later. The politically expedient imposition of a selective national amnesia regarding the Gulag—its causes and consequences—undermines the integrity of the collective memory and further marginalizes and victimizes the dwindling generation of

Gulag survivors. By contrast, the issue prioritized by Russia's past and present rulers was not confronting this criminal history but rather strengthening the stability and legitimacy of the regime.

Nevertheless, to the surprise of many, the head of the Presidential Human Rights Council stated in 2010 that the agency's main purpose was the "de-Stalinization of public opinion," however ill-fated that initiative turned out.[18] That Russia would face this problem twenty years after the fall of the Soviet Union had not been anticipated, for the condemnation of Stalinism during glasnost had been so extensive and seemed so profound. Thus, for example, no comprehensive educational tools were put in place that might have countered the present, positive reinterpretation of the country's (mis)fortunes under Stalin. In consequence, the adulation of Stalin that appeared as an aberration around the celebration of the sixtieth anniversary of the victory in the Second World War became nearly the norm, or was at least perceived as innocuous, ten years later. In 2005, a portrait of Generalissimo Stalin on a trolleybus in St. Petersburg caused a furor, but in 2015, his image emblazoned on private cars, advertising boards, and posters no longer provoked outrage. The liberal intelligentsia reacted to the emergence of Stalin nostalgia with a mixture of shock, aversion, and incomprehension. Even though independent historians—if they can be identified as a cohesive group in today's Russia—are better equipped to explain this phenomenon than anyone else, their abilities to confront it are constrained.

The ongoing crackdown has generated countercurrents, even if they are only ripples. One of the most prominent such initiatives has been Memorial's "Last Address" campaign, which enables individuals to place name plaques on the buildings where their relatives were arrested, often never to be seen again. These plaques display eight lines, for example: "HERE LIVED VLADIMIR ABRAMOVICH NIKOLAEV; PEDIATRICIAN, BORN 1902, ARRESTED 1936, EXECUTED ON 19/12/1938; REHABILITATED IN 1961."[19] A starkly empty square cut to the left of the text represents the void the repression created in the families of millions of Soviet citizens through arrest, exile, and/or execution. It also represents the void created by the official silence. In addition, in commemoration of the Day of Political Prisoners on October 29, Memorial holds an annual ceremony at the monument to victims of totalitarianism in Moscow. The ceremony, Vozvrashchenie Imen (Returning of Names), consists of reading aloud, from ten in the morning until ten at night, the names of executed individuals, which is barely enough time to recite two thousand names, let alone the names of tens of thousands of executed Moscovites. In 2018, the Moscow city government only reluctantly granted permission to hold the event.[20]

Juggling mixed messages, in October of 2017, President Putin unveiled the state- and crowd-funded Wall of Grief, a monument to the victims of Stalinism, in Moscow.[21] The state did not give the green light to the monument until

Fig. 0.1. Returning of Names ceremony, Lubyanka Square, Moscow, October 29, 2016. Photo by Nanci Adler.

Fig. 0.2. Wall of Grief plaque, Moscow, November 2018. Photo by Nanci Adler.

2015. The plaque that marks the entrance states: "Monument to the Victims of Political Repression Wall of Grief. Erected by decree of the President of the Russian Federation Vladimir V. Putin through government's funding and popular donations." The inscription conspicuously fails to address the issue of agency, as if Stalinism were a natural disaster. Furthermore, it largely credits Putin and his government for their efforts.

In his remarks, Putin, standing next to Patriarch Kirill, invited the audience to mourn the victims but not to destabilize the country through confrontation and score settling.[22] The abstract reference to the "victims of political repression" in the memorial's name goes back to the official interpretation of Stalin's crimes as set forth in 1956 by Nikita Khrushchev in his "Secret Speech" denouncing Stalin's "cult of personality." Khrushchev never raised the issue of the state's responsibility for the crimes, which he attributed to Stalin and his (deceased) henchmen, thus limiting it to the political purges of 1937–38. Putin's speech at the monument's opening ceremony sixty-one years later was even more oblique. Without mentioning Stalin by name, he spoke vaguely of the "tragedy," "terrible past," "cruel blow," and "dark events" that should never be forgotten or justified. In essence, such circumspect references frame the dark events as some sort of disaster that hit the country rather than a deliberate Soviet policy targeting its own population.[23] Politically, drawing a line under Communist mass crimes—especially during the centennial of the Bolshevik Revolution—served Putin well. The Russian Orthodox Church has been a faithful ally of the Kremlin not least because of their focus on the martyrs, which helps the state draw a thick line when it comes to the discussion of perpetrators. Such reconceptualization of the past has served as a short-term remedy to circumvent any obligation for Russia to undertake transitional justice—the generally accepted norm for successor states in the aftermath of conflict, repression, or dictatorship.[24]

Factors such as the Russian annexation of Crimea, the targeted destabilization of Ukraine's eastern regions, and a more aggressive posture against the West generally have fueled speculations about a new Cold War in the making. One can effectively argue that an inability or unwillingness to decisively break with the Soviet past is among the most essential determinants of Russia's policymaking. The concept of a hostile encirclement, which is a staple of current Russian propaganda, had been a defining feature of the Bolshevik mindset. In this vein, Marxist insistence on the control of the means of production had been subconsciously translated into the monochromatic interpretation of history promoted by Putin's government.

Putin, formerly a KGB officer, has helped facilitate the Soviet myth of the Soviet security police as a professional organization predating Stalin with no innocent blood on its hands. Although it was actually Yeltsin who introduced the Day of Secret Service Workers, Putin took it a step further by honoring the

Federal Security Service (FSB) in the Kremlin. The new monuments to the head of the Cheka, Felix Dzerzhinsky, that keep popping up in Russia (although with less frequency than those to Stalin) coincide with calls to return the "Iron Felix" statue to Lubyanka Square. The 1991 toppling of this monument from its perch in front of KGB headquarters in Moscow was the iconic symbol for the fall of the Soviet Union. Nearly three decades later, the term *chekist* is being used not derogatorily but rather as an honorary designation for the security police personnel. This is a telling illustration of the disproportionate authority enjoyed by law enforcement agencies and the military (*silovye struktury*; *siloviki*) in Russia. The head of the FSB, Alexander Bortnikov, exhibits pride in the continuity of the Cheka/OGPU/NKVD/KGB/FSB, as attested to by the evidence he cites of the agency's good work. In a December 2017 interview with *Rossiiskaia gazeta*, he claimed that "archival materials testify to the existence of an objective side in a significant portion of the criminal cases, including those underlying the well-known public trials."[25] He further reinforced the FSB self-image as a select group of people devoted to protecting the interests of the state. This siege mentality is accompanied by attempts to suppress civil society that hark back to Soviet propaganda images of capitalist encirclement, with internal enemies aided and abetted by foreign enemies. When coupled with the unchecked power the FSB wields, that mentality informs political decisions that further isolate Russia from the rest of the world.

Memorial's Alexandra Polivanova observed that Putin's regime, with the FSB as its prime instrument, is postideological. They are neither Stalinist nor anti-Stalinist, neither pro-Soviet nor neo-Communist, in their world outlook. Their priority lies in the preservation of state power.[26] This is, of course, also true for all the predecessor regimes, which used ideology to mobilize popular support and maintain legitimacy. Some of Putin's comments during his exclusive interview with Oliver Stone offer insight into his ambivalent stance.

"Stalin was a product of his era," stated Putin, who warned against "demonizing" the dictator. "We are trying to talk about his merits in achieving victory over fascism," he said.[27] What it seems Putin intended to convey, however, was the ideal of a strong state (*derzhavnost*), which he attributes to the Russian people.[28] Ruthless czars, victorious military commanders, and assertive Communist Party first secretaries, for that matter, all share a singular positive trait in the eyes of Putin—namely, the ability to hold on to power, the art of survival. Repression has been their common maintenance tool.[29]

Interestingly, the centennial of the Bolshevik Revolution was not a big affair. In fact, the government nearly passed it—and the ideological divide that framed the subsequent civil war—in silence. This reflected the unease of the current regime with fitting the revolution into the paradigm of a continuum of Russian history. According to Alexander Chubarian, head of the Institute of World History of the Russian Academy of Sciences, the major lesson of the Bolshevik Revolution is that violence is only acceptable when it is directed against foreign intervention but not when one population group is pitted against another.[30] This interpretation is effectively a variation on current policymaking, which seeks interethnic unity within the country in the face of perceived encroachments by the West. Historical revisionism in contemporary Russia has two sides. On the one hand, a pantheon of military victories, real or mythical, is undergoing an expansion. On the other hand, there is a tendency to legitimize, directly or indirectly, specific acts of aggression by the Soviet Union, such as the division of Poland in 1939, the annexation of the Baltic states in 1940, the invasion of Czechoslovakia in 1968, and the war in Afghanistan in 1979–89. Hence, the Soviet war in Afghanistan has been recast as a "heroic deed" and Brezhnev's period of rule as the years of stability.

At the same time, few original studies of earlier Russian history have emerged that are utilizing hitherto untapped sources and novel interpretations. In recent years, one of the more interesting, as well as controversial, such works to appear was Evgenii Ponasenkov's *The First Scholarly History of the 1812 War*.[31] Typically, early Russian history is advanced by means of faceless monuments (often incorporating factual and/or pictorial mistakes) installed en masse by the likes of the Russian Military Historical Society (see chap. 2).

Triumph as a Unifying Narrative

Validated by Putin, the idiosyncratic concept of history designates both the ruling regime and the Russian people as the bearers of a great historical tradition that rests on the achievements of pre- and postrevolutionary Russia. The survival of this narrative depends on the careful monitoring of selected omissions.[32] As Nikita Petrov explains in his chapter, the history of the state-sponsored mass murder and systematic oppression of its citizens runs counter to the mythologized Soviet victory over the barbaric Nazi regime. Indeed, nearly all contributors to this volume emphasize the centrality of the Soviet victory over Nazi Germany in Russia's self-image as cultivated by Putin's regime. In the narrative promoted by the state, the war is stripped of gore and blood, cleansed of numerous gray zones, and reframed into a story of exceptional heroism displayed by the Soviet people. Reference to Soviet mass crimes is undesired, as it is antithetic to industrialization, the eradication of illiteracy, and other achievements of the Stalinist era that are foundational to many citizens even today. Loyal subjects are expected to cherish these triumphs and not to raise inconvenient questions about troublesome episodes in their common history.[33] The dominance, and acceptance, of this state-sponsored narrative makes it easier to acquiesce to the systematic denial of freedoms in today's Russia.

The Soviet state was built on contradiction, well reflected in oxymorons such as "Socialist legality," "Socialist international law," and "reform Communism." These kinds of contradictions, one may argue, are as numerous and as entrenched in modern Russia as they were under Soviet rule. One of the editors of this volume earlier identified this as defensive self-righteousness—that is, the inherent inability to admit faults routinely attributed to others.[34] In 2013, during one of Putin's signature marathon conferences, Alexei Venediktov, editor in chief of the liberal Ekho Moskvy radio station, asked the president if he thought Stalinism might stage a comeback in Russia. Putin replied to the effect that times were different now and the people would simply not let that happen. In so answering, it apparently did not occur to Putin that the illiberal democracy he had been upholding in Russia cultivates the exact same collective traits in the population—self-censorship, political withdrawal, vigilance, hostility toward all things foreign—that had facilitated Stalin's rule of terror. And while "things may be different now," an implicit message by the government is that the survival of the state presupposes the suppression of individual rights.

The trend toward re-Stalinization casts a long shadow over Russia and has assumed all kinds of forms. Take, for example, the case of the British-French feature film *The Death of Stalin*. Two days before its scheduled release in Russia, on January 23, 2018, the Ministry of Culture suspended its license. What made it problematic in the eyes of Russian bureaucrats was not its subject but its genre—comedy. Had it not been for such a strong reaction, the film would have likely gone largely unnoticed: a B movie of limited artistic and historical value. The reasoning given by top Russian officials for banning the film made even seasoned observers raise their eyebrows. Radio Liberty ran the headline: "Stalin's Death Cancelled." A group of lawyers employed by the Ministry of Culture recommended that Vladimir Medinskii postpone the release until summer 2018. The lawyers found the movie extremist because of its aim to "arouse hatred and hostility, to humiliate dignity of the Russian (Soviet) people, to promote human inferiority." They further insinuated that the film creators intended to "falsify our country's past, so that the life of the Soviet people during the 1950s would only invoke dread and aversion." What they essentially objected to was the comical, unflattering portrayal of Stalin's entourage engaged in a life-saving operation in the wake of their boss's death. Not surprisingly, the Russian Communist Party urged the banning of the film as an "instrument of the information war waged against Russia."[35]

In all its complexity, the push for a revised history curriculum is a telling indicator of what the government wants students to learn about and from the past.[36] As a Duma deputy once complained, negative versus positive events in twentieth-century Russian history in the older history books exist in a five-to-one ratio. Such a portrayal, in his view, makes it next to impossible to raise proud citizens of the country.[37] It is relevant to note that although educational materials are fashioned to reflect the views of the government, in practice, teachers still feel more or less free to disregard the content of the official textbooks. It is not clear to what extent they do so. What is clear is that the patriotic lessons advocated from the top down have also resonated from the bottom up in numerous pro-Soviet, even pro-Stalin, youth groups. So despite the introduction of Solzhenitsyn's *Gulag Archipelago* into the high school curriculum—an initiative supported if not driven by Putin—the fact that some such organizations today proudly proclaim "we leapt forward, we created a country of tanks from a country of plows" attests to the effectiveness of this history lesson—namely, that the political ethos is not (yet) ready to change.[38]

Moreover, state-sponsored efforts aside, as Anna Sanina argued, the value system and ingrained attitudes of many teachers and local school administrations remained largely preserved despite the collapse of the Soviet Union. The teachers she interviewed revealed they did not even bother reading the programmatic documents on patriotic education with which they had been bombarded. Rather, they drew instead directly from their professional experiences in the USSR in the 1980s.[39]

If this is the case, there was a great disconnect with the expectations of Gulag survivors who reemerged as relatively prominent voices in those same years. After the collapse of the Soviet Union, many a returnee who gave testimony pinned their hopes on the first graders of that time who had been born in an already independent Russia. They believed it would take a generation for real changes to occur in both the mentality and long political tradition that suppressed the dignity of the individual. Their hope was that this cohort—now in their late twenties—would be able to fully confront the Stalinist past.[40] In reality, in the course of one generation, the opposite seems to have occurred.

Accordingly, the approved account of history presently taught in Russian high schools offers a sanitized version of the Stalinist past. Putin, who famously described the collapse of the Soviet Union as the "greatest geopolitical catastrophe of the twentieth century" in a nationally broadcast address in 2005, has been an influential advocate of this narrative.[41] He later argued that Russia should not be made to feel guilty about the Great Purge of 1937 because "in other countries, even worse things happened."[42] Putin admitted to certain "problematic pages" in Russia's history yet rhetorically asked what state could possibly claim it had none.[43] This stance is both the cause and effect of Russia having made no substantial attempts to come to terms with the legacy of Soviet Communism. On the one hand, prominent Russians such as Alexander Solzhenitsyn and Andrei Sakharov have compelled the state to publicly disavow repression. On the other hand, the country's leadership and many of its citizenry have become dependent on repression to maintain stability.[44]

In 2008, in an effort to promote patriotism among young people, the government approved of a teachers' manual covering the period from 1900 to 1945 for use in schools.[45] Achieving such a goal for a period that encompasses the Great Terror required a considerable manipulation of the facts as well as contriving creative interpretations. For example, the manual instructed teachers to address the period of Stalin's terror by focusing on "what we built in the 1930s"; they were urged to explain that "Stalin acted in a concrete historical situation; as a leader, he acted entirely rationally—as the guardian of the system."[46] Since the scope of the repression does not readily fit into the concept of "rational governance," the manual suggested working the numbers a bit. It recommended, for example, that a "formula could be used wherein only those who received death sentences and those who were executed would be counted."[47] These figures are significantly lower than the additional millions who languished and then died from disease and forced labor in the Gulag or were released to die outside the camp. Other history texts published around that time advanced similar views.[48]

Finally, the patriotic swing in history education reached a point in 2014 wherein the government initiated the creation of a textbook whose narrative would present a "unitary vision," emphasizing the role of Stalin as an "effective manager" (see chap. 1). Putin proscribed "dual interpretations" to the central message that could be formulated as follows: "We are citizens of a Great Country with a Great Past."[49] Earlier, the Moscow Russian History Teachers' Association circulated a list of no less than thirty-one controversial subjects from the seventeenth century onward. When it came to Stalin, attention was to be directed to the role of his personality, with no reference to Stalinist repressions. Guidelines that suggested interpreting his behavior within the framework of a "one-party system dictatorship and the autocracy of Stalin" were a further attempt at obfuscation.[50] In other words, one-party rule endowed this autocrat with excessive power. Whereas Khrushchev blamed Stalin to save the party, this approach seems to be doing the opposite. Although a culture of repression persists, there have been important changes, including the publication and ready availability of works such as *Gulag Archipelago*.

Authoritarian History

The extraordinary number of initiatives, legal acts, and official statements on issues regarding history might be best understood within the framework of a state policy. If there was a particular point in time when an official Russian policy on history came into existence, it would probably be 2005. Following a 2004 spat between the Russian and Latvian Foreign Ministries concerning the Latvian Waffen SS Division and a subsequent Russian-sponsored resolution in the UN Commission on Human Rights on a related subject, the Duma on May

27, 2005, issued a statement, "On Attempts at Falsification of History." Aiming at domestic audiences, the Russian parliamentarians used street language to nail their counterparts in the Baltic states and Poland. The message was that holding the Soviet Union as partly responsible for the outbreak of the Second World War was immoral and asking present-day Russia to repent for military occupation, cynical. The first comprehensive effort by the post-Soviet Russian state to manage the historical narrative came in the shape of the Presidential Commission of the Russian Federation to Counter Attempts to Falsify History to the Detriment of Russia's Interests, established by Dmitrii Medvedev on May 15, 2009.[51] Presidential decree no. 549—which was not immediately made public—spoke of the deliberate falsification of historical facts and events for the purpose of belittling Russia's international prestige. The commission was expected to analyze alleged attempts at falsification and come up with counterproposals. The commission, chaired by Sergei Naryshkin, head of the Presidential Administration and a former KGB operative, was composed primarily of high-level state bureaucrats and a few historians, who were charged with looking for misrepresented or manipulated historical facts that cast Russia in a negative light. Coordination would proceed mainly on the federal and regional levels, which was reflected in the commission's makeup. Civil society organizations expressed concern that the "struggle against the falsification of history" was becoming an "affair of the state" because, they cautioned, the state cannot be the arbiter of the "truth."[52]

As Medvedev was clearing his office in anticipation of Putin resuming his duties as president, the work of the commission also came under review. It turned out that in the three years of its existence, the commission had achieved precious little. A largely bureaucratic mode of operation, an insufficient PR campaign, and a rather symbolic contribution by professional historians and academic institutions all contributed to the February 2012 decision to dissolve the ill-founded commission. (In 2016 there was talk of resurrecting that commission or one with a similar mandate.)[53]

Policymaking on matters of history in Russia has demonstrated a number of things, among them commitment to the cause by the state and a firm grip on academia at home. Since 2012 the Russian government has been making extra efforts to strengthen its control over history. Putin began his third presidential term in the wake of unprecedented pro-democracy protests in what was officially pronounced the Year of History in Russia. A top-level meeting convened by the Federation Council at the end of 2012 aimed to develop a uniform policy on historymaking. As before, the objective was framed as a countermeasure to the perceived threat of "history falsification." Instead of delegating this issue to a special commission, this time around different government agencies pledged to act in unison toward a common goal. Among the participating agencies were the Foreign Ministry, the Defense Ministry, and the Prosecutor General's Office.[54]

On the basis of the November 2012 roundtable, the Federation Council issued a series of practical recommendations, many of which had long been reflected in educational practice and the public domain. The document proceeded from the premise that Russia is a great state and constitutes a unique civilization. Among its many achievements, Russia played a major role in saving the world from fascism and positively contributed to the social and economic development of a number of countries. Like other great powers in history, Russia had experienced great victories but also "tragic events and political mistakes." The well-being of Russian society and the state depends on respect for its history in its entirety, among other things. Building on traditional spiritual and moral values, the document prescribed that all elements of Russian society—including state institutions, scholars, and history instructors—should come together in preserving historical memory and strengthening patriotism. This would serve to counter the falsification of Russian history that had been attempted abroad, including in the former Soviet republics, during the past two decades. Among the particular faults it highlighted were the "tendentious description of the Soviet period of Russian history as an uninterrupted sequence of mistakes and crimes committed by the state against its people," belittling the decisive contribution of the USSR to the defeat of Nazi Germany, equipoising Nazism and Stalinism, and questioning the positive impact that incorporation into the Russian state had on numerous nationalities.[55] Each participating agency received specific instructions on how to proceed.

The year 2012 also saw the entrance of mass-membership government-funded bodies into the field of historymaking. First to arrive on the scene was the Russian Historical Society (RIO), which conveniently assumed the mantle of the Russian Imperial Historical Society. Nominally a nongovernmental organization, it was obviously not the first such entity to come into existence. The Historical Memory Foundation and World without Nazism were established in 2008 and 2010, respectively, to support the work of the aforementioned Presidential Commission of the Russian Federation to Counter Attempts to Falsify History to the Detriment of Russia's Interests. A sleek website and local chapters are not what primarily set RIO apart from its predecessors. The government unambiguously asserted its influence on RIO by determining its structure and leadership. The individuals staffing the organization's presidium, advisory board, and board of trustees are a who's who of Russian academia. Presiding over academics, however, is Naryshkin, presently head of intelligence and a member of the Security Council.[56]

Coupling state bureaucracy with academia was expected to yield good results as far as an official Russian position on issues of history was concerned.

Yet it did not. For one, the present regime has failed to superimpose its version of Soviet history, including Stalin's crimes and the USSR's role in the Second World War, beyond Russia's borders. Bureaucrats who owe their careers personally to Putin lack the imagination that would enable them to penetrate Western public opinion, let alone the pluralistic world of academia. What such Russian policymaking on history has succeeded at is destroying academic institutions and the very tradition of academic research within Russia. Deprived of foreign funding as a consequence of the 2012 Foreign Agent Law and forced to look over their shoulder when it comes to pursuing "sensitive" topics of research, professional historians find themselves pushed into a corner. Indeed, historian can be a dangerous profession in today's Russia, as manifested in the harassment and even arrests of researchers.

The current grip on history is a variation on a zero-sum game Putin has played politically. Insofar as the survival of the regime partly depends on curbing dissent, an interpretation of history at variance with that advanced by the Kremlin is subject to being labeled as "falsification." This is both a subversion of the idea of history and an obstruction to independent research. In its (un)willingness to rigorously confront the past, the current regime is not unlike its predecessor. It apparently recognizes that such an inquiry could unsettle the foundations of the present state and could also be expensive because a full acknowledgment of historical wrongdoings would ordinarily encompass compensation (greater than the paltry sum allotted to exonerated returnees since 1991).[57]

Volume Overview

To the extent that the contributing authors devote less explicit attention to the history and memory of the repression and the entrenched culture of repression, we hope this introductory chapter identified some of the more salient impediments to confronting the Stalinist past and embedded this discussion in its larger, as well as current, context. We also hope to have drawn attention to the importance and timeliness of these questions. In order to narrow its focus, this collection does not journey in any depth into the historical memory questions surrounding the Romanov years, the revolutions of 1917, the Civil War, Bolshevism, Lenin, and a host of other periods. Rather, it examines the phenomenon and consequences of entrenched Stalinism (see prior) as a defining feature of the Soviet period. The volume is divided into three parts, each examining an overarching set of issues. All the contributors urge a nuanced understanding of the politicized history and historicized politics surrounding the Soviet past. While a number of the chapters focus on the cult of the Great Patriotic War, others closely examine the flip side—namely, the amnesia of Stalin's repressions. Part 1 focuses on the present memory of the past; part 2 looks at museums, pop culture, and other memory battlegrounds; and part 3 deals with remembering and framing the Soviet past beyond Russia's borders. Ivan Kurilla sets the tone by approaching history-making in contemporary Russia as a manifestation of *presentism*—the tendency to view both past and future through the prism of today. The phenomenon of presentism as such, according to Kurilla, demonstrates the inability of a society to come to terms with its painful past. Kurilla argues that, beginning in the 1990s, an individual's position on issues of history came to increasingly define his or her political preferences—the way forward to democracy or a reroute to authoritarianism. Putin's government gradually extended its influence onto the history discipline. Most unambiguously, it expressed itself in a push for a unified school textbook, which would endorse one particular interpretation of history. Kurilla, as well as the rest of this volume's contributors, identify the Great Patriotic War as the single most important, sacrosanct narrative misappropriated by the state in lieu of self-legitimization.

The stranglehold on history greatly increased with the establishment of the Presidential Commission of the Russian Federation to Counter Attempts to Falsify History to the Detriment of Russia's Interests in 2009 and reached a crescendo with the passing of a law proscribing the "glorification of Nazism" in 2014. Tellingly, even progovernment historians expressed their concern about the dangerous path set forth by the commission; the upsurge of political repression during Putin's third presidential term has muffled the voices of dissent. Despite the exponential growth of censorship, Kurilla finds hope in the emergence of grassroots history initiatives. As successful examples he cites the Immortal Regiment project launched in 2012 by a group of journalists in Tomsk, the creation of the Free Historical Society (of which he is a member) in 2014, and individual family history projects set in the context of Stalin's mass terror. Time will tell if Kurilla's optimistic prognosis—that is, popular initiatives chipping away at the history prerogative claimed by the state—is grounded in reality.

While Kurilla sees Russia as a battleground between different actors vying for control of the historical narrative, Anton Weiss-Wendt discerns a rigid top-down system in which the state lets its proxies superimpose the politically correct storyline. As Weiss-Wendt argues in his chapter, Putin's regime feels confident enough to outsource history to a broad group of supporters, from the Russian Military Historical Society to a biker club to so-called patriotic organizations. All these entities manage to get a piece of the pie in the form of governmental grants. In return, they peddle the state-approved historical narrative, to which they genuinely appear to subscribe. By so doing, these proxies help enforce uniformity and eventually consolidate state power. Historymaking as such is not a priority to the regime, obviously. The Kremlin uses the same toolkit with respect to history as it does, for example, to foreign policy. Regardless, history as a discipline is being tailored exclusively for domestic consumption in Russia. And here lies the greatest peril, contends Weiss-Wendt. By acting through proxies, Putin's regime has compromised—wittingly or unwittingly—the integrity of academic research and academic institutions. In this respect, revoking Kirill Alexandrov's PhD degree in history in late 2017 created a dangerous precedent that should sound alarms in Russia and beyond.

Moving away from governmental policies and the dignified efforts to check them by a select few, Nikita Petrov, in his chapter, examines the discursive mechanisms by which the memory of Stalin's repression has faded into the background and that of the Great Patriotic War has come to dominate the Russian historical landscape. As the successor state to the Soviet Union, Russia has inherited the same enemy list with its attendant subconscious fears and confrontational posture, argues Petrov. On the other side of the spectrum is the traditional disregard for the rule of law, which would conversely have led to a general conclusion that Stalin's repression was unconstitutional. The best opportunity for proving the regime's criminality, according to Memorial's vice president, Petrov, arrived in 1992. Unfortunately, the newly independent Russia failed the test presented by the deliberations of the Constitutional Court on the question of the legality of Yeltsin's ban on the Communist Party. With no further attempts at adjudicating Stalin's mass crimes, the only chance at restoring historical justice was missed.

Petrov draws attention to the Kremlin's fixation on improving Russia's image. The structural inability to shake off authoritarian traits, however, makes the regime emphasize the only positive historical achievement it can muster—the Soviet contribution to the defeat of Nazi Germany. Insofar as the name of Stalin is associated with victory, the Soviet terror takes a backseat. In effect, the entire Soviet repressive regime gets exonerated. The messianic vision of a collective Soviet sacrifice in the war serves geopolitical ends and simultaneously helps quash internal descent. Needless to say, Russia's neighbors refuse to accept this interpretation. Coming back to the issue of legality, Petrov makes a case that the Kremlin's efforts to put history in a straitjacket by means of so-called patriotic education or legal acts such as article 354.1 are plainly unconstitutional. As long as a majority of Russian citizens tend to accept the primacy of the state (Russian: *derzhavnost*), promoted in various ways by Putin's regime, Petrov concludes that the Soviet period will remain a "glorious past."

One particularly dramatic episode in modern history that has seen a marked change in the official Russian position, Kirill Feferman argues in his chapter, is the Holocaust. Feferman formulates his thesis as a question: what motivates contemporary Russia to claim leadership in the global fight against antisemitism and Holocaust denial? He sees it as a side effect of the current standstill in Russian-Western relations in the wake of the annexation of Crimea. Despite claims to the contrary, the Russian government has been desperately searching for allies, which it had found in Israel and its significant Soviet/Russian Jewish population. The Jewish contribution to the armed struggle against Nazi Germany (neglected in historiography) is one aspect of the Holocaust that both Russia and Israel are eager to emphasize. References to Holocaust denial, meanwhile, reinforce the self-righteous indignation at the alleged belittling of the Soviet role in the ultimate defeat of Nazi Germany. The superimposed comparison between the lowly status of Jews throughout history and Russia's present status as a pariah state ultimately serves to break its international isolation. At the same time, Feferman warns against viewing this exclusively as expediency. Levels of popular antisemitism did indeed decrease in recent years in Russia, and Putin has displayed a certain affinity for Jews.

In Russia, the memory culture surrounding the Nazi past is thus as much subject to reconceptualization as is the Soviet past, depending on which way the political winds are blowing. Some of these turns were anticipated while others were not. In 2002, one of the present editors argued that "postwar Europe made the concentration camps an important theme in its efforts to expose the ideology and practices of fascism. Post-Soviet Russia has the potential to do the same. The beginnings are evident."[58] One of the prominent examples was the effort to transform the labor camp at Perm, which Gorbachev closed in 1987, into a museum. Dedicated in 1995, the former camp site was developed over the following two decades. Observers and participants in those years did not foresee the shift in policy that made the government view the camp itself as a threat that ought to be eliminated. In 2014, when the authorities shut off the power and water and bulldozed the camp's watchtower, it was evident that Perm 36's physical survival was in peril.

Steven A. Barnes, in his chapter, furthers our understanding of these events at the hitherto independent Perm 36 Gulag Museum of Political Repression and points out that the state takeover paralleled the establishment of a central museum in Moscow dedicated to the victims of political repression. The hostile takeover, argues Barnes, reflects a decisive turn to dictatorial rule in Russia. The goal was to delegitimize and eventually reshape the museum in conformity with the present doctrine of Soviet history. Established in 1946, Perm 36 became infamous as a site of incarceration of Soviet dissidents in the 1970s and 1980s. Among tens of thousands of former Gulag camp sites, Perm 36 is one of the best preserved. Beginning in 1994, a group of activists started what became a lifetime project: preserving the camp site for posterity and educating the public about the Soviet repression. Furthermore, consecutive museum directors—husband and wife Viktor Shmyrov and Tatiana Kursina—had conceived of Perm 36 as a living institution promoting liberal values and human rights. The annual civic forum Pilorama, launched in 2005, became the premier arena for the museum's comprehensive agenda. That is what unnerved the authorities the most, according to Barnes.

Half of the museum's funding came from the regional budget and the rest from private sources, including foreign donors. That was later used against Perm 36. In the wake of unprecedented pro-democracy protests in the winter of 2011–12, a newly appointed governor slashed the funding, which meant the end of Pilorama. Consequently, the Perm 36 leadership was forced out, and the permanent exhibition was purged of all references to the Gulag, Communist repression, and the Soviet dissident movement. Moscow's aggression against Ukraine in 2014 generated a barrage of insinuations that the former management sought to portray as "dissidents" those Perm 36 inmates who truly were habitual criminals and war criminals. In its curtailed form, Perm 36 has lost its significance as a unique public institution in Russia. An important independent voice has been stifled. There are indications that the decision to dismantle the Perm 36 museum came from the very top and was motivated by ideology. Only massive mobilization on behalf of the museum in Russia and abroad has forestalled its closure. For Barnes, particularly troubling is the ambiguous position on the revamped museum by professional historian Iulia Kantor, who was subsequently appointed curator.

Johanna Dahlin, in her chapter, casts a glance at nonprofessional curating efforts, namely by a Russian volunteer movement of young men and women who use their spare time to unearth and identify Soviet soldiers fallen on Second World War battlefields. Although the volunteers belonging to the particular group under investigation operate within the state-approved framework, they claim divergent reasons for joining the movement and feel uneasy about the form of commemoration promoted by the government. The dedication required in the act of searching for human remains binds volunteers to the personal stories they help unearth of the dead soldiers and their families. Most volunteers enthusiastically join the annual Immortal Regiment march yet at the same time recognize the living memory of the war is disappearing, with the state playing a not entirely helpful role. The hard work—and its low yield (i.e., only a minority of all unearthed soldiers ever are identified by name)—invested by the volunteers contrasts sharply with the militant rhetoric of Russian officialdom; indeed, the 1945 victory brought no relief to literally millions of unidentified Soviet soldiers still not properly buried. Hence, volunteers offer a minor corrective to the uniform story of heroism preferred by the Kremlin. The romantic, somewhat sentimental outlook of Dahlin's volunteers does not project the same kind of virility as Kurilla's grassroots enthusiasts. In both cases, the historical narrative advanced by Putin's regime appears to be under no threat.

Working with the media of television series, Boris Noordenbos examines how Russian popular culture has reclaimed the Soviet juxtaposition of "good intelligence officers" versus "evil foreign infiltrators." The spy thrillers and police series that populate Russian television have one thing in common, argues Noordenbos: the claim that the country is constantly at war, harking back to the Soviet experience in the Second World War. The fixation on an ever-present (and ill-defined) "fascist threat" resonates with current politics, specifically the way the Russian state propaganda has been serving up the 2014 attack on Ukraine's sovereignty. Although set in the postwar period and wrapped in a Hollywood gloss, the television series under review comply with the state-sponsored interpretation of the Great Patriotic War. As Noordenbos contends, "These contemporary spy and detective series, by forging intricate links and connecting disparate events, eras, and cultural narratives, engage in a form of cultural memory that leans heavily on the logic of myth."

Stephen M. Norris engages with yet another form of historical representation: film. The three recent Russian movies Norris analyzes in his chapter effectively tell how cinema, politics, and remembrance practices intersect. Their respective subject—heroism of the Soviet soldiers in the Battle of Moscow and the Battle of Stalingrad versus mass deportation of Chechens—has determined the path and reception of these movies in Russia. The minister of culture, Vladimir Medinskii, personally endorsed *Stalingrad* and *Panfilov's 28* as "socially meaningful blockbusters" yet refused to certify *Ordered to Forget*, labeling it as "falsification of history." The faithful portrayal of the February 1944 massacre of some seven hundred Chechens in *Ordered to Forget* obviously did not fit the status of a "sacred legend" that Medinskii vowed to defend, as in the case of *Panfilov's 28*. Otherwise, as Norris points out, none of the three movies break any new ground in terms of cinematic representation or problem setting. The analysis advanced in his chapter leads Norris to conclude that the "future of the Soviet past under Putin 2.0 is no longer a source of guarded optimism."

Moving the discussion to the broader European context, Nikolay Koposov offers a comparative perspective on Russian history politics. The notorious article 354.1 of the Russian penal code makes punishable contravening the 1946 judgment of the international criminal tribunal at Nuremberg, disseminating false information about the role of the Soviet Union in the Second World War, and defiling symbols of Russian military glory. Adopted in May 2014 in the wake of Russia's annexation of Crimea, the new article has been increasingly used by the courts to pin down political dissent. According to Koposov, article 354.1 is an extension of the present cult of the Great Patriotic War, which incorporates the postwar world order agreed upon (in Stalin's favor) at Yalta. This linkage, in its turn, serves to legitimize Putin's neoimperial ambitions.

Koposov situates article 354.1—popularly known as the law against the glorification of Nazism—in the context of European memory laws. The term *memory law* designates legal acts criminalizing certain enunciations about the past. Remarkably, the text of the 2014 Russian law came close to including a ban on Holocaust denial, which is more prevalent in Western Europe. Otherwise, the enactment came in response to a series of memory laws condemning Communist crimes that were earlier passed in a number of Eastern European countries. By comparison, article 354.1 imposes by far the strictest punishment: up to three years of imprisonment for individuals and five years for officials. The only other comparable examples would be the 2018 Polish "Holocaust law," which proscribed mentioning the Poles in the same breath with the Nazis, and the 2005 Turkish law, which criminalized designating the extermination of Ottoman Armenians as genocide.

George Soroka, in his chapter, examines the tortured path of a Polish-Russian historical commission that operated under different names from 1987 to 1990, briefly in 2002 and 2005, and again in 2008–13. At its most productive, this bilateral body identified the most contested issues in joint history and generated an informed exchange of opinions backed by primary sources. Despite the best efforts of academicians on both sides, domestic and international politics came to constantly interfere with the commission's work. From the Polish perspective, even the central matter of the 1940 Katyn massacre did not find proper closure. The dismemberment of Poland in 1939 and the reimposition of Soviet rule in the wake of the Second World War, among other issues, also failed to bring about consensus. Most regrettable, according to Soroka, was that the Polish-Russian Group on Difficult Issues did not have a mandate to extend their expert conversation into the public domain. Without political goodwill, a more fundamental coming to terms with history as an essential element in Polish-Russian relations never came to fruition. As Soroka observes, after over thirty years of bilateral discussions, history remains subservient to geopolitics, which is particularly true in the case of Russia.

Štěpán Černoušek continues the discussion developed by Soroka by examining how Russian state propaganda manipulates popular opinion with respect to particular historical events. Černoušek takes a close look at a 2015 documentary, *The Warsaw Pact: Declassified Pages*, which portrays the Communist bloc's military alliance as a conventional peacekeeping force. The invasion of Czechoslovakia in August of 1968 serves as a major example that purports to substantiate that claim. The documentary, as Černoušek ascertains, blatantly uses elements of Soviet propaganda to prove that a pro-democracy movement in Czechoslovakia was actually a coup masterminded by the West and that many among the Czechoslovak citizens who stood up to the invading force were former fascists and Nazi collaborators. None of the individuals interviewed on camera are Czechs or Slovaks, who might have provided a very different perspective on the suppression of the Prague Spring.

Černoušek sees the valorization of the Warsaw Pact as a means to foster Soviet nostalgia, nurture the popular perception of the USSR as a positive force in the international arena, and ultimately vindicate Russia's current, expansionist politics. The Russian progovernment media went so far as to declare the Prague Spring the first attempt at so-called color revolution engineered by the West. The universal condemnation of the documentary in both the Czech Republic and Slovakia, including by (Moscow-friendly) president Miloš Zeman, made Russian authorities back down. The Foreign Ministry distanced itself from the controversial television production, emphasizing instead the official position of the Russian government on the 1968 events, as expressed in the 1993 treaty on cooperation between the two countries. The problem, according to Černoušek, is that the majority of Russians get their news from television and probably never heard of this and similar bilateral documents. How much the Russian government itself cares for such treaties, he writes, has been vividly demonstrated by the brazen Russian aggression against Ukraine in 2014. "The unfortunate tendency in today's Russia to uncritically reflect on the past may have grave consequences for the future," Černoušek concludes.

According to a Soviet aphorism, it is easy to talk about the present and future, but the past keeps changing every day. The composite picture in this volume suggests that the history of the Soviet past, including the role of Stalin, is still a battleground and may remain so for some time to come. The few countercurrents identified by the editors and contributors—Ivan Kurilla's grassroots initiatives, Johanna Dahlin's volunteers, Memorial, or the stance against antisemitism and Holocaust denial observed by Kirill Feferman—have been gradually marginalized or appropriated by the state as elements of realpolitik. What has happened even in the course of preparing this book for publication indicates, perhaps in microcosm, the fragile ground on which critical investigation of the Soviet past still rests. The European University at St. Petersburg—Kurilla's home institution—was nearly put out of commission by the authorities; another Russian scholar who was writing a chapter for this collection had to ultimately withdraw her contribution due to the pressure exercised by her university administration; Feferman was denied an entry visa to Russia; Nikolai Koposov has effectively been living in self-imposed exile in the West; and Nikita Petrov's Memorial is locked in a perennial struggle for its right to exist. There are, however, conceivable and constructive ways to move forward from the not-so-bright past to a brighter future. An inclusive history that recognizes the victims and their heirs while it verifies, analyzes, records, acknowledges, and seeks to understand the competing narratives of the Soviet past could facilitate a shift from dueling monologues to engaging dialogues. This might offer a future agenda on which society and the state could work in unison—or at least alongside each other. Such a common undertaking might move Russia, however fragilely, beyond the post-Communist impasse and shorten the long shadow of repression. In the absence of such an effort, the future of the Soviet past is predictable.

Notes

1. Nanci Adler, "The Future of the Soviet Past Remains Unpredictable: The Resurrection of Stalinist Symbols amidst the Exhumation of Mass Graves," *Europe-Asia Studies* 8, no. 57 (December 2005): 1093–119.

2. See, among others, Berber Bevernage, "Writing the Past Out of the Present: History and Politics of Time in Transitional Justice," *History Workshop Journal* 69 (2010): 111–31.

3. Aaron Korewa, "Putin's Goal is a New Yalta," Atlantic Council, December 8, 2015, http://www.atlanticcouncil.org/blogs/ukrainealert/putin-s-goal-is-a-new-yalta.

4. Sarah Raisford, "Putin-Backed Bikers Begin Controversial Ride to Berlin," BBC, April 25, 2015.

5. See "20th Bike Show. Sevastopol. 2015," Night Wolves Motorcycle Club, June 25, 2016, video, 43:58, https://www.youtube.com/watch?v=_2Zc60-sY-E.

6. "Bolee 40% rossiian nazvali stalinskie repressii vynuzhdennoi meroi," BBC, July 5, 2017, https://www.bbc.com/russian/news-40460762; "Rol Stalina v istorii Rossii," Levada, January 13, 2016, http://www.levada.ru/2016/01/13/rol-stalina-v-istorii-rossii; "Praviteli v otechestvennoi istorii," Levada, March 1, 2016, http://www.levada.ru/2016/03/01/praviteli -v-otechestvennoj-istorii/.

7. "Stalin i ego rol v istorii strany," Levada, March 31, 2015, http://www.levada.ru/31-3 -2015/stalin-i-ego-rol-v-istorii-strany; "Rol lichnosti v istorii Rossii," Levada, January 20, 2015, http://www.levada.ru/20-01-2015/rol-lichnostei-v-istorii-rossii.

8. "Rol Stalina v istorii Rossii"; "Praviteli v otechestvennoi istorii."

9. "Praviteli," Levada, February 15, 2017, http://www.levada.ru/2017/02/15/15388/.

10. Eva Sohlman and Neil MacFarquhar, "A Diary from Inside the Gulag Meets Evil with Lightness," *New York Times*, January 3, 2018.

11. Denis Abramov, "Russian Justice Ministry Searches Human Rights Group Memorial," *Moscow Times*, September 7, 2016.

12. "Miniust obvinil 'Memorial' v podryve konstitutsionnogo stroia RF," *Novaia gazeta*, November 10, 2015, http://www.novayagazeta.ru/news/1697854.html.

13. Anna Dolgov, "Russian Senator Introduces Bill Criminalizing Pro-Stalin Propaganda," *Moscow Times,* September 22, 2015.

14. "Lider KPRF ob'iavil o nastuplenii 'stalinskoi vesny,'" Dozhd TV, December 21, 2015, https://tvrain.ru/articles/lider_kprf_objavil_o_nastuplenii_stalinskoj_vesny-400547.

15. Alec Luhn, "What Stalin Owes Putin," *International New York Times*, March 12–13, 2016.

16. Interview with Sergei Kovalev in Nanci Adler, *The Gulag Survivor: Beyond the Soviet System* (New Brunswick, NJ: Transaction, 2002), 256–57.

17. "Russia Marks Day of Victims of Political Repressions," *Itar-TASS*, October 30, 2009.

18. "Odnoi iz pervoocherednykh zadach Soveta pri prezidente po pravam cheloveka stanet destalinizatsiia obshchestvennogo soznaniia," Ekho Moskvy, October 12, 2010, https:// echo.msk.ru/news/717770-echo.html.

19. Semen Charnyi, "Odno imia, odna zhizn, odin znak," *30 oktiabria* 123 (2014): 2, https://nkvd.tomsk.ru/content/editor/30%20Oktabrja/123_30oct-2014.pdf.

20. "Meria Moskvy otozvala soglasovanie 'Vozrashcheniia imen,'" Memorial, October 19, 2018, https://www.memo.ru/en-us/memorial/departments/intermemorial/news/200.

21. The Moscow City government bore over 90 percent of the construction cost, with the remainder raised through private donations.

22. "Strashnoe proshloe nelzia opravdat nikakimi vysshimi tak nazyvaemymi blagami naroda: Vladimir Putin otkryl 'Stenu skorbi,'" *Novaia gazeta*, October 30, 2017.

23. Paraphrase of Arsenii Roginskii's eloquent characterization of this conceptualization of the terror (*Prava na pamiat* documentary film), Ludmila Gordon, 2018.

24. Nanci Adler, "On History, Historians, and Transitional Justice," in *Understanding the Age of Transitional Justice: Crimes, Courts, Commissions, and Chronicling*, ed. Nanci Adler (New Brunswick, NJ: Rutgers University Press, 2018), 1–17.

25. "FSB rasstavliaet aktsenty," *Rossiiskaia gazeta*, December 19, 2017, https://rg.ru/2017/12/19/aleksandr-bortnikov-fsb-rossii-svobodna-ot-politicheskogo-vliianiia.html.

26. Sergei Medvedev, "Reabilitatsia repressii," Radio Liberty, January 10, 2018.

27. See, for examples, Jenna Scherer, "10 Most WRF Things We Learned from Oliver Stone's Putin Interview," *Rolling Stone*, June 16, 2017.

28. Cf. Oliver Stone's *The Putin Interviews* (Showtime Networks, June 2017).

29. See Adler, *The Gulag Survivor*.

30. Elena Loriia et al., "Bolshe chem istoriia," *Izvestiia*, June 20, 2018, https://iz.ru/755596/elena-loriia-elena-ladilova-ekaterina-veto-roman-kretcul/bolshe-chem-istoriia.

31. Evgeny Ponosenkov, *Pervaia nauchnaia istoriia voiny 1812 goda* (Moscow: AST, 2018).

32. Arsenii Roginskii et al., "Predlozheniia ob uchrezhdenii obshchenatsionalnoi gosudarstvenno-obshchestvennoi programmy 'Ob uvekovechivanii pamiati zhertv totalitarnogo rezhima i o nationalnom primerenii,'" Memorial, March 29, 2011, https://rg.ru/2011/04/07/totalitarizm-site.html.

33. Dmitry Volchek, "Anatomia Chekizma," Radio Liberty, December 9, 2017.

34. Anton Weiss-Wendt, *The Soviet Union and the Gutting of the UN Genocide Convention* (Madison: University of Wisconsin Press, 2017), 10–13, 26–40, 70–75.

35. "Iuristy minkulta poprosili ne vypuskat v Rossii 'Smert Stalina,'" BBC Russian Service, January 23, 2018.

36. Elizabeth A. Cole, "Transitional Justice and the Reform of History Education," *International Journal of Transitional Justice* 1 (2007): 115–37.

37. Sergei Chuev quoted in Pavel Gutiontov, "Zabvenie neotrvratimo, no nevozmozhno," *Novaia gazeta*, August 24, 2018, https://www.novayagazeta.ru/articles/2018/08/24/77589-zabvenie-neotvratimo-no-nevozmozhno.

38. "Ensuring Stalin's Victims Are Not Forgotten," BBC, February 22, 2016.

39. Anna Sanina, *Patriotic Education in Contemporary Russia: Sociological Studies in the Making of the Post-Soviet Citizen* (Stuttgart: Ibidem, 2017), 83–94.

40. Adler, *Gulag Survivor*.

41. See video of Putin's speech at "Putin: 'Collapse of the Soviet Union Was a Major Geopolitical Disaster of the Century' (Eng 2005)," WorldNews, Annual Address to the Federal Assembly of the Russian Federation, April 25, 2005, video, 9:31, January 12, 2014, https://www.youtube.com/watch?v=nTvswwU5Eco&feature=youtu.be&ab_channel=WorldNews.

42. Douglas Birch, "Vietnam Worse than Stalin Purges," *Associated Press*, June 21, 2007.

43. Leon Aron, "The Problematic Pages," *New Republic*, September 24, 2008.

44. Adler, *Gulag Survivor*; Nanci Adler, *Keeping Faith with the Party: Communist Believers Return from the Gulag* (Bloomington: Indiana University Press, 2012).

45. Alexander Danilov and Alexander Filippov, *Istoriia Rossii 1900–1945 gg.: Kniga dlia uchitelia* (Moscow: Prosveshchenie, 2009).

46. Ibid., 19, 267.

47. "Uchiteliam istorii veleno prepodnosit stalinskii terror kak ratsionalnyi instrument razvitiia strany," News.ru, August 25, 2008, https://www.newsru.com/russia/25aug2008 /koncept.html.

48. Alexander Barsenkov and Alexander Vdovin, *Istoriia Rossii 1917–2009* (Moscow: Aspekt, 2010).

49. Lyudmila Aleksandrova, "Work on Standard Russian History Manual Proves Really Daunting Task," TASS, September 26, 2013, https://tass.com/opinions/763057.

50. Svetlana Bocharova, "Experty perepisivaiut istoriiu Rossii," *Vedomosti*, June 11, 2013.

51. Ukaz no. 549, May 15, 2009, http://www.kremlin.ru/acts/bank/29288.

52. Paul Goble, "Medvedev Historical Falsification Commission 'Harmful' or 'Useless', Memorial Expert Says," *Window on Eurasia*, May 20, 2009; Vladimir Ryzhkov, "History Under Lock and Key," *Moscow Times*, June 9, 2009; "Medvedev Seen Making History More 'Politicized' with Creation of Commission," *Vedomosti*, May 19, 2009.

53. Nanci Adler, personal interview with Arsenii Roginskii, Moscow, October 31, 2016.

54. Russian Federation Council, *O protivodeistvii popytkam falsifikatsii istorii narodov v ushcherb interesam Rossii, sbornik materialov*, March 2013, 1–52, http://council.gov.ru/media /files/41d54c47347ee1e7b7ea.pdf.

55. Russian Federation Council, *O protivodeistvii popytkam*, 34–36.

56. Cf. RIO's website, http://historyrussia.org. Note that RIO has appropriated the domain of Russian history.

57. Adler, "The Future of the Soviet Past," 1104.

58. Adler, *Gulag Survivor*, 261.

NANCI ADLER is Professor of Memory, History, and Transitional Justice at the NIOD Institute for War, Holocaust, and Genocide Studies and the University of Amsterdam. She has authored or edited, among others, *Keeping Faith with the Party: Communist Believers Return from the Gulag*, *The Gulag Survivor: Beyond the Soviet System*, *Victims of Soviet Terror: The Story of the Memorial Movement*, and *Understanding the Age of Transitional Justice: Crimes, Courts, Commissions, and Chronicling*. Her current research focuses on transitional justice and the legacy of Communism.

ANTON WEISS-WENDT is Research Professor at the Norwegian Center for Holocaust and Minority Studies. He works mainly in the field of comparative genocide studies. He is author of *Murder Without Hatred: Estonians and the Holocaust*, *The Soviet Union and the Gutting of the UN Genocide Convention*, and *A Rhetorical Crime: Genocide in the*

Geopolitical Discourse of the Cold War. He is editor (with Rory Yeomans) of *Racial Science in Hitler's New Europe, 1938–1945, The Nazi Genocide of the Roma: Reassessment and Commemoration,* and the two-volume *Documents on the Genocide Convention from the American, British, and Russian Archives.*

PART I
THE PRESENT MEMORY OF THE PAST

1 Presentism, Politicization of History, and the New Role of the Historian in Russia

Ivan Kurilla

THE ACADEMIC STUDY of history and common views on its relevance to the present are rapidly changing. This evolution has been marked by the growing number of actors engaged in history politics; heightened attention to the traumatic history of the previous century, underlined by cultural and political agendas; and the emergence of a burgeoning new discipline, memory studies. French historian Francois Hartog has linked the emergence of memory studies to the phenomenon of *presentism*—the cultural context, or "regime of historicity," that makes the present virtually dominate over both past and future.[1] Within the existing analyses of the relationship between history and memory, I emphasize the significance of the recent past on memory; many of the traumas considered in memory studies deal with the experience of the last three or four generations—a typical generational horizon of the traditional "ahistorical" society.[2]

Presentism is in part a result of the inability of any given society to cope with its painful past, to establish a distance between now and then, especially when *then* refers to mass murder. The traumatic experience continues into the present without ever becoming past. Societies trapped in the unprocessed memory of twentieth-century violence cannot establish distance from that time and lose a sense of historical progression, which, in its turn, hinders the "vector of progress."[3]

The Russian case both illustrates this particular perspective on the past and helps historians better understand the general challenges facing all countries.[4] In Russia, presentism is aptly characterized by the intensified struggle over history among different actors within the politics of history: the state, business elites, professional historians, and, most recently, grassroots and family-oriented organizations.

Among the groups claiming their right to control historical narratives are various supranational actors united on an ethnic or geographic basis, for-profit history-related businesses, and professional historians. These cleavages contribute to the international "history wars" fought between Russia and its neighbors.[5] Institutionally, there are currently two state-controlled historical societies and an independent professional group in Russia. However, the field of memory has also been shaped by recent grassroots initiatives at local and family levels. The battleground has increasingly shifted into new domains and includes building monuments, demarcating holidays, changing city and street names, rewriting history textbooks, and establishing master narratives.

I differentiate between the political use of history and the business of history, although they overlap at times. Thus, governors and mayors use the historical significance of their respective administrative units not only to attract tourists but also to claim additional funds from the federal budget—for example, to celebrate a city's jubilee (confusingly, in 1977, Kazan celebrated eight hundred years since its foundation and, in 2005, one thousand years). In 2010, Volgograd governor Anatolii Brovko demanded adoption of a special all-Russian program of patriotic upbringing that would require every high school student to visit Volgograd, formerly Stalingrad, known as the patriotic capital of the country.

Historian Alexei Miller, who studied these processes for many years, suggested differentiating among the "politicization of history" as the "inevitable and unescapable" impact of a political agenda on professional historians and all those interested in history, "memory politics" as a body of "social practices and norms regulating collective memory," and "historical policy" as choosing one interpretation of history over others for political reasons as well as attempts to "convince the public that the interpretation is correct."[6] To my mind, this terminology does not take into account the social aspect. Besides, "memory politics" incorporate norms and practices that diffuse the border between "memory politics" and "historical policy." I tend to agree with Nikolay Koposov, who divides historical memory into "cultural memory" linked to the "legacy industry" and "political memory" supported by institutes of "historical policy."[7]

Using this conceptual framework, this chapter examines the changing role of historians in circumstances determined by the rise of presentism and current politics, as well as a new reality shaped through the entry of new actors into history politics.

State Appropriates History for Political Purposes

History used to be a major ideological discipline in the USSR. Joseph Stalin's *Short Course of the History of the All-Union Communist Party (Bolsheviks)* was a one-volume exposé of the dominant ideology that included everything the Soviet citizen needed to know about politics and society. Stalin's death did not alter the situation; indeed, his successors had to deal with his legacy adding complexity to the canonic vision of the past. During Nikita Khrushchev's Thaw and Mikhail

Gorbachev's perestroika, revelations about mass crimes committed under Stalin's rule made politicians even more committed to reforms, thus making the debate about the past a vital part of politics.

The collapse of the USSR was at the same time a failure of Marxism. Among other things, however, the ruling ideology also shaped historical methodology. The critique of Marxism, by initially incorporating the history politics of the Soviet regime, inadvertently demolished part of academic history and drastically altered the landscape of memory.

During the 1990s, history practically disappeared from public debate in Russia. Social reformers no longer needed the past to justify their policies, and the globalizing economy appeared to reject national histories. The first decade after the collapse of Communism focused on the future, not on the painful or heroic past. (Russian intellectuals' tradition of comparing the Russian experience to the German one rested on an insufficient knowledge of the German story.)[8] However, since the language of politics has been distorted by its arbitrary use in the 1990s (e.g., *liberal* and *democratic* have become the name of a populist right-wing party led by Vladimir Zhirinovskii), political identities in Russia tend to be defined in historical terms. Today, the best way to understand the political outlook of ordinary Russians is to ask them about their attitude toward historical figures such as Stalin or Peter the Great or historical events such as the Bolshevik Revolution of 1917 or the unraveling of the Soviet Union in 1991. The transformation of the language of historians into the language of politicians did not attract much attention at first, but eventually it came to negatively affect the academic field of history as society began to perceive any public statement with reference to history as a political one.[9]

After a decade marked by crisis in Russia's attitude toward its past, the new government of Vladimir Putin began a process of consolidating the nation's past in order to establish Russia firmly in the present. It also gradually reclaimed control over the historical domain as the main source of ideology, propaganda, and national identity.

More than anything else, the history of the Second World War has been (re)politicized in Russia since 2000. It remains the focal point of Russian history. The Great Patriotic War constitutes the core historical memory for Russians and hence endows it with great symbolism. This is eagerly exploited by politicians, who describe the Soviet victory over Nazi Germany—which most Russians consider the country's highest achievement—in a terms that had been adopted in Leonid Brezhnev's USSR. The victory narrative has ossified, and any attempt to challenge it even marginally meets political rebuttal.[10] In recent years, however, this narrative has acquired new characteristics, including an anti-Western tone and an emphasis on the great organizing capacity of the state.

Notably, in the history promoted by Russian politicians, victory in the war is much more significant than the plight of the population during those years and the sky-high death toll (typically mentioned only in passing). In 2010, when Volgograd governor Anatolii Brovko sought a federally funded center of patriotic education in Volgograd (as mentioned earlier), the project was named Victory Center despite the common knowledge that the memory of the Battle of Stalingrad includes not only celebration but also mourning. The generic image of the "Stalingrad victory," with no reference to suffering and death, has been clearly selected for political purposes.[11]

"Victory" is a core element politicians want to see in each and every period of Russian history. It is rather symptomatic that the chair of the academic council of the Russian Military Historical Society, Vladimir Churov, insisted during the preparations for the commemoration of the First World War that Russia should "participate in a parade of the victorious nations."[12] In that particular case, the First World War was refashioned in accordance with the official Russian narrative of the Second World War.

The Russian state uses various methods to impose its vision of the Second World War and command historical interpretations: school textbooks, TV documentaries, museum exhibitions, legislation, and so on. Beginning in 2004, the government started regaining control over history textbooks. The first casualty was a textbook by Igor Dolutskii that challenged high school students by including a provocative assessment of Putin's regime by two opposition figures. The Russian Ministry of Education struck the textbook from a recommended literature list, and it was eventually purged from the classroom.

In 2007, President Putin endorsed a different school textbook that provided students with the emerging "official" interpretation of recent Russian history. The main purpose of the textbook—*History of Russia, 1945–2007*, by Alexander Filippov, Alexander Danilov, and Anatolii Utkin—was to erase any harsh criticism of Russia's twentieth-century ruling regimes.[13] Critical assessments were "counterbalanced" by a list of positive achievements. Putin and his associates repeatedly insisted that raising a "patriot" requires teaching a heroic history of the country and that dark pages of the national past are not appropriate subjects for school textbooks. Many Russian historians and human rights activists have condemned this position and the new textbook. Others have been more cautious when stating that, while such a view (read: Putin's) of Russian history is possible, the state's prerogative in determining which version of history will be taught at school is problematic.

In early 2013, Putin returned to the problem of history textbooks, now suggesting the production of a "unified" textbook for schools that would replace the variety of texts available to teachers. He expressed concern over the existence of conflicting narratives of the past in various history textbooks published in

Russian regions. The state response was in a sense predictable: it tried to expunge alternative narratives. However, it is common wisdom that contemporary society has space for multiple narratives and that the only way to address a controversy is to use analytical skills to examine conflicting views. Putin's initiative has gone through many twists and turns to eventually produce a "historical-cultural template" and shorten the list of publishers permitted to publish new history textbooks.

Russian state-controlled television has been producing quasi-historical programs with a subtle political message. A prime example of this practice is a "documentary" entitled *Death of an Empire*, filmed by Father Tikhon (Shevkunov), an Orthodox priest and allegedly Putin's spiritual counselor. Built on the comparison between medieval Byzantium and contemporary Russia, the hour-long film delivered the message that Russia should not place too much trust in the West. According to the film, it was this mistake—and not the Ottoman Turkish conquest—that destroyed the Byzantine Empire in the fifteenth century, the implication being that Russia in the twenty-first century should learn the same lesson. After the film aired in early 2008, the British *Economist* noted that "in the minds and language of the ex-spooks who dominate Russia, history is a powerful tool."[14] While controversial, the official Russian approach to history is not unique, and there was no direct link between being a "spook" and using history as a political tool. The use of the state coercive apparatus and lawmaking to limit historians' freedoms poses an immediate and much larger threat.

During his visit to Volgograd on Defender of the Fatherland Day in 2009, one of the leaders of United Russia Party, Sergei Shoigu, proposed criminalizing "denial of the victory of the USSR in the Great Patriotic War," citing as precedent laws in some European states prohibiting denial of the Holocaust. On the eve of Victory Day, the Russian State Duma considered a piece of legislation, On Countering the Rehabilitation of Nazism, Nazi Criminals, and Their Accomplices in the Newly Independent States of the Former Soviet Union. The draft law included punishment of up to five years in prison for committing that offense. It also proposed the creation of a special public commission that would track pro-Nazi policies in neighboring states and advise Russian authorities how to react. Those professing revisionism would be denied entry to Russia or tried in Russian courts.

This piece of legislation was apparently considered too harsh by "liberal" president Dmitrii Medvedev, who refused to endorse it. Ten days after the legislation was introduced, Medvedev reworked it into presidential decree 549, which created a Commission for Countering Attempts to Falsify History to the Detriment of Russia's Interests. In his video blog, Medvedev attacked various analyses of the Second World War, calling recent interpretations increasingly rigid and malicious, and asserted a need to defend historical truth. This video recording was subsequently posted on the official presidential website along with the text of the decree. The commission established in accordance with the decree consisted of twenty-eight individuals, including several professional historians and members of the Duma and the Federal Council, as well as representatives of the Foreign Intelligence Service (SVR), Federal Security Service (FSB), Ministry of Defense, and Ministry of Foreign Affairs. The commission was expected to expose "falsifications of history detrimental to Russia" and elaborate measures to counteract them.

Russian historians and human rights activists assailed the decree. Lev Ponomarev, the executive director of a nongovernmental human rights organization, stated that the decree was essentially totalitarian. He argued that the decree went beyond "standard authoritarian police measures, because it aimed at regulating a field that only totalitarian regimes dare to control." Ponomarev claimed that it gave credence to "Stalin's policy and pro-Stalin historical mythology." He expressed hope that the decree "would unite not only historians but also civil society, different ideological camps for whom the very idea of bureaucratic ideology and ideological censorship is unacceptable." Ponomarev called for the opening of archives and a complete denunciation of the crimes of the Stalin regime.[15] Another nongovernmental organization, Memorial, issued a statement that offered a list of what it considered historical falsifications, including the denial of the NKVD mass execution of Polish officers at Katyn in 1940 and the assertion of a "military-fascist conspiracy" against Stalin in 1937. Memorial insisted that historical falsifications should be combated with "open and free academic discussions, including [at an] international [level]."[16] The state's role in the process— the statement continued—is to ensure free and open access to archives and not to interfere with the substance of historical studies. Memorial expressed deep concern that the commission was set up to counteract not the falsification of history but the opinions, assessments, and concepts that run counter to government policy. The group warned that such a use of the commission's powers would be unconstitutional.[17] An open letter against the decree and draft law was also published online on polit.ru. Signed by 221 prominent scholars, mainly historians, the letter bore the title "In a democratic society, freedom of history means freedom for all."[18]

The most sophisticated, philosophical justification of the decree was provided by Alexander Dugin, who sought the creation of state axioms of history and the imprisonment of those who equate Stalin to Hitler. Dugin asserted that the notion that "Stalin was a good guy" is part of Russia's "national myth," thus concealing the fact that the majority of the Russian population consider Stalin's rule to be criminal.[19] The ill-fated commission was quietly dissolved in the winter of 2012 at the peak of public protests against the electoral fraud.

The state strengthened its control over history when, in the spring of 2014, a group of pro-Kremlin Duma deputies introduced the first "memorial law" in Russia. The Russian Criminal Code was amended to include a new article, 354.1, making it a criminal offense "to deny facts recognized by the international military tribunal that judged and punished the major war criminals of the European Axis countries, to approve of the crimes this tribunal judged, and to spread intentionally false information about the Soviet Union's activities during the Second World War." The law cited "artificially creating evidence for the prosecution" (i.e., manufacturing false evidence) as an aggravating circumstance and along the way criminalized the "spreading of information on military and memorial commemorative dates related to Russia's defense that is clearly disrespectful to society, and to publicly desecrate symbols of Russia's military glory."[20] Commentators traced the appearance of this latter part of the law to popular opposition bloggers who have criticized the use of St. George ribbons as a symbol of Russian "loyalists." Under the law, the rehabilitation of Nazism is punishable by a fine of up to 300,000 rubles (ca $8,400 at the time) or three years in jail. If a state official were to commit the offense, he or she could be sent to prison for up to five years or face a fine of up to 500,000 rubles ($14,000) and be barred from government posts for up to three years. Publicly desecrating symbols of Russian military glory or spreading information disrespecting public holidays related to the country's defense would be punishable by a fine of up to 300,000 rubles or up to one year of community service.

One particular argument the authors of the law have used in its favor is that Germany, Austria, France, and other European states have similar memorial laws. Such laws prohibit Holocaust denial; in France, they also recognize slavery as a crime against humanity. These laws, however, were propagated by left-wing political forces aiming to preserve the memory of oppressed groups and the crimes of their respective states. The Russian version (like memorial laws adopted in several Central and Eastern European states) is backed by pro-state right-wing politicians who seek to create a heroic national narrative and legislate away any doubt about the state's historical righteousness.

The law uses exceedingly vague language. The ban against desecrating symbols "of Russia's military glory" goes far beyond the "rehabilitation of Nazism." Equating hooliganism to the whitewashing of Nazism effectively undermines the latter's meaning. The clause concerning "spreading information on military and memorial commemorative dates related to Russia's defense that is clearly disrespectful of society" is simply incomprehensible. How can information possibly be "clearly disrespectful of society"? The problem of interpretation remains acute, especially after the first criminal case applied the new law, in September 2016, by instituting a fine for an entry posted on a blog.

Essentially, Putin's regime has reversed the gains in the field of history that took root during perestroika and in the early 1990s. In 2013, the most distinguished organization dealing with the Stalinist past, Memorial, was labeled a "foreign agent" by the Russian Ministry of Justice. Despite protests and attempts to defend itself in Russian courts, in September 2016, Memorial joined the Levada Center and numerous independent nongovernmental organizations (NGOs) added to the list of "foreign agents" since the law to that effect had been adopted two years earlier.[21] The head of the Karelian branch of Memorial, Iurii Dmitriev, who had located the mass graves of prisoners executed during the late 1930s at Sandarmokh, was arrested in December 2016 on trumped-up charges that independent observers considered absurd.[22] Meanwhile, the local (Karelian) authorities mobilized local historians and federal media to question the NKVD responsibility for the murder, claiming that the individuals executed at Sandarmokh were, in fact, victims of Finnish atrocities during the Second World War.[23]

State control over the history domain is implemented by two institutions: the Russian Historical Society (RIO), created in June 2012 (nominally a successor to the Imperial Russian Historical Society that had dissolved in 1917), and the Russian Military Historical Society (RVIO), founded the following winter.[24] RIO is formally a nongovernmental association that was founded on the initiative of twenty-seven state-funded organizations, including the Russian Academy of Sciences, several leading universities, museums, and libraries. RIO is funded through a special fund, Istoriia Otechestva (history of fatherland), created by presidential decree in April 2016. Yet another presidential decree gave it the responsibility for the commemoration of the centennial of the Russian Revolution in 2017. RVIO is even closer bound to the state structures, as it was established by the presidential decree as a "public-state" organization (*obshchestvenno-gosudarstvennaya*) with two official founders—the Ministry of Culture and the Ministry of Defense. RVIO has its own post in the state budget; in addition, it attracts private funds from big Russian companies. It supports so-called patriotic moviemaking, military reenactments, regional military museums, the erection of monuments, and so on. The former society is headed by Duma speaker Sergei Naryshkin (currently director of the Foreign Intelligence Service) and the latter by the minister of culture, Vladimir Medinskii.

Medinskii is notorious for his numerous ahistorical statements, such as the following: "You are naïve to think that facts are the main thing in history. Open your eyes: nobody pays attention to them! What matters is its interpretation, point of view, and mass propaganda" and "If you love your Motherland, your people, you will only write positive history. Always!"[25] Another bureaucrat of history, the Russian Historical Society's secretary, Andrei Petrov, had the following response to Medinskii's Facebook commenters: "It looks like only professional historians have the right to express themselves. Perhaps those bookish (detached from life) and for long time unnecessary historians should heed their society at last?"[26] In fact, what Petrov was criticizing was the negative stance toward the politicization of history prevalent among historians. Meanwhile, Medinskii has become the herald of the new approach to history in Russia. Thus, he repeatedly proclaimed that "useful myths" are more important than facts and that heroic myths trump facts. The only validation of historical research, according to Medinskii, is the national interest of Russia.[27]

Professional Historians' Response

One of the most troubling signs for the contemporary Russian historical community is the rupture between professional historians and society. The public acquires historical knowledge not from scholarly monographs but from the mass media, criticism leveled against the authors of school textbooks is typically ahistorical, and the political usage of history is omnipresent. The lack of set criteria for who qualifies as a historian is yet another aspect of the problem. Self-styled historians dominate the media and demand to be included in the profession. The state (bureaucracy) has acquired nearly full control when it comes to reviewing dissertations, textbooks, and research projects. The expertise itself became less rigid, reflecting the deterioration of state-controlled institutions generally. Certainly this is also a problem of trust, the general quality of education, and the strength of the professional community.

Russian historians were not quick enough to respond to the challenges from the politicians. For a long time, they entertained hope of academic independence and therefore stayed back as the process of political appropriation of their field accelerated. They became more proactive following certain events, such as the controversy surrounding the textbook by Moscow historians Alexander Vdovin and Alexander Barsenkov (who were accused of nationalism) and the aforementioned governmental initiative to establish a commission against the falsification of history and produce a unified history textbook.

The state's attempt to interfere with history interpretations provoked the first instance of opposition to the politicization of history. In 2009, the most respected members of the historical guild criticized the very idea of a commission "against falsification of history," and academician Valerii Tishkov—whose office issued a letter that marked the beginning of the campaign against "falsifiers of history"—was forced to modify his original statement under pressure from his fellow historians.[28] Academician Alexander Chubarian, then director of the Institute of World History of the Russian Academy of Sciences and later a member of the commission ex officio, tried to change the commission's mandate so it could fight for the depoliticization of historical research instead. Even the director of the Institute of Russian History—academician Andrei Sakharov, known for his conservative views on history writing—supported the creation of the commission with reservations, stating that it could "easily slide from academic discussions to mutual accusations that certain points of view could undermine state's security."[29]

The state's encroachments on the historians' discipline made the practitioners vigilant. Thus, their response to the idea of a unified textbook in 2013 (one of the RIO's projects) was unexpectedly unanimous. Tishkov wrote on his Facebook page that he knew of two such attempts, in 1934 and 1949 respectively, and that he, as an academic secretary of the Russian Academy of Sciences history and philology branch, "would not encourage the third attempt."[30] Chubarian did not openly oppose the idea, but he explained that producing the unified textbook would take a long time while the task at hand was improving current historical education in schools.[31] Iurii Petrov, the new director of the Institute of Russian History, commented that "unified did not mean the only possible,"[32] and his predecessor, Sakharov, also criticized the idea: "My attitude toward the creation of a unified textbook is negative, because I believe that a teacher should have at least some choice how to teach. Controversial problems, different interpretations and points of view—everything must be there. In the unified textbook all of these will be levelled and subsequently disappear. That should not be the case."[33] The reaction of yet another academician—Iurii Pivovarov, then director of the Institute of Scientific Information on Social Sciences of the Russian Academy of Sciences— was negative as well ("I do not like it").[34] Pivovarov added that "our historical profession is not the worst of what we have in our society. Some of its members acknowledge their responsibility before the society."[35] The only prominent historian who supported a unified textbook was medievalist Sergei Karpov, then dean of the Moscow State University history department, who expressed his wish to "teach points of view that overlap with the geopolitical interests of Russia."[36] In the final analysis, while there are many among thousands of Russian historians who are ready to support "history by politicians," the high-ranking members of the historical community, including academicians, were united in their opposition.

The major step in historians' consolidation against these political infringements was the creation of the Free Historical Society (VIO) in February of 2014. This group of experts in their respective subfields of history founded the professional association to shield history from the attacks of politicians, sustain professional integrity, and promote historical education in Russia. Many prominent historians joined VIO's ranks by the time of its first conference, which took place in the summer of 2015 in Moscow (the second conference took place in 2017, when membership surpassed one hundred people). Despite operating under the cloud of tense Russian politics, the society's message made it into the open.[37]

VIO advances its agenda through public lectures and media publications about essential historical problems. In cooperation with the leading Russian publisher of intellectual literature, NLO (New Literary Observer), the society launched a popular book series—What Russia Is—written by professional historians. VIO essentially operates as a volunteer project and as such does not receive state funding, although the two conferences and the website of the society were made possible through the support of the Committee of Civic Initiatives.

Recently, historians have started to wage campaigns to defend their professional integrity. An early battle for the meaning and substance of history was fought by a group of historians who sought to strip the minister of culture, Vladimir Medinskii, of his doctorate in history. Medinskii's 2011 dissertation was titled "Problems of Objectivity in the Foreigners' Accounts of Russia in the Second Half of XV–XVII Centuries." His research method involved sorting out positive and negative accounts and subsequently proclaiming the latter to have been the result of anti-Russian bias and conspiracy. The positive stories told by foreign visitors were obviously historical truth. Professional historians identified numerous factual mistakes and biased interpretations by the author, which prompted a group of scholars to file a formal complaint in 2016.[38]

According to Russian law, all postgraduate degrees are approved by the All-Russian Attestation Commission (VAK); VIO filed a complaint with VAK listing the ahistorical and unscholarly content of Medinskii's dissertation. VAK initially sent the dissertation to the dissertation council at Urals Federal University in Ekaterinburg but later withdrew it in anticipation that local historians were likely to vote the minister's thesis down. For the next attempt, VAK forwarded the dissertation to the Moscow State University dissertation council, but the council refused to send it for further review. Finally, the dissertation was assessed by the dissertation council of Belgorod State University. The council did not review the text of the dissertation yet ruled against the complaint.

However, the final decision was to be made by VAK itself. Shortly before the VAK expert committee considered Medinskii's dissertation, *Novaia gazeta* published an article speculating that the whole procedure of thesis defense might be fraudulent.[39] Experts voted to strip Medinskii of his degree, but at the eleventh hour, the Presidium of VAK overruled that recommendation. Medinskii, a public relations pro, attempted to mobilize public opinion but clearly failed to convince professional historians (just three historians were willing to risk their reputations by publicly defending Medinskii). The case received enormous attention from historians in Russia; despite VAK's ultimate decision to let Vladimir Medinskii keep his doctorate, it proved an important symbolic victory for historians as a profession.

In the case of Medinskii's dissertation, historians scored a symbolic victory: the minister kept his degree, but the public learned it was despite the opinion of professional historians, including the expert council of VAK. Simultaneously, historians lost another battle—that for the doctoral dissertation on Russian Nazi collaborators written by St. Petersburg historian Kirill Alexandrov. In March 2016, Alexandrov was awarded his degree by St. Petersburg Institute of History, Russian Academy of Science. However, "patriotic" vigilantes denounced the study of collaborators as a step toward their rehabilitation and subsequently filed several complaints with the prosecutor's office, the Ministry of Education and Science, VAK, and other state organizations. Consequently, VAK sent the dissertation to the Ministry of Defense Academy for review. The Ministry of Defense found fault with the dissertation, which led to the ultimate decision, in July 2017, to revoke Alexandrov's degree. This example illustrates the clash between historical research and the state propaganda narrative. Hence, the state makes it possible to sustain a canonical interpretation of the Second World War—the major source of its "historical legitimacy."

Historians have demonstrated their resolve not to participate in the dissemination of myths, which the state wanted to use for propaganda purposes. Hence, in a recent development, history politics turned away from textbooks and/or primary research, where professional historians dominate. Instead, Father Tikhon, who stood behind the *Death of an Empire* documentary mentioned earlier, has emerged as one of the major actors in Russian history politics. In 2017, he received huge funding from Gazprom (presented by the donor as an act of philanthropy) to build interactive multimedia exhibitions in twenty-seven Russian cities under the name "Russia: My History." The exhibition presents Russian history from an anti-Western, anti-liberal, and church-centered perspective. It tells the story of Ivan the Terrible according to Medinskii's fantasies and the story of Soviet-era dissidents according to a KGB-inspired book from the late Brezhnev era (*CIA against USSR*, by Nikolai Yakovlev). Despite numerous factual inaccuracies, oversimplifications, and outright falsifications, the exhibition makes use of the newest digital technologies to attract scores of visitors.[40]

The Grassroots Historical Movement

Besides the appropriation of history, state history politics, and professional historians' resistance, a new claim to ownership of the nation's past has quietly emerged. It came from the grassroots level in the shape of local initiatives, genealogy studies, and family histories. The authors of a recent study called it "second memory" as distinguished from the "first," "official" memory promoted by the state.[41]

The report, "Which Past the Russian Future Needs?," was commissioned by the Committee of Civil Initiatives (KGI) and prepared by a group of sociologists, historians, and philosophers from the Free Historical Society. Published in January 2017, the final report consists of two parts: a sociological study based on research carried out in a number of Russian cities under the leadership of Grigorii Yudin and an analytical study written by a group of scholars under Alexander Rubtsov. The latter study proved controversial because it contained an element of ideology and sounded polemical rather than academic (e.g., the authors excessively used metaphors such as "immune system of the nation" or "ptomaine of Stalinism"). Consequently, at its conference in June 2017, VIO refused to endorse the entire report. The sociological study, on the other hand, received universal praise and is recommended to anyone who wants to assess the status of memory studies in Russia today. The report substantiated the earlier hypothesis concerning the extent of nongovernmental, nonpolitical forms of memory developed within families and/or local communities. The rest of this chapter is an attempt to interpret some of the most important examples of that "second memory."

The Second World War is, indeed, the biggest event that shaped the Russian people's memory. As the generation of war veterans is fading away, their children and grandchildren feel a mixture of pride and sorrow. On May 9, 2012, a group of journalists in Tomsk working for the independent TV2 channel proposed holding a parade with the relatives of those who took part in the Great Patriotic War carrying their portraits during the Victory Day celebration. The authors of this initiative—Sergei Lapenkov, Igor Dmitriev, and Sergei Kolotovkin, who gave it the name Immortal Regiment—were motivated by their own family stories. Lapenkov recollected about his grandfather: "[He] went through two wars, returned without legs. He fought for real, [he was awarded] Hero of the Soviet Union, [and served in] a battalion reconnaissance unit."[42] Lapenkov recalled seeing his grandfather's photo and said this was the image he had in mind when he came up with the idea for the parade. The atmosphere at the parade was very emotional. The images televised by TV2 were broadcast by other television stations, spreading the idea across the country.

This grassroots initiative was immediately appropriated by the authorities, who created a bureaucratic structure that came to supervise the Immortal Regiment march across Russia in the subsequent years. Putin took part in the 2016 Immortal Regiment march in Moscow. At that point, many commentators concluded that Immortal Regiment was merely a form of mass mobilization and a constituent of state history politics. Consequentially, a majority of the liberal intelligentsia lost interest in the event. In 2017, former Crimean prosecutor and currently Duma deputy Natalia Poklonskaia participated in the Immortal Regiment march with an icon of Czar Nikolai II (instead of her own relative), as others did. Despite criticism by participants and organizers, that (widely televised) appearance further alienated a liberal segment of the population from the march. As a response to the march, journalist Andrei Desnitskii proposed a new project—Immortal Barrack—in 2015 to commemorate the nameless prisoners of the Gulag, which is soon to become an actual database.[43]

Meanwhile, the TV2 channel was shut down. The founder of the studio was "absolutely convinced" the decision had been made at the Presidential Administration level. Specifically, he referred to a source who stated that one of the three reasons for the closure was the channel's "unsanctioned interference in the historical politics of the state for the purpose of undermining its ideological foundation [*namerevaias rasshatat ego glavnuiu ideologicheskuiu skrepu*]. They meant our 'Immortal Regiment' initiative."[44]

An explanation can be found in the history of the Second World War, which has been used by the state for propaganda purposes, as well as a political language of power. The state appropriated the entire war memory for its nefarious goals (including popular mobilization against neighboring Ukraine in 2014). Such brazen misuse has misfired: some people felt something important and dear to them had become subject to manipulation. The very idea and extreme popularity of Immortal Regiment are essentially a popular attempt to reclaim the memory of the Great Patriotic War. Poklonskaia's appearance with the icon—if her appearance can be regarded as part of the state manipulation and not merely an expression of her own beliefs—was a calculated move to turn Immortal Regiment into a religious procession. From this perspective, the original Immortal Regiment can be seen as the largest protest movement in modern Russian history, which the liberal intelligentsia failed to recognize.

Another widely discussed example of grassroots activism is the story of Denis Karagodin, a young man (coincidentally also from Tomsk) who started his own investigation into the murder of his great-grandfather by the NKVD at the peak of the Great Terror in 1938. During the campaign of de-Stalinization under Nikita Khrushchev, Stepan Karagodin was rehabilitated posthumously. Denis was now asking why the murderers had gone unpunished and unidentified. Karagodin spent several months working in the archives (many of them still classified), looking for any evidence and publishing the reports of his investigation online.[45] He succeeded in documenting the entire chain of command, from Stalin at the top to the names of the executioners at the Tomsk NKVD prison. Karagodin's investigation prompted many people to follow his example and pushed society to engage in an open dialogue about the past.

Memorial, for its part, has published the lists of the NKVD operatives, thus making similar personal investigations into family history easier for descendants of the victims as well as the perpetrators.[46] Activists and historians at Memorial work to recover the names of the victims buried in mass graves during Stalin's terror: Butovo near Moscow, Levashovo near St. Petersburg, Sandarmokh in Karelia, Miasnoi Bor near Novgorod, and many other sites across Russia. Another activist group, the Last Address (Poslednii Adres), has since 2015 been placing small plaques on buildings from where the victims of state terror were taken to their death. In each of these cases—Immortal Regiment, Immortal Barrack, Karagodin's investigation, Last Address, and marking mass execution sites—the main purpose is to recover individual names so society can remember each and every one of them.

Conclusion

Grassroots memory initiatives may provide an antidote to the extreme form of presentism embedded in history politics. However, it is unlikely for society to return to the optimistic "progressive" regime of historicity that collapsed in the twentieth century. Professional historians' role in society is rapidly changing, too. One of the most important tasks is trying to patch conflicting narratives of the past produced by various interest groups. Although compromise is not always possible, historians must provide the substance that ensures mutual respect. Historians also need to find new ways to function within a new reality described as presentism, which blurs the border between the past and the present. Historians must take into account grassroots movements, which are typically misrepresented by the state actors engaged in history politics, the media, and the general public alike. Above all, they have to accept responsibility and become a real force capable of changing society, thus taking a step forward from merely being interpreters of the past. With their intricate understanding of the relationship between the past and the present, historians could help put an end to culture and history wars.

For Russia, the "latest catastrophe" was not the Holocaust but the double impact of the Second World War and Stalin's terror. However, the mass crimes carried out by the Soviet state are overshadowed by the Second World War, which incorporates the mass murder of Jews in German-occupied territories, the plight of the civilian population, and the huge death toll of twenty-seven million overall. Victory in the war was an answer to the traumatic past, a remedy or even justification for all the sacrifices endured. Victims were the price paid for victory, thus vindicating the regime's murderous policy toward its own population. Forgetting was chosen as the best strategy to deal with the catastrophic past. The last decades saw these attitudes changing, as attested by the attention received by the projects seeking to establish the names of each and every victim killed by either an invading force or their own government.

The Russian case suggests that presentism is an extant form of historicity. Grassroots organizations and their interest in the past can eventually make us rethink the function of history in contemporary society. But we do not yet know if this inevitable change is for good or bad.

Notes

1. See Francois Hartog, *Regimes of Historicity: Presentism and Experiences of Time* (London: Cambridge University Press, 2015).

2. Geoffrey Cubitt contests the very possibility of establishing a boundary between history and memory since both are dependent on the context. See Geoffrey Cubitt, *History and Memory* (Manchester: Manchester University Press, 2007), 62.

3. According to Henry Rousso, "The major catastrophes of the twentieth century produced new historiographical figures that kept the near past alive and rooted it in the social imaginary. . . . The revelation of the major mass crimes, foremost among them the extermination of the Jews, no doubt played a central role in the importance granted to recent history." Henry Rousso, *The Latest Catastrophe: History, the Present, the Contemporary* (Chicago: University of Chicago Press, 2016), 143–44.

4. For a recent analysis of the Russian memory trauma, see Alexander Etkind, *Warped Mourning: Stories of the Undead in the Land of the Unburied* (Redwood City, CA: Stanford University Press, 2013). On Russian history politics, see Olga Malinova, *Aktualnoe proshloe: Simvolicheskaia politika vlastvuiushchei elity i dilemmy rossiiskoi identichnosti* (Moscow: Rosspen, 2015); Nikolay Koposov, *Pamiat strogogo rezhima: Istoriya i politika v Rossii* (Moscow: Novoe Literaturnoe Obozrenie, 2011); Nikolay Koposov, *Memory Laws, Memory Wars: The Politics of the Past in Europe and Russia* (London: Cambridge University Press, 2017); Ivan Kurilla, "The Symbolic Politics of the Putin Administration," in *Identities and Politics during the Putin Presidency: The Discursive Foundations of Russia's Stability*, ed. Philipp Casula et al. (Stuttgart: Ibidem, 2009), 255–69.

5. See, for example, Dan Stone, "Memory Wars in the 'New Europe,'" in *The Oxford Handbook of Postwar European History*, ed. Dan Stone (Oxford: Oxford University Press, 2012), 714–31; Ivan Kurilla, "Memory Wars in the Post-Soviet Space," *PONARS Eurasia Policy Memo* 63 (September 2009), http://www.ponarseurasia.org/sites/default/files/policy-memos -pdf/pepm_063.pdf.

6. Alexei Miller, "Rossiia: Vlast i istoria," *Pro et Contra* 3–4 (2009): 6–23.

7. Nikolay Koposov, "Memorialnyi zakon i istoricheskaia politika v sovremennoi Rossii," *Ab Imperio* 2 (2010): 273.

8. Mischa Gabowitsch, "Foils and Mirrors: The Soviet Intelligentsia and German Atonement," in *Replicating Atonement*, ed. Mischa Gabowitsch (London: Palgrave Macmillan, 2017).

9. As a result of political appropriation of historical language, political topics in the speeches of politicians are increasingly framed as historical narratives. Thus, President Putin mentioned Prince Vladimir in the tenth century in an effort to justify the annexation of Crimea while Foreign Minister Sergei Lavrov explained contemporary Russian foreign policy by making references to the one thousand years of Russian history. Cf. President of Russia, "Meeting with Young Academics and History Teachers," November 5, 2014, http:// kremlin.ru/events/president/news/46951/videos; Sergei Lavrov, "Russia's Foreign Policy in a

Historical Perspective," *Russia in Global Affairs* 2 (2016), https://eng.globalaffairs.ru/articles
/russias-foreign-policy-in-a-historical-perspective.

10. Irina Shcherbakova, "Wenn Stumme mit Tauben reden: Generationendialog und
Geschichtspolitik in Russland, *Osteuropa* 5 (2010): 17–25.

11. Cf. Natsionalnyi tsentr "Pobeda," http://web.archive.org/web/20160101153601/http://
nc-pobeda.ru. Brovko eventually failed to secure funding, in part due to the budget
limitations but also because Putin wanted Stalingrad to remain his own symbolic pet
project. In early 2018, the new Volgograd governor, Andrei Bocharov, once again approached
Putin with the request to fund a patriotic center in the city. See "Andrei Bocharov
rasskazal Vladimiru Putinu o sudbe Lysoi gory," Volga-Media, February 2, 2018, https://
vlg-media.ru/2018/02/02/andrei-bocharov-raskazal-vladimiru-putinu-o-sudbe-lysoi-gory
-69263/amp/.

12. "Churov peresmotrel itogi Pervoi mirovoi voiny—vkluchil Rossiiu v riady pobeditelei,"
Svobodnie novosti—n2ru, May 31, 2013, http://n2ru.info/story/5387/.

13. To give just one example, the authors of the ninth-grade textbook *Istoriia Rossii XX
vek* (Moscow: Prosveshchenie, 1995), Alexander Danilov and Liudmila Kosulina, describe
the "political system of Stalinizm" as totalitarian and repressive (126–36). Danilov was also
a member of the team that created a new text, more benign to Stalin and Stalinism, twelve
years later. Cf. Alexander Filippov, Alexander Danilov, and Anatolii Utkin, *Istoriia Rossii,
1945–2007* (Moscow: Prosveshchenie, 2008).

14. "A Byzantine Sermon," *Economist*, February 14, 2008.

15. "V Rossii sozdadut Ministerstvo pravdy?," Kharkivska Pravozakhisna Group, May 20,
2009, http://khpg.org/1242768468.

16. Mezhdunarodnoe obshchestvo Memorial, "O novoi komissii pri Presidente Rossiiskoi
Federatsii," May 22, 2009, http://old.memo.ru/2009/05/22/komissia.htm.

17. Mezhdunarodnoe obshchestvo Memorial, "O novoi komissii."

18. "V demokraticheskom obshchestve svoboda istorii eto svoboda vsekh," Polit, June 1,
2009, https://polit.ru/article/2009/06/01/let/.

19. Since 2009, the popular image of Stalin has been steadily improving. Still, according
to an opinion poll conducted by Levada Center in September 2017, a majority of Russians
condemn the Stalin-era terror while 60 percent find Stalin personally responsible for the
crimes. See "Great Terror and Oppression," Levada Center, September 7, 2017, https://www
.levada.ru/2017/09/07/16561/.

20. "Article 354.1 of the Criminal Code of the Russian Federation. (Rehabilitation of
Nazism)," accessed January 26, 2021, Codes & Laws, https://www.zakonrf.info/uk/354.1/.

21. "'Memorial' on the 'Foreign Agent' List: Court Litigation to Continue," International
Memorial, April 2, 2017, https://www.memo.ru/en-us/memorial/departments/intermemorial
/news/22.

22. Having spent over a year in jail, Iurii Dmitriev was eventually acquitted—even if only
temporarily—by Petrozavodsk court on April 7, 2018.

23. Anna Yarovaia, "Perepisat Sandarmokh," 7x7—Horizontal Russia, December 13, 2017,
https://lr.7x7-journal.ru/sandarmokh/.

24. The Russian word *obshchestvo* can be translated as both "society" and "association."

25. Mark Solonin, "Vy naivno schitaete, chto fakty v istorii—glavnoe . . . ," February
6, 2011, *Mark Solonin* (blog), http://www.solonin.org/blogs_vyi-naivno-schitaete-chto;
Vladimir Medinskii, *Voina: Mify SSSR, 1939–1945* (Moscow: OLMA, 2012), 658.

26. Andrei Petrov, comments on Facebook entry by Ivan Kurilla, February 27, 2013, https://www.facebook.com/ivan.kurilla.9/posts/10152546961980018?comment _id=38614353&offset=0&total_comments=19.

27. See, for example, Vladimir Medinskii, "Pamiatniki kulturnogo naslediaia—strategicheskii prioritet Rossii," *Izvestia*, November 22, 2016.

28. See, for example, interview of Pavel Uvarov of the Russian Academy of Sciences, "Nuzhna sovmestnaia kropotlivaia rabota uchenykh, a ne chinovnye prikazy," Polit, August 10, 2009, https://polit.ru/article/2009/08/10/istorija/; Alek Epstein, "Akademiku Tishkovu ne nuzhny otvety na 'direktivy s trebovaniem,'" July 5, 2009, http://alek-epstein.livejournal .com/45964.html.

29. "Eksperty: U komissii po protivodeystviiu falsifikatsii istorii mnogo raboty," Russian Academy of Sciences, May 21, 2009, http://www.ras.ru/news/shownews.aspx?id=92ec0991 -e540-4b2d-8554-9cccbf6dbeb7.

30. Valery Tishkov, Facebook entry, February 27, 2013, https://www.facebook.com /permalink.php?story_fbid=344482752337752&id=100003280900276.

31. "Chubarian: soderzhanie edinogo uhebnika istorii Rossii ne politizirovano," RIA Novosti, June 19, 2013, https://ria.ru/20130619/944337138.html.

32. Marina Lemutkina, "Edinyi uchebnik pridet v shkoly uzhe cherez paru let," *Moskovskyi komsomolets*, March 4, 2013.

33. "Rossiya bez Putina: Edinyi uchebnik istorii 'privedet stranu k Kitaiu,'" *RBC*, June 18, 2013, http://rbc.ru (page discontinued).

34. The Institute of Scientific Information is essentially a research library that provides bibliographical services, which was perhaps more important in the pre-Internet era and certainly so during Soviet times when foreign literature was off-limits.

35. "Uchenye khitree ideologov: Istorik Pivovarov schitaet, chto edinyi uchebnik istorii udivit zakazchikov," Dozhd TV, June 17, 2013, https://tvrain.ru/teleshow/coffee_break /uchenye_hitree_ideologov_istorik_pivovarov_schitaet_chto_edinyj_uchebnik_istorii _udivit_zakazchikov-345914/.

36. Svetlana Bocharova, "Eksperty perepisyvaiut istoriiu Rossii," *Vedomosti*, June 11, 2013.

37. For activities of the Free Historical Society, see the organization's website, http:// volistob.ru.

38. A list of major problems with Medinskii's dissertation and the links to the main critique was compiled by Meduza, "Pochemu Vladimir Medinskii ne istorik," October 4, 2016, https://meduza.io/feature/2016/10/04/pochemu-vladimir-medinskiy-ne-istorik.

39. "A byla li voobshche zashchita dissertatsii Medinskogo?" *Novaya gazeta*, October 18, 2017.

40. Daniil Sotnikov, "Arkhipelag Shevkunova: Kak 'dukhovnik Putina' stroit patrioticheskie tsentry po vsei strane," Meduza, November 20, 2017, https://meduza.io /feature/2016/10/04/pochemu-vladimir-medinskiy-ne-istorik.

41. "Publikuem doklad Volnogo istoricheskogo obshchestva: Kakoe proshloe nuzhno budushchemu Rossii," Komitet grazhdanskikh initsiativ, January 21, 2017, https://komitetgi .ru/analytics/3076/.

42. Sergei Lapenkov, oral interview, Tomsk, May 22, 2016.

43. "Internet Database of Political Repression Victims Launched in Russia," *Moscow Times*, October 29, 2015.

44. Viktor Muchnik, "Telekompaniia TV-2 unichtozhalas po politicheskomu resheniiu," Open Town, January 17, 2017, https://www.opentown.org/news/139249/.

45. Denis Karagodin, "Rassledovanie v otnoshenii sudby Karagodina Stepana Ivanovicha," Investigation of Karagodin, accessed January 26, 2021, https://karagodin.org/

46. Memorial, "Kadrovyi sostav organov gosudarstvennoy bezopasnosti SSSR, 1935–1939," last modified February 18, 2017, https://nkvd.memo.ru/index.php.

IVAN KURILLA is Professor of History and International Relations at the European University at Saint Petersburg. He is editor (with Victoria I. Zhuravleva) of *Russian/Soviet Studies in the United States, Amerikanistika in Russia: Mutual Representations in Academic Projects* and author of further five books in Russian. His articles have appeared in a number of Russian historical journals and in the *Journal of American History, Nationalities Papers, Demokratizatsiya, Journal of Cold War Studies,* and *Problems of Post-Communism.*

2 Secondhand History: Outsourcing Russia's Past to Kremlin Proxies

Anton Weiss-Wendt

THE WORD PROXY has several interrelated meanings. For the purposes of this chapter, *proxy* will be defined as an agency authorized by the state to act on its behalf. *Proxy warfare* is a concept that entered circulation during the Cold War and signified armed factions that carried out Soviet and American bidding in the global ideological struggle between the Communist bloc and the West. It began in postcolonial Africa but quickly spread to Asia, the Middle East, and Latin America. In the 1980s, not a day passed without the Soviet population being reminded of the US-backed Contras in Nicaragua or Mujahideen in Afghanistan. However, war by proxy has more than just foreign political and/or military connotations. It can come in the form of soft power and within a country's borders.

Authoritarian regimes draw multiple benefits from their association with proxy groups. First, proxies render useful services by intimidating critics of the regime. Second, they help create a false sense of unity within a society. Third, they help feign a semblance of plurality of opinion and thus undermine democratic processes and institutions. Finally, the noise they generate helps divert public attention from the actual problems facing the state. As this chapter argues, in the past decade, Putin's regime has successfully incorporated proxy groups into his brand of policymaking, including history politics. Under the guise of fostering patriotism, nationalist and religious groups got a free hand to impress their opinion on Russia's past. In a matter of years, state-sponsored and manipulated vox populi has effectively taken over what has traditionally been a domain of select professionals—history. Due to space limitations, this chapter examines a selection of the great many proxy groups populating the Russian historical landscape: the Russian Military Historical Society (RVIO), the Night Wolves biker club, and some key nationalist/religious organizations.

Vladimir Medinskii's RVIO, a "Nongovernmental" Organization in the Service of the Government

When it comes to all things history, one particular entity has dominated the news in recent years: the Russian Military Historical Society. What may sound like a professional historians' association is anything but that. For all means and purposes, RVIO is a state-run organization. On December 29, 2012, a presidential decree established RVIO for the purpose of "consolidating state and public efforts" in the study of Russian history and "countering attempts at its falsification," "promoting patriotism and raising the prestige of military service."[1] In 2014, RVIO received 285 million rubles from the state budget, and the following year 325 million. In addition, the organization draws support from "private" donors, including such giants as Russian Railways and Transneft.[2] Judging by its membership, RVIO is indeed a continuation of the state. For example, the head of the Crimea chapter is none other than Sergei Aksenov, who has been steering the peninsula since the Russian annexation of 2014.

RVIO's status as a nongovernmental organization occasionally forces it to engage in role-play by seeking formal agreements on cooperation. For instance, in June 2018 a Voronezh chapter signed such an agreement with the local office of United Russia. RVIO pledged to coordinate its activities with the party while the latter agreed to represent the former's interests at central and regional levels.[3] Office space for RVIO local chapters is typically procured through the Ministry of Culture, and the minister himself supervises all aspects of RVIO's work. When RVIO initiated collection of funds for a monument dedicated to "heroes of the First World War"—bound to be the organization's biggest such project—the Ministry of Culture backed it by instructing theaters to support the initiative with one gratis performance for the benefit of RVIO.[4]

The Ministry of Culture's special care of RVIO is not coincidental, for both are headed by one and the same person, Vladimir Medinskii.[5] Medinskii's career path makes him the perfect spokesperson for the kind of historical ideology promulgated by the Kremlin. An active Komsomol member and later member of the Communist Party, Medinskii studied international journalism at the School of International Relations of the Soviet Foreign Ministry (MGIMO) in Moscow in the late 1980s. His 1999 doctoral dissertation was on Russian foreign policy in the context of a globalized media. In 2004 Medinskii entered the Duma on the United Russia ticket. He is known as a history buff and in his years as a Duma member ran his own program on the federal channel TV Center. The program addressed traditional stereotypes about the Russian people such as heavy drinking and docility. The *Myths about Russia* program, which has been serialized into books since 2007, eventually became the basis for Medinskii's second dissertation. Despite his lack of formal training, in 2011 he completed a doctoral thesis in history, "Problems of Objectivity in the Fifteenth–Seventeenth Century Writings on Russian History," at the Russian State Social University in Moscow.

Defended a few months prior to the 2011 pro-democracy protests, Medinskii's PhD thesis may be read as a statement of purpose. Toward the end of his study, Medinskii gives a series of practical recommendations, many of which he subsequently implemented first as minister of culture and then as head of RVIO. His writings show an eagerness to draw a link between the past and present. Here, Medinskii expresses the hope that his conclusions will be taken into consideration by government agencies to counter a negative portrayal of Russian history. He conveys his concern that the media has contributed to rewriting history and creating myths. As a result, he argues that the numbers of university students who feel pride in Russia's history are decreasing. To arrest that development, Medinskii proposes elevating "historical consciousness" among undergraduate and graduate students and thus raising them as "patriots of Russia." Furthermore, he makes a plea in his thesis for a state policy on history. To that end, he proposes creating a historical association that would work closely with, and be supported by, the Duma and the Ministry of Education. More than just an academic association, it ought to be a "state historical and propaganda organization" that would deal with historical memory and "historical propaganda."[6] In short, Medinskii seeks an active role for the state in historymaking as a means of changing the negative perception of Russia in the West.

Medinskii regards history as both an academic discipline and a tool. "History is politics projected into the future," he once quipped, "because the contours of the future are drawn from historical myths."[7] Medinskii is the exponent par excellence of the current regime's idiosyncratic view of history. Hence, he consistently described odious characters in Russian and Soviet history such as Ivan the Terrible, Stalin, and Dzerzhinsky as "complex historical figures." Preaching relativism, Medinskii insists one and the same historical figure may be judged differently within a hundred-year span—good and/or bad, a hero and/or a monster. The very word *monument* (Russian: *pamiatnik*) comes from *memory* and thus, according to this chief history bureaucrat, is by default nonjudgmental. When asked about new monuments to Stalin, Medinskii had this to say:

> Here's another divisive issue. My attitude toward Stalin has changed ten times over the past thirty years. A new aspect necessarily emerges every time I read a new book, new documents, or just memoirs. . . . I would not make any unequivocal statements about Stalin right now. But neither would I ever endorse a state-sponsored monument to Stalin. I believe it would split the nation, which is always a bad thing, especially since 2014, since Crimea. . . . I mean erecting monuments to Stalin is undesirable not because it's in itself bad, or very bad, but because it divides the nation.[8]

In short, Medinskii endorses an instrumental use of history. Whatever works to keep the population united in the face of an adversary (read: keep it docile) defines any given perspective on history. Accordingly, historical viewpoints may change along with political circumstances. Those professional historians who reject this algorithm automatically fall into the category of adversary, the kind of people who swim against the tide of history. Although Medinskii defines himself as a "latent monarchist" and identifies with the "liberal wing" of the United Russia Party—if such a thing exists—with respect to history he essentially practices the "creative Marxism" of Stalin and Vyshinsky. Listening to Medinskii is like reading George Orwell: "the past is always a reconstruction of the present"; "he who controls history also controls the future" (this is indeed a variation on Orwell's); "frankly, any history is a history of today"; "history can never be unbiased"; "the true historian . . . is analyzing the present through the prism of past experiences"; "the historian is a hostage of his own beliefs."[9]

Despite this unambiguous message, Medinskii on occasion manages to contradict himself within a single sentence. Such was the case, for example, when he described RVIO's objectives. In response to a question from a *Rossiiskaia gazeta* journalist on what sorts of stances RVIO maintains in the ongoing history war, Medinskii stated, "RVIO is not so much a propaganda outlet as it serves to promote [*propagandirovat*] our military and historical achievements." Further, he claimed that raising the level of patriotism was not a goal in its own right. Yet "patriotic education" is explicitly listed in RVIO's statute.[10]

In many respects, Medinskii is a quintessential historian turned government official who promotes the virtues of historical fiction. Deep at heart, he seems to see himself as an artist, someone who brings history to the masses. In a mirror-image worldview adopted in Russia under Putin, Medinskii, the mythmaker, poses as a myth buster. That is what essentially drew attention to him in the first place.

If historical research can advance national interests—as Medinskii has insisted—then substituting a work of fiction for history is legitimate, too. As photographs attest, the minister of culture was elated attending the premier of the play *Sedition, 1609–1611* at the State Academic Malyi Theater in Moscow on May 10, 2018. Medinskii came on the stage to receive a huge bouquet of flowers as the author of the original novel that provided the storyline. Published in 2012 and listed as a historical adventure novel, *The Wall* marked Medinskii's debut as a fiction writer. The book tells the story of the siege of Smolensk during the Polish-Muscovite War of 1609–18. According to the author, the defense of Smolensk is "cooler than Stalingrad, the siege of Leningrad, and the Brest fortress rolled into one."[11] The theme of high-minded Russians battling morally corrupt Europeans is strikingly close to the dominant political discourse. Take, for example, one of the characters, a venerable old man named Savvatii who has incorporated some of Putin's neologisms in his speech: "We'll relentlessly pursue the bastards, be it on the road or elsewhere. If we catch them in the outhouse, so we'll put an end to them in the outhouse all the same." The heroic pathos of *The Wall* echoes Soviet-era theater pieces lambasting German fascists. Ironically, one spectator audibly reacted to a scene of betrayal in the play as follows: "aren't they fascists!" One of the play's central ideas is that all troubles and foreign invasions in Russia are due to sedition. The dialogue is replete with jokes on what sort of barbarians the peoples of Europe consider Russians to be.[12]

Like its chief, RVIO has been brazenly mixing history and current politics, as in, for example, a temporary exhibition, "1941–1945: No Retreat," opened by RVIO at the Manezh in Moscow in late 2016. Inexplicably, the way the exhibition was organized, the names of Adolf Hitler and Joseph Goebbels stood side by side with those of Leonid Gozman, Mark Solonin, Andrei Zubov, and Gavriil Popov. RVIO's research director, Mikhail Miagkov, explained away this shocking juxtaposition by citing the dissenting views on the Second World War expressed at different times by these Russian historians and public figures. He disputed certain episodes—for example, the burning alive of 750 Chechens in the village of Khaibakh by the NKVD (People's Commissariat for Internal Affairs) on February 24, 1944. He considered this fact damaging to the reputation of Russia. He further claimed that such information corrupted historical memory, offended war veterans, and confused young people at the same time. Otherwise, Miagkov insisted, the exhibition superimposes no conclusions but lets visitors decide for themselves.[13]

Among the different types of activities pursued by RVIO (i.e., exhibitions, historical reenactments, public talks, publications, etc.), the most visible is memorialization. By its own count, RVIO has commissioned over two hundred monuments in its five years of existence, 2012–17. These monuments essentially fall into two categories: one-off statues of Russian statesmen such as Ivan III and Prince Vladimir or serialized markers of Russian military glory. The disregard for historical accuracy, not to mention artistic quality, has led to many an embarrassing faux pas. For instance, it turned out that the monument to the designer of the eponymous Kalashnikov assault rifle (2017) featured a blueprint of a German gun in its design.[14] A similar problem occurred three years earlier with a sculptural group known as *Slavic Girl's Farewell* (*proshchanie slavianki*).[15] Also in Moscow, the Alley of Rulers (2017) is a singular example of plagiarism (the sculptor, Zurab Tsereteli, copied facial features from known works of art). Among the forty-three busts of Russian rulers on display are Lenin and Stalin—personally inaugurated by Medinskii and the first such in post-Soviet Moscow to be officially sponsored. As radio host Matvei Ganapolskii remarked, the regime does not care for details in its desire to make yet another "patriotic" statement.[16]

Putin's Jackals Make History

The patriotic fervor generated by RVIO may receive substantial media coverage but not necessarily public attention, particularly from youth. Medinskii and his ilk are apparently too bland for this cohort, who are more captivated by "patriotic bikers." The Night Wolves are formally registered as an "autonomous youth NGO," even though their core is composed of men in their forties. Like all other "patriotic" entities in Russia, the Night Wolves and their leader, Alexander Zaldostanov (who goes by the nickname "the Surgeon"), cannot claim a stellar reputation. Artemii Troitskii recalled Zaldostanov (born in 1964 in Soviet Ukraine) and his fellow bikers in the late 1980s and early 1990s sporting American and Confederate flags and doing petty crime. A particular source of pride for Zaldostanov, according to Troitskii, was his West German wife. But this adoration of all things Western at some point turned sour.[17]

Biker groups have traditionally been outlaws with a pronounced anarchist ethos (the most famous and biggest is Hells Angels). The Night Wolves, on the other hand, are primarily known for their close links to the Russian government and to Vladimir Putin personally. What began in 1989 as the Soviet Union's first biker club has by now become a highly centralized quasi-paramilitary force with substantial business interests. Zaldostanov has since long rewritten the Night Wolves charter, installing himself as the club's permanent president. The club has chapters in nearly all bigger cities while its business entity has offices in over one hundred of them. Several thousand among its members have firearms licenses.[18] The Night Wolves first shot to fame in 2010, when then prime minister Putin was filmed riding along with the bikers in Ukrainian Crimea, a feat he repeated in subsequent years. Why was there now an alliance between Putin, a former KGB officer, and Zaldostanov, a representative of what in the heyday of perestroika was deemed counterculture? Outwardly, posing alongside bikers seems just like Putin's other photo ops—an opportunity to advance his macho image as a strongman. There is more to this, however, as Mark Galeotti has explained. Putin first met Zaldostanov in 2009 while the latter was organizing a biker festival in Sevastopol—with the blessing of Patriarch Kirill. Before Putin openly did so, Zaldostanov advocated "reunification" of Crimea with Russia. The neo-Orthodox, anti-Western, militant type of nationalism professed by Zaldostanov and his men perfectly fit the Russian government's agenda. Moreover, as Galeotti pointed out, the Night Wolves are an asset because they can keep in check groups that are similar yet genuinely independent and thus potentially hostile to the regime.[19] Back in 2011 Putin made an appearance at a biker festival in Novorossiysk, just across from Crimea. In his speech, Putin praised the Night Wolves for helping promote patriotism and "historical memory." By historical memory he meant the heroic deeds of the Soviet soldiers who fought against Nazi Germany—the backbone of Great Russia.[20] It was Putin who proposed the theme for the biker festival to Zaldostanov.[21] Putin and Zaldostanov share their evaluation of the role of Stalin in Soviet history: the Soviet victory over Nazi Germany eclipses mass deportations and the Gulag.[22]

As far as the subject of this chapter is concerned, the Night Wolves have inserted an interactive element into Russian historymaking, essentially turning it into a freak show. The Night Wolves position themselves in the heroic template that has been superimposed on the Great Patriotic War as a new generation of the defenders of the motherland. The projected generational continuity, however, is typically expressed as a threat: "Banderite, I'll chop your head off for granddad" (*Banderovets, za deda, zagryzu!*).[23] In 2013, Putin personally decorated the Surgeon with a state honor after the group helped restore a Stalin-era fountain in Volgograd. In the midst of the Russian takeover of Crimea, Zaldostanov showed up in the regional capital, Simferopol, where he spoke of a "fascist" danger and the resolve to defend the rights of the Russian speakers. Wherever Night Wolves tread, he declared, is Russia. Subsequently, the Night Wolves joined the notorious "green men" in patrolling the streets in Crimea.[24] It was also Zaldostanov's men who erected the first barricade in Luhansk in Donbass.[25] The leader of the Night Wolves subsequently proposed resuscitating Kievan Rus with the capital in either Sevastopol or Kiev.[26] Consequently, the United States, Canada, and a number of EU states put Zaldostanov on the sanction list for his role in destabilizing the situation in Ukraine and the annexation of Crimea. Taking the news as a badge of honor, in January of 2015 he cofounded a pro-Kremlin anti-Maidan movement. The next month, Zaldostanov, in his trademark custom-made bear leather jacket, joined the Crimean administration and the speaker of the Russian Duma in unveiling a monument commemorating the 1945 Yalta Conference. Commonly referred to as the "Yalta betrayal" during the Cold War but described by Putin at the United Nations General Assembly as a "cornerstone of the post-war world order," the tripartite summit effectively sanctioned Soviet expansion into Eastern Europe.[27] Until recently, the two-meter-tall figure of Stalin (sitting alongside Roosevelt and Churchill) was the only monument to the Soviet dictator sponsored by the Russian state.

Since then, the Night Wolves have firmly established their presence in Russian history politics. The biker club of some five thousand, including Chechen strongman Ramzan Kadyrov and his second-in-command, Magomed Daudov, resort to performance art to fashion an eclectic version of the Soviet past. Not surprisingly, their main means of expression is the motorcycle—the American Harley Davidson, at least for those who can afford it. As if to address this contradiction, the club's division, Wolf Engineering, built its own bike model, based on the Soviet Ural, which they christened Stalinets (Stalinite in English, although it is just a prototype not slated for mass production).[28] The flags emblazoned with Stalin, and a wartime chant "For victory, for Stalin!" accompanied the Night Wolves' provocative stunts and generated extensive foreign publicity. Each spring since 2015, the club has arranged a bike ride to Berlin. According to the organizers, they seek to commemorate the Second World War dead and pay tribute in Soviet war cemeteries. The Polish and German authorities were caught unprepared in trying to negotiate between their instinctive desire to bar entry to Russian bikers and the international norms regulating border crossing. From the perspective of Russian propaganda, however, this was secondary: the Night Wolves were mainly playing to domestic audiences. The Night Wolves' ride to Berlin in 2018 was cosponsored by RVIO. As far as RVIO is concerned, the biker ride is meant to alert the people of Russia and Europe to the attempted falsification of the history of the Great Patriotic War. A Night Wolves Kaliningrad chapter modified the concept of a ride into Berlin to fit the local context. There, each biker was joined by a Russian Orthodox priest holding a banner. The biker-priest duos then crisscrossed the Russian enclave to visit all the international border crossings—accompanied by a religious ceremony.[29]

Having been involved with the Second World War memorials, the biker club eventually decided to directly contribute to memorialization. In September 2014, in separatist-controlled Luhansk in Ukraine, the Night Wolves unveiled a monument symbolizing their vision of a new Russia. The freestanding granite stela features the crude contours of the Soviet coat of arms with a double-headed eagle in the middle. The ribbon-wrapped stalk of wheat no longer carries the inscription "Proletariat of all countries, unite" in the languages of the fifteen national republics. Instead, an accompanying plaque declares "Russia's destiny is to rise as a Eurasian giant." The leader of the club's Donbass chapter explained on camera that one president, Zaldostanov, had approached the other president, Putin, with a request to make the Night Wolves' design into Russia's new coat of arms.[30] Since then the Night Wolves have incorporated the new design into the Russian flag they regularly display, and the man in the video received a medal for bravery from the self-proclaimed Luhansk People's Republic.[31]

The Night Wolves, through their leader, regularly sing accolades to the leaders of Chechnya, Abkhazia, South Ossetia, Transnistria, Crimea, Donetsk People's Republic, and Republika Srpska (not to mention their annual birthday wishes to Patriarch Kirill and President Putin) and occasionally receive decorations from the latter's hands.[32] Zaldostanov often receives, and proudly advertises, invitations to attend formal gatherings under the patronage of the Federal Security Service (FSB) and the Defense Ministry. He was also among the invited guests attending Putin's (fourth) inauguration as Russia's president in May 2018. Perhaps not surprisingly, among the Night Wolves' well-wishers are Duma members Vladimir Zhirinovskii and Irina Yarovaia. Among other destinations, they have traveled to a Russian air base in Syria. When asked about Russian opposition leader Alexei Navalny and his investigation of corruption, Zaldostanov replied that he thinks it is a smokescreen and that he otherwise associates Navalny with the kind of people who brought the Soviet Union to ruin.[33]

Quid pro quo, since 2013 the Night Wolves have received over 80 million rubles in presidential grants, most recently 3 million for the project "Slavic World" and 9 million for organizing Christmas tree fests for children. According to their grant application, bike and car rides and pilgrimages have the purpose of "uniting brotherly Slavic peoples through popular diplomacy." As for the Christmas tree fest, its purpose is to "explain to children the historical and spiritual heritage of Russia and Russia's challenges in a clear, fairytale manner."[34] The fairy tale, as understood and executed by the Night Wolves, is populated by grotesque characters loosely painted to portray Nazis fighting it out with the forces of good—all on wheels—presided over by St. George and the Soviet-style Grandfather Frost. According to Zaldostanov, the show blends history and myth in order to "save the country."[35] Even the adults in the audience find the evil entourage frightening: "We'll pay in bucks to get your strength—to conquer the Russian lands and populate it with bastards."[36] The "infernal Christmas tree"—as it was once advertised on the club's website—is typically sold out.

Rumors that Zaldostanov has fallen out of favor with Putin have been exaggerated. In August of 2017, for example, the president was seen chatting with the biker in chief in Sevastopol. While dodging the question of whether governmental grants for his children's Christmas fest have dried out, the Surgeon insists he is driven solely by the desire to promote "Russian traditional values and patriotism." Meanwhile, the Night Wolves have been aggressively advancing their business interests.[37] The Night Wolves cash in on patriotism every time they feel undercut by rival groups. They do so by resorting to the tried and tested Soviet method of denunciation. In particular, they have a bone to pick with Bandidos, presented by the group as a Satanist narco syndicate. The story goes back to a gang-related murder of a Night Wolves member in Sevastopol in 2012. Three years later, under the aegis of anti-Maidan, Zaldostanov proposed to ban Hells Angels and Bandidos from the territory of Russia, maintaining that those "foreign agents with headquarters in the USA" allegedly took part in the popular uprising in Ukraine and might one day stir up unrest in Russia as well. The same year in Saratov, Zaldostanov backed a local businessman cum deputy for the United Russia Party in the latter's conflict with a journalist. In his amicus curiae, Zaldostanov pulled out all the stops by evoking the fifth column, fascism, mockery of Orthodox values, and so on. Interestingly, the journalist in question, not unlike Zaldostanov, had endorsed Russia's intervention in Ukraine and routinely praised Putin.[38]

The Night Wolves also act as proxies in the subtle state takeover of the Immortal Regiment initiative and the volunteer search movement, which has been working since Soviet times to identify the remains of soldiers who died in battle. A new memorial day commemorating the Unknown Soldier, December 3, was introduced in Russia at the beginning of 2014 (see chap. 6). Three years later, the leader of the Night Wolves Cheliabinsk chapter handed over copies of the archival documents to the relatives of a soldier who had been listed as missing in action.[39]

Still, a major arena for the Night Wolves remains the annual biker festival, which they have been organizing since 1995. Zaldostanov endows Sevastopol—the site of the show since 2009—with the same meaning Stalingrad had back in 1943. The enormous coverage the state media gives to the biker festival in Crimea has turned it into one of the major and most anticipated cultural events in Russia.

The 2014 biker show, "The Return," served a Russian propaganda narrative of the events in Ukraine, albeit in a grotesque, theatrical form.[40] The 2015 edition, "Forging Victory," served up another dose of maddening eclectics, portraying the Soviet military triumph over Nazi Germany as God's will. According to a Night Wolves press release, the show would prove that "Victory is Christ." Playing himself, Zaldostanov appeared on the stage and shared with the audience that the "great Stalin and the Soviet people emerged victorious in that terrible, religious war and thus barred hell from earth." Evoking religious imagery, he described the Soviet Union as a "enormous red monastery" and major urban centers as the twelve cities/apostles blessed by "God's mother Moscow" (one of the apostles, Kiev, proved to be Judas).[41] At a press conference, Zaldostanov spoke of psychological warfare allegedly waged by the West against Russia. He regards himself a soldier and "Forging Victory" his counteroffensive in that war.[42] The 2016 edition, "The Fifth Empire," pitched a "morally corrupt" West against a "strong in spirit" Russia in a dystopian setting worthy of a *Mad Max* movie. As the name of the show suggests, the Night Wolves and their leader celebrate the ascent of Putin's Russia, which they regard as heir to the fourth and mightiest reincarnation of the holy empire: Stalin's Soviet Union.[43] One episode in the biker show, accompanied by Georgy Sviridov's suite *Time, Forward!* was lifted from the closing ceremony of the Winter Olympic Games at Sochi the previous year. Indeed, with a total of one thousand participants, Zaldostanov compared the scale of the biker show to that of the Olympics.[44]

Zaldostanov explained the concept of the show as follows: "I give people what they want, I share the idea that I've run through myself. This is a rebuttal to the enemies of Russia and the humiliation to which they subject our country by discrediting our victory. . . . This is an extension of our ride onto Berlin. Consider all the hatred toward those who don't want to forget the Great Patriotic War, our victory, our heroes, our traditions. . . . Not a play or a reconstruction, but the history of the war as I and the Night Wolves see it." All who have seen the show, including a handful of foreigners, will take back with them a sense of Russian "affability [*radusheie*], a part of the Russian soul," according to Zaldostanov.[45]

The Night Wolves' vision of Russian history is conspicuously close to that advocated by Putin's regime. The similarity does not end there. Zaldostanov borrowed "Russian Reactor," the name of the 2017 biker show and now feature film, from Alexander Prokhanov. As if it were coordinated, President Putin, in a televised address to schoolchildren on September 1, 2017, spoke of an "inner nuclear reactor of the Russian people that enables it to move forward." According to Zaldostanov, that statement made him decide to produce a film on the theme of the latest festival.[46] Zaldostanov advertises his show as a "people's miracle-play [*narodnaia misteria*]" and the short film as a "chronicle of a hundred years of Russia's history." To promote their cinematic creation, the Night Wolves drove around a replica steam locomotive built on a track chassis and a crude scaled-down copy of the monument to the Soviet soldier in Berlin's Treptower Park.

After years of experience, Zaldostanov feels comfortable in his role as stage director and messianic storyteller. As the narrator and main character, Zaldostanov apparently takes cues from a Soviet cinematic portrayal of Grigory Rasputin. The film is essentially one long shot of Zaldostanov wandering zombielike along the railway tracks and narrating, in menacing voice, his version of Russian history from February 1917 until today. From an elevated rostrum decorated with composite state symbols of Russia, Zaldostanov ruminates about "mixed-up facts of history" and a mythical "Russian Reactor that has been set in motion to advance the truth and save the world." What follows is the history of an apocalypse, staved off first by Stalin and now by Putin: the February Revolution brought about destruction; the abdication of Tsar Nikolai II threw Russia into anarchy; plotted by the "West," the Bolshevik Revolution pushed Russia into a civil war; the conspiring forces dismembered the empire by triggering the independence of the borderland regions. The segment on Stalin's period of rule that followed is worth citing in full: "By means of repression and terror, Stalin halted the burning magma of destructive popular energy and channeled it into modernization. He restored justice, revived the people's precious dream of ideal existence. That energy, in the iron grip of Stalin, turned into thousands of factories, smashed Hitler's fascist empire, and painted the entire world the Soviet color red."[47] After listing postwar Soviet achievements, with emphasis on the space program, Zaldostanov arrives at another rock bottom in Russian history—August 1991 and the dissolution of the Soviet Union. As a result of the persistent efforts of the cunning enemies, he tells the audience, the Soviet empire collapsed, never to rise again: "The great red kingdom, which was the center of the world, was no more." Yet, in the end, the Russian people have embraced God's ways, professes the alpha wolf. It will continue on the straight road to victory, as the entire historical experience has demonstrated, and will no longer stray off the "May 9 path." Russia killed the fascist dragon and put its sword to rest—until the next enemy attack, that is. Zaldostanov ends his forty-odd-minute invocation with the Soviet/Russian anthem playing in the background.[48]

As far as storytelling is concerned, it has been a downward spiral for Zaldostanov and his band. The 2018 showpiece was essentially two uninterrupted sequences, one apocalyptic (Russia surrounded by forces of evil) and another uplifting (Russia breaking through the encirclement). In terms of historical references, all that was left was a copy of the 1930s fountain the Night Wolves helped restore in Volgograd.[49]

Patriotic Hitmen Seeking Out Fifth Columnists

Despite their wild appearance informed by heavy metal aesthetics, the Night Wolves do not normally go around hurting people. Zaldostanov's bikers appear comfortable just doing the theatrics. Ordinary-looking men with the St. George ribbon belonging to various "patriotic" organizations represent a much more ominous force in today's Russia. The impact of their actions far exceeds their numbers. It is they who physically drive the vestiges of free speech, including the interpretation of history, underground. Whatever their formal affiliation or funding sources, they are all essentially doing the state's bidding.

With the myriad of nationalist entities currently operating in Russia, the evolution of the Kremlin patriotism project can be traced by focusing on some of the major organizations. Among the first such organizations created by Putin's spin doctors was Molodaia gvardiia (Youth Guard) in the mid-2000s. As the youth wing of United Russia Party, it offered an easy career path. Almost simultaneously, in 2005, Kremlin ideologists created Nashi (Our Own). The influence of Vladislav Surkov, who oversees Nashi's operations, is manifested in the organization's stated goal: to help advance "sovereign democracy." While its structure and agenda are similar to Molodaia gvardiia's, Nashi functions more like shock units, harassing pro-democracy activists and foreign diplomats. Its attempts to develop any sort of ideology beyond militant patriotism have failed; the Nashi Orthodox Corps did not last long. By 2014–15, Nashi had effectively run its course. The Kremlin assembled an organization of a new kind to address political challenges in the wake of Russia's aggression against Ukraine. Ideologically driven, Sut vremeni (Essence of Time) attracted a share of nationalist youth with a tinge of intellectualism. The idea of Soviet imperialism promoted by the group's leader, Sergei Kurginian, worked well in cofounding the anti-Maidan movement on the one hand and launching projects such as Stalinobus (drawing attention to Stalin's perceived achievements) on the other. An effective model of compartmentalized, pseudointellectual opposition, Essence of Time features too many ideological subcurrents to make it a mass organization.[50]

In late 2012, a new organization, the National Liberation Movement (NOD), made its entrance. It was a hybrid between Nashi and Essence of Time created with the specific purpose of keeping the liberal opposition in check. Uninterested in intellectual pursuits, NOD went straight after so-called fifth columnists. In comparison to Essence of Time, NOD boasts a larger membership and employs more brutal methods. Both organizations joined forces under the anti-Maidan umbrella, alongside patriotic bikers, Orthodox extremists, Nikolai Starikov followers, and others. Since the beginning of hostilities in Ukraine, the anti-Maidan movement welcomed various hit squads to its ranks, the most infamous of which is the Russian Liberation Movement (SERB). Battle-hardened SERBs are focused only on beating people up.[51] All these entities evoke history when playing out their conspiratorial vision of Russia as surrounded by enemies. If further proof is necessary as to the political use of history—in this particular case the Polish-Muscovite War—consider NOD coming out in force during the 2015 Day of National Unity walk in Moscow. One of the banners on display evoked the liberation of Moscow from Polish invaders in 1612 as a rallying cry to "join Putin in liberating [Russia] of American invaders." A quotation from Putin that followed superimposed the ultimate conclusion: "The people liberated Moscow and the country from invaders and those who had betrayed Russia. Subsequently, by their own free will, the people established strong, viable rule." Other NOD activists carried slogans calling for the "cleansing of the fifth column."[52]

In 2016 alone, patriotic nongovernmental organizations received a total of 4.6 billion rubles in presidential grants. To name but a few entities that received federal funding that year: Brothers in Arms, with the project of uniting the peoples of Russia around the heroic mission of Molodaia gvardiia; Memory of Victory, with a goal of fostering Eurasian integration on the basis of traditional values and the living memory of Soviet victory in the Second World War; and the historical play *Shield of Russia*, which portrays the heroic struggle of the Russian people against the German and Swedish oppressors (with the example of Alexander Nevsky).[53] This incomplete list is enough to establish that proxy groups take inspiration from the Soviet propaganda of the late 1930s and 1940s in their rendition of Russian history, a narrative that has apparently found enthusiastic support at the governmental level.

Counterintuitively, it was not the centennial of the Bolshevik Revolution and the deposition of the last monarch that dominated Russian news in 2017. Rather, it was a controversy surrounding the feature film *Matilda* based on a true story of the intimate relationship between Tsar Nikolai II and ballerina Mathilde Kschessinskaya in the 1890s. The official trailer of the film that came out in late 2016—featuring an erotic scene, among other concerns—mobilized militant Orthodox groups in protest. The church and a few politicians who were professed believers joined in. King's Cross, a virulently nationalistic, monarchist entity, deemed the movie an "anti-Russian and antireligious provocation" and turned to Natalia Poklonskaia for help. A longtime official in the Ukrainian Prosecutor's Office, Poklonskaia rose to fame for her support of the Russian annexation of Crimea, where she was briefly installed as prosecutor general. In 2016 she was elected to the Duma on Putin's United Russia ticket. A telegenic, soft-spoken lawyer-cum-politician, Poklonskaia brandished her faith and admiration for the slain tsarist family. Poklonskaia subsequently requested that the Russian Prosecutor's

Office check the film on the basis of article 148 of the penal code law that pro-scribes "offending religious sentiments of the believers" (essentially blasphemy) and more generally privacy laws.[54]

Meanwhile, vigilantes took the matter into their own hands. In early 2017, a hitherto unknown organization—Christian State, Holy Russia—distributed threatening leaflets to movie theaters, warning them against screening *Matilda*. Any decision otherwise would be regarded as an "intent to humiliate the Orthodox Church saints and a provocation leading up to 'Russian Maidan.'" The group's leader, born-again Christian Alexander Kalinin, insinuated in an interview that potential viewers might interpret the film's message as a call for revolution.[55] That was also the underlying idea that informed a "prayer protest" across Russia in the summer of 2017, coordinated by King's Cross and an organization with a similar ideology, Forty Forties. Among the slogans carried by protestors were "Anathema to those who plot uprising and treason against Orthodox rulers" and "Against lies and falsification of history."[56] Typically, perhaps, none of the op-ponents had actually watched the film; some, like Poklonskaia, explicitly refused to do so.

The religious extremists of Christian State turned from words to action. On August 31, 2017, the St. Petersburg studio of the film's director, Alexei Uchi-tel, was firebombed. Days later, two cars were set ablaze outside his lawyer's of-fice in Moscow. In an unrelated incident, a minivan loaded with gas cylinders rammed into an Ekaterinburg movie theater set to show *Matilda*.[57] This act was carried out by Kalinin; the police discovered gas canisters and leaflets titled "For Matilda—Burn!" when conducting a search of his house. Kalinin earlier had de-fended his right to burn movie theaters and even threatened to break Uchitel's legs or impale him. Tellingly, Christian State, Holy Russia has linked its religion-inspired activities to its support of Putin.[58] Under pressure, some movie theaters canceled their film screenings. In other cases (e.g., in Novosibirsk), security was beefed up at screenings. The Orthodox Church, as it had done before in other contexts, (publicly) distanced itself from some groups (Christian State) while it continued endorsing others (Forty Forties). Some dioceses initiated a signature-gathering campaign against *Matilda* on their own.[59] As if by coincidence, several weeks prior to the planned countrywide release of *Matilda*, a series of billboards under the heading "Nikolai and Alexandra Fedorovna: Words of Love" went up in Moscow. The billboards featured images of the tsar and his wife, interspersed with quotations celebrating the virtues of love, marriage, and family. The project was sponsored by the Orthodox Church.[60]

Until recently, Kremlin proxies have mainly fought for larger historical causes without ganging up against individual historians and their scholarship. The un-precedented attack on Kirill Alexandrov in 2016–17 that ultimately led to the re-vocation of his doctorate marks a dangerous escalation. St. Petersburg historian

Alexandrov is a recognized expert on Russian collaborationist forces in the Second World War. On March 1, 2016, Alexandrov defended a PhD that examined the motivational factors that made a small segment of the Soviet officer corps join General Andrei Vlasov's army fighting on the German side. Based on archival sources and scholarly analysis, Alexandrov's dissertation is by far the most comprehensive piece of research produced on this subject in Russia. Outside scholarship, Alexandrov has been outspoken in his political views: in 1991, he defended the Lithuanian parliament; along with historian Andrei Zubov, he belongs to a quintessential anti-Communist organization, the National Alliance of Russian Solidarists (NTS); and his collected works appeared in 2003 under the title *Against Stalin*.

A summary of the thesis published prior to the defense greatly irritated "patriots" of various kinds. People's Assembly (Narodnyi sobor), which styles itself as a nationalist, patriotic, and religious movement, concluded that Alexandrov was trying to whitewash Vlasov. Consequently, it asked the prosecutor's office to check if the dissertation violated article 354 of the penal code ("public calls to launch aggressive war"). As the leader of People's Assembly and aide to the notorious Duma deputy Vitalii Milonov explained: "I don't want him executed or imprisoned. I simply want that such dissertations were no more. I want that individual to change his subject." The St. Petersburg war veteran organization took this battle one step further: "The dissertation serves those who seek to conquer Russia. The thesis effectively tests the mechanisms of treason, of which there are many examples: Serbia, Iraq, Libya, Ukraine, Yemen, Syria. In all those countries the US and NATO made use of a fifth column to create Vlasov-style opposition, and subsequently depose the legitimate governments, dismember them, and install regimes of their liking."[61] The street protestors included such dissimilar entities as the Communist Party and the Russian Way (Russkii lad) movement. Slogans carried by elderly protestors read: "No dissertation praising Vlasov," "Whitewashing Vlasov today—denying the Holocaust tomorrow," and "Bandera in Ukraine—Vlasov in Russia."[62] Subjected to this barrage of accusations, Alexandrov's dissertation was eventually sent for academic expert review. Meanwhile, the scholar claimed that some of his archival notes had been stolen in order to discredit his research. Shortly thereafter, St. Petersburg city court, taking cues from St. Petersburg State University, opened an investigation into a newspaper article Alexandrov had published back in 2014 in *Novaia gazeta*.[63] Alexandrov's piece on Ukrainian nationalist Stepan Bandera allegedly contravened article 351.1 of the penal code ("denial of facts established by the Judgment of the International Military Tribunal at Nuremberg"). Notwithstanding the apparent incompetence and bias shown by the reviewers, the Russian Ministry of Education and Science in October 2017 rescinded Alexandrov's degree, which had been awarded by the Institute of History of the Russian Academy of Sciences.[64]

To make matters worse, two months later St. Petersburg court ruled that Alexandrov's article from 2014 constituted "extremist material."[65]

With nearly thirty years of experience and several hundred publications to his name, Alexandrov is unlikely to be discouraged, let alone intimidated.[66] But schoolchildren may be. For almost twenty years, Memorial in Moscow has organized a competition for high school students titled "People in History: Russia, XX Century." The idea of the competition is to encourage children and youth to collect evidence and critically reflect on the history of Russia through the prism of family. Memorial takes extra effort to engage school pupils in provincial Russia. Out of about two thousand texts submitted, the forty best are nominated at an annual ceremony in Moscow. In the past few years, the award ceremony has been brazenly sabotaged by the pro-Kremlin National Liberation Movement (NOD), with the connivance of police.

On April 28, 2016, a few dozen members of NOD—mainly males in their late teens sporting May 9 paraphernalia—hurled abuses and eggs at the people arriving for the award ceremony. Several of the attendees, including writer Liudmila Ulitskaia, had Brilliant Green (an antiseptic commonly used in the former USSR) thrown in their face. "Liberal bastards," "You came here for money," and "We don't need alternative history," shouted the assailants while the police stood by without intervening. Although the Memorial officials tried to put on a brave face, the schoolchildren were visibly shaken by the ugly incident.[67] The following year, NOD used more refined methods in their attempt to disrupt the event. They broke into the Memorial electronic system and stole the names and addresses of the winners. Subsequently, they called the respective school administrations and, in the name of the Ministry of Education, demanded that the students cancel their trip to Moscow. The organizers were also forced to change the venue of the award ceremony at short notice.[68]

It is remarkable that Alexandrov's earlier publications on Vlasov's army (from the early to mid-2000s) prompted no public outcry. Obviously it is not the tenet of his analysis, but the political climate in the country, that has changed so dramatically. More than just politicization of history, there is a willingness to apply criminal justice to stamp out inconvenient views on history, to cultivate self-censorship, and ultimately to put a stranglehold on independent research. At this point in time in Russia, the persistent condemnation of Stalin by a historian may prove a liability in the eyes of the "patriotic" proxies or, even worse, be construed as binary opposition between war heroism and high treason. Not coincidentally, newly instituted public celebrations in Russia—including the Day of National Unity, which came to replace commemoration of the Bolshevik Revolution—take the opportunity to evoke discredited historical tradition. During the 2015 Moscow City Fest, guests were treated to a historical reenactment of the public execution of a "traitor of the nation" (*natsional-predatel*); Muscovites could also try out make-believe corporal punishment such as stocks and birching.[69] Tellingly, the same day in April 2016 that National Liberation Movement activists attacked participants of the history competition organized by Memorial, they also used Brilliant Green against the opposition leader, Alexei Navalny. The message communicated from the top down appears to be this: exposing traitors is a civic duty and can also be fun.

Conclusion

In the early 1990s, in an attempt to explicate the radicalization of Nazi racial policy, Ian Kershaw came up with the concept "working toward the Führer." According to Kershaw, Nazi officials progressively raised the stakes by trying to outbid each other in anticipation of Hitler's will.[70] Although Kershaw was careful to lay out the differences between Hitler and Stalin, historians since then have successfully applied Kershaw's analysis to the Soviet dictator during the Great Terror. In fact, "working toward the leader" would serve well with regard to just about any authoritarian regime, and certainly Putin's Russia. A corporate system entails subordinates vying for privileges in exchange for loyalty. That loyalty can take on different forms, including politically correct interpretations of history. Opaque as he can be, Putin made himself understood on issues of history, particularly the Soviet period. The president, who had picked his favorite tsar, participated in the Immortal Regiment march, and made advanced nuclear weapons a part of his 2018 reelection bid, could not but appreciate celebration of strongmen in Russian history, bike rides onto Berlin by the Night Wolves, and clamping down on research allegedly celebrating the archetypical traitor Vlasov.

Repackaged by Kremlin proxies, Russia's history has been turned into a commodity and an acquired market value. It is reasonable to suggest that history in Russia has inadvertently become a part of a nepotistic, corporate system in the making since the early 1990s. The 2000s have witnessed the universal phenomenon of progovernment groups morphing into shadowy structures with extensive business and political interests. In such a power relationship, statements on history are predictably shaped by a client to satisfy or anticipate the interests of a patron. Although emphasizing the Soviet victory over Nazi Germany alone would not cause one to win lucrative governmental contracts and political appointments, it now appears somewhat in sync. Conversely, no group or agency dependent on governmental largess would dare challenge the established historical narrative. The new tradition of wearing the St. George ribbon on May 9 in Russia may resemble that of the remembrance poppy on Armistice Day in select British Commonwealth countries. Yet the consequences of publicly disallowing this tradition are different.[71] Complacency informs public views on history and is also reflected in political participation. Like politics, history is a means to an end for the present regime. Coincidentally, the underlying principle of Marxism was also that the means justify the goal, especially as interpreted by Lenin and Stalin. Soviet Russia was proclaimed to be a country of workers, peasants, and soldiers whereas contemporary Russia can be described as a state propped up by oligarchs, clerics, and soldiers. Militarism is the factor that binds the two Russias together. Yet there is also one substantial difference: the older constituents were able to make history but left professional elites to tell the story; the present constituents have license to do both.

Historymaking may also be viewed as a bonus that Putin's regime has given to its proxies. By so doing, Putin has demonstrated that he regards history as belonging to auxiliary services—useful but not essential. The outward impression of pluralism conveyed by progovernment entities and their views on Russian history is pure fiction, of course. And so is the notion of grassroots movements when applied to Kremlin proxies. Consider, for example, a debate regarding the site of a future Prince Vladimir monument. The Night Wolves, Forty Forties, Kirill Frolov of the Association of Orthodox Experts—all of them vowed to fight to the bitter end to have the monument situated on Sparrow Hills in Moscow, as long as authorities approved of that location. When the decision was made to place the monument next to the Kremlin, the voices of protest ceased at once.[72]

In essence, it is a manifestation of a general pattern in Russian policymaking, both domestic and foreign. A slight deviation between fundamentally similar perspectives on history measures the extent of (inconsequential) debate allowed to be stirred by the so-called systemic opposition. Regulated at the top, it is harmless at worst. The populist, uncritical presentation of the country's history appeals to the masses, who are actively discouraged from challenging the authorities politically. Multiple actors pushing a unified agenda in the field of history is merely an extension of the hybrid warfare practiced by the Kremlin at the international level. It also comes cheaper than paying salaries to thousands of historians pushing the party line, as in the former Soviet Union or currently in countries like Poland. The unspoken policy adopted by Putin's regime in respect to history mimics policies regulating other aspects of life of the Russian people. In the long run, it serves the very same objective of keeping the population docile and the present regime entrenched in power.

Kremlin proxies have the numbers on their side: the 2017 edition of the Night Wolves biker festival was reportedly seen by two hundred thousand spectators, their children's Christmas fest (biker festival lite) is typically sold out, the Rossiia 24 reporting besmirching Kirill Alexandrov's scholarship reached millions, and serialized monuments installed by RVIO across Russia have created a new standard for memorialization. In contrast, the number of participants in the "People in History: Russia, XX Century" competition run by Memorial does not exceed a few thousand. Likewise, the handful of other professional, independent institutions, such as the Free Historical Society, the Sakharov Center, and the Yeltsin Center, find themselves constantly under fire and therefore stand no chance of staving off the upsurge of secondhand history backed by the considerable power of the Russian state.

Notes

1. See full text of Putin's decree no. 1710 at RVIO, "Decree No. 1710," December 29, 2012, https://rvio.histrf.ru/officially/ukaz-1710.

2. Leondi Velekhov, "Mrakobesie na marshe," Radio Liberty, December 5, 2016, https://www.svoboda.org/a/28157613.html.

3. RVIO, "Evgenii Revenko: Nasha zadacha—aktivizirovat voenno patrioticheskuiu rabotu," June 5, 2018, https://rvio.histrf.ru/activities/news/item-5046.

4. Svetlana Reiter and Ivan Golunov, "Rassledovanie RBK: Zachem Medinskomu Voenno-istoricheskoe obshchestvo," RBK, July 13, 2015, https://www.rbc.ru/society/13/07/2015/559e8f459a7947860ab1f73a.

5. Another RVIO sponsor is the Ministry of Defense.

6. Vladimir Medinskii, "Problemy obiektivnosti v osveshchenii Rossiiskoi istorii vtoroi poloviny XV–XVII vv," abstract (Moscow State Social University, 2011), 6, 10, 40–45.

7. "Vladimir Medinskii: 'Mogu rasskazat i vsiu pravdu, i vsiu nepravdu,'" *Novaia gazeta*, December 16, 2016, https://www.novayagazeta.ru/articles/2016/12/15/70908-vladimir-medinskiy-mogu-rasskazat-i-vsyu-pravdu-i-vsyu-nepravdu.

8. "Vladimir Medinskii," *Novaia gazeta*, December 16, 2016.

9. "Interesnaia istoria: Vladimir Medinskii vpervye otvechaet kritikam svoei dissertasii," *Rossiiskaia gazeta*, July 7, 2017, https://rg.ru/2017/07/04/vladimir-medinskij-vpervye-otvechaet-kritikam-svoej-dissertacii.html.

10. Cf. Medinskii's interview, "Iz vsekh isskustv vazhneishim dlia nas iavliaetsia istoriia," *Rossiiskaia gazeta*, August 26, 2015, https://rg.ru/2015/08/26/pravda.html; for RVIO's statute see RVIO, "Charter of the Russian Military Historical Society," 2018, https://rvio.histrf.ru/officially/ustav-rvio.

11. Viktor Zhukov, "Kritiki raznesli spektakl po romanu Medinskogo: 'Vygliadit kak son ministra,'" URA.ru, May 12, 2018, https://ura.news/news/1052334488?fromtg=1.

12. Alexandra Zerkaleva, "Volshebnyi son ministra kultury," Meduza, May 11, 2018, https://meduza.io/feature/2018/05/11/volshebnyy-son-ministra-kultury. Savvatii's monologue bears an unmistakable resemblance to Putin's crass remark from 1999 with respect to Chechen separatists.

13. Velekhov, "Mrakobesie na marshe." On the atrocity committed in February of 1944 at Khaibakh and its current interpretations, see Stephen M. Norris's chapter in this volume.

14. "S pamiatnika Kalashnikovu spilili fragment vintovki Shmeissera," Radio Liberty, September 22, 2017, https://www.svoboda.org/a/28751543.html.

15. "S pamiatnika russkomu soldatu v Moskve spilili nemetskie mauzery," RBK, May 13, 2014, https://www.rbc.ru/society/13/05/2014/57041c9e9a794761c0ce9cb8.

16. Matvei Ganapolskii, "Chelovek i avtomat," Ekho Moskvy, September 25, 2017, https://echo.msk.ru/blog/partofair/2061538-echo/.

17. Artemii Troitskii, "Volchii vals," BBC Russian Service, May 18, 2015. Troitskii is perhaps the best-known Russian rock music critic and since 2014 has resided in Estonia.

18. Oleg Raldugin, "Kak baikery 'Nochnye volki' stali politicheskoi staei," *Sobesednik*, June 30, 2014, https://sobesednik.ru/rassledovanie/20140630-kak-baykery-nochnye-volki -stali-politicheskoy-staey.

19. Mark Galeotti, "An Unusual Friendship: Bikers and the Kremlin," *Moscow Times*, May 19, 2015.

20. "Predsedatel Pravitelstva Rossii V. V. Putin posetil mezhdunarodnoe baik-shou v Novorossiyske," Government of Russia, August 29, 2011, http://archive.premier.gov.ru/events /news/16325/.

21. "Glavnyi motovolk RF rasskazal, pochemu Putin ezdit na traike i o kaprizakh Volochkovoi," Segodnya.ua, July 1, 2011, https://www.segodnya.ua/interview/hlavnyj -motovolk-rf-racckazal-pochemu-putin-ezdit-na-trajke-i-o-kaprizakh-volochkovoj-255061 .html.

22. Cf. Alan Jourdan, "Une Nuit enflammée dans la tanière des Loups de Vladimir Poutine," *Acteurs*, January 22, 2018. The translation of the article is available at Night Wolves, "Zimnie prikliuchenia shveitsarskogo zhurnalista v Moskve," March 3, 2018, http:// nightwolves.ru/nw/news/4628/.

23. That was the slogan sported by the Night Wolves, for example, at the Day of National Unity March in Moscow on November 4, 2015. See Night Wolves, "Foto: Den narodnogo edinstva 4 Noiabria 2015. Nochnye Volki v edinom shestvii," April 11, 2015, http:// nightwolves.ru/nw/gallery/2300/. The term *Banderovites* denotes members of the nationalistic Ukrainian military organization OUN-B, which did commit a series of war crimes against Jews and ethnic Poles during the Second World War and fought against the Soviets well through the 1950s. In the former Soviet Union and currently in Russia, *Banderovites* has been used as a generic word of abuse vis-à-vis Ukrainian nationalists.

24. Simon Shuster, "Russia Ups the Ante in Crimea by Sending in the 'Night Wolves,'" *Time Magazine*, February 28, 2014.

25. Raldugin, "Kak baikery 'Nochnye volki' stali politicheskoi staei."

26. "Baiker Hkirurg predlagaet perenesti stolitsu Rossii v Sevastopol ili Kiev," Politnavigator, October 1, 2015, https://www.politnavigator.net/bajjker-khirurg-predlagaet -perenesti-stolicu-rossii-v-sevastopol-ili-kiev.html.

27. "Vladimir Putin's 2015 Address to the United Nations," September 28, 2015, Scribd, https://www.scribd.com/doc/283010015/Vladimir-Putin-s-2015-Address-to-the-United -Nations.

28. "V Sevastopole presentovali mototsikl 'Stalinets,'" Lenta.ru, August 23, 2015, https:// lenta.ru/news/2015/08/23/motociklfe.

29. Kirill Sinkovskii, "V Kaliningrade 'Nochnye volki' proveli kresnyi khod," BBC Russian Service, June 17, 2015.

30. See Night Wolves, "Foto. Den narodnogo edinstva 4 noiabria 2015: Nochnye Volki v edinom shestvii," December 6, 2016, http://nightwolves.ru/nw/gallery/2300/.

31. See Night Wolves, "Nochnye volki podarili Lugansku granitnyi monument, simvoliziruiushchii svobodu LNR," November 19, 2015, https://nightwolves.ru/nw/news/2332; Night Wolves, "Prezident motokluba 'Nochnye Volki-Donbass' Vitaly 'Prokuror' nagrazhden medaliu 'Za otvagu' II stepeni," February 21, 2018, https://nightwolves.ru/nw/news/4616.

32. Cf. Night Wolves, "News," http://nightwolves.ru/nw/news/.

33. Night Wolves, "2-ia chast interviiu s Khirurgom: O patriotizme, Navalnom, Staline i probleme smeniaemosti vlasti," August 17, 2017, http://nightwolves.ru/nw/news/4371/. A high-profile member of the Duma for United Russia Party, Irina Yarovaia has sponsored multiple legal acts that limit freedom of expression, including the so-called foreign agent law (2012), the law against "rehabilitation of Nazism" (2014), and an antiterrorism law (2016).

34. Night Wolves, "Interviiu 'Sobesedniku,' Khirurg: 'Pochemu v nashei druzhbe s Putinym vse vidiat tolko dengi?," November 23, 2012, https://nightwolves.ru/rms/news/1638.

35. Jourdan, "Une Nuit."

36. Elena Chinkova, "Baiker Khirurg zhaleet, chto ne vybil iz Sobchak dur poezdkoi na mototsikle," Kuban.kp.ru, January 7, 2018, https://www.kuban.kp.ru/daily/26777.1/3812283/.

37. Cf. "'Nochnye volki' na okhraniaemoi territorii," RBK, February 3, 2017, https://www.rbc.ru/newspaper/2017/02/06/58931c099a79472d0683cad1; Alexander Litoi, "Samolety, vystrely i 'Nochnye volki,'" Radio Liberty, January 30, 2018, https://www.svoboda.org/a/29007264.html.

38. Roman Arbitman, "Slovo za slovo, ili kak 'Khirurg' na patriotizme zarabatyvaet," Radio Liberty, August 18, 2015, https://ru.krymr.com/a/27195115.html.

39. See Night Wolves, "Sokhraniaia pamiat," December 3, 2017, http://nightwolves.ru/nw/news/4505/. For more on the Immortal Regiment, see chapters by Johanna Dahlin and Ivan Kurilla in this volume.

40. See the video at Night Wolves, "The Return," December 8, 2014, 45:26, https://www.youtube.com/watch?v=McvxG5kebwA&ab_channel=wolfnomad.

41. See the video at Night Wolves, "Forging Victory," August 22, 2015, 57:40, https://www.youtube.com/watch?v=WrwsJAqo7Jk&ab_channel=Thesavspb. See also Anton Mesnianko, "Poslushniki 'krasnogo monastyria,'" Radio Liberty, August 31, 2015, https://www.svoboda.org/a/27214715.html.

42. "Khirurg: 'Kuznitsa Pobedy'—eto bitva, a ia—voin," NSN, July 22, 2015, http://nsn.fm/hots/khirurg-kuznitsa-pobedy-eto-bitva-a-ya-voin.php.

43. See the video at Night Wolves, "The Fifth Empire," October 29, 2016, 42:46, https://youtu.be/mXcqQZ45F_c.

44. Documentary on the making of the of the 2016 edition of the Night Wolves biker show aired on Zvezda, the Defense Ministry TV channel, "Nochnye Volki: Sevastopol, 2016," 16:52, https://www.youtube.com/watch?v=rNlAE09vQu4.

45. See a documentary about the making of the 2015 edition of the Night Wolves biker show, Night Wolves, "Film o sozdanii baik-show 2015," June 26, 2016, 21:17, https://www.youtube.com/watch?v=43rr-MR4iFk.

46. See Night Wolves, "Reaktor rossiiskogo naroda," September 1, 2017, http://nightwolves.ru/nw/news/4385/. Zaldostanov and Prokhanov share their mutual admiration. The leader of the Night Wolves has adopted the latter's idea of contemporary Russia as the Fifth Empire, which he made into the theme of the 2016 edition of the biker festival. Among their other joint projects is renaming Volgograd back to Stalingrad.

47. See the video at Night Wolves, "Russian Reactor," August 19, 2017, http://nightwolves.ru/nw/news/4374/. The show and the film, which Zaldostanov claims are largely self-financed, involved laying one hundred meters of railway tracks and bringing in a giant port crane, among other equipment.

48. Night Wolves, "Russian Reactor."

49. See the video at Night Wolves, "23 baik-show: Sevastopol, 2018 'Russkaia Mechta,'" August 17, 2018, 1:13:31, https://www.youtube.com/watch?v=Gp686LowmQg.

50. Kseniia Kirillova, "Kremlevskaia gvardiia," Radio Liberty, April 26, 2018, https://www.svoboda.org/a/29188787.html. Molodaia gvardiia is the name of a clandestine wartime Soviet cell that operated for a few months in 1942–43 in the city of Krasnodon in Nazi-occupied Ukraine. The story was immortalized in a novel (1946) and a movie (1948) and thus became part of the Soviet foundational myth of the Great Patriotic War. Molodaia gvardiia was the subject of two different TV series aired in 2006 and 2015 respectively. The word *nashi* is typically associated with Soviet forces fighting against Nazi Germany and/or ethnic Russians residing in the former Soviet republics.

51. Kirillova, "Kremlevskaia gvardiia."

52. Cf. Elena Rykovtseva and Ivan Trefilov, "Den narodnogo edinstva," November 4, 2015, Radio Liberty, https://www.svoboda.org/a/27344456.html.

53. Liubov Chizhova, "Ritualnye tantsy patriotov," Radio Liberty, December 28, 2016.

54. "Minkult prokommentiroval prosbu Poklonskoi proverit film 'Matilda,'" RBC.ru, November 2, 2016, https://www.rbc.ru/rbcfreenews/581a4ebe9a794766597464c7. From a legal point of view, Polonskaia's request has validity only if supplemented with an affidavit from the person who claims a violation of privacy—that is, Tsar Nikolai II.

55. Elena Poliakovskaia, "Kinoteatry nachnut goret," Radio Liberty, February 1, 2017.

56. Anastasiia Tishchenko and Mumin Shakirov, "Postoiat protiv 'Matildy,'" Radio Liberty, August 7, 2017.

57. "Rage at Tsar Film Suspected in Russia Car Blaze," BBC, September 11, 2017, https://www.bbc.com/news/world-europe-41225387.

58. Liubov Chizhova and Mark Krutov, "Radikaly pod prikrytiem," Radio Liberty, September 20, 2017, https://www.svoboda.org/a/28746680.html; Sergei Medvedev, "Arkheologiia: Gospod, zhgi!," Radio Liberty, October 1, 2017, https://www.svoboda.org/a/28739870.html.

59. "Hanty-mansiiskaia eparkhiia RPTs nachinaet sbor podpisei za zapret filma Alekseia Uchitelia 'Matilda,'" Ekho Moskvy, June 29, 2017. Forty Forties—which in 2015 was personally commended by Patriarch Kirill—showed its mettle in recent years in delivering "humanitarian goods" to Donbass, breaking up protests against the erection of a monument to Prince Vladimir, seeking prison terms for the "propaganda of homosexuality," and advocating the prosecution of select members of Russian opposition parties.

60. "V Moskve ustanovleno poriadka 300 stendov s tsitatami Nikolaia II i ego suprugi," Ekho Moskvy, September 27, 2017.

61. "Zashchita s generalom Vlasovym," *Fontanka*, March 2, 2016.

62. "Spory o Vlasove: Ideologiia protiv nauki," video posted on Radio Liberty, April 6, 2016, https://www.svoboda.org/a/27657991.html.

63. Kirill Alexandrov, "Bandera i banderovtsy: Kto oni byli na samom dele," *Novaia gazeta*, September 12, 2014.

64. Tatiana Voltskaia, "Khochu, chtoby mne podavali ruku," Radio Liberty, November 3, 2017.

65. See St. Petersburg court decision no. 33–13964/2017, December 14, 2017, https://sankt-peterburgsky--spb.sudrf.ru/modules.php?name=sud_delo&srv_num=1&name_op=doc&number=16965244&delo_id=5&new=5&text_number=1.

66. Cf. Interview with Alexandrov, "Lozh daet kratkovremennyi effect, a zatem razrushaet," *Novaia gazeta*, January 12, 2018.

67. Svetlana Pavlova and Valentin Baryshnikov, "Provokatsiia pod prismotrom politsii," Radio Liberty, April 28, 2016.

68. Anton Nosik, "Upyri iz NOD protiv shkolnikov: Istoriia odnoi provokatsii," Ekho Moskvy, April 26, 2017.

69. Alia Ponomoreva, "Rubka kapusty, porka shpitsrutenami i sgon oblakov," Radio Liberty, September 7, 2015.

70. Cf. Ian Kershaw, "Working towards the Führer: Reflections on the Nature of the Hitler's Dictatorship," *Contemporary European History* 2, no. 2 (July 1993): 103–18.

71. In May 2017, Russian Railways threatened a disciplinary action against train conductors who did not wear St. George ribbons. Liberal member of St. Petersburg's city government Boris Vishnevskii was formally reprimanded by the speaker for refusing to display the ribbon. See "V Peterburge deputata otchitali za otsutstvie georgievskoi lentochki," BBC Russian Service, May 3, 2017; "RZhD nakazhet provodnikov za otsutstvie georgievskoi lenty na forme," Radio Liberty, May 11, 2017.

72. Medvedev, "Gospod, zhgi!"

ANTON WEISS-WENDT is Research Professor at the Norwegian Center for Holocaust and Minority Studies. He works mainly in the field of comparative genocide studies. He is author of *Murder Without Hatred: Estonians and the Holocaust*, *The Soviet Union and the Gutting of the UN Genocide Convention*, and *A Rhetorical Crime: Genocide in the Geopolitical Discourse of the Cold War*. He is editor (with Rory Yeomans) of *Racial Science in Hitler's New Europe, 1938–1945*, *The Nazi Genocide of the Roma: Reassessment and Commemoration*, and the two-volume *Documents on the Genocide Convention from the American, British, and Russian Archives*.

3 The Soviet Past and the 1945 Victory Cult as Civil Religion in Contemporary Russia

Nikita Petrov

ONE OF THE fundamental initiatives that emerged from the nascent civil society in the Soviet Union in the late 1980s was erecting a monument to the victims of Stalin's terror. The idea, which was first pronounced in 1987, brought together different segments of the population and precipitated the creation of a new organization, Memorial. Gorbachev's democratic reforms disavowed Communist dogma and inevitably prompted a comprehensive reevaluation of the Soviet past. Public opinion at that time was particularly ill-disposed toward the Soviet bureaucratic system and the omnipotent Communist Party. For the first time in decades, the daily press began writing about Stalin's crimes, the Great Terror of 1937–38, ethnic deportations, and other hitherto censored topics. This period also ushered in, for the first time in the Soviet Union, the publication of banned books such as Alexander Solzhenitsyn's *The Gulag Archipelago*.

Continued political reforms and a reassessment of Soviet history thus appeared unavoidable. Beginning in 1988, the present author participated in (for the Soviet Union) groundbreaking academic conferences, civic initiatives, and scholarly and public programs organized by Memorial, which by then had resolved not only to seek full exoneration and restoration of names of the victims of Stalin's repression but also to create an archive and a museum telling the story of Soviet terror. This mission seemed possible at the time. In 1989–91, the public appeared ready to fully confront the legacy of Soviet totalitarianism; a majority of Russians were sincerely trying to come to terms with history while expressing shame for the mass crimes committed by the Soviet government against its own citizens.

No one could have imagined that the country that appeared to be on the brink of shaking off its totalitarian legacy would once again manifest so many of its tendencies. The past, complete with the notion of a sacral, all-powerful state, in particular, is making a strong comeback in Russia. Sadly, most of the population appears willing to swap individual rights and freedoms for ephemeral pride in the might of the Soviet empire. This inevitably brings back the historical figure of Stalin, who is now regularly portrayed as a great statesman.

This chapter seeks to explain why and how the shadow of the past still/again hangs over Russia. More specifically, it traces the change in popular sentiments and the efforts to once again limit access to archival records documenting Soviet crimes. Fundamentally, the chapter engages with the enduring question of why Russia did not learn lessons from the past.

Until recently, two mutually exclusive tendencies have been on display in contemporary Russia.[1] On the one hand, a state development program was set in motion in the aftermath of the failed coup in August 1991. That program aimed to build a democratic political system, complete the transition to a market economy, and safeguard human rights. On the other hand, a growing monopoly of the state over public life and the economy—typical of Russia—inevitably resulted in suppression of individual rights and freedoms in the name of "common" (actually state) interests. The tension between these two tendencies, "democratic" and "state protective," still constitutes the subject of heated public debates. The supporters of a strong state (*gosudarstvenniki*), imbued with imperial tradition, came out on top in that struggle. Political confrontation predictably informed the process of reevaluation of the Soviet legacy and consequently the framing of a state policy in the field of history. The class approach to evaluating past events and the place of the individual in history, inherent in the Communist doctrine, has undergone a transformation. We now have a new doctrine in the making, according to which the Soviet state succeeded the Russian Empire and post-Soviet Russia is the legitimate successor of the USSR. Such a rationale makes Russia inherit not only "external enemies" but also a confrontational posture and all the archetypical fears and misconceptions that come with it.

Rehabilitation

During the last years of the Soviet Union, Stalin's criminality and the need to reevaluate the Soviet past became the subjects of public debate. In November 1987, Soviet leader Mikhail Gorbachev stated that the "responsibility of Stalin and his inner circle before the party and the people for mass repressions and unlawful acts is both immense and inexcusable."[2] Perestroika set off the process of reevaluation not only of the role of Stalin but also of Soviet history generally. The process of rehabilitation of victims of Stalin's terror resumed. However, a special commission that had been created for that purpose by the Central Committee of the Communist Party focused mainly on former opposition leaders and high-ranking party officials who had been sentenced in the infamous trials of the late 1930s. The 1920s trials, not to mention the extrajudicial executions of the Lenin period, were never reviewed by the commission. Such notorious court cases as the Industrial Party Trial of 1930 or the Menshevik Trial of 1931 fell by the wayside, too. During the Gorbachev period, the ideological postulate introduced at the Twentieth Communist Party Congress in 1956, according to which unlawful repressions were launched in 1934 by Stalin, still rang true. The broader term *Stalinism*, however, was also taken into circulation, in contrast to the Khrushchev period, when it was maintained that Stalin's cult of personality "could not corrupt the essence of socialist state."[3] Hence, Stalin was still held singlehandedly responsible for all the crimes committed during the Soviet period. The head of the KGB, Vladimir Kriuchkov, in his November 4, 1989, report, spoke of the "serious, destructive consequences of Stalinism, which had deformed socialism and corrupted the Leninist concept of a new society." When talking of mass repression and "innocent victims," however, Kriuchkov said nothing about rehabilitation.[4] The KGB was clearly opposed to extensive rehabilitation, especially when the dissidents sentenced from the 1960s to the 1980s entered the conversation.

Of particular significance was the decree of the Presidium of the Supreme Soviet of the USSR from January 16, 1989, On Additional Measures to Restore Justice to the Victims of Repressions That Took Place in the 1930s–1940s and the Early 1950s. That decree recognized all decisions by the extrajudicial bodies (i.e., NKVD Special Board, NKVD "troika," OGPU Collegium, NKVD Commission, and Chief Prosecutor's Office) as unconstitutional and thus invalid. Yet the decree contained a clause that made it inapplicable to "traitors to the Motherland and henchmen during the Great Patriotic War period, Nazi war criminals, members of armed bands and their accessories, officials who had falsified criminal investigations, as well as individuals who committed premediated crimes and other criminal acts."[5] This clause still applies, thus validating the decisions by "unconstitutional" extrajudicial bodies.

Further acts have been passed with the purpose of deepening and simultaneously speeding up the process of rehabilitation. The decree by president of the USSR Mikhail Gorbachev from January 13, 1990, On Restoring [Civil] Rights to All Victims of Political Repressions of the 1920s–1950s, expanded the chronological limits of the rehabilitation process and condemned repressions carried out against peasants during the collectivization of agriculture in the late 1920s and early 1930s. Yet this decree also contained a clause regarding "crimes against the Motherland."[6] A resolution of the Supreme Soviet of the USSR from November 14, 1989, invalidated all normative legal acts that created a basis for ethnic deportations and obliged state authorities to "implement by the end of 1991 actual restoration of legal rights to the repressed peoples."[7]

In the wake of the collapse of Communism in August of 1991, the process of rehabilitation was expected to continue without hindrance. Declassified archival documents have proved that mass killings carried out in the Soviet Union qualify as crimes against humanity. Alas, the new Russian authorities, focused on multiple other problems facing them, never provided a judicial evaluation of the Soviet past. Furthermore, the new law on rehabilitation, which was passed on October 18, 1991, still contained clauses that prevented reviewing criminal cases of "traitors to the Motherland" and "spies," even if they had been sentenced extrajudicially. This remnant of Stalinist justice still exists today. That said, the October 1991 law as a whole provided impetus to the rehabilitation process. A crucial difference is that, in accordance with that law, exoneration only requires the prosecutor's sanction, versus judicial review of a case in the 1950s.

Judgment on the Communist Past

One of the main factors that made the Soviet imperial renaissance possible is the missing judgment on the Communist past. Soviet crimes have never been adjudicated. In August 1991, Russian president Boris Yeltsin signed a decree that banned the Communist Party's activities and provided access to the Communist Party and KGB archives. Yeltsin's decrees created a precondition for a subsequent review of the Communist Party case by the Russian Constitutional Court.

In essence, that legal case did not specifically take aim at the Soviet regime's crimes. At the core of the case was a suit filed by the Communist Party of the Russian Federation on the alleged unconstitutionality of Yeltsin's ban on the Soviet and Russian Communist Party's activities and a countersuit filed by the presidential administration to proclaim the Soviet Communist Party an unconstitutional organization. The review of the case began in July of 1992. My Memorial colleagues Nikita Okhotin and Arsenii Roginskii and I, together with Sergei Mironenko, prepared an amicus curiae brief, which was supported by numerous archival documents that attested to the multiple crimes of the ruling Communist Party from Lenin to Gorbachev and specifically the crimes committed by Stalin. The brief ascertained that the party was not a public organization but the nucleus of state power and that it grossly violated constitutional norms by subsuming executive, legislative, and judicial authority. Each of these points was backed by extensive evidence based on our archival investigations.[8]

The Constitutional Court, however, did not intend to establish whether the unlimited power exercised by the Communist Party was in and of itself criminal. Still, the judgment of November 30, 1992, proved Yeltsin right in his decision to ban the party. Specifically, it stated: "During the long time the country was ruled by the regime that exercised unlimited power propped by violence, the regime consisting of a small group of Communist functionaries incorporated in the Politburo of the Central Committee of the Communist Party with Secretary General at the top."[9] Nevertheless, the Constitutional Court avoided judging the constitutionality of the Communist Party and the crimes committed by the party leadership. The case was dismissed, and a critical chance at restoring historical justice was missed.

The negative judgment of Stalin that was pronounced loud and clear during perestroika is all but forgotten now. The leaders of modern Russia avoid discussing

Stalinist crimes and violations of constitutional norms—that is, the laws of their own country. At a press conference on September 6, 2010, a British journalist asked Putin what he thought of Stalin. Putin countered by posing another question: "Was Cromwell better or worse than Stalin?"[10] Russian leaders are incapable of engaging in a direct discussion about Stalin and his legacy, preferring historical relativism; they fail to understand that historical figures like Cromwell and Stalin cannot be judged by the same yardstick. What appeared natural during Cromwell's time may look different in the twentieth century. Cromwell lived four hundred years ago, and the international situation, the essence of the rule of law, and respect for multilateral agreements and universal human rights—all have radically changed since then. Stalin drove the country back into the Middle Ages by means of the Great Terror, mass murder, torture, and forced labor. In many a postdictatorial society in the twentieth century, such deeds, and the attendant question of the criminal responsibility of the dictators and tyrants, have been the focus of international justice and accountability mechanisms.[11]

The Constitution is understood to be the supreme law of the land. All other laws and normative documents should conform to the articles of the Constitution. Conversely, laws and normative acts in conflict with respective articles of the Constitution must be declared invalid or brought in conformity with the Constitution. The 1936 Constitution, on paper, guaranteed Soviet citizens extensive rights, including secret ballots and immunity for deputies of the Supreme Soviet of the USSR, as a guarantee against arbitrary rule. Stalin personally signed the lists of persons sentenced to death. By so doing, he usurped judicial authority. It is hard to think of a graver violation of the Constitution.[12]

The position taken by contemporary Russia not only forestalls the possibility of prosecution (by evoking the statute of limitations) of the former Soviet Communist Party and security police officials who were responsible for gross violations of human rights or abused judicial authority during the Soviet period but also makes sure that no such trials take place in the former Soviet republics and now independent states. In the 1990s and 2000s, several former Soviet security police officials stood trial in the Baltic states on charges of war crimes and genocide, specifically mass murder and deportations. For example, in Latvia sentences were meted out to Evgenii Savenko, a former MGB (Ministry of State Security) investigator who put together deportee lists, and Vassilii Kononov, who was charged with the murder of the inhabitants of Malye Baty village in 1944, including a pregnant woman.[13] In Estonia, Arnold Meri, a former Communist Party official who participated in the 1949 deportation, stood trial.[14] In these and similar cases—every time Lithuanian, Latvian, and Estonian judicial authorities put a Soviet official implicated in Stalinist mass deportations on trial—the Kremlin counteracted by initiating a noisy propaganda campaign and hiring defense lawyers.

Revising History and Image Campaigns

A good indication that Russia has been descending into historical relativism is the exponentially growing sympathy toward Stalin displayed by the general population. At the beginning of the 2000s, opinion polls rendered a predominantly negative attitude toward Stalin, but by 2008 the number of those who approved of his role in history equaled those who did not. As of January 2017, approval rates reached 46 percent (those who described their attitude toward Stalin as "appreciation," "respect," or "sympathy") compared with 21 percent who harbored a negative attitude toward the Soviet dictator.[15] Those figures are a direct result of a new Russian history politics informed by ideology. As one observer correctly pointed out: "We no longer deal here with attitudes toward a particular individual but rather with a model, albeit in a subtle form. It is not that we once again learned to appreciate Stalin; on the contrary, we are being taught to appreciate Stalin, as the regime has embraced that prototype for the lack of any other element of historical legitimacy."[16]

Not coincidentally, the Kremlin developed the idea of standardizing history education, creating a "unified" history textbook that conforms to a chosen concept and "logic of uninterrupted Russian history, interconnectedness of all [historical] periods, and respect to all elements of our past."[17] According to this thesis, enemies of Russia deliberately distort its history, which prompts counteraction in the form of an attempt to "create a positive image of modern Russia in the world, also among Russians themselves."[18] Professional historians in Russia have been ascribed the role of propagandists who are required to promote the official patriotic doctrine. Alexander Chubarian, head of the Institute of World History, has no qualms stating that "we have received a request from the president: to intensify and broaden contacts with foreign scholars with the purpose of promoting historical truth and countering the attempts to distort Russia's role."[19]

The Kremlin is fixated on improving the image of Russia. Back in the day, this task was delegated to commercial public relations agencies. Changing the nature of an authoritarian state—whose very existence is preconditioned by limitations imposed on the free flow of information—is, however, a nearly impossible task. Even when President Putin said something to the effect that "I believe it is a matter of principle to secure broad access to archival documents, to secure their publication, to have the opportunity to peruse primary sources—this is an effective means against all sorts of conjectures and myths," newspaper propagandists immediately corrected him, arguing that "historical knowledge gives experts an upper hand in debates, and politicians an instrument to manipulate public opinion. Knowledge is useful, for it helps to separate the truth from lies, yet it can also be dangerous, for you never know in whose hands the truth ends up and to what use they are going to put it."[20] The perception that historical knowledge and historical facts in and of themselves constitute a danger to the regime serves as a basic postulate that keeps archives, and Russian society as a whole, closed. Moreover, this perception further contributes to the growth of xenophobia in Russia. The media increasingly promotes theories that justify closing off the Russian space to Western news outlets (the West is reportedly waging a virtual war against Russia) and their ideological impact: "We risk ending up in a situation in which the basic values of our society that had been formed in the course of centuries may be facing destruction."[21]

Tracing collective state identity back to the Soviet period backfired on Russian history politics. It is based on the postulates of "national interests" and "patriotic education." The program of patriotic education adopted by the Russian government not only ill fits a free and democratic country but also contravenes article 13, paragraph 2 of the (recently rewritten) Russian Constitution, which reads: "No ideology can de declared as official and/or obligatory."[22] In spite of that, the purpose of school and college textbooks is identified as bringing forth the "best civic and patriotic values" in students. This caveat effectively rules out objective historical analysis and places such books outside scholarship. The very attempt to ascribe educational function to history textbooks is unconstitutional. Otherwise, it prompts tendentiousness (a preferred line of interpretation), whereas the actual goal of any history textbook, beside the study of history per se, is to foster critical thinking and consequently help develop civic consciousness.

In recent years the Kremlin has doubled its propaganda efforts in thrusting new ideologically tinted values on Russian society. Authorities proclaimed the need to formulate a "national idea," with President Putin joining in the search, placing an emphasis on patriotism.[23] Furthermore, there was talk about entering in the Constitution the notion of the "Russian nation," an initiative that has received support from the Kremlin.[24]

Along with the collapse of Communism in 1991, the Soviet value system also perished. The concept of the Soviet people as a new historical entity was left for dead. The ideology of Soviet imperial grandeur was utterly exhausted, and it seemed to have disappeared for good. However, the deep-seated instinct of the ruling elite required a reference point, a single date that would be accepted by the general population and simultaneously unite it. Independence Day, June 12, did not fit the profile, as a portion of the pro-Soviet population of Russia had refused to accept it as their own.[25] The only date all Russians can relate to is May 9.

The 1945 Victory Cult as a New Civil Religion

Every year on May 9, war veterans got together in town squares across the Soviet Union to reminisce. With each passing year, fewer and fewer of them gathered on Victory Day. Although the celebration did have an element of pathos to it, it was largely a contemplative event. The formula of victory signified the memory of men at war—their suffering, their resilience, and their trust in ultimate victory. Victimhood and the inhumane nature of war were topics of conversation. For the population at large, it was the day of commemoration of the fallen, the day of compassion. Public commemoration was humane and carried strong antiwar sentiments.

During Soviet times that date obviously carried an ideological weight, apart from the popular perceptions and sentiments. In the immediate postwar years, Stalin turned victory in the Second World War into his personal achievement, letting his image be engraved on the commemorative medal. Those medals were awarded to war veterans and those in rear services. Stalin let it be known that he personified Victory. After Stalin's death, however, the meaning of victory quickly shifted away from extolling his role. The front-page story in *Pravda* on May 8, 1955, tellingly titled "The Great Heroic Deed of the Soviet People," mentioned Stalin only once. State propaganda had recalibrated its message. Now it was the Communist Party that had "organized and inspired" victory in the war. The exposure of Stalin's crimes at the Twentieth Communist Party Congress entirely removed the name of the "great leader" from the Victory Day narrative.

The year 1994 proved crucial as Russian television returned to the old Soviet practice of filling the airtime on the eve of May 9 with war-themed movies. Since then, the Russian state propaganda machine has invested disproportionately in infusing Victory Day with special meaning. Arranged for the first time in independent Russia in 1995, the military parade in Red Square has now become an annual feature. The May 9 celebration reached its apotheosis during Putin's presidency. Victory Day has now received top status as nearly the most important state holiday. Newspaper articles, TV and radio programs, public concerts, and mass distribution of St. George ribbons—all these have become ubiquitous features of the Victory Day celebration. As Polish journalist Vaclav Radzivonovič correctly characterized it, "The cult of victory over Nazism has transformed into a mandatory civil religion."[26]

In spite of the sacralization of victory in the war and the unwillingness of the Russian government to reevaluate Soviet foreign policy, the question of Soviet responsibility refuses to go away. Essentially, when Nazi Germany invaded Poland on September 1, 1939, it was bound by agreement with the Soviet Union, strengthened by the bilateral friendship and boundary agreement signed on September 28. Although the Congress of People's Deputies of the USSR in December 1989 condemned the Nazi-Soviet Pact, this is only infrequently mentioned in history textbooks.

The archaic train of thought of Russian leadership is evident not only in its interpretation of Soviet history but also in its foreign policy. It is commonplace in Russia today to speak of certain "principles of geopolitics" as a universal

Fig. 3.1. Moscow metro, November 2018. Photo by Nanci Adler.

explanation of everything and anything. Yet geopolitics is just a notion that, if any given state dearly wishes a neighboring state's territory, settled by people different from its own, the former should use all possible means to conquer and/ or reconnect the latter without scruples. The third and last edition of *Bolshaia Sovetskaia Entsiklopedia* published during the Brezhnev period identified geopolitics as a "reactionary bourgeois concept" based on the notion of the state as a geographic and biological entity with proclivity for expansion, mentioning along the way that geopolitics has become an "official doctrine of fascism."[27]

Yet the politicians and political scientists of today are not ashamed to speak of the geopolitical interests of Russia. That may be both the cause and the explanation of the adamant attempts to justify the expansionist policy of the Soviet Union, circumvent the subject of the Gulag and political mass terror, and present as benevolent the Sovietization of neighboring countries and accompanying deportations. All this naturally serves to justify Russia's current aggressive posture. Statements that appear in today's Russian newspapers are more than just outrageous; this is essentially a manifestation of Imperial Russian Nazism. As Maxim Kononenko put it, "Russian is not an ethnicity. Russian signifies belonging to the Russian World. Hence, I hesitate thinking that a person who requests something from the president of Latvia is Russian. The Russian can only demand from the president of Latvia."[28]

Today's rulers of the Kremlin perceive the victory over Nazi Germany in 1945 as a means of whitewashing the Soviet regime and preserving its symbols: "History is not defined by symbols—history fills the symbols with meaning. The red star has been washed in the blood of soldiers in the Great Patriotic [War]. That has redeemed many, if not all, sins."[29] Sacralization of the Soviet victory over Nazi Germany serves the cause of battling historical dissent. By now the 1945 victory has acquired a truly universal significance. Contemporary Russian propagandists of history surely acknowledge that the leading Western countries also fought against Hitler, yet only "in pursuit of their own interests," while the "Soviet people fought in the name of all of mankind."[30] This supposedly reveals the "messianic nature of the Russian" and makes the "Russian Victory the central event of the twentieth century." Consequently, Stalin should be credited for "returning the country to the Russian geopolitical doctrine."[31]

Filling Victory Day with new ideological meaning has not proceeded without difficulties, however. On the one hand, many previously classified documents that expose dubious Stalinist foreign policies and facilitate an accurate historical analysis of the war have resurfaced. On the other hand, neighboring countries are showing resolutely negative reactions to the growing imperial rhetoric and foreign policy of the Kremlin. Both these factors deepen the intrastate cleavages for the simple reason that Moscow has identified acceptance of its historical interpretation as an indication of its neighbors' loyalty and friendship toward Russia.

Assessing the consequences of the Second World War is impossible without an analysis of its causes and an understanding of the role and place of Stalin's Russia in the postwar settlement. In this context, the Kremlin spin doctors have particular difficulties in explaining forcible Sovietization and the imposition of totalitarian rule on the countries of Eastern and Central Europe. This is a major stumbling block that prevents the former Communist countries from enthusiastically embracing May 9, 1945, in its current Russian interpretation.

Top Russian officials within the field of history are trying to find a way out of this quagmire, typically by seeking to excuse the Soviet Union. For example, Alexander Chubarian gingerly admits that "yes, we do bear responsibility for the countries of Eastern Europe following in our path." By so doing, he draws a strict line between the liberation of Eastern Europe from Nazism and the process of Sovietization that immediately followed, shifting the blame to the victim in the process: "One has to segregate what happened before and after May 9, 1945. A Soviet model was indeed imposed on Poland, with all the manifestations of Stalinism. However, first, it took place during the Cold War. Second, Polish officials played an active part, too, in that Poland did not become a democracy but a part of the totalitarian system."[32]

Even such cautious interpretations are no longer acceptable in today's Russia. The present form of address is frontal attack. When speaking before a group of history teachers and researchers, Putin unequivocally stated, "One can read that in the aftermath of the Second World War Eastern Europe had descended in the darkness of Stalinism. But what if fascism had won? Some nations would have ceased to exist, they would have simply been destroyed."[33] Such a simplification of history is typical of contemporary Kremlin propaganda. The Kremlin's key thesis can be formulated as follows: we defeated the greatest evil the world had ever seen, and hence our own crimes must be all but purged from memory. The Kremlin instantly placed those who did not forget the forcible Sovietization in the category of "accessories to Nazis." The old Soviet ideological stratagem— "Those who do not sing along sing against"—made a comeback.

By the early 2000s, Russian columnists had formulated a propaganda triad advanced by the Kremlin: "patriotism–loyalty–tolerance [*terpimost*]."[34] However, in the intervening period, tolerance proved an ill-fitting quality. Since February 2014, the Kremlin resolved to intimidate those who disagreed with the regime and suppress all manifestations of peaceful resistance. During Soviet times, as some observers have argued, "citizens who did not openly oppose the Soviet power might take for granted that their basic social and economic rights would be guaranteed by the state."[35] Currently, a guarantee of one's rights (i.e., material benefits distributed by the state) must be earned by taking part in the persecution of all those who oppose the Kremlin's policies. During the Soviet period, criticism was possible only within the context of Socialist choices, but now one is allowed to criticize the ruling regime exclusively within the patriotic paradigm. Those who display "antipatriotic" sentiments and dare to express them publicly are now vulnerable to prosecution.

The fateful year 2014 saw the introduction of article 354.1 in the Russian penal code, which frames the so-called rehabilitation of Nazism as a punishable offense. The most ominous is part three of the article, which can be easily evoked to prosecute the regime's opponents: "Public distribution of information expressing manifest disrespect toward society regarding Russia's days of military glory and the commemorative dates associated with the defense of the Fatherland or public insults to the symbols of Russia's military glory are punishable by a fine of up to three hundred thousand rubles . . . or by corrective labor for up to one year."[36] Herein lies the ability to prosecute anyone who expresses themselves disparagingly about Victory Day or any other holiday. As of this writing (March 2018), article 354.1 has been applied in tens of cases. To give just one example, Igor Dorogoi of Magadan was indicted in 2017 under article 354.1 for views he shared on social media. At the core of the indictment was "disrespect toward symbols of Russian military glory," even though Dorogoi's criticisms were regarding the conduct of Marshall Georgy Zhukov and the Soviet judge on the Nuremberg Military Tribunal, Roman Rudenko.[37]

The study and evaluation of Soviet history can be roughly divided into two periods: prior to 2014, when critical, independent interpretations were still possible, and after 2014, when expression of views not preapproved by the Kremlin about the role of the Soviet Union in the Second World War could land one in prison.

Article 354.1 is clearly unconstitutional, for freedom of speech—guaranteed by the Constitution—has never been abrogated. This law is in and of itself anachronistic as it takes aim at heterodox opinions.

Occasionally, Kremlin rulers speak common sense. Thus, President Putin recently stated, "In the aftermath of the Second World War we attempted to superimpose on many East European countries our development model. We did it by force and, it should be admitted, it was not a good thing."[38] Yet this acknowledgment does nothing to modify the aggressive tone of the Kremlin propaganda. Officialdom has taken over the popular character of the May 9 commemoration. The state has appropriated Victory Day by emphasizing the Soviet contribution to the defeat of Nazism, unwittingly reviving the former adoration of the country's "supreme leader," Stalin, in the process. Each year, Stalin's image reappears under the guise of Victory. Each spring—like a bad dream or a bad joke—busses and fixed-route cabs adorned with the face of Stalin make their way in one Russian town or another. Curiously, with each passing year, the dictator's portrait becomes more and more glamorous. The image of Stalin in the gorgeous white uniform of generalissimo was especially popular. Along with the imagery, the historical debate on the role of Stalin in the 1945 victory is rekindled each spring—the last and only argument advanced by those who seek his historical rehabilitation.

The victory is being used to whitewash not only Stalin but also the entire Soviet repressive regime. It reclaims its legitimacy precisely through the 1945 victory. Some Russian citizens suffer so-called Stockholm syndrome by justifying Stalin's deeds and presenting him as the "savior of the motherland" in trying times of war. The train of thought of those who defend Stalin is fairly unsophisticated, if not primitive: "denouncing Stalin casts a shadow on victories and prevents the population from taking pride in just anything at the moment of unity in the face of confrontation with the outside world."[39]

The means of presentation of Stalin are predictable in that they are fairly modern. Advertisements have long been used on public transport, and Stalin's image appears there regularly. City dwellers are used to seeing advertisements for cell phone operators, soft drinks, laundry detergent, and pet food. According to modern Stalinists, adoration of the "military and state genius" of Stalin must be public and mandatory, and hence they advocate publicizing the image of the despot in public spaces wherever possible.[40] It goes further than that, however. Year after year, arguments reemerge in favor of renaming Volgograd "Stalingrad." Lately, a suggestion was aired to start erecting monuments to Stalin across Russia. This is yet another phase in the process of imposing totalitarian values on Russian society.

Moscow bookstores today provide a wealth of popular history books. Here one can plainly see that the general population is being fed the mythologized image of the "strict and just" leader.[41] Works praising Stalin dominate the section

Fig. 3.2. 2017 Stalin calendar, RGASPI book kiosk, Moscow.
Photo by Nanci Adler.

dedicated to Soviet history. The book titles are self-explanatory: *A Different Stalin* (*Inoi Stalin*), *Stalin the Great* (*Stalin velikii*), *Stalin as a Reflection of Our Youth* (*Stalin—nashei iunosti polet*), and so on. Furthermore, an entire series of publications attempt to whitewash Lavrenty Beria, Viktor Abakumov, and other odious leaders of the Secret Police under Stalin. All these beg the question of what the Russian authorities and the population at large think of Stalin today.

The Russian government avoids giving an official evaluation of the Soviet past in general and of Communist leadership in particular. It is a complex question for them. In his inaugural speech in May 2000, Putin set historical reference points by stating that "our history had both tragic and bright moments."[42] Since then, this thesis has been elaborated. Since August 2015, Russia has had a "Program of Commemorating the Memory of the Victims of Political Repression," and on October 30, 2017, a city-sponsored monument to the victims of Soviet political repressions—the Wall of Grief—was unveiled in Moscow. The fact that such a monument exists is an important milestone that attests that the state has admitted the scale and gravity of mass repressions. The monument is bound to serve as a reminder of a tragic past. At the same time, many civil rights activists have expressed a justified skepticism as to the ability of the Russian authorities to draw a line under the past and provide a legal assessment of the crimes of the Soviet regime. Activists have emphasized the ongoing, actually growing, systematic violations of human rights in Russia and have criticized the political setting in which archives that could provide evidence of the crimes committed by the state security remain off-limits while Stalin is being venerated. There is a need for a legal act that provides assessment of the crimes of Soviet totalitarianism.

Yet the authorities do not dare qualify Stalin's deeds as crimes. Instead, they refer to "mistakes" or "excesses," typically explained away by "difficulties of the prewar period" and the "need to prepare the country for war." Their calls to "understand Stalinism" are another way of saying that the history of the Soviet Union is not defined by the Gulag.

The "historical and cultural standard" that prescribes to schools how to teach history recommends referring to "mistakes," rather than mass crimes, committed by the Soviet regime. History textbooks typically sketch the Great Terror of 1937–38 without qualifying it by providing numbers of those arrested and executed.[43] Alternatively, textbooks state that Stalin had decided on a "purge from Soviet society of potential fifth-columnists."[44] A reference to the "fifth column" prompts rationalizing Stalin's designs and thus serves as an indirect justification of mass terror. Such textbooks are capable of neither providing a larger picture of the Great Terror nor fostering analytical thinking among school pupils. The state, which does not regard history as a legitimate branch of knowledge but rather as an instrument that services its ideology, just keeps applying pressure by administrative means. This constitutes the biggest problem of Russian education and society at large.

At the family level, the memory of relatives killed by the Soviet regime certainly lives on. Although people speak freely about it, this memory often coexists with the conviction that "such were the times." Just a handful of people would identify state authorities as the perpetrator. In the popular mind, the Great Terror appears as a natural disaster of sorts—a hurricane, perhaps. Only few Russian citizens comprehend, even less dare to publicly state, that the mass Soviet political terror of 1937–38 was a premeditated crime of the state, and personally of

Stalin, against his own people. A majority of Russians are altogether uncomfortable having a conversation on the horrors of Stalinism, for it violates their wholesome, patriotic perception of both the motherland and those in power.

The discussion of whether Stalin can be qualified as a criminal is important for the following two reasons. First, today Stalin appears as a man of the media. People in Russia increasingly speak of Stalin as a great state figure who carried out a consistent, if debatable, policy in the name of strengthening the country's might. For example, the controversial textbook by Alexander Barsenkov and Alexander Vdovin, *Istoriia Rossii, 1917–2009*, contains the following statement: "from the perspective of statehood, Stalin is a hero; from the perspective of human rights—a murderer and villain."[45] This quotation, not coincidentally, pitches "statehood" against the rule of law and human rights, for the Russian population has continuously regarded the state as a sacral notion, an object of adulation worth sacrificing lives. Hence, the popular mind struggles to reconcile two parallel histories: the archaic yet "glorious" history of the state that demanded human sacrifice and the tragic history of the people who bore that sacrifice. This calls forth a discussion on the essence of the Soviet state. In a nutshell, did Stalin's dictatorship prompt or violate the rule of law? Second, formal admission of the criminality of Stalin and the Stalinist system is a prerequisite for stamping out, once and for all, the forms of state governance that had been used by Stalin's regime. Alas, contemporary Russia displays a recurrent tendency of authoritarian rule.

It is fair to speak of a new Russian ideology. It rests on patriotism, militant isolationism, and a certain paternalistic conception of the role of the state on the one hand and glorification of the past, including the Soviet period, on the other. The underlying principle of this ideology is straightforward: authorities always do the right thing, and even if it creates victims, it is justified in the name of the chosen "special path." In consequence, the state can superimpose its ideology and exercise a monopoly on history education, effectively stamping out dissent.

Conclusion

Following the collapse of Communist rule in August 1991, popular consensus on the Soviet period abruptly came to an end. Declassified archival documents attested that from the 1930s to 1950s, the country was ruled by a criminal clique with Stalin at the helm. What they did to their own people falls under the category of crimes against humanity. Alas, new Russian authorities, facing a myriad of problems, did not provide a legal assessment of the Soviet past and did not call a spade a spade. Simultaneously, the major achievement in 1990s Russia—freedom of speech—ironically made it possible for Stalinists of all kinds to state their point.

The current revival of pro-Stalin sentiments in Russia is grounded in an idealized perception of the orderliness, justice, and lack of conflict during late

Stalinism. Disappointed with the results of economic reforms and perturbed by rampant corruption among the present Russian authorities and their distance from the people, the average person is missing the "strong hand," the leader who would put the house in order. Those sentiments go back to a particular trait of Soviet education that insisted on the exclusiveness of the Soviet people and their alleged superiority over citizens of capitalist countries. People in their forties and above still remember the slogans from their childhood: our political system is the most advanced in the world, we are treading the right path, we will show the way for all of mankind. These and similar ideological postulates are all dead now. The deeply seated crowd instinct and latent monarchism and paternalism come through in the attempts to make the very notion of the state sacral. The idea of a dominant state popular in conservative quarters can be rendered as follows: we do not need the state serving its subjects; we need the state posing as a father, perhaps a strict father. Although such sentiments were prevalent during the Brezhnev era, the then political elite was afraid of and therefore did not seek the return of Stalin and the attendant Stalinist form and methods of rule. Currently, the Kremlin is using the growing Stalin nostalgia to further increase the divide between Russia and the West, which is now once again regarded as hostile.

The well-oiled propaganda machine that goes into high gear in the run-up to the May 9 commemoration each year reserves no place for an honest conversation over the price of victory, millions of victims, and ethnic mass deportations. In Russia, it is the holiday itself that celebrates its victory. Trying to make sense of an improbably high death toll, grieving millions of dead—all this faded into the background. Victory Day has become a hollow celebration where individual pride turns into nationalistic intoxication.

Notes

1. The chapter has been translated from Russian by Anton Weiss-Wendt.

2. Mikhail Gorbachev, *Izbrannye statii i rechi* (Moscow: Politizdat, 1988), 5:402.

3. Resolution of the Central Committee of the Community Party from June 30, 1956, "On Superseding the Cult of Personality and Its Consequences," *KPSS v rezoliutsiiakh i resheniiakh sezdov i plenumov TsK* (Moscow: Gospolitizdat, 1960), 4:231.

4. Vladimir Kriuchkov, *Velikii oktiabr i obnovlenie sovetskogo obshchestva* (Moscow: Politizdat, 1989), 6.

5. Supreme Soviet of the Russian Federation, *Sbornik zakonodatelnykh i normativnykh aktov o repressiakh i reabilitatsii zhertv politicheskikh repressii* (Moscow: Respublika, 1993), 186–87.

6. *Sbornik zakonodatelnykh i normativnykh aktov*, 187–89.

7. *Sbornik zakonodatelnykh i normativnykh aktov*, 191–94.

8. Cf. Nikita Okhotin, Nikita Petrov, Arsenii Roginskii, and Sergei Mironenko, "Ekspertnoe zalkiuchenie k zasedaniiu Konstitutsionnogo Suda RF 7 iiulia 1992 g. po 'delu

KPSS,'" 1–63. Cited after Kristina Gorelik, "Delo KPSS—byl li upushchen shans?" Radio Liberty, July 11, 2014, https://www.svoboda.org/a/25452052.html.

9. Fedor Rudinskii, *"Delo KPSS" v Konstitutsionnom Sude* (Moscow: Bylina, 1999), 485.

10. Elena Shishkunova, "Lenin poka ostanetsia v Mavzolee: Vladimir Putin otvetil na voprosy uchastnikov Valdaiskogo kluba," *Izvestia*, September 8, 2010.

11. It is important to point out that Stalin and the Soviet authorities in general were aware of modern "European" legal norms by the 1930s. As an indirect proof, the 1936 Soviet Constitution enumerated rights and freedoms without referring to the extraordinary revolutionary situation, as was the case earlier.

12. Nikita Petrov, "Byl li Stalin prestupnikom?," in *Istoricheskaia politika v XXI veke*, ed. Maria Lipman and Alexei Miller (Moscow: Novoe literaturnoe obozrenie, 2012), 396–416.

13. Viktoria Sokolova, "Starik i gore," *Izvestia*, March 11, 2000; Viktoria Sokolova, "Meniaem chekista na fashista," *Izvestia*, March 14, 2000; Viktoria Sokolova, "Deti iavitsia postesnialis," *Izvestia*, July 10, 2000; Alexei Vsilivetskii, "Partizan pobedil Latviiu," *Izvestia*, June 27, 2008.

14. "Poslednii geroi Estonii: Interviu s Arnoldom Meri," *Izvestia*, June 11, 2008.

15. Igor Plugaterev and Vladimir Zuev, "Muzei Pobedy priros 'domikom Stalina,'" *Nezavisimoe voennoe obozrenie* 7 (February 23, 2018): 12–13.

16. Alexander Rubtsov, "'Stalinism bez Stalina': Novaia mechta rossiiskoi elity," *Izvestia*, August 2, 2017.

17. Alexander Iunashev, "Vladimir Putin poruchil sozdat edinyi uchebnik istorii," *Izvestia*, February 20, 2013.

18. Konstantin Pukemov, "Shkolnyi kurs istorii izbaviat ot iskazhenii," *Izvestia*, May 16, 2012.

19. "'Protiv nashei strany vedetsia informatsionnaia voina': Interviiu s Alexandrom Chubarianom," *Izvestia*, May 30, 2016.

20. "Putin ne otkroet iashchik Pandory," *Nezavisimoe voennoe obozrenie* 15 (April 28, 2017): 2.

21. Piotr Tolstoy, "Na voine kak na voine," *Izvestia*, February 4, 2016.

22. See text of Article 13 of the Russian Constitution, accessed January 25, 2021, https://www.zakonrf.info/konstitucia/13/.

23. Egor Sozaev-Guriev, "Patriotizm—eto i est natsionalnaia ideia," *Izvestia*, February 4, 2016.

24. Natalia Zotova, "Poniatie 'rossiiskaia natsia' dolzhno byt zakrepleno v Konstutsii," *Novaia gazeta*, November 2, 2016.

25. The declaration of national sovereignty of Russia was passed on June 12, 1990, which has been a state holiday since 1991.

26. Wacław Radziwinowicz, "Niepokalane rosyjskie zwycięstwo," *Wyborcza, Magazyn Świąteczny*, April 4, 2015, http://wyborcza.pl/magazyn/1,124059,17700646,Niepokalane _rosyjskie_zwyciestwo.html.

27. *Bolshaia Sovetskaia Entsiklopedia*, 3rd ed. (Moscow: Sovetskaia Entsiklopedia, 1971), 6:316.

28. Maxim Kononenko, "Russkii, vozvrashchaisia v Rossiiu," *Izvestia*, February 18, 2015.

29. Elena Iampolskaia, "Rubinovyi skandal," *Izvestia*, October 19, 2010.

30. Leonid Ivashov, "Na skrizhaliakh mirovoi istorii," *Nezavisimoe voennoe obozrenie* 24 (July 1, 2011): 6–7.

31. Ivashov, "Na skrizhaliakh mirovoi istorii."

32. Alexander Chubarian, "Opravdanie sotrudnichestva s natsiskim rezhimom nedopustimo," *Izvestia*, February 21, 2005.

33. "Prezident prizval izbavitsia ot ideologicheskogo musora v uchebnikah istorii," *Izvestia*, January 17, 2014.

34. Victor Toporov, "Kak podredaktirovat grafa Uvarova," *Izvestia*, October 23, 2012.

35. Anatolii Kucherena, "Pravovoi nigilizm i infantilism," *Izvestia*, August 24, 2017.

36. Federal Law no. 128-FZ of May 5, 2014, O vnesenii izmenenii v otdelnye zakonodatelnye akty Rossiiskoi Federatsii [On the introduction of changes to certain legislative acts of the Russian Federation].

37. "'Edinstvennoe, o chem ia sozhaleiu,—ne uchel razvitie v strane stukachestva': Interviu s Igorem Dorogim," *Novaia gazeta*, February 14, 2018.

38. Fedor Lukianov, "K mirnomu sosushchestvovaniiu," *Rossiiskaia gazeta*, April 21, 2015.

39. Alexander Rubtsov, "Stalin umer zavtra," *Novaia gazeta*, July 12, 2017.

40. Cf. Vladimir Sukhodeiev, *Stalin: Voennyi genii* (Moscow: OLMA, 2015).

41. See, for example, Sergei Kremlev, *Zachem ubili Stalina? Prestuplenie veka* (Moscow: Eksmo, 2008), 191.

42. Vladimir Putin, *Priamaia rech* (Moscow: Zvonnitsa-MG, 2016), 2:94.

43. Sergei Karpachev, Piotr Romanov, and Oleg Volobuev, *Istoriia Rossii: Nachalo XX— nachalo XXI veka. 10 klass* (Moscow: Drofa, 2018), 115.

44. Mikhail Gorinov, Alexander Danilov, and Mikhail Morukov, *Istoriia Rossii. 10 klass* (Moscow: Prosveshchenie, 2016), 1:144.

45. Alexander Barsenkov and Alexander Vdovin, *Istoriia Rossii, 1917–2009* (Moscow: Aspekt-Press, 2010), 13. On November 22, 2010, the faculty of the History Department of Moscow State University voted against using this textbook in the classroom. Cf. Moscow State University History Department, November 22, 2010, http://www.hist.msu.ru/Science /DISKUS/2010/index.html.

NIKITA PETROV is a historian and board member of Memorial: An International Historical, Educational, Charitable and Human Rights Society. He served as an expert witness in the legal case against the Soviet Communist Party considered in 1992 by the Russian Constitutional Court. He is author (with Marc Jansen) of *Stalin's Loyal Executioner: People's Commissar Nikolai Ezhov, 1895–1940, Die sowjetischen Geheimdienstmitarbeiter in Deutschland (1945–1954)*, and numerous books in Russian.

4 Russia as a Bulwark against Antisemitism and Holocaust Denial: The Second World War according to Moscow

Kiril Feferman

Is it justified for modern-day Russia to portray itself as a bulwark against antisemitism and Holocaust denial? This may ring true, to a certain extent, with respect to Holocaust denial given the fact that the country bore the brunt of the war against Nazi Germany, of which the Holocaust was an integral part. It may be harder to argue when it comes to antisemitism, specifically state-sponsored anti-Jewish discrimination and violence, which had a long history in Russia. This chapter examines contemporary trends in official Russian posturing about antisemitism and Holocaust denial. I situate these trends within the context of the Russian and Soviet past and current entanglements between Russia and the West, with a special emphasis on Israel.

State-Sponsored Antisemitism and the Holocaust in Russia: A Historical Overview

Russia has a long history of anti-Jewish bias. Originally predicated on religious foundations and strongly connected with Byzantine Orthodox intolerance toward the Jews, over the centuries it evolved into an essentially Russian phenomenon.[1] In the first part of the nineteenth century, Russian officialdom viewed Jews in the empire as an obscurantist and alien element to be reformed and acculturated.[2] In the second half of that century, Russian views evolved to take stock of Jewish economic rise on the one hand and their prominence in opposition politics and especially in revolutionary movements bent on toppling the government on the other.[3] Consequently, state authorities came to conclude that the Jews constituted a high and permanent security risk.[4] This view culminated in the appearance of the "Protocols of the Elders of Zion"—the catechesis of modern antisemitism—at the beginning of the twentieth century, which was sponsored by one of the branches of the imperial security service.[5] The classical religious solution by means of Jewish conversion to Christianity was increasingly challenged in the last years of the Russian Empire, with powerful figures and institutions advocating racially based discrimination against Jews.[6] Last but certainly not least, violent pogroms against the Jews and blood libel, frequently instigated and sometimes supervised by the authorities, were unique in scope and intensity in the last decades of the Russian Empire.[7]

The interwar period added new and unknown layers to Russian anti-Jewish sentiments. The Soviet state viewed manifestations of antisemitism with apprehension and publicly denounced it.[8] State-sponsored antisemitism seems to have dwindled to the point that, by the mid-1930s, some high-ranking Soviet functionaries claimed it had entirely ceased to exist in the country.[9] At the same time, the Soviet state cracked down on what it regarded as manifestations of Jewish particularism, specifically Zionism and Judaism.[10] Soviet methods in dealing with the Jews accused of Zionist or religious links combined persecution inside the country and enforced emigration.[11]

On the whole, the Bolshevik regime regarded Soviet Jews not only as natural allies internally but also as an asset in the global struggle for the hearts and minds of world Jewry.[12] Only by the end of the 1930s did the regime start to gradually purge Jews from positions of power in the Soviet political and security establishment.[13] Alongside the desire to get rid of the old elite, the regime now regarded Jews occupying sensitive positions with suspicion.

The Nazi mass murder of the Jews in the occupied Soviet territories is characterized by several unique features that informed the ways the Soviet regime and the local population alike came to treat Jews for the generations to come.[14] First, it was visible. Killing operations were carried out within localities where Jews lived; some local people witnessed massacres while the rest instantly learned of the Jews' fate.[15] The high number of extermination sites matched the number of local collaborators involved in the "Final Solution of the Jewish Question."[16] On top of that, a high number of Soviet military personnel saw the atrocities sites on their march westward.[17] All of this contributed to widespread knowledge of the Holocaust among the Soviet people even during the war—and certainly in its aftermath.

Meanwhile, a considerable number of Soviet Jews survived the Holocaust. Many were able to escape eastward as part of the Soviet evacuation program.[18] Their prominence among the refugees in the Soviet hinterland and later among those who returned to the liberated territories fueled anti-Jewish sentiments among the general Soviet population.[19] At the same time, a considerable number of Soviet Jews were involved in fighting the Germans and their allies within the Red Army ranks and Soviet partisan units.[20] Arguably, the latter factor did not change dramatically classical Russian perceptions about Jews as war dodgers. These sentiments were notably enunciated by Alexander Solzhenitsyn, who argued that there were few Jews on the front line.[21] The ensuing Russian attitudes toward the Holocaust were shaped in part by the suffering and misery many non-Jewish citizens had experienced.

Coming back to the issue of antisemitism, one should make allowance for the long occupation period during which the local population was exposed to intensive, vicious Nazi antisemitic propaganda. That propaganda mixed Nazi racial theory with the traditional antisemitism prevalent in the Russian Empire while capitalizing on the existing resentment against the Bolshevik regime, which the local population associated with the Jews.[22] It appears that this propaganda message exerted a lasting effect on the Soviet population beyond the war period.

The Soviet government pursued an ambiguous policy toward the Jews during the war. On the one hand, it viewed the Jews as loyal subjects who, due to the program of extermination set in motion by the Nazis, had no choice but to align themselves with Moscow.[23] Furthermore, it capitalized on Jews' international networks by establishing a Jewish Anti-Fascist Committee.[24] On the other hand, despite the string of relevant publications that had appeared in the wartime Soviet Union, Moscow was cautious not to draw excessive public attention to the ongoing genocide for fear of alienating the general population and unwittingly strengthening Nazi claims of the nexus between the Bolshevism and the Jews.[25]

For the entire Cold War period, the Soviet state downplayed the unique features of the Holocaust by situating it within the tragic experience of the Soviet people.[26] Furthermore, the Holocaust issue turned out to be a minefield with so many potential international implications and repercussions on Soviet internal affairs that the regime increasingly preferred to sideline the Holocaust theme entirely. Communist dogma proscribed manifestations of nationalism while state antisemitism remained poorly concealed. Consequently, the Soviet government continued viewing the Holocaust and its commemoration as potentially perilous instruments of Jewish and international intervention in its own affairs.

Postwar Soviet antisemitism implied an awareness and tacit recognition of world Jewish power. The establishment of the state of Israel in 1948 and its support by Soviet Jews was interpreted by the regime as a sign of the latter's untrustworthiness. A minor form of Jewish national awakening, nurtured by the "Israel factor" and Holocaust awareness, made Jews into a liability or even a security risk in Moscow's eyes. Soviet authorities tackled this perceived problem through various repressive methods, depending on the period, from purging the Jews from broadly defined "sensitive" industries to discriminating against them in education and forcing all those regarded as troublemakers to emigrate. However, since the regime remained committed to the ideological postulate of "proletarian internationalism" on paper, it never admitted the existence of discrimination against the Jews as such, portraying it instead as an anti-Zionist campaign.[27]

The Second World War according to the Russian Government

After a short period of ineptitude in the 1990s, the Russian government gradually returned to using the Second World War legacy for political purposes.[28] This policy has intensified in recent years, mainly due to the Russian-Ukrainian crisis and the subsequent deterioration of Russia's relations with the West. The official Russian position on the Second World War takes cues from the old Soviet Russian position. It views itself as the rightful heir to the Soviet Union and claims to still be a superpower that should be reckoned with, especially within the sphere of its vital interests, which covers the entire post-Soviet space (with the exception of the Baltic states). However, in contrast to the Soviet Union, after 2014, contemporary Russia seems to attach less importance to the principle of the inviolability of post–Second World War borders. At most, in the Russian thinking, this principle only applies to the areas outside the former Soviet Union. The reason is self-explanatory: Russia itself has contributed to changes in postwar borders vis-à-vis Ukraine and Georgia. The principles outlined prior cater to both foreign political goals and domestic audiences that value what is regarded as a restoration of Soviet grandeur. Russian leader Vladimir Putin did a lot to personally promote the legacy of the Second World War.[29]

Another trend in the Russian government's policies is discernible in its attempts to employ legal means to control the discourse on the war and its legacy. In 2009, then president Dmitrii Medvedev announced the formation of a Commission to Counter Attempts to Falsify History to the Detriment of Russian Interests. Some observers hoped the commission's activities could be harnessed to sideline or probably even censure those advocating Holocaust denial. However, the commission accomplished little during the three years of its existence and was eventually disbanded in 2012. Along these lines, in May 2014, the Russian president signed a law banning the "glorification of Nazism." The new law imposed penalties on individuals accused of denying the crimes committed by the Nazis during the Second World War, including the Holocaust.

These policies are reminiscent of what some other Eastern European countries (e.g., Poland, Ukraine) do to preserve some aspects of war memory and downplay others, particularly those that present the country in a negative light. Particularly noteworthy in this respect is the highly publicized case revoking a doctoral degree of Kirill Alexandrov, a well-known Russian historian who had done extensive research on the officer corps of the so-called Russian Liberation Army under Nazi German command.[30] This unduly harsh reaction demonstrates that the image of anti-Soviet forces in the Second World War fighting for freedom against Stalinist despotism is no longer tolerated in Russia. This interpretation, widespread in the 1990s and influenced by anti-Communist sentiments that flourished in the immediate post-Soviet period, gradually gave way to the concept that the only force Soviet patriots could identify with during the war was the Soviet Union. Still, the latter perspective does not automatically rule out new studies on Russian collaboration with the Germans, including in the Nazi mass murder of Jews.[31]

While these government initiatives tentatively outlaw Holocaust denial, the situation with antisemitism is less clear-cut. Anti-Americanism, and to a lesser extent anti-Westernism, became an essential component of Russia's new old worldview actively promoted by Russian propaganda since 2014 and shared by many ordinary Russians. Almost inevitably, these trends led to the resurgence of conspiracy theories in which antisemitism is one of the key ingredients.[32]

A Bulwark against Holocaust Denial

Vladimir Putin has been Russia's indisputable chief policy maker for twenty years. Therefore, like with many other issues, in order to understand the contemporary Russian position vis-à-vis the Holocaust and its denial, it is essential to try to understand his views.[33] His publicly voiced opinions are complex, but some trends are discernible. Unlike the Soviet stance, his viewpoint contains a clear recognition of the Holocaust and—an extraordinary admission for any Russian leader—its exceptionality.[34] Predictably, the theme of Russian victimhood still populates Putin's statements. However, it is now hailed as something that enables the Russian people to properly understand the dimensions of the Jewish tragedy.[35]

A special emphasis on the Jewish contribution to the armed struggle against Nazism is also noteworthy. This aspect is rarely addressed in the context of the Holocaust, and presumably the only other place where it has had and continues to play an important role is Israel. Therefore, it is little wonder that this issue has contributed to a rapprochement between the two countries.[36] For the Russians, who are eager to present themselves as the country that bore the brunt of the war and paid for the victory with the lives of millions of its citizens, it is a natural subject. In short, viewing the Jews, at least those who served within the military ranks, on par with the rest of the Soviet people is a clear departure from the classical Soviet narrative.[37]

The following presents several recent state-sponsored initiatives that came to fruition in 2018. The first initiative involves the promotion of the movie *Sobibor,* which tells the story of the 1943 uprising in the Sobibor death camp led by Jewish Red Army officer Alexander Pechersky.[38] The screenplay was cowritten by none other than the minister of culture, Vladimir Medinskii, otherwise known for his conservatism. The second initiative, a traveling exhibition on the liberation of Nazi death camps by the Red Army, was created in cooperation with the Russian Jewish Congress. The exhibition was displayed in a number of countries, in addition to the UN and UNESCO headquarters, with the official Russian representatives using it to reiterate the country's leading role in the fight against Nazi Germany.[39]

Another important Holocaust-related message conveyed by Putin involves a juxtaposition of Holocaust denial and what he refers to as "belittling the decisive contribution of the Soviet Union to the victory over Nazi Germany."[40] This effectively means that the issue of Holocaust denial had entered the Russian foreign political discourse and to a lesser extent the domestic political discourse. At the same time, the issue of Holocaust denial remains instrumentalized and even weaponized by the contemporary Russian state in pursuit of its own political goals. It is no different from the recurrent emphasis on the role of the Soviet army in liberating certain Nazi exterminations camps, specifically Auschwitz.[41] Historically speaking, even though the liberation of Auschwitz did little to stop the Holocaust (simply because it came too late), it was an important act that enabled the Allies for the first time to assess the scale and dimensions of the industrial genocide of the Jews and later use it as incriminating evidence against the Nazis.[42]

The special emphasis on the Holocaust and Holocaust denial in the context of Russian foreign policy indicates that the government considers it largely a foreign policy issue. This may have to do with its assessment of worldwide Jewish power, which in a way is a continuation of the Soviet thinking pattern of the 1970s and 1980s. It may also stem from the realization that advancing this topic domestically may prove counterproductive. To put it differently, the authorities fear that Russian public opinion might view laws prohibiting Holocaust denial as promoting Jewish interests. Apparently, the Russian government and the circles close to it feel they are on firm ground while directing such accusations at other countries. This proposition can be illustrated through numerous examples. In one such case, an influential Russian TV show frequently associated with the government went to great lengths to criticize the Polish Holocaust law by accusing the Poles who "have forgiven themselves for killing Jews during Nazi occupation" and thus implicitly accusing Poland of state-sponsored Holocaust denial.[43] Russia's accusation of Poland as the nation that was actively involved in the Nazi mass murder of Jews and is currently denying it is considerably harsher than the criticism voiced in Israel in connection with the Polish Holocaust law.[44]

In another accident, Maria Zakharova, a sharp-tongued spokeswoman for the Russian Ministry of Foreign Affairs, lashed out at Bulgaria after anonymous Bulgarian vandals defaced the monument to the Soviet Army in central Sofia with antisemitic graffiti. According to Zakharova, "This is especially cynical considering that during World War II our soldiers prevented the deportation of Jews from Bulgaria and saved some 50,000 people from imminent death."[45] This statement is historically inaccurate, of course: the rescue of Bulgarian Jews can be attributed to the Soviet Army only if we choose to believe the Bulgarians reversed their decision to deport the country's Jewish population in 1943 solely as a result of the Soviet victory at Stalingrad.[46] Historical accuracy aside, it is noteworthy that not only do the Russian authorities not shy away from being associated with the fight to save Jews during the Holocaust, but they also endeavor to appropriate it even when it is not due.

Russia's new policy came to the fore when legislation was proposed in Israel to recognize the Holodomor—a man-made famine in 1932–33 that severely affected Ukraine—as genocide of the Ukrainian people. Russian diplomats tried to influence Israeli public opinion by implying that such recognition would be tantamount to diluting the uniqueness of the Holocaust and would thus make it more difficult for Russia to stand up against Holocaust denial.[47] This notion demonstrates Russia's new self-perception, at least for foreign consumption, as the major bulwark against Holocaust denial (ironically, perhaps even more resolute than Israel's, which is bound by political constraints).

A Bulwark against Antisemitism

When it comes to antisemitism—and the prior Holocaust legacy—insight into Putin's mindset is in order here. An attempt to interpret his views was made by a high-ranking Russian rabbi associated with the Chabad movement, which stands close to the Kremlin.[48] According to him,

> Putin's nationalism, unlike its Soviet predecessor, incorporates and claims ethnic minority groups, including Jews, weaving "ours" into the narrative governing Russia's history and future in an effort to unite the Russian people and restore the former empire. When viewed from this angle, logically, antisemitism, as a kind of religious or ethnic-based enmity undermines the foundations of such an ethnically and religiously heterogeneous country as Russia. As soon as we let the seeds of antisemitism, neo-Nazism, national intolerance, and chauvinism sprout, we will be facing severe consequences for the state and for the entire country. It is a destructive force.[49]

Thus, Putin's approach may be partly explained as a sort of indispensable imperial etatism.[50] However, given its permanent presence in Russian history, motives such as Putin's personal predilection for Jews may be also at play. If not for Putin's long-standing contacts with his Jewish neighbors, his teachers, and, most important, his judo coach, the odds are high that he might have embraced antisemitism much like other KGB officers from his cohort did.[51]

As in the case of Holocaust denial, the Russian leader instrumentalizes the issue of antisemitism to advance Russia's foreign political goals. Given Russia's tense relations with the West, emphasis on the need to combat antisemitism appears to be an important tool in attempting to break through the present isolation. By so doing, Putin tries to enlist, with a significant degree of success, Israeli support as well as the backing of certain elements within the Jewish world; as he once stated, "Rejection of antisemitism, of any form of xenophobia and ethnic animosity, brings Russia and Israel closer together."[52] Along these lines, he also invoked the issue of antisemitism in conjunction with other phobias, specifically Russophobia.[53] The Russian self-perception of an unduly ostracized nation, not unlike the Jews prior to the Holocaust, informs the message delivered to domestic and foreign audiences alike.[54]

Presenting today's Russia as the bulwark against antisemitism is an important element of Russian foreign policy. In this respect, the situation is quite complex. Russia has invested considerable efforts in cozying up to Israel. It is then all the more surprising that Russia turned out to be the only Organization for Security and Co-operation in Europe (OSCE) country to vote against, and thus block, the international definition of antisemitism in January 2017. Russia's no vote created uproar in Israel and beyond and cast doubt on its commitment to fighting antisemitism.[55] The motives behind the Russian move are obscure but may suggest a lack of synchronization in Russian foreign policy; its disregard for international forums, especially OSCE; and finally its failure to influence the OSCE in adopting a general declaration denouncing antisemitism alongside other phobias, including Islamophobia and Russophobia.[56] If the last presupposition is correct, it may be interpreted as Russian desire not to alienate the Muslim world.[57] Finally, Russia's self-promotion as a defender of Jewish rights grew exponentially in the course of its aggression against Ukraine.[58]

Building on my previous research on the rabbinic responses in Russia and Ukraine to the conflict when it broke out in Ukraine in 2014, I provide the following analysis to account for the subsequent period.[59] The Ukrainian crisis laid bare the growing Russian isolation from the West. Despite the consistent message of Russian propaganda that emphasizes the country's ability to withstand the treacherous West, for all purposes, Russia's search for allies in the rapidly changing, ominous situation never ceased. It is against this backdrop that one should understand the Russian government courting Jewish communities and institutions, with which it has created stable, workable relations in the intervening period.

For their part, Jewish organizations reacted positively to the government's overtures. For one, it was an expression of gratitude. There was also a desire to secure more government protection against homegrown Russian antisemitism and probably even to secure the support of conservative and "patriotic" elements within the Russian population—which were traditionally the most guarded—toward Jews. It also presented a rare opportunity to capitalize on the government support to advance their own agenda. Simultaneously, Russian Jewish organizations by and large refrained from advancing their position as pro-Russian but rather presented it—depending on their expertise and affiliation—as historically grounded and morally justified. Such a measured response further reinforced the official Russian position, according to which the country was engaged in a just battle for the right cause.

In the ensuing war of words, Russian propaganda frequently took up the theme of Ukrainian Jews being under attack in the new Ukrainian state.[60] The Ukrainian government, for its part, while acknowledging antisemitic accidents, ascribed them to Moscow's manipulation and thus effectively absolved itself of any wrongdoing.[61] Furthermore, it accused Russia of showing indulgence to antisemitism within its own borders and among Russian-supported separatists in East Ukraine.[62]

Returning to the issue of antisemitism, the current Russian posture appears more twisted than that on Holocaust awareness. A lingering consciousness of the Holocaust—as so many Russians in the occupied German territories witnessed it firsthand—helps contemporary Russian public opinion embrace it as a tragedy on par with the one that befell the Russian people. In contrast, many Russians are not yet ready to forget their old scores with the Jews. According to a 2017 report prepared by the Tel Aviv University Kantor Center, Russian society has experienced a marked decline of grassroots antisemitism, which is effectively regarded as passé.[63]

When it comes to contemporary Russia coming to grips with the issue of antisemitism, the recently inaugurated Museum of Tolerance in Moscow serves as a good example.[64] The museum received the blessing of Putin, who even contributed one month's salary (a fact widely cited by the museum yet, to the best of my knowledge, omitted from official statements) and visited it several times. Yet it remains a private Jewish initiative, with no state funds allocated to its construction and activities. The museum fits well with Russian foreign policy by portraying the country as an island of interethnic and interreligious harmony. Important in Russian overtures to the Jewish world, this ambitious undertaking also aims at reaching out to domestic Russian audiences. This is achieved by showcasing Jews as ordinary and interesting people and highlighting their victimhood and concomitantly their contribution to the Russian state, thus taking a jab at anti-Jewish stereotypes. Several years ago, the present author observed the museum's advertisement on a Moscow bus stop—"It's cool to be Jewish"—viewed with astonishment by onlookers.

That the Russian public still has a long way to go as regards anti-Jewish bias is further indicated by several recent statements by high-profile public figures (e.g., Piotr Tolstoy, prominent lawmaker, deputy speaker of the Russian Duma, and the great-grandson of Leo Tolstoy).[65] Tellingly, all those statements were made in the context of the intensified struggle over property rights waged by politicians close to the Orthodox Church against what can be broadly defined as liberals. The most outrageous was an allegation made public by the influential Bishop

Tikhon Shevkunov, who suggested that Tsar Nicholas II's execution in 1918 was in fact a ritual murder.[66]

These and similar anecdotes create the picture of a group that feels particularly empowered in contemporary Russia to publicly engage in poorly disguised anti-Jewish rhetoric—namely, conservative groups allied with the Russian Orthodox Church. The lack of public outcry to that type of rhetoric outside certain pro-Jewish groups suggests general indifference bordering on antipathy.[67] However, even though this is a relatively new development, the government has demonstrated its ability to impose constraints on public discourse on Jews and antisemitism. The participating public figures who expressed themselves on the slaying of the tsarist family (i.e., Pyotr Tolstoy, Vitaly Milonov, and Bishop Tikhon) stopped short of uttering the words *Jew* or *Judaism*. This omission enabled them to later explain away their statements as directed at anonymous figures and groups, not Jews per se. Furthermore, the row was only over when these explanations were publicly accepted by figures associated with the Russian Chabad. Then and only then did the stories finally fade from the headlines.[68] My guess is that their disappearance was not due to public opinion but rather was a result of pressure exerted by the Kremlin. Presumably, it came because of clout wielded by Russian Jewish groups. More likely, though, was a realization that continuing the dispute would be detrimental to the government's domestic and foreign policies.

Contemporary Russian public discourse on Jews is also characterized by frankly bizarre and disconnected interpretations of real and mythical episodes in recent Jewish history, including classical conspiracy theories (e.g., a group of Jews, freemasons, and "illuminati" sinking the *Titanic* to provoke an international crisis and install themselves as leaders of a world government; blaming the Jews for disasters that resulted in a huge death toll; and allegations of Jews masterminding the Bolshevik Revolution).[69] Another peculiarity is replacing the words *Jews* and *Judaism* with *Zionists* and *Zionism* as a way of explaining the satanic "Zionist" influence on Russia's historical trajectory.[70] As a rule, these verbal attacks do not generate much media attention and are routinely hushed up, with the instigators sometimes castigated by local officials. According to Alexander Verkhovskii of the independent think tank Sova in Moscow, "xenophobia creeps into official discourse, which until now had been controlled from the top."[71] When it comes to ordinary offenders, however, the government may occasionally prosecute some (on account of "inciting public hatred") or relieve others of their duties.[72]

When examining the Russian brand of antisemitism, one should be aware of the blurred boundaries between antisemitism as a phenomenon and the missing notion of political correctness in Russia. As always, the tone is set by none other but Putin himself, who once suggested that "Jews with Russian citizenship were behind US election interference."[73] This speculation was aptly picked up by Maria Zakharova of the Russian Ministry of Foreign Affairs.[74] In most other countries, such statements would be immediately qualified as antisemitic. Contemporary Russia and its leader have gained a reputation for being pro-Jewish, however, and thus no furor ensued. Hence, commercial advertisements for a sauna in Siberia—"Auschwitz is nothing compared to us" (*Osventsym otdykhaet*)—or an ice cream called "A poor Jew" in central Russia were primarily interpreted as the tactlessness or lack of sensitivity characteristic of contemporary Russian culture.[75]

One should also consider that Russian *Judenpolitik* is not completely synchronized and that not everything is dictated from the Kremlin. Jews are occasionally viewed with suspicion because of their international networks. That is how one should interpret the consistent policy of Russian security agencies to deport rabbis not in possession of Russian passports.[76] This policy is in place despite the rabbis' affiliation with Russian Chabad—which, in turn, maintains a direct line of communication with the Kremlin—and the potential damage such deportations could cause to Russia's self-image as the bulwark against antisemitism. Another example is a Justice Ministry review of Jewish sacred texts and religion textbooks at the behest of "concerned citizens" on account of potential "extremism."[77] (In late 2015, however, Russian authorities put a halt to this practice, which was apparently also applied to the sacred books of other religions.)[78] Along similar lines are Russian law enforcement agencies reviewing statements by a Jewish activist.[79] To the detriment of the country's reputation, such stories pop up despite the protests of Jewish communities and public figures in Russia and abroad.

The last story that warrants discussion here is the response of the Russian public to the downing of a Russian jet by Syrian antiaircraft weapons in mid-September 2018. Leaving aside the bizarre handling of the episode by the Russian government, it also unleashed a wave of anti-Jewish sentiment.[80] The accusations of "Israeli perfidy" and "Israeli ingratitude" were first circulated by the Russian Ministry of Defense and discussed for several days on federal TV channels.[81] In the Russian blogosphere, however, this soon gave way to the notions of "*Jewish* perfidy" and "*Jewish* ingratitude." The story culminated in letters sent to all major Jewish organizations across the country in which unanimous Russian nationalists promised to settle accounts with the Russian Jews for the purported belligerent actions of Israel against Russia in Syria.[82] Notably, just one head of a Jewish organization agreed to publicly disclose the outburst of antisemitism, with no official reaction to his exposé. The lack of official response is perhaps the most significant aspect here. It identifies Russian preferences in dealing with such stories—namely, providing no comment in the hope that the entire episode will disappear from the headlines—and probably also Russian reluctance or inability to crack down on antisemites in the current situation. In such a reality, it is difficult to anticipate a propaganda campaign that would enlighten the population of the moral wrongs associated with attacking the Jews.

Conclusion

Russia has come a long way from being a country associated with a history of antisemitism and a patchy collective memory of the Holocaust to its current self-portrayal as a bulwark against Holocaust denial and antisemitism. This newly acquired image has been actively promoted by the Russian government, which deems it both necessary and just as well as providing concrete political dividends. It would be erroneous, however, to see it solely as a function of the government's realpolitik. Putin's personal predisposition toward the Jews appears to be an independent factor. The Russian government did, on occasion, yield to pressure exerted by various Jewish groups, both local and international, which argued that highlighting the Russian image as a defender of Jewish rights goes hand in hand with the government's own goals. That said, the shift in Russian policies did not prompt a change in public opinion. While there is a tendency to view the Holocaust as an unprecedented human tragedy, the general population is not yet ready to detect and unequivocally condemn antisemitism. Still, owing to overwhelming government control, these sentiments are off-limits in the current political configuration.

Notes

1. Shmuel Ettinger, "The Muscovite State and Its Attitude towards the Jews," *Zion* (1953): 136–68 (in Hebrew).

2. Eliyahu Stern, "Catholic Judaism: The Political Theology of the Nineteenth-Century Russian Jewish Enlightenment," *Harvard Theological Review* 109, no. 4 (October 2016): 483–511. Cf. Alexander Fried, "Gavriil Romanovich Derzhavin, 'An Opinion Regarding the Prevention of Famine in White Russia and the Organization of the Way of Life of the Jews' (1800)," *Aschkenas* 14, no. 2 (2004): 229–312.

3. Oleg Budnitskii, "The Jews and Revolution: Russian Perspectives, 1881–1918," *East European Jewish Affairs* 38, no. 3 (December 2008): 321–34.

4. John D. Klier, "Why Were Russian Jews Not Kaisertreu?," *Ab Imperio* 4 (2003): 41–58.

5. See, for example, Michael Hagemeister, "The Protocols of the Elders of Zion: Between History and Fiction," *New German Critique* 103 (Winter 2008): 83–95.

6. See, for example, Eugene M. Avrutin, "Racial Categories and the Politics of (Jewish) Difference in Late Imperial Russia," *Kritika: Explorations in Russian and Eurasian History* 8, no. 1 (Winter 2007): 13–40.

7. Robert E. Johnson, "Russians, Jews, and the Pogroms of 1881–1882," *Canadian Journal of History* 50, no. 1 (Spring–Summer 2015): 155–57. Cf. Viktoria Khiterer, "The October 1905 Pogroms and the Russian Authorities," *Nationalities Papers* 43, no. 5 (September 2015): 788–803. Cf. Robert Weinberg, *Blood Libel in Late Imperial Russia: The Ritual Murder Trial*

of *Mendel Beilis* (Bloomington: Indiana University Press, 2014); Edmund Levin, *A Child of Christian Blood: Murder and Conspiracy in Tsarist Russia, The Beilis Blood Libel* (New York: Schocken, 2014).

8. Michael Beizer, "Antisemitism in Petrograd/Leningrad, 1917–1930," *East European Jewish Affairs* 29, no. 1 (1999): 26–28. Cf. Arkadii Zeltser, "Inter-War Ethnic Relations and Soviet Policy: The Case of Eastern Belorussia," *Yad Vashem Studies* 34 (2006): 106–8.

9. Arkadii Zeltser, "Inter-War Ethnic Relations and Soviet Policy: The Case of Eastern Belorussia," *Yad Vashem Studies* 34 (2006): 113–14.

10. Robert Weinberg, "Demonizing Judaism in the Soviet Union during the 1920s," *Slavic Review* 67, no. 1 (Spring 2008): 120–53.

11. Ziva Galili and Boris Morozov, *Exiled to Palestine: The Emigration of Soviet Zionist Convicts, 1924–1934* (New York: Routledge, 2006).

12. Daniel Soyer, "Back to the Future: American Jews Visit the Soviet Union in the 1920s and 1930s," *Jewish Social Studies* 6, no. 3 (2000): 124–59. Cf. Allan L. Kagedan, "American Jews and the Soviet Experiment: The Agro-Joint Project, 1924–1937," *Jewish Social Studies* 43, no. 2 (1981): 153–64.

13. Arkadii Zeltser, "Jews in the Upper Ranks of the NKVD, 1934–1941," *Jews in Russia and Eastern Europe* 52 (2004): 64–90.

14. See, for example, Mordechai Altshuler, "The Unique Features of the Holocaust in the Soviet Union," in *Jews and Jewish Life in Russia and the Soviet Union*, ed. Yaacov Ro'i (Ilford, Essex, UK: F. Cass, 1995), 171–88.

15. See, for example, Daniil Romanovskii, "The Soviet Person as a Bystander of the Holocaust: The Case of Eastern Belorussia," in *Nazi Europe and the Final Solution*, ed. David Bankier and Israel Gutman (Jerusalem: Yad Vashem, International Institute for Holocaust Research, 2003), 276–306.

16. See, for example, Rebecca L. Golbert, "'Neighbors' and the Ukrainian Jewish Experience of the Holocaust: Profiles of Local Police Collaborators," in *Lessons and Legacies: The Holocaust in International Perspective*, ed. Dagmar Herzog (Evanston, IL: Northwestern University Press, 2006), 233–52.

17. Arkadi Zeltser and Erina Megowan, "Differing Views among Red Army Personnel about the Nazi Mass Murder of Jews," *Kritika: Explorations in Russian and Eurasian History* 15, no. 3 (Summer 2014): 563–90.

18. See, for example, Kiril Feferman, "A Soviet Humanitarian Action? Centre, Periphery and the Evacuation of Refugees to the North Caucasus, 1941–1942," *Europe-Asia Studies* 61, no. 5 (July 2009): 813–31.

19. Oleg Leibovich, "Antisemitskie nastroeniia v sovetskom tylu," in *SSSR vo Vtoroi mirovoi voine: Okkupatsiia, Kholokost, Stalinism*, ed. Oleg Budnitskii and Liudmila Novikova (Moscow: ROSSPEN, 2014), 280–96; Zeev Levin, "Antisemitism and the Jewish Refugees in Soviet Kirgizia, 1942," *Jews in Russia and Eastern Europe* 50, no. 1 (2003): 191–203.

20. See, for example, Yitzhak Arad, *In the Shadow of the Red Banner: Soviet Jews in the War against Nazi Germany* (Jerusalem: Yad Vashem, International Institute for Holocaust Research, 2010).

21. Alexander Solzhenitsyn, *Dvesti let vmesti* (Moscow: Russkii put, 2002), 2:136.

22. Dmitri Zhukov and Ivan Kovtun, *Antisemitskaia propaganda na okkupirovannykh territoriiakh RSFSR* (Rostov-on-Don, Russia: Feniks, 2015); Yuri Astashkin, "Antisemitskaia

propaganda na okkupirovannoi territorii Leningradskoi oblasti (po materialam gazety 'Za Rodinu' 1942–1943 gg.)," *Vestnik NovGU* 83, no. 2 (2014): 9–12.

23. Cf. Feferman, "A Soviet Humanitarian Action?," 826–29.

24. Theodore H. Friedgut, "Stalin's Bureaucracy in Action: The Creation and Destruction of the Jewish Anti-Fascist Committee," *Yad Vashem Studies* 26 (1998): 419–31.

25. Mordechai Altshuler, "The Holocaust in the Soviet Mass Media during the War and in the First Postwar Years Re-examined," *Yad Vashem Studies* 39 (2011): 121–68; Karel C. Berkhoff, "'Total Annihilation of the Jewish Population': The Holocaust in the Soviet Media, 1941–1945," *Kritika: Explorations in Russian and Eurasian History* 10, no. 1 (Winter 2009): 61–105.

26. See, for example, Kiril Feferman, *Soviet Jewish Stepchild: The Holocaust in the Soviet Mindset, 1941–1964* (Saarbrücken, Ger.: VDM, 2009); Zvi Gitelman, "Politics and the Historiography of the Holocaust in the Soviet Union," in *Bitter Legacy: Confronting the Holocaust in the USSR*, ed. Zvi Gitelman (Bloomington: Indiana University Press, 1997), 14–42.

27. See, for example, Robert S. Wistrich, *A Lethal Obsession: Anti-Semitism from Antiquity to the Global Jihad* (New York: Random House, 2010) 103–13; Jonathan Frankel, *The Soviet Regime and Anti-Zionism: An Analysis* (Jerusalem: The Hebrew University of Jerusalem, 1984).

28. See, for example, Alexei Miller, "The Turns of Russian Historical Politics, from Perestroika to 2011," in *Convolutions of Historical Politics*, ed. Alexei Miller and Maria Lipman (Budapest: Central European University Press, 2012), 253–78.

29. See, for example, Elizabeth A. Wood, "Performing Memory: Vladimir Putin and the Celebration of World War II in Russia," *Soviet and Post-Soviet Review* 38 (2011): 172–200; Stephen M. Norris, "Memory for Sale: Victory Day 2010 and Russian Remembrance," *Soviet and Post-Soviet Review* 38 (2011): 201–29.

30. Act of the Ministry of Education and Science no. 834/nk, June 23, 2017, cited after Georgy Ippolitov, *Otpor pokusheniiu na podvig naroda: protiv falsifikatsii istorii Velikoi Otechestvennoi voiny* (Moscow: Direct Media, 2020), 87.

31. Cf. Kiril Feferman, "Studying Russia or the Soviet Union? Holocaust Scholarship in Contemporary Russia," *Dapim: Studies on the Holocaust* 31, no. 2 (2017): 165–70.

32. See, for example, Marlène Laruelle, "Conspiracy and Alternate History in Russia: A Nationalist Equation for Success?" *Russian Review* 71 (October 2012): 565–80.

33. Michael Eltchaninoff, *Inside the Mind of Vladimir Putin* (London: Hurst, 2018).

34. President of Russia, "Meeting with the Representatives of International Public and Religious Organizations," July 9, 2014, http://kremlin.ru/events/president/news/46180.

35. President of Russia, "Meeting with the Representatives."

36. Lahav Harkov, "Israel-Russia Tensions Put Aside for Joint Holocaust Remembrance Event," *Jerusalem Post*, April 12, 2018, https://www.jpost.com/israels-70th-anniversary /israel-russia-tensions-put-aside-for-joint-holocaust-remembrance-event-549507.

37. Charles Dunst, "How Russian Nationalism Explains Putin's Outreach to Jews and Israel," Jewish Telegraphic Agency, July 19, 2018, https://www.jta.org/2018/07/19 /news-opinion/russian-nationalism-motivates-putins-jewish-outreach-home-towards -israel?utm_source=JTA%20Maropost&utm_campaign=JTA&utm_medium=email&mpw eb=1161-5291-3693.

38. Cnaan Liphshiz, "Why a Gory Holocaust Film is a Blockbuster in Russia," *Times of Israel*, May 12, 2018, https://www.timesofisrael.com/why-a-gory-holocaust-film-is-a -blockbuster-in-russia/.

39. Council of Europe, "Opening of the Exhibition 'The Holocaust: Annihilation, Liberation, Rescue' Organized by the Permanent Representation of the Russian Federation," July 3, 2018, https://www.coe.int/en/web/secretary-general/-/opening-of-the-exhibition-the -holocaust-annihilation-liberation-rescue-organised-by-the-permanent-representation-of -the-russian-federation.

40. "Putin Speaks against Holocaust Denial and Anti-Semitism," *Moscow Times*, January 30, 2018, https://www.themoscowtimes.com/2018/01/30/putin-speaks-against-holocaust -denial-and-anti-semitism-a60326.

41. Ministry of Foreign Affairs of the Russian Federation, "Permanent Representative of the Russian Federation to the OSCE A. K. Lukashevich's remarks at the OSCE Permanent Council meeting on International Holocaust Remembrance Day, Vienna, February 1, 2018," February 2, 2018, http://www.mid.ru/web/guest/foreign_policy/rso/osce/-/asset_publisher /bzhxR3zkq2H5/content/id/3052994.

42. See, for example, Michael Fleming, *Auschwitz, the Allies and Censorship of the Holocaust* (Cambridge: Cambridge University Press, 2014). Cf. Rebecca E. Wittmann, "Indicting Auschwitz? The Paradox of the Frankfurt Auschwitz Trial," *German History* 21 (2003): 505–32.

43. "Russian TV Show Talks Holocaust Bill, US Sanction," BBC Monitoring Former Soviet Union, February 12, 2018, https://search.proquest.com/docview/2000971261?accountid=40023 (password required).

44. Daniel Blatman, "Diverse Narratives or Separate Histories: The Polish-Israeli Debate over the So-Called Polish Holocaust Law" (paper delivered at the conference Genocide in Twentieth Century History: The Power and the Problems of an Interpretive, Ethical-Political, and Legal Concept, University of Toronto, October 19, 2018).

45. "Russia under Fire after Claiming Credit for Saving Bulgaria's Jews from Holocaust," *Haaretz*, November 6, 2017, https://www.haaretz.com/world-news/europe/.premium -russia-under-fire-after-claiming-credit-for-saving-bulgarias-jews-1.5463431.

46. Cf. Steven F. Sage, "The Holocaust in Bulgaria: Rescuing History from 'Rescue,'" *Dapim: Studies on the Holocaust* 3, no. 2 (2017): 139–45.

47. "Russian Embassy Slams Israel's Draft Law on Soviet-Era Famine in Ukraine," TASS, February 7, 2018, https://tass.com/politics/988863.

48. Chabad, a Chassidic movement founded at the beginning of the nineteenth century in East Europe, expanded after the Second World War to become the worldwide Jewish movement. It is very influential in many post-Communist countries, including Russia. Cf. Philip Wexler, "Chabad: Social Movement and Educational Practice," in *Educational Deliberations: Studies in Education Dedicated to Shlomo (Seymour) Fox*, ed. Mordecai Nisan and Oded Schremer (Jerusalem: Keter, 2005), 196–205; Sue Fishkoff, *The Rebbe's Army: Inside the World of Chabad-Lubavitch* (New York: Schocken, 2003).

49. Ministry of Foreign Affairs of the Russian Federation, "Neo-Nazism—A Dangerous Threat to Human Rights, Democracy and the Rule of Law," Coordination Forum for Countering Antisemitism, April 18, 2016, https://antisemitism.org.il/?p=105240. See also Dunst, "How Russian Nationalism Explains Putin's Outreach."

50. "Attempts to Deny the Holocaust, Belittle USSR's Role in Victory over Nazis Must be Foiled—Putin," Interfax, January 29, 2018, http://www.interfax-religion.com/?act=dujour&div=199&page=3.

51. Cf. Jonathan Adelman, "Russians and Jews: The Odd Couple," *Jerusalem Post*, October 12, 2018; Ulf Walther, "Russia's Failed Transformation: The Power of the KGB/FSB from Gorbachev to Putin," *International Journal of Intelligence and Counter-Intelligence* 27, no. 4 (2014): 666–86; Evgeniia Albats, *The State within a State: The KGB and Its Hold on Russia's Past, Present, and Future* (New York: Farrar, Straus & Giroux, 1994).

52. President of Russia, "Meeting with the Representatives."

53. "Putin: Politicians, Religious and Public Activists Must Condemn Antisemitism and Russophobia," Interfax, January 29, 2018, http://www.interfax-religion.ru/judaism/?act=news&div=69161; President of Russia, "Plenary Session of the St. Petersburg Economic Forum," June 2, 2017, http://kremlin.ru/events/president/news/54667.

54. On the conference "Russophobia and Information War against Russia," September 26, 2015, Pravorf.org, http://pravorf.org/index.php/news/1842-0-konferentsii-rusofobiya -i-informatsionnaya-vojna-protiv-rossii. Cf. Ambassador of the Russian Federation to Macedonia O. N. Sherbak's article, "'The McCarthyism of the Twenty-First Century' Published in the Country's Oldest Newspaper, 'Noa Macedonia' on June 20," Ministry of Foreign Affairs of the Russian Federation, June 22, 2017, http://www.mid.ru/web/guest/maps /mk/-/asset_publisher/Bx1lWHr8ws3J/content/id/2793998.

55. "In Rare Criticism, Israeli Envoy Raps Russia for Blocking Anti-Semitism Definition," *Times of Israel*, February 15, 2017, http://www.timesofisrael.com/in-rare-criticism-israeli -envoy-raps-russia-for-blocking-anti-semitism-definition/.

56. Ministry of Foreign Affairs of the Russian Federation, "Russian Foreign Minister S. V. Lavrov Holds a Press Conference on Russian Diplomatic Activities in 2016," January 17, 2017, http://www.mid.ru/web/guest/meropriyatiya_s_uchastiem_ministra/-/asset_publisher /xK1BhB2bUjd3/content/id/2599609.

57. On the Russian foreign policy vis-à-vis the Muslim world, see Roman Silantev, *Musulmanskaia diplomatiia v Rossii: istoriia i sovremennost* (Moscow: IPK RGLU "Rema," 2010), 193–276.

58. On the use and misuse of the Jewish factor in the Russian-Ukrainian conflict, see the forthcoming book by Sam Sokol. I am grateful to the author for sharing his unpublished manuscript with me.

59. Kiril Feferman, "The Ukrainian Crisis and the Attitudes of the Russian and Ukrainian Jewish Communities," *Israel Journal of Foreign Affairs* 9, no. 2 (2015): 227–36.

60. For example, Masha Kondrachuk, and Stephen Ennis, "Jews Reject Russia Claims of Ukraine Anti-Semitism," BBC, November 12, 2014, https://www.bbc.com/news/world -europe-29991777.

61. Halya Coynash, "Debunking Russia's Narrative of Rampant Anti-Semitism in Ukraine Again," Atlantic Council, August 4, 2015, https://www.atlanticcouncil.org/blogs /ukrainealert/debunking-russia-s-narrative-of-rampant-anti-semitism-in-ukraine-again/.

62. Consulate General of Ukraine in Chicago, "Deputy Foreign Minister of Ukraine Danylo Lubkivsky met with a Delegation of the American Jewish Committee," April 23, 2014, https://chicago.mfa.gov.ua/en/news/21966-zastupnik-ministra-zakordonnih-sprav-ukrajini -danilo-lubkivsykij-proviv-zustrich-z-delegacijeju-amerikansykogo-jevrejsykogo-komitetu.

63. "'Levada Tsentr' zafiksiroval snizhenie urovnia antisemitizma v Rossii," Dozhd TV, November 1, 2016, https://tvrain.ru/news/jews-420115/.

64. Olga Gershenson, "The Jewish Museum and Tolerance Center in Moscow: Judaism for the Masses," *East European Jewish Affairs* 45, nos. 2–3 (2015): 158–73.

65. "Russian Lawmaker: Ancestors of Jewish Politicians 'Boiled Us in Cauldrons'" (in Hebrew), *Makor Rishon*, February 13, 2017, https://www.makorrishon.co.il/nrg/online/1/ART2/863/736.html. Cf. "State Duma Vice-Speaker Pyotr Tolstoy Makes Anti-Semitic Statement, Then Accuses Journalists of Anti-Semitism," Meduza, January 24, 2017, https://meduza.io/en/feature/2017/01/24/state-duma-vice-speaker-pyotr-tolstoy-makes-anti-semitic-statement-then-accuses-journalists-of-anti-semitism.

66. "FJCR Shocked by the Emergence of the 'Judeophobe Myth' of the Ritual Murder of the Tsar 100 Years after the Revolution," Interfax, November 28, 2017, http://www.interfax-religion.ru/judaism/?act=news&div=68706.

67. "Pinchas Goldschmidt: Jews Are the First to be Targeted by Terrorists in Europe," RIA, February 8, 2017, https://ria.ru/religion/20170208/1487377206.html.

68. "Bishop Tikhon Explained That on the Issue of Nicholas II's Ritual Murder One Does Not Mean Ethnicity or Religious Beliefs of the Perpetrators," Interfax, November 30, 2017, http://www.interfax-religion.ru/judaism/?act=news&div=68736.

69. Daniel Leons-Marder, "Russian TV Blames Jews for Sinking of Titanic, Chernobyl and 9/11," Everyday Antisemitism, November 8, 2016, http://everydayantisemitism.com/2016/08/11/russian-tv-blames-jews-for-sinking-of-titanic-chernobyl-and-911/?mc_cid=eb4c9d8eba&mc_eid=042d32eadf; Artur Priimak, "The Tragedy at Kemerovo Is Followed by 'Blood Libel,'" *Nezavisimaia gazeta*, April 4, 2018, http://www.ng.ru/facts/2018-04-04/10_440_kemerovo.html; Ekaterina Makhotina, "Verordnete Versöhnung: Geschichtspolitische und gesellschaftliche Perspektiven auf die Russische Revolution," *Jahrbücher für Geschichte Osteuropas—East European History* 65, no. 2 (2017): 295–305.

70. Walter Laqueur, "Anti-Semitism and the New Russian Idea," *Mosaic*, June 25, 2015, https://mosaicmagazine.com/observation/politics-current-affairs/2015/06/anti-semitism-and-the-new-russian-idea/.

71. Statement by Alexander Verkhovskii of the NGO Sova, "Russian Lawmaker: 'Jews Destroyed Russia,'" Israel National News, February 14, 2014, http://www.israelnationalnews.com/News/News.aspx/177443#.Uv4UopuYaM9.

72. "A Resident of Yekaterinburg Sentenced to Compulsory Community Service after Being Convicted of Sharing a Video with Extremist Content and Drawing Graffiti in an Elevator," Coordination Forum for Countering Antisemitism, May 28, 2017, https://antisemitism.org.il/?p=114952; "Resident of the City of Barnaul Was Convicted of Disseminating Antisemitic Materials," *Altaiskaia pravda*, August 6, 2016, http://www.ap22.ru/paper/Barnaulets-osuzhden-za-publichnoe-vozbuzhdenii-nenavisti-k-evreyam.html; "Russian Judge Dismissed for Antisemitic Post," Israel National News, July 23, 2015, http://www.israelnationalnews.com/News/News.aspx/198535.

73. "Putin: I Don't Care If Russians Intervened in the US Elections, Possibly Jews Did It," *Maariv* (in Hebrew), March 10, 2018, http://www.maariv.co.il/news/world/Article-627133.

74. "Russian Government Spokeswoman Suggests Trump Won thanks to 'the Jews,'" Coordination Forum for Countering Antisemitism, November 18, 2016, https://antisemitism.org.il/?p=109864.

75. Cf. "Russian Court Orders 'Poor Jew' Ice Cream Line Pulled," *Times of Israel*, August 10, 2018, https://www.timesofisrael.com/russian-court-orders-poor-jew-ice-cream-line -pulled/.

76. "American Chabad Rabbi in Sochi Called Security Risk, Ordered to Leave," Jewish Telegraphic Agency, February 8, 2017, https://www.jta.org/2017/02/08/news-opinion/world /american-chabad-rabbi-called-security-risk-in-russia-ordered-to-leave.

77. "Textbooks on Jewish Tradition Will Be Reviewed on Account of Containing Extremist Content," Politsovet, June 1, 2015, http://politsovet.ru/48710-uchebniki -po-evreyskoy-tradicii-proveryayut-na-ekstremizm.html.

78. In November 2015, Putin signed the law that proscribed reviewing the sacred books of four Russian "accepted" religions, including Judaism. Official Internet Portal of Legal Information, "Federal Law of 23.11.2015 No. 314-FZ 'On Amendments to the Federal Law' On Countering Extremist Activity," November 23, 2015, http://publication.pravo.gov.ru /Document/View/0001201511230050.

79. "Proverku na ekstremizm lidera evreiiskogo dvizheniia v RF sviazali s ego postom v seti," Interfax, August 13, 2018, https://www.interfax.ru/russia/625087.

80. "Russia Blames Israel after Military Plane Shot Down off Syria," BBC, September 18, 2018, https://www.bbc.com/news/world-europe-45556290.

81. "Ingratitude and Criminal Negligence: Russian Ministry of Defense Accused Israel of Downing IL-20," *Vesti* (Tel Aviv), September 23, 2018, https://www.vesty.co.il /articles/0,7340,L-5356515,00.html.

82. Andrei Melnikov, "Nationalists Threaten Jews with Revenge for Il-20 Downed by the Syrians," *Nezavisimaia gazeta*, October 9, 2018, http://www.ng.ru/faith/2018-10-09/100 _il20_0910.html.

KIRIL FEFERMAN is Senior Lecturer in History and Director of the Holocaust History Center at Ariel University. He is author of *"If We Had Wings, We Would Fly to You": A Soviet Jewish Family Faces Destruction, 1941–42* and *The Holocaust in the Crimea and the North Caucasus*. He is editor (with Crispin Brooks) of *Beyond the Pale: The Holocaust in the North Caucasus*.

PART II
Museums, Pop Culture, and Other Memory Battlegrounds

5 Keeping the Past in the Past: The Attack on the Perm 36 Gulag Museum and Russian Historical Memory of Soviet Repression

Steven A. Barnes

MEMORY POLITICS AROUND the history of the Gulag and Soviet repression defies easy generalization in Russia today.[1] Evidence abounds for those who would paint Vladimir Putin and Russia as beholden to the Soviet past, wanting to restore its memory and greatness to buttress the legitimacy of a formally democratic yet fundamentally dictatorial form of power. State terror, as Nanci Adler argued, is "marginalized in today's official version of Russia's history" as the Russian leadership fashions a "usable past" through "repressing the memory of repression."[2] Other evidence points to at least some official recognition of the public presence of the memory of the Gulag and Soviet repression. From 2012 to 2015, the Perm 36 Gulag Museum was brazenly attacked through a hostile takeover that threw out its leadership and threatened to close the museum. On October 30, 2015, Moscow's small Gulag Museum reopened in a gleaming new facility with more than nine times its original exhibit space and the substantial public support of the Moscow city government. Simultaneously, in recent years, monuments to and images of Stalin seem to be reappearing all over Russia. On October 30, 2017, President Vladimir Putin personally spoke at the opening of the Wall of Grief, Moscow's new monument dedicated to the victims of political repression. While still subsumed in a broader narrative of Soviet successes, especially the sacralization of the victory in the Great Patriotic War, Putin's Russia seems at least somewhat attuned to criticism of its handling of the history of Soviet repression. Perhaps echoing its neighbor, Kazakhstan, the Russian government has concluded that official state acknowledgment of the history of repression need not entail reduction in authoritarianism or even respect for human rights.[3]

In short, memory politics in Russia is complex and multifaceted. While Putin can certainly be the final arbiter at the national level when he so chooses, decisions and debates over the historical memory of the Gulag and Soviet repression and its relationship to contemporary Russian politics are often fought most fiercely at the local level as civil society actors clash with regional authorities and with one another. This chapter examines Russian historical memory through events in the Perm region. Located on the western slopes of the Ural Mountains, the Perm region is notorious for its role in Soviet and post-Soviet forced labor imprisonment.[4] In the village of Kuchino, some one hundred kilometers northeast of the city of Perm, a forced labor camp dating to the Stalin era operated until the late 1980s as one of the last Soviet detention institutions for political prisoners. After the collapse of the Soviet Union, local activists and the organization Memorial claimed the site and, in a remarkable public-private partnership, turned it into a historical site and museum with a strong commitment to civic engagement and defense of human rights in contemporary Russia. After 2012, a new governor of the Perm region turned on the museum, forcing out its founders and the nongovernmental organization that had restored the site and administered the museum for two decades. Former employees of the Perm 36 camp, along with Perm Communists and self-styled "left patriots" from an organization called the Essence of Time (*Sut vremeni*), eagerly collaborated with Perm government officials and nationwide state-controlled television in an attempt to delegitimize and destroy the museum. The slanderous attacks on the museum and its founders led to a widespread outcry in Russia and beyond. While the mass public response failed to return control of the museum to the original leadership, it was instrumental in preventing regional officials from closing the museum, although it now exists in a fundamentally altered form.

Alexander Etkind likened different components of cultural memory to a computer's hardware and software: "*Soft memory* consists primarily of texts (including literary, historical, and other narratives), whereas *hard memory* consists primarily of monuments. Of course, the soft and the hard are interdependent. Museums, cemeteries, commemorative festivities, guided tours, and history textbooks are complicated systems that demonstrate multilevel interactions between the hardware (sculptures, obelisks, memorials, historical places) and the software (songs, films, guidebooks, inscriptions, historical studies) of cultural memory. It is not the mere existence of the hardware and the software but their interaction, transparency, and conduct that give cultural memory life."[5] The interdependency of hardware and software is evident in the Perm 36 Museum under its new leadership. While its hardware has been preserved, the changes in the software have been so extensive that the museum's relevance in contemporary Russia has been lost.

Perm as a Site of Remembrance and Musealization

Founded in 1946 as a timber felling operation in Stalin's empire of forced labor camps, what came to be called Perm 36 outlived the dictator by more than thirty years before closing as part of reformist Mikhail Gorbachev's attempt to turn the country away from its history of oppression. By the time it closed in 1987, Perm 36—along with its sibling camps, Perm 35 and Perm 37—was famous as a place of incarceration for Soviet human rights activists and other dissidents in the 1970s and 1980s. Soviet authorities specifically chose the three Perm camps for this purpose in the early 1970s due to the remoteness of their location in the western Ural Mountains. They thought this would prevent political prisoners from smuggling information about the horrific conditions in the camps to the West, even though reports continued to trickle out nonetheless. In 1980, an even stricter special regime division was built to further isolate the most incorrigible inmates, who were now locked away in cramped cells they could only leave once a day for exercise in a "yard" not much bigger than their cells. Special regime prisoners worked assembling electronics components and were punished with solitary confinement and a reduction in already meager food rations for failure to meet work norms.[6]

The Perm 36 camp held some of the Soviet Union's most famous dissidents, including Sergei Kovalev, Balys Gajauskas, Natan Sharansky, Vladimir Bukovsky, Vasyl Stus, and many others. In 1985, the Ukrainian poet and advocate for Ukrainian independence Stus was the last prisoner to die in the camp. In 1989, a group of Ukrainians—including Vasyl Ovsienko, recently released Perm prisoner and member of the Ukrainian Helsinki Group—traveled to Kuchino, where they filmed the former camp's facilities and sought to exhume Stus's remains for return to Ukraine. In response, local officials took bulldozers to the site and razed much of the camp to the ground.[7] In the following years, camp infrastructure was pillaged to meet resource needs for a psychoneurological boarding school that had been assigned to one of the former camp buildings. The local population, which bore the brunt of the economic collapse that accompanied the fall of the Soviet Union, scavenged the site for building materials.[8]

By 1994, the camp site was in an advanced stage of decay, with most buildings wrecked and stripped of anything that might be of value. At that time, local activists affiliated with the International Memorial Society—an organization dedicated to preserving the history of Soviet political repression—recognized the unique value of the Perm 36 site, which they identified as the "sole preserved zone out of the tens of thousands of camp zones that existed in the 1930s–1950s on the territory of the USSR."[9] Many Gulag camps had only been temporary structures, built to complete a particular economic project like felling timber or building roads and railways. Once the projects were completed, the camps were abandoned and the facilities left to either deteriorate or be ransacked for building materials. Some of the more permanently built structures of the Gulag continue to operate today as part of the Russian penal system, although in a heavily altered form. Occasionally, original stone or steel structures like barracks walls and watchtowers can be found in remote locations. However, only the Perm

36 labor camp contains a more or less intact structure dating to the Stalin era that was intimately involved with the Soviet political repression of the later decades.[10]

Viktor Shmyrov, a history professor at the Perm State Pedagogical Institute and a local museum director, spearheaded the preservation effort and is generally regarded as the founder of what became the Perm 36 Museum.[11] Tatiana Kursina, Shmyrov's wife and herself a professional historian, served as the museum's director until 2014. For twenty years, Shmyrov and Kursina were the heart and soul of the Perm 36 project. The first order of business was site preservation, repair, and reconstruction. Volunteers funded much of the initial reconstruction work. In the fall of 1994, activists rented a plot in the forest, bought chainsaws and gasoline, recruited a work brigade from nearby villages, and in that first winter felled some two thousand cubic meters of timber, which was then processed in Perm 36's own sawmill, which they had restored to working order. Timber was used to both fund and complete reconstruction.[12]

The emerging Perm 36 Museum operated as a public-private partnership. The activists formed an "autonomous noncommercial organization" (the Russian version of a nongovernmental organization, or NGO) called Perm 36 to lead the museum.[13] The Perm regional government owned the site and all the buildings but granted its use without charge to the NGO Perm 36 for the purpose of reconstruction and museum operations. Furthermore, starting in 1996, the Perm regional government began financially supporting the museum. Shmyrov estimates that the Perm regional government provided just under half of estimated restoration costs in the late 1990s and early 2000s. The rest was funded through the work of NGO Perm 36. NGO staff and volunteers felled and processed their own timber construction materials, did much of the carpentry, and carried out other reconstruction activities.[14]

While the regional government financially supported maintenance and reconstruction, all other activities of the museum were privately funded. The NGO Perm 36 obtained substantial funding from Russian and foreign businesses and foundations. Among the foreign donors, the Moscow office of the Ford Foundation was a large early supporter of the project. At other times the museum received support from the Open Society Institute, the TACIS Democracy Program, the American Jewish World Service, the Charles Stewart Mott Foundation, and the National Endowment for Democracy.[15] Critics later capitalized on the museum's foreign funding in their attempt to delegitimize its existence.

The results were remarkable. Over the course of two decades, some twenty buildings totaling nearly five thousand square meters of floor space were either preserved, restored, or totally rebuilt. In addition, museum staff and volunteers reconstructed nearly one and a half kilometers of wooden, steel, and barbed wire fencing along with watchtowers, searchlights, and perimeter lighting. By 2011, as they embarked on the reconstruction of the last two buildings from the former camp (a bathhouse and a workshop), government support was withdrawn. As of this writing, the two buildings remain incomplete.[16]

With reconstruction and preservation efforts underway, activists started working on a museum to provide necessary historical context for visitors. The museum officially opened on September 5, 1995, with a single exhibit mounted in the former barrack of the camp's now-reconstructed special regime division. Meanwhile, staff started a research program to expand the museum's expertise and collections on the history of the Gulag and Soviet repression. The museum engaged in archival research, recorded oral histories with former prisoners and eyewitnesses, and undertook expeditions to former Gulag sites in search of artifacts for the museum's collections and exhibits. Over the next decade, the research and expeditions paid off with a series of new and increasingly sophisticated exhibitions on the political prisoners of Perm 36, Gulag history, forced labor, daily life in camps, and broader approaches to Soviet history and life under totalitarian rule.[17] From the founders' perspective, though, the most important aspect of the museum was the site itself. As Shmyrov wrote in 2001: "[Visitors] can tread the same path as every newly arrived prisoner. They can feel the terrifying atmosphere of isolation which surrounded the prisoners for years."[18]

The Perm 36 Museum's founders had been affiliated with the International Memorial Society, for whom preservation of history was as much means as it was end. The founders envisaged the museum as a civically engaged institution preserving the memory of the Gulag and Soviet repression as a warning against totalitarianism in general and state violations of human rights in particular. While the museum's subject matter was firmly rooted in the past, its approach was not antiquarian but forward looking, focusing on contemporary Russia and the world. It was critical to the founders, therefore, to find ways to overcome the site's isolation.[19] Consequently, the Perm 36 Museum developed an extensive outreach program within the Perm region and beyond. Museum staff sent traveling exhibitions to village clubs and secondary schools and crisscrossed the Perm region to organize lectures, meetings with victims and witnesses of repression, and screenings of feature and documentary films.[20]

Particularly concerned with raising historical awareness in a new post-Soviet generation, the museum engaged broadly with teachers. As part of their curriculum, future history teachers studying at the Perm Institute of Education were required to visit the museum. Once the museum could provide overnight accommodation and classroom space, it began offering weeklong on-site courses for teachers from the Perm region and around the country. Museum staff, textbook authors, and experienced educators led these seminars to improve methodology for teaching the history of twentieth-century Russia.[21]

In addition, the museum organized training courses for state and local museum professionals and held annual monthlong practicums for dramaturgs, actors, and artists interested in portraying the history of the Gulag and repression in their works. In 2003, they mounted a two-month exhibition, "History Lessons in the Museum of the Gulag," in the State Central Museum of Contemporary History of Russia in Moscow. Between 2005 and 2012, the museum hosted a highly anticipated annual civic forum, Pilorama (Russian for *sawmill*). With its focus on contemporary Russia, Pilorama was particularly despised by the museum's critics, and, as discussed later, it became a special target in the 2012 attack on the museum. All activities combined brought an estimated forty thousand visitors to the museum annually.[22]

Outreach efforts extended well beyond Russia, and the museum proved adept at cultivating international support, cooperation, and recognition. As early as 1997, the *New York Times* published an extensive piece on the museum.[23] In 1999, the museum was one of the seven founding members of the International Coalition of Historic Site Museums of Conscience, an organization founded on the belief that such institutions have an "active role to play in contemporary issues."[24] In 2003, the museum hosted a small exhibition in the US Capitol Building.[25] The World Monument Fund placed the Perm 36 site on its 2004 list of One Hundred Most Endangered Sites. The Perm 36 Museum leadership exchanged visits and expertise with public historians of the US National Park Service, and the two organizations cooperated on a traveling exhibition, "Gulag: Soviet Forced Labor Camps and the Struggle for Freedom," that opened at Ellis Island in 2006 before traveling to Boston, upstate New York, California, and Georgia. The Perm 36 Museum, along with the International Memorial Society in Moscow, were key partners of the Roy Rosenzweig Center for History and New Media at George Mason University in the development of a major online exhibition on the history of the Gulag.[26]

In short, up until 2011 the story of the Perm 36 Museum was a story of resounding success. The museum had been named one of three "national memorial-museum centers of memory of victims of repression" as part of the Russian federal government's "program of memorialization of victims of political repression" for 2011–13. This designation came with a promise of federal funding to the tune of some 500 million rubles.[27] The museum and historic site was under consideration for inclusion in the UNESCO World Heritage List. With promises of a budget increase, the museum began planning for further development of the museum and the surrounding territory, including a five-hectare natural map of the Gulag and a memorial park—the "Forest of Memory of the Victims of Political Repression." When the museum came under attack, it was almost ready to sign a contract with Ralph Appelbaum Associates, one of the world's largest and most famous museum design firms responsible for projects such as the US Holocaust Memorial Museum, the US Capitol Visitor Center, the American Museum of Natural History, and the Moscow Jewish Museum and Tolerance Center.[28]

The Politics of Perm: The Battle over the Past

Supported by successive Perm regional governors, the museum was largely allowed to work without political interference.²⁹ Yet in the aftermath of public protests in Russia in the winter of 2011–12, marked by growing state pressure on civil society organizations, and the arrival of a new Perm regional governor, the public-private partnership collapsed. Appointed to his position in May 2012, Viktor Basargin immediately cut funding for reconstruction activity at Perm 36, the first time the museum had been without government reconstruction support since 1996. Reconstruction of the last two camp buildings was halted, and the museum was forced to cut many of its other projects. Although governor Basargin did not publicly state his position on the museum until mid-2014, his actions were uniformly hostile. When the vice president of Ralph Appelbaum Associates traveled to Perm to continue negotiations on a museum development contract, Basargin left the delegation sitting in his reception area for over an hour before refusing to meet with them.³⁰ All this was just a hint of the trouble to come.

Basargin's hostility toward the Perm 36 Museum reflected the emerging sentiment of Putin's newest presidential term. Driven by notions that foreign-funded NGOs fomented the "color revolutions" and Russian protests in the winter of 2011–12, Putin's government stepped up pressure by adopting a law in July 2012 requiring any NGO that receives funds from foreign sources and engages in political activities to register as a "foreign agent." The law has since been evoked to harass Russian NGOs and ultimately was one of the weapons used against the Perm 36 Museum.³¹

Whether taking cues from the new governor's hostility to the museum or mobilized by his bid to delegitimize the museum, a veritable coalition of former Perm 36 wardens and guards, Perm Communists, and self-styled "left patriots" launched a smear campaign against the NGO in July of 2012.³² The coordinated attack occurred as the Perm 36 Museum was preparing for its annual Pilorama civic forum. The Pilorama forum was high profile and overtly political and therefore one of the most dangerous activities of the Perm 36 Museum in this new era of Putin's Russia. Pilorama started in 2005 as a festival of so-called author's songs, or Russian Bard poetry, performed to simple musical accompaniment. This was an important and popular feature of the Soviet dissident movement as the songs gave powerful voice to the very types of nonconformist thinking that landed many prisoners in Perm 36. Thus, a festival of author's songs was a natural extension of the work of the Perm 36 Museum.

In 2007, the format of Pilorama was expanded to become an all-encompassing civic forum featuring music, film, theater, and discussion panels. The discussion panels proved popular and controversial; like the museum as a whole, Pilorama did not limit itself to history but focused on related human rights issues in contemporary Russia and around the world. In the aftermath of the previous winter's protests, some in Putin's Russia came to perceive the forum's agenda as a threat.

A mecca for Russian liberals, Pilorama was open to anyone. It drew celebrities, politicians (both members of the opposition and of the Putin administration), civil society activists, and human rights advocates from all around the world. It also drew opponents. Perm Communists attended Pilorama, albeit primarily as provocateurs seeking to disrupt and criticize the forum, its organizers, and the museum.[33] Members of a self-styled "left patriotic" organization, Essence of Time, attended the 2012 Pilorama forum, where they set up their own separate "AntiPilorama."[34] While Pilorama uncomfortably but in a principled fashion accepted the presence of critics at the forum, its opponents attacked Pilorama's very existence.

The vociferous public attacks on the Perm 36 Museum emerged in the lead-up to Pilorama shortly after Basargin took office. In mid-July 2012, a group of about one hundred picketers from a club calling itself "Patriot" gathered in front of the Perm regional government buildings, calling on the government to cut its funding for Pilorama and carrying signs like "No NATO base at Perm 36!" In an interview, one of the picketers, Sergei Vilisov (who reemerged identified merely as a "student" in the scurrilous 2014 NTV television program about the Perm 36 Museum discussed later), slandered human rights activist, former human rights commissioner, and former dissident Sergei Kovalev as a spy and complained that the Pilorama forum and the museum more generally were using foreign funds to "brainwash our citizens" and "propagandize 'orange revolution.'"[35]

Despite Basargin's hostility to the museum, opposition to the museum brought together just a handful of picketers. Their message, however, was amplified later that month by the popular Russian weekly *Argumenty i Fakty*. In its July 25 Perm regional supplement, days before the start of Pilorama, the newspaper published an interview with the former warden of the Perm 36 camp. Dripping with venom disguised as a search for hidden truth, Olga Volgina introduced the interview by asking why Pilorama never invited former camp employees to participate: "What are the Memorial tour guides hiding?" Volgina described Pilorama as a place where "tourists and human rights advocates from Germany, the Netherlands, America, France, etc." and fans of "camp exotica" were afforded the opportunity to freely explore the site with the "enthralling stories of volunteers about the suffering and tortures of the camp's last prisoners." She lamented that Vladimir Kurguzov, the head of the Perm 35-36-37 complex, was never invited to share his version of the dissident-era events because he might tell an inconvenient story.[36]

The remainder of the article is mostly direct quotations from Kurguzov. Kurguzov hit all the buttons of what has become the standard Perm 36 counternarrative. First, the prisoners in the Perm 36 camps were genuine enemies, not prisoners of conscience. Second, conditions in the camp were not only humane but were actually better than the living conditions experienced by free Soviet citizens. Finally, the Perm 36 Museum was a foreign-funded effort to make Russia look bad. While these elements of criticism were amplified and intensified over the next two years, the counternarrative remained basically unchanged. Hence, the following takes a closer look at Kurguzov's interview.

First, Kurguzov sought to demystify the camp's prisoners, emphasizing that they were not human rights heroes but "traitors to the Motherland [Article 64] . . . , forest brothers, Banderovites, Vlasovites, and our own Russian traitors . . . , those who sold secret documents abroad . . . , [and] anti-Soviet people [Article 70]."[37] Critics later expanded Kurguzov's critique and emphasized that the camp held prisoners other than just dissidents, including recidivist criminals and bandits. After the start of hostilities in Ukraine, critical attention focused on the allegedly "Banderovite" and "forest brother" prisoners, generally subsumed under the catch-all word *fascists*.

Second, Kurguzov likened Perm 36 to a "sanatorium" and emphasized that comparisons with the Gulag made his "blood boil." In the Gulag of the 1930s–1950s, he noted, thousands of people died working on "major construction projects, logging, and the Kolyma road." Perm 36, on the other hand, "with its clean, well-nourished little prisoners," was engaged in the manufacturing of electric components. Camp administration could not have treated Perm 36's prisoners like the Gulag inmates of the Stalin years, he asserted: "These were . . . people with tremendous support from abroad" who lived in "ideal conditions," dressed in brand-new clothes, and were "fed better than the majority of the population in the country." Foreign backing ensured good conditions in the camp, for any failure on the part of the administration would immediately echo "over there" (e.g., foreign radio broadcasts), and investigators would come running to preserve the country's image. Essentially, Kurguzov painted a picture of Perm 36 prisoners as coddled, while those who were justly punished with solitary confinement committed violations intentionally so they could "trumpet [their suffering] to the whole world."[38]

Finally, Kurguzov emphasized that "any normal person" understands the museum is a "plainly ideological operation, aimed at creating a certain image of the country and paid for out of foreign pockets." Here Volgina jumped in with an absurd comment that the museum, "like Memorial," is 99.5 percent financed by foreign sponsors, latching on to the accusations of foreign funding commonly used against NGOs in the aftermath of the foreign agent registration act. "And that's the whole deal," argued Kurguzov. "Why? To show that everything for us has been bad, is bad, and will always be bad." Worse yet, according to Kurguzov, the Pilorama festival included rock concerts just to attract youth who could then be brainwashed. Kurguzov concluded that the Perm 36 founders did not love their country, as they took grants to falsify history for foreign amusement.[39]

The article is basically a series of lies from beginning to end. It hardly seems necessary to remind readers that prisoners suffered and died in this camp, often for nothing more than the things they wrote and the ideas they expressed. Although conditions in Perm 36 were certainly better than in many Stalin-era forced labor camps, this does not mean the prisoners were fed and dressed better than free Soviet citizens.[40]

Negotiating Perm's Present and Future

Starting in November 2012 and extending well into 2013, the self-styled "left patriots" of Essence of Time, who seek the "development of Communist ideas in the 21st century and in search of a synthesis of the red project with national traditions," ran a fourteen-part series under the title "Perm 36: Truth and Lies."[41] When compared to this treatise, even Kurguzov appears sober in his assessment of the museum. Sections like "How SS Men and Criminals Became Political Prisoners" reveal the thrust and slanderous nature of the argument. The series develops and amplifies the standard Perm 36 Museum counternarrative, drawing heavily on interviews with former staff members.

Basargin's enmity toward the Perm 36 Museum and specifically Pilorama continued in 2013. At the last minute, the Perm regional government cut the funding for Pilorama 2013 in half, effectively requiring the organizers to cancel the event.[42] Then, in the winter of 2013–14, Ukrainian protestors overthrew the pro-Russian government of Viktor Yanukovych and Russia seized Crimea and intervened in Ukraine's easternmost region amid the denunciations of "fascists," "Nazis," and "Banderovites" who allegedly led the Euromaidan movement. Denunciations of all things Ukrainian gained ground, which also affected the Perm 36 Museum.

In 2014, the confrontation between Basargin's Perm regional government and the Perm 36 Museum came to a head. Without a contribution from the regional budget, the museum was completely nonfunctional for the first half of the year. Museum employees stopped receiving salaries in early 2014; in April, water and electricity were cut off for nonpayment; and in May, Tatiana Kursina was fired as the museum's director. The new director appointed by Basargin, Natalia Semakova, was a bureaucrat with no particular interest in—or experience related to—the work of the museum. Simultaneously, the NGO Perm 36 was replaced with a governmental agency to administer the museum. Shmyrov and Kursina, meanwhile, were essentially accused of embezzlement. The Perm regional government claimed the museum had not made any improvements despite the allocation of over 89 million rubles from the regional budget over the previous five years.[43] With Kursina and Shmyrov cast aside for a loyal bureaucrat, the museum was literally on the verge of extinction.

In June 2014, shortly after Kursina's firing, the Russian television station NTV—infamous in recent years for its hatchet job on opponents of Russian actions in Ukraine and anti-Putin protestors, along with its uncanny ability to arrive at NGOs simultaneously with Russian government officials carrying out raids under the foreign agent registration act—ran an episode of its program *Profession: Reporter*. The episode, "Fifth Column," viciously attacked the Perm 36 Museum and its leadership for allegedly "teach[ing] children that Ukrainian fascists are not as bad as history textbooks portray them, whilst their grandchildren caused genocide in eastern Ukraine." The program closely followed the Perm 36 counternarrative, emphasizing the Ukrainian angle and allegations that the museum was largely funded by the United States government with the intention of splitting Siberia from Russia or carrying out a coup d'état, as supposedly had been done in Ukraine.[44]

The appearance of "Fifth Column" on national television could be taken as an indication of support for the destruction of the museum by Putin's government. Few doubt that the museum's dismemberment was Basargin's plan. Criticism of Kursina's firing and the scurrilous "Fifth Column" program was fierce and constant in and out of Russia. Several articles reporting the attack on the museum took it as a sign that the Kremlin had decided to erase the memory of the Gulag. The founders of the Perm 36 Museum, however, believed they had found powerful patrons in the presidential administration: Mikhail Fedotov, chair of the presidential administration's human rights council, and Vladimir Lukin, commissioner for human rights in Russia. Indeed, *Komsomolskaia Pravda* and Gazeta.ru speculated that only intervention from the presidential administration prevented the museum's imminent closure. Ultimately, in July 2014, Basargin broke his silence and publicly announced that the museum would be preserved and that he was willing to engage in a dialogue concerning the future of the museum.[45]

Meetings, negotiations, and discussions over the museum's fate effectively continued from the fall of 2013 through the fall of 2015. Yet even with the active participation of Fedotov, Lukin, and other well-placed federal officials, negotiations to resume cooperation between the NGO Perm 36 and the Perm regional government and to restore the NGO's (and the original leadership's) control over the museum failed.[46] With the NGO Perm 36 sidelined, a new state agency slated to run the museum took over the property and buildings. Basargin withdrew from the informal agreement that had granted use of the property and buildings to the NGO Perm 36, and the newly established state agency seized the museum's collections—artifacts, archives, and library—all of which had been acquired by the NGO from financial sources beyond those provided by the government. In effect, the state seized not only the property and facilities of which it was the legal owner but also all the materials collected by the NGO over the course of twenty-odd years.[47]

The state's takeover of the NGO's property is still a major source of disagreement. Shmyrov has repeatedly stated that the museum's founders will only consider cooperation with the new museum leadership after the property has been returned and a suitable agreement on its use has been reached. The new director of the museum, Natalia Semakova, has disputed this account and essentially accused Kursina of theft of museum property: "Tatiana Kursina came and took away things [from the museum] personally. During the summer, her employees came in cars and took things away. I do not even know exactly what they took. They carried things out in black bags and left with full trunks. . . . Throughout the summer [of 2014] they had free access."[48] Absent pressure from her superiors, Semakova seems unlikely to budge on this issue.

Even after gaining control of the museum, the Perm regional government remained hostile toward the NGO Perm 36 and the museum's founders, who continued to speak out against the direction taken by the new museum leadership. Ordered to register as a "foreign agent," the NGO decided to "self-liquidate" in March 2015, and thus it no longer formally exists.[49] Regardless, in May 2015, the new Perm 36 Museum leadership demanded 1.5 million rubles from the NGO Perm 36 for its alleged failure to return (unspecified) property in a timely fashion.[50] Two months later, a Perm court ordered the NGO Perm 36 to pay 300,000 rubles for its refusal to register as a foreign agent. As the NGO's director, Kursina was personally fined an additional 100,000 rubles.[51] Given that the government had already established control over the museum, these moves seem to have been designed to shut up Kursina and Shmyrov.

In 2017, the whole sorry affair received renewed coverage with the release of director Sergei Kachkin's documentary film *Perm 36: Otrazhenie* (*Perm 36: Reflexion*). The first half of the film features interviews with three former Perm 36 prisoners, and the second focuses on Pilorama 2012 and the attack on the museum. Press coverage and reviews of the film have reenergized old debates, with defenders of the museum's founders praising the film and museum critics denouncing the film and any institution brave enough to screen it.[52]

Basargin's departure from his position as Perm's regional governor in February 2017 briefly raised hopes that the incoming administration might reopen negotiations for the return of the original museum leadership. Kursina, too, expressed hope that things were about to change.[53] However, in May, the new Perm regional governor reappointed Semakova for another term as the director of Perm 36. *Kommersant* reported that Memorial would continue its policy of refusing to cooperate with the museum under the new leadership.[54]

The question persists of why Basargin attacked the Perm 36 Museum in 2012–14 in the first place. Basargin never explained his actions. In 2017, *Kommersant* carried a brief statement by Basargin's regional minister of culture, Igor Gladnev, who said that the former directors of Perm 36 "with funding of foreign sponsors organized questionable events justifying Banderovites," although this does not directly reflect on Basargin's actions.[55] Shmyrov writes that for him the whole affair is quite clear. An order was given to destroy the "museum, which was built by a group of enthusiasts and volunteers with tremendous public support and even, at an earlier stage, with the support of particular government structures. Above all, that order was carried out in spite of powerful public opposition. . . . However, the order was not for destruction but for the restructuring [*pereprofilirovanie*] of the museum. It was supposed to become a new museum—a museum that was under control [*podkontrolnyi*], a museum acceptable to those in power." Shmyrov took the very process of legitimizing the seizure of the museum as an indication that the museum had lost "meaning and perspective." Shmyrov is certain that someone in power gave an order to seize control of the museum from the independent group of activists, museum professionals, and historians. Ultimately, the museum was not necessarily meant to be closed: Perm 36 was to come under government control, and its content was to become more convenient and more useful for those in power.[56] Sergei Kovalev explained the state takeover as follows: "They very much need a museum that is absolutely under control and reliably censored but has the same name and better yet with the participation of some of those non-government people who were closely affiliated with it, obviously."[57]

The Content(s) of the Museum

The crucial question is how the hostile takeover of the museum's management has affected the content of the museum's exhibits and the nature of its work. Although the present author has not been able to visit the Perm 36 Museum since its seizure by the state, journalistic accounts and the museum's online presence suggest the museum no longer pursues its original mission, especially its commitment to serve as a platform for civic discussions and engage with questions of human rights in contemporary Russia. If the new museum leadership indeed sought to create a museum devoted exclusively to the practice of incarceration and/or the laudable service provided by camp guards and staff—as repeatedly alleged by the museum's founders—the museum has apparently backed off from that plan, at least for the time being.[58] The headlines declaring that the museum had erased all evidence of Stalin's crimes appear to be a gross overstatement. What we do know about the museum and its new direction, however, is troubling enough.[59]

Certain aspects of the museum's online presence are concerning. For example, one current exhibition presented on its website is titled "Between Dream and Reality." It promises to mark the one hundredth anniversary of the Russian Revolution by recounting the "history of the communist idea, its implementation, and the fates of people and entire countries. Particular attention is paid to the revolution in Russia, the embodiment of the ideas of communism in our country." The exhibition further shows how the communist idea played out in different countries and features a section on Soviet ideological literature from the 1950s to 1980s that projects Soviet attitudes "toward world politics, socialist bloc countries, the understanding of communism and socialism, the Victory of the Soviet people in the Great Patriotic war, the exploration of space, etc." The description of the exhibition does not mention the Gulag, Soviet repression, or the Soviet dissident movement—no indication whatsoever that mass state violence was part of Soviet history. To be fair, the museum is currently displaying an exhibition devoted to the eightieth anniversary of the Great Terror. The short description provides a fair discussion of the basic history of the Great Terror, which is told in the exhibition through NKVD investigation files from the Perm State Archives of Social and Political History.[60]

In 2015, the museum hired Iulia Kantor as an external curator and historian. Kantor is a serious scholar specializing in the history of the Second World War, military history, and international relations during the interwar period. She serves as head of research at the Hermitage Museum in St. Petersburg and is also a frequent guest on Ekho Moscow radio, where she typically provides commentary on a wide range of historical topics. She was a leading figure in the Council of Russian Museums and a member of the Interdepartmental Commission on the Perpetuation of the Memory of Victims of Political Repression.[61]

In an interview Kantor provided an interesting take on the museum's current activities, although it was clearly from an insider's point of view and therefore supportive of the status quo. However, even her defense of the museum is disconcerting. The interview appeared in October 2016 in the St. Petersburg online newspaper *Fontanka*. The interview got off to a troubling start with *Fontanka* journalist Irina Tumakova's sarcastic introduction. She informed readers that "two years ago, we learned that . . . the authorities decided [to turn the Perm 36 Museum into] a 'museum of the screws' [*vertukhai*, Russian slang word for prison guards] so as to honor the memory not of the victims but of the victimizers." Tumakova continued describing events at the museum, laying out a story she clearly thinks was all too easily believed. The museum's founders were expelled and replaced by "obedient officials who had no relationship to culture or history." This story, she concluded, fit with a trend to erect monuments to the "leader of the peoples" (read: Stalin). Yet, on the eve of October 30—the annual day of commemoration of the victims of political repression—the new museum staff held a conference dedicated to the history of the Gulag. Tumakova feigned shock that such a thing could happen given what the press had reported over the course of two years, so she proceeded to interview Kantor to find out what was really happening at the museum.[62]

Kantor set out to defend the museum, condemning the way the takeover was handled yet endorsing the current activities of the new museum leadership. She called the government's closure of the museum "undignified." According to her, the government was displeased with the status of the museum, in particular the pro-opposition views that dominated the Pilorama forum. When the government attacked the museum, Kantor asserted, historians and museum workers across the country rose to its defense.

Kantor clearly believed the Perm regional government wanted to either destroy the museum or turn it into a depoliticized museum of the penitentiary system. Kantor contended that Perm 36 museum workers, through the Council of Russian Museums, asked her to intervene due to the threat from a new leadership of loyal bureaucrats with no interest in the museum's work. Kantor claimed that she was alarmed about the new direction of the museum when she went to meet with the new director, Semakova, whom she described as a *chinovnik* (hard-core bureaucrat). When she toured the museum, however, Kantor discovered that the "main exposition tied to the history of the Gulag had been preserved." Moreover, she noticed that Shmyrov's name was still displayed as the author of the exposition's concept: "I walked around the museum and saw that nothing terrible was happening." Furthermore, new temporary exhibitions on certain aspects of Gulag history were in the making. She ultimately concluded that the new employees were building an "honest museum."

Hence, Kantor presented herself as a skeptic turned supporter of the work of the new museum, establishing her bona fides by condemning the seizure of the museum but quickly reassuring readers that nothing extraordinary had happened. After visiting the museum, Kantor said she returned to St. Petersburg and reported the situation to Mikhail Piotrovskii, the director of the Hermitage Museum and the president of the Council of Russian Museums. Piotrovskii subsequently decided to visit the Perm 36 Museum alongside other museum experts.

At that point, Kantor's defense of the museum became a bit tortured. By the time she returned with Piotrovskii, one of the original exhibits dealing with Perm 36's political prisoners had been removed. Kantor explained it away as a desire on the part of the new museum leadership to present a more balanced picture. According to Kantor, Perm 36 held not only dissidents and human rights activists but also Nazi collaborators, hardened criminals, and spies. Simultaneously, Kantor argued that Soviet authorities treated bandits and dissidents as one and the same. The founders of the museum, she asserted, did much the same except that they reversed the moral evaluation by regarding Perm 36's prisoners all as heroes, thus ignoring the presence of real enemies among them. Kantor thought this was unacceptable from both a moral and a professional point of view. Now, Kantor argued, the exhibition covered all categories of the camp's prisoners, and the museum as a whole was "hiding nothing." From now on, she avowed, individuals with "impeccable dissident reputations," like Vasyl Stus and Valerii Marchenko, could no longer be confused with "criminal recidivists or 'forest brothers.'"

According to Kantor, Piotrovskii decided to collaborate with the new museum. He invited the entire Perm 36 staff to St. Petersburg for training and organized a roundtable at the Hermitage to discuss how to present complex historical issues, emphasizing that "respect for history" does not mean "retouching its shameful pages." During those meetings, the Perm minister of culture proposed to the Perm 36 director that Kantor serve as an external curator for the museum. Kantor inferred that Semakova came to understand that closing or radically transforming the museum would be "blasphemy." Kantor perceived herself as a mediator of sorts between those who wanted the museum closed and those who worked with the "former" Perm 36 and now boycotted it. The founders of the museum, Kantor lamented, continue to give interviews asserting that Perm 36 has become a museum of the camp guards and/or the NKVD. Yet she said they refused to set foot in the museum or join the museum's expert council; none of the critical journalists had been to the museum either. Kantor invited the museum's founders to get over their hurts, accept that they would not be returned to their previous positions of leadership, and recognize that their continued criticism only increased the chances the museum might be shut down entirely.[63]

In late 2016, journalist Vladimir Sokolov backed up Kantor's account to a certain degree, stating that he found that the museum itself as well as director Semakova's attitude toward the museum had changed for the better since his previous visit earlier that year. He praised the museum for a large number of new temporary exhibitions and found the tour guides more professional and less hostile to the museum and former camp prisoners than they had been on his previous visit. While Sokolov concluded that "life goes on" in the museum, he admitted some troubling signs—changes in the museum's policies that "could be perceived as ambiguous." In particular, he noted that the museum carefully avoided serving as a public square or platform for debate—a role it had previously cultivated. He quoted several individuals on the incredible loss of the demise of the annual Pilorama forum.

Shmyrov's article in *Zvezda* cited extensively in this chapter was written in response to Kantor's interview and Sokolov's article. Shmyrov remained critical of the new museum leadership, noting that the sheer number of new exhibitions was a bad sign since each exhibit ideally should be the subject of extensive research and preparation. Shmyrov asserted these exhibitions were instead hastily assembled in just days or even hours. Given that the museum was forced to apologize, in early 2016, for its overly positive presentation of the "effectiveness" of *sharashki* in an exhibition devoted to these Gulag scientific research and development laboratories employing prisoner scientists, it appears they were indeed moving too fast and with too little care.[64] Shmyrov was particularly offended that some of the new exhibits were placed within the cells of the special regime prison, thus taking attention away from their real purpose. The main exhibit of the museum, he said, is the "prison itself with its monstrous interiors." Instead, the new leadership has filled the space with temporary exhibitions and even painted directly on the walls, beautifying the "monstrous" rooms that served as prisoner barracks.[65]

Conclusion

On the one hand, if we take Kantor at her word, the outcome of the hostile takeover of the museum is not as destructive as initially feared for Gulag remembrance. It is likely that outcry over the attack on the museum from within Russia and around the world, combined with the patronage of a few highly placed officials in the presidential administration, prevented the total demise of the museum. The continued existence of the Perm 36 Museum keeps open the possibility that its message and the story of the Gulag and Soviet-era political repression of dissidents and human rights activists will reach future generations. Should the political regime in Moscow ever change and an honest and balanced account of the Soviet past become possible, the museum will be well positioned to contribute. Yet the entire episode also emphasizes the fragility of even the hardware of historical memory under an authoritarian regime that is at best ambivalent to (and at worst dismissive of) the darker pages of the Soviet past. If the presidential administration saved the museum today, it could destroy it tomorrow. The general atmosphere of hostility toward civil society organizations in Putin's Russia—worsened in the aftermath of the 2011–12 protests—combined with a change in the regional governor led to unrelenting assaults on the Perm 36 Museum, spearheaded by the newly appointed regional governor. Voices of slanderous criticism were amplified to unprecedented levels in state-controlled media after Russian aggression in Ukraine. As a result, a group of people who had devoted more than twenty years of their lives to preserving, restoring, and reconstructing this unique site of historical memory were forcibly removed from the museum they had literally built with their bare hands.

Even though the museum continues to exist and to a certain degree still engages with the history of the Gulag and Soviet repression, real damage has been done. After all is said and done, Kantor works for the museum's new leadership and thus cannot credibly pass as a third party, especially given her willingness to justify what many observers consider troubling changes to the museum's content. Furthermore, her calls for the museum's founders to get over it, mute their criticism of the museum, and cooperate with its new leadership are rather disingenuous insofar as she makes them out to be the true threat to the museum's existence.

Even if we were to assume that Kantor is correct and nothing terrible is happening at the museum, she fails to acknowledge all that has been lost—something Sokolov at least hints at. While the hardware and many of the lines of code in the software of historical memory have been preserved, its essence has been irrevocably altered. Exhibits have been changed in subtle but important ways. Insofar as Soviet dissidents are placed alongside "bandits," "hardened criminals," "spies," and "Nazi collaborators" without proper explanation of the differences, the museum makes use of the standard Soviet rhetorical device, thus validating and reinforcing the slanders of former camp guards and public organizations critical of the museum. The elimination of the Pilorama forum further recontextualizes the museum's work. The new museum certainly will not include civic engagement and observance of human rights in its mandate. In some ways, this is the most troubling outcome of all. Putin's Russia appears to have found the proper place for the history of Soviet repression—in the past, never to be associated with the present, authoritarian form of rule.

Notes

1. Scholarship on the Russian historical memory of Stalin's mass crimes, and specifically the Gulag, is voluminous. In addition to the work of Nanci Adler and Alexander Etkind cited later, the studies most influential to my approach are the following: Elisabeth Anstett, "Memory of Political Repression in Post-Soviet Russia: The Example of the Gulag," SciencesPo, Mass Violence and Resistance Research Network, September 13, 2011, https:// www.sciencespo.fr/mass-violence-war-massacre-resistance/en/document/memory-political -repression-post-soviet-russia-example-gulag.html; Dina Khapaeva, "Historical Memory in Post-Soviet Gothic Society," *Social Research* 76, no. 1 (Spring 2009): 359–94; Dina Khapaeva, "Triumphant Memory of the Perpetrators: Putin's Politics of Re-Stalinization," *Communist and Post-Communist Studies* 49, no. 1 (March 2016): 61–73; Arsenii Roginskii, "The Embrace of Stalinism," Open Democracy, December 16, 2008, https://www.opendemocracy.net/en/the -embrace-of-stalinism/; Thomas Sherlock, "Russian Politics and the Soviet Past: Reassessing Stalin and Stalinism under Vladimir Putin," *Communist and Post-Communist Studies* 49, no. 1 (March 2016): 45–59; Maria M. Tumarkin, "The Long Life of Stalinism: Reflections on the Aftermath of Totalitarianism and Social Memory," *Journal of Social History* 44, no. 4 (Summer 2011): 1047–61; Sarah J. Young, "Historical Memory of the Gulag (3): Contested Memory," *Dr. Sarah J. Young* (blog), September 17, 2015, http://sarahjyoung.com/site/2015 /09/17/historical-memory-of-the-gulag-3-contested-memory/; Greg Yudin, "History in Russia: Two Memories and Multiple Pasts," Raam op Rusland, accessed January 21, 2021, https://www.raamoprusland.nl/debat/geschiedschrijving-als-politiek-instrument; and Nanci Adler, "The Future of Unwanted Histories," Raam op Russland, accessed January 21, 2021,

https://www.raamoprusland.nl/debat/geschiedschrijving-als-politiek-instrument/564-the
-future-of-unwanted-histories.

2. Nanci Adler, "Reconciliation with—or Rehabilitation of—the Soviet Past?," *Memory Studies* 5, no. 3 (2012): 327–38.

3. Cf. Steven A. Barnes, "Remembering the Gulag in Post-Soviet Kazakhstan," in *Museums of Communism: New Memory Sites in Central and Eastern Europe*, ed. Stephen Norris (Bloomington: Indiana University Press, 2020), chapter 4. Specifically, Putin stated: "Indeed, we and our descendants must remember the tragedy of repression and what caused it. However, this does not mean settling scores. We cannot push society to a dangerous line of confrontation yet again. Now, it is important for all of us to build on the values of trust and stability. Only on this basis will we be able to achieve the goals of our society and our country, which is one for us all." "Otkrytie memoriala pamiati zhertv politicheskikh repressii 'Stena skorbi,'" President of Russia, October 30, 2017, http://www.kremlin.ru/events /president/news/55948.

4. Judith Pallot, "Forced Labour for Forestry: The Twentieth-Century History of Colonization and Settlement in the North of Perm Oblast," *Europe-Asia Studies* 54, no. 7 (2002): 1055–83; Ola Cichowlas, "The Zone," Open Democracy, November 9, 2013, https:// www.opendemocracy.net/en/odr/zone/.

5. Alexander Etkind, "Post-Soviet Hauntology: Cultural Memory of the Soviet Terror," *Constellations* 16, no. 1 (2009): 182–200, here at 194.

6. Viktor Shmyrov, "The Gulag Museum," *Museum International* 53 (2001): 23–27.

7. See V. Ovsienko, "Memorial Museum in Kuchino," Kharkiv Human Rights Group, May 21, 2000, http://khpg.org/en/958939878.

8. Ovsienko, "Memorial Museum in Kuchino"; Viktor Shmyrov, "'Perm-36': Reabilitatsiia repressii," *Zvezda*, December 13, 2016.

9. Shmyrov, "'Perm-36': Reabilitatsiia repressii."

10. Shmyrov, "The Gulag Museum." See also Judith Pallot, "The Topography of Incarceration: The Spatial Continuity of Penality and the Legacy of the Gulag in Twentieth- and Twenty-First-Century Russia," *Laboratorium* 7, no. 1 (2015): 26–50.

11. Although the museum generally referred to itself as the Gulag Museum in its early years, its formal name is the Museum of the History of Political Repression Perm 36. To avoid confusion with the Gulag Museum in the city of Moscow, I use the designation Perm 36 Museum.

12. Shmyrov, "'Perm-36': Reabilitatsiia repressii"; Shmyrov, "The Gulag Museum."

13. I refer to the organization as NGO Perm 36 in order to distinguish it from the Perm 36 Museum, which until 2014 was operated by this particular NGO.

14. Shmyrov, "'Perm-36': Reabilitatsiia repressii."

15. Shmyrov, "The Gulag Museum."

16. Shmyrov, "'Perm-36': Reabilitatsiia repressii."

17. Shmyrov, "'Perm-36': Reabilitatsiia repressii."

18. Shmyrov, "The Gulag Museum." See also Joel Chalfen, "Performances of Conscience at Three Historic Site Museums" (PhD diss., University of Manchester, 2010).

19. Cf. Barnes, "Remembering the Gulag in Post-Soviet Kazakhstan."

20. Shmyrov, "'Perm-36': Reabilitatsiia repressii."

21. Shmyrov, "'Perm-36': Reabilitatsiia repressii."

22. Shmyrov, "'Perm-36': Reabilitatsiia repressii."

23. Alessandra Stanley, "Lest Russians Forget, a Museum of the Gulag," *New York Times,* October 29, 1997.

24. See articles by the founder of the organization: Liz Sevcenko, "Sites of Conscience: New Approaches to Conflicted Memory," *Museum International* 62, nos. 1–2 (May 2010): 20–25; Liz Sevcenko, "Activating the Past for Civic Action: The International Coalition of Historic Site Museums of Conscience," *George Wright Forum* 19, no. 4 (2002): 55–64. See also the International Coalition of Sites of Conscience, http://sitesofconscience.org.

25. "Perm-36 Museum Helping to Overcome Gulag Legacy," Radio Liberty, October 9, 2003.

26. The author served as a consultant for the US National Park Service in the creation of the traveling exhibition and later as the project historian at George Mason University in building its online version (http://gulaghistory.org). Cf. Martin Blatt, "Remembering Repression: The GULAG as an NPS Exhibit," *Perspectives on History,* November 2008; Louis P. Hutchins and Gay E. Vietzke, "Dialogue between Continents: Civic Engagement and the Gulag Museum at Perm 36, Russia," *George Wright Forum* 19, no. 4 (2002): 65–74.

27. Aleksandr Kalikh, "'Perm-36': Unichtozhenie pamiati," Memorial, March 4, 2015, http://www.pmem.ru/4055.html. Kalikh likens the Perm government's takeover of the museum to corporate raiding, suggesting that control of the substantial federal funding might have been part of the motivation. At the very least, the federal funding might have allowed the museum to expand its activities in ways its opponents feared.

28. Shmyrov, "'Perm-36': Reabilitatsiia repressii." Cf. Paul Williams, "Treading Difficult Ground: The Effort to Establish Russia's First National Gulag Museum," *National Museums and the Negotiation of Difficult Pasts: Conference Proceedings from EuNaMus, Brussels January 26–27, 2012,* https://ep.liu.se/ecp/082/007/ecp12082007.pdf.

29. Arsenii Roginskii, the director of the International Memorial Society, called the museum project "a unique example of an ideal partnership of state and society." Aleksei Krizhevskii, Nataliia Mitiusheva, and Tatiana Sokhareva, "Ostorozhno, zona zakryvaetsia," Gazeta.ru, July 25, 2014, https://www.gazeta.ru/culture/2014/07/25/a_6145885.shtml.

30. Shmyrov, "'Perm-36': Reabilitatsiia repressii."

31. "Russia: A Year On, Putin's 'Foreign Agents Law' Choking Freedom," Amnesty International, November 20, 2013, https://www.amnesty.org/en/latest/news/2013/11/russia-year-putin-s-foreign-agents-law-choking-freedom/.

32. The criticism of the museum was not entirely new but was greatly amplified in the political atmosphere of 2012. As Ivan Kukushkin, a former Perm 36 guard, put it in 1997: "We believed they were here for a good reason. . . . Nobody knew anything, even if now some people say the prisoners were right." Quoted in Stanley, "Lest Russians Forget."

33. In the documentary film *Perm 36: Otrazhenie,* which includes extensive footage from the 2012 Pilorama, Sergei Andrianov, a leader of the Perm Komsomol, belligerently interrupts Sergei Kovalev speaking on a panel. Andianov was interviewed by the filmmaker about his scuffle with Kovalev at the 2008 Pilorama forum, when he accused the human rights activist of having the blood of Russian soldiers on his hands through his opposition to the war in Chechnya.

34. Cf. *Perm 36: Otrazhenie.*

35. "Pikety kluba 'Patriot' protiv foruma 'Pilorama,'" *Ekho Moskvy v Permi,* July 17, 2012.

36. Olga Volgina, "Byvshii nadziratel 'Perm-36' ulichil 'Piloramu' v falsifikatsii istorii," *Argumenty i Fakty* 30, July 25, 2012.

37. Volgina, "Byvshii nadziratel 'Perm-36.'"

38. Volgina, "Byvshii nadziratel 'Perm-36.'"

39. Volgina, "Byvshii nadziratel 'Perm-36.'"

40. Ivan Kovalev, "Nemnogo faktov k vashim argumentam," Grani, August 10, 2012, https://graniru.org/blogs/free/entries/199607.html. Kovalev was a prisoner in Perm 35 who was arrested, along with his father and his wife, for their involvement in the publication of the underground Soviet newsletter *Chronicle of Current Events*. For more on conditions in the Perm camps, see Ivan Kovalev, "8 dekabria—25 let so dnia smerti Anatoliia Marchenko," December 4, 2011, https://hro.org/node/12591.

41. For more information see the website of Essence of Time, http://eotperm.ru.

42. "'Piloramy' v etom godu tochno ne budet," Properm.ru, July 10, 2013, https://properm.ru/afisha/news/62483/.

43. Krizhevskii et al., "Ostorozhno, zona zakryvaetsia."

44. The episode is available on YouTube at "Pro Perm-36. Professiia reporter: piataia kolonna," NTV, June 7, 2014, video, 29:26, https://youtu.be/W99Y9aZ6C_o. The English translation of the quoted text from the program comes from Ola Cichowlas, "The Kremlin Is Trying to Erase Memories of the Gulag," *New Republic*, June 23, 2014. In February 2015, a civil society collegium that reviews complaints about the press declared the program "quasi-journalistic libel." See Stefan Savelli, "Siuzhety o 'Permi-36' na NTV sochli 'kvazizhurnalistskim paskvilem,'" 59.ru, Perm Online, February 13, 2015, https://59.ru/text/gorod/2015/02/13/62503271/.

45. Dmitrii Mikheenko, "Viktor Basargin: Muzei 'Perm-36' budet sokhranen," *Komsomolskaia Pravda*, July 8, 2014. See also "Viktor Basargin zaiavil, chto 'Perm-36' budet sokhranen," *Argumenty i fakty Prikamie*, July 9, 2014. *Argumenty i fakty* stated that Kursina had been fired "as an ineffective manager." For a sampling of the criticism, see Cichowlas, "The Kremlin Is Trying" and Krizhevskii et al., "Ostorozhno, zona zakryvaetsia"; articles on the "scandal surrounding the Perm 36 Museum" published between May 2014 and November 2015 are listed at Ura.ru, http://ura.news.

46. Shmyrov, "'Perm-36': Reabilitatsiia repressii"; Kalikh, "'Perm-36': unichtozhenie pamiati."

47. Shmyrov, "'Perm-36': Reabilitatsiia repressii"; Vladimir Sokolov, "'Perm-36': Teper vse po-drugomu," *Zvezda*, November 9, 2016.

48. Sokolov, "'Perm-36': Teper vse po-drugomu."

49. "Organizatsiia-sozdatel muzeia 'Perm-36' obiiavila o samolikvidatsii," Deutsche Welle, March 3, 2015, https://www.dw.com/ru/организация-создатель-музея-пермь-36-объявила-о-самоликвидации/a-18290405.

50. "Nesvoevremennoe zakrytie muzeia politicheskikh repressii otsenili v 1,5 mln rublei," *Slon*, May 15, 2015.

51. "Permskii muzei GULAGa oshtrafovali po zakonu ob inostrannykh agentakh," *Slon*, July 22, 2015.

52. Compare a convincing scholarly review by Frederick C. Corney, "Sergei Kachkin: *Perm 36: Reflexion (Perm 36: Otrazhenie*, 2016)," *KinoKultura* 57 (2017) with hysterical attacks like "V Eltsin-tsentre reabilitiruiut banderovskii natsizm," *Novorossiia Informatsionnoe Agenstvo*, January 16, 2017.

53. "Stalin umer vchera?," Radio Liberty, March 5, 2017.

54. Viacheslav Sukhanov and Valentina Efremova, "Vpered s repressiiami: Nataliia Semakova prodolzhit rukovodit 'Permiu-36,'" *Kommersant*, May 19, 2017.

55. Sukhanov and Efremova, "Vpered s repressiiami."

56. Shmyrov, "'Perm-36': Reabilitatsiia repressii."

57. Shmyrov, "'Perm-36': Reabilitatsiia repressii."

58. Shmyrov, "'Perm-36': Reabilitatsiia repressii."

59. Perhaps the most alarmist article around the time the NGO Perm 36 decided to disband was Laurence Peter, "Stalin Wiped from Soviet Gulag Prison Museum," BBC, March 3, 2015. Much Western news coverage at that moment confused the closing of the NGO with the closing of the museum itself.

60. Memorial Museum of the History of Political Repressions, Perm 36, accessed January 12, 2020, http://itk36-museum.ru.

61. See interviews with Iulia Kantor on Ekho Moskvy, https://echo.msk.ru/guests/11284/.

62. Irina Tumakova, "'Perm-36': Muzei GULAGa i Minkulta," *Fontanka*, October 30, 2016.

63. Sokolov, "'Perm-36': Teper vse po-drugomu."

64. "Muzei repressii izvinilsia za publikatsiiu ob effektivnosti 'sharashek,'" *Slon*, April 14, 2016.

65. Shmyrov, "'Perm-36': Reabilitatsiia repressii."

STEVEN A. BARNES is Associate Professor of Russian History at George Mason University. He is author of *Death and Redemption: The Gulag and the Shaping of Soviet Society* and is currently finishing a book on women prisoners in the Gulag, *The Wives' Gulag: Gender, Family, and Survival in Stalin's Terror*. He is founder of the website Gulag: Many Days, Many Lives (gulaghistory.org).

6 Known and Unknown Soldiers: Remembering Russia's Fallen in the Great Patriotic War

Johanna Dahlin

ONE APRIL EVENING in 2010, Alexander returns later than everyone else to the camp at Siniavino near St. Petersburg. He usually does that, digging on his own, going places others find impassable. The rest of the group are already sitting around the table, having supper. It is dusk and getting dark: in late April in northwestern Russia that means it is about ten at night. Alexander is looking grim, hardly moving a muscle in his face as he carries a thighbone in his hand and walks off to where the search unit Ingria keeps their finds: human remains and wartime artifacts. This is the first soldier this particular expedition (*vakhta*) has unearthed. There is very little of him left, but there is a medallion—the Soviet equivalent of a name tag.

By examining the work on finding remains and identifying and memorializing soldiers from the Second World War in Russia, this chapter explores the symbolism of named and unnamed soldiers. My discussion focuses on the Unknown Soldier in its symbolical and memorial form, as well as those unknown soldiers whose identities have not been established due to necessity, neglect, or accident. I also look into the process of making those soldiers known. The remains unearthed by the kind of search unit Alexander belongs to can be identified primarily through medallions. Hence, finding medallions is central to the search as the most tangible link between remains and name. I discuss the significance of this link, as well as the bond being formed between members of the search units and the fallen soldiers.

The Siniavino camp belongs to the search unit Ingria, which is based at St. Petersburg State University. It is part of a Russia-wide voluntary search movement (*poiskovoe dvizhenie*). The national organization is simply called the Russian Search Movement. It was formally constituted in 1988, along with many other nongovernmental organizations that emerged during Gorbachev's glasnost. Relatively autonomous units such as Ingria have been doing search work throughout Russia for three decades now. During this time, members of the movement have found the remains of nearly half a million soldiers throughout Russia. Ingria frequents the Siniavino area, which is in the Kirov district east of St. Petersburg. This area saw intense battles for more than two years as the Red Army tried to break through the German lines and establish a land connection to the besieged city. Helmets, splinters, and barbed wire still lie on the ground. Trenches pierce the forest, and the sun is reflected in the water-filled bomb craters. Less visible, often a mere few inches below the ground, are the remains of soldiers who lost their lives in battle. Here, and on former battlefields all across the former Soviet Union, lie the remains of dead soldiers, sometimes rudimentarily covered in dirt in so-called sanitary burials hastily organized by the Germans, who threw bodies into trenches as they advanced.[1]

But let us return to Siniavino on that particular April evening. At the conclusion of the daily routine, Ingria's leader, history professor Evgenii Ilin, rewards Alexander for finding the expedition's first unearthed soldier with the tongue-in-cheek award (*nagrada*) bestowed on those who find a medallion: five tins of condensed milk. It is a freezing cold spring night, but everyone is lured away from the warming campfire as the medallion is opened. Once placed in water, the black capsule disgorges a rolled paper. Alexander uses needles to handle the tightly compressed paper. All present look nervously at the piece of paper when it is once again placed in water, and the layers begin separating from one another almost immediately. He then places the paper strip on a sheet of white paper and at once starts unrolling it. The writing is well preserved, and Alexander and Evgenii Ilin are able to establish, with the help of torchlight, that the medallion belonged to Vasilii Apolonov, born in 1903 in the village of Kubenskoe, Volgograd Oblast.

The next morning, the search unit finds out from OBD Memorial (*Obobsh-chennyi bank dannykh*) that Apolonov was reported as missing in action in February 1942. OBD Memorial is an online database of scanned military records created to preserve the memory of those who perished in the war and give their relatives an opportunity to find vital information.[2] A few more days of investigation yield further personal information. Apolonov was married with no children. His wife died in the 1990s. Apolonov reportedly had a nephew, whose whereabouts the search unit has as yet been unable to establish.

In early May 2010, Vasilii Apolonov was buried on memorial grounds in the Siniavino Heights. As the remains of all the exhumed soldiers are prepared for burial, Apolonov's are separated from the rest. He will have his own coffin with his vital information attached. Still, he will not be buried alone but along with 285 others in a common grave (known as a "brotherly" grave in Russian). At the burial, Ingria and the other search unit members perform the symbolic role of relatives of Apolonov and all "their" nameless soldiers buried alongside him. The search unit will carry the coffins and throw the ceremonial handful of soil.

The unearthed soldiers are often called "brothers," "close ones" (*blizkie*), or "loved ones" (*rodnye*). At the end of the burial ceremony, members of the search unit toast to the memory of the fallen. Of the soldiers buried that day, Apolonov is one of just eleven whose names will appear on the headstone to be later erected. The relatives, if ever found, can install a memorial plaque of their own.

I came in contact with Ingria while doing dissertation research in 2009, and I maintained contact with the group after my 2012 defense. Ingria is comprised of twenty-five active members, mainly current and former university students. While numbers remain constant, members of the search unit come and go. As new members join, former members, due to work or family obligations, may be put on the reserve list. They all have different motivations for joining the unit and dedicating so much of their time to its work. Some have family members who died or went missing in the war, while others have developed a profound interest in history. Still others enjoy the outdoors and appreciate the spirit of a close-knit community that sustains dedication to a cause. The sense of duty and obligation universally expressed in public also comes to the fore in informal day-to-day interaction within the unit. Since its establishment in 2000, Ingria has exhumed the remains of 2,627 soldiers and found 148 medallions; 68 of the soldiers have been identified.[3] Originally trained as a social anthropologist, my main research method was ethnographic fieldwork and participant observation of the unit's activities. Ingria annually conducts three major search expeditions, referred to as "memory watches" (*vakhta pamyati*). The expeditions last for up to two weeks and are held in spring, summer, and early fall. Some of the group's members spend the entire two weeks in the camp, while others commute back and forth to the city for work or take classes in between. I took part in twelve expeditions as a participant observer. In addition, I also took part in some of the smaller expeditions and tours organized by the search unit and spent time at its headquarters (*shtab*) in the university. Through Ingria, I met other individuals active in the search movement.

War and Remembrance in Russia

The Second World War—or the Great Patriotic War, as it is commonly known in Russia—had tragic consequences for the Soviet Union. Most families in Russia lost one or several members in the war. The immense death rates made it nearly impossible to provide accurate estimates.[4] The memory of the war remains important for both the Russian state and ordinary Russians.[5] There are still hundreds of thousands, perhaps millions, of unidentified soldiers lying on the former battlefields.[6] Most have been officially designated as "missing in action." Figures can be controversial, for the high death toll can be seen as a testimony to both the sacrifice of the Soviet people and the disregard for human life.

Fig. 6.1. Search work in the Gaitolovo area, May 2015. Photo by Johanna Dahlin.

The memory of the war has gone through several phases in the Soviet Union and later in Russia. Although shifts in the interpretation of history are a universal phenomenon, the changes introduced in the Soviet Union were especially abrupt and swift, despite claims to the contrary.[7] The war was almost immediately called "sacred," as in the famous 1941 song "Sviashchennaia voina," but initial attempts at commemoration were abandoned shortly after the end of the war. The Soviet Union was effectively in ruins, and the leadership was keen on returning to what might be called normalcy. The first Victory Day—May 9, 1946—was a public holiday, yet by the following year it was a normal working day marked by modest celebrations. The Cold War and the worsening relationship between the Soviet Union and its former allies framed a new perspective on the war. A large number of memorials erected in the Soviet Union during the 1950s emphasized a continuity between the Bolshevik Revolution and the Great Patriotic War; war memory was integrated into the history of the Communist Party and thus contributed to its legitimacy. During these years, May 9 continued to be a normal working day, although it was celebrated and commemorated with meetings, informal gatherings, and fireworks in the evening.

The twentieth anniversary in 1965 not only made Victory Day a public holiday again but also saw the emergence of what might be called a Soviet war cult. The figure twenty million—the officially accepted Soviet death toll in the war—gained prominence as a testimony to the sacrifice of the Soviet population that placed the country highest in a "hierarchy of suffering," as historian Nina Tu-markin put it.[8] During the following two decades, the Great Patriotic War assumed the status of a dominant foundational myth. War monuments erected across the Soviet Union attest to the high status of war memory. While the enormous death toll could not be easily dismissed, the regime denied the existence of unburied remains up until the 1980s.[9] The policy of glasnost introduced by Mikhail Gorbachev in the late 1980s put parts of the war myth, like all other aspects of Soviet history, under a magnifying glass so that even the heroic image of the war veterans came into question. The search movement came into existence during that period through its work identifying and giving importance to those denied and neglected bones.

Post-Soviet Russia initially held war memory in low regard. Much of the official pomp was gone, along with the parades in Red Square. Celebrations continued but in a more informal, subtle way.[10] Since the mid-1990s, the war has increasingly regained its formal status, and today the Victory Day parade is as grand an affair as it was in Soviet times. Victory Day retains its dual character of personal grief and official ceremony, but as the war generation is nearly gone, the latter is taking precedence over the former.

The outgoing war generation is one of the factors that led to the creation of the Immortal Regiment march (*Bessmertnyi polk*), which in recent years has become a prominent part of Victory Day celebration. The search unit Ingria has taken part in the march since 2014, as will be discussed later in this chapter. The origins of the Immortal Regiment can be traced to the Siberian city of Tomsk and the local TV station TV2. The first march brought together around six thousand participants, who marched down the main street of the city carrying photographs of relatives who took part in the war. Obviously this was not the first time such photographs were carried in a commemorative march. The significance of this particular initiative was the massive scale of participation. Another component of the Immortal Regiment involves entering a name into a virtual *Bessmertnyi polk*, a website that collects data on Soviet servicemen in the Second World War.[11]

From Tomsk, the Immortal Regiment initiative spread all over Russia. Mischa Gabowitsch called it a "copycat movement"—that is, a locally initiated drive later taken up by others, who may not have any links to the organizers and who implement it once again locally with no central coordination (in this particular case, the organizers in Tomsk did their best promoting the original idea).[12] As Russia celebrated the seventieth anniversary of the victory, the Immortal Regiment had already become a mass phenomenon. According to the organizers, the 2015 march in St. Petersburg brought together anywhere between 150,000 and 300,000 people (the high estimate is by the police).[13] In Moscow, at least 250,000 people are estimated to have participated in the march, with media focusing on

President Putin, who carried a portrait of his father, who was severely wounded on Nevsky bridgehead east of besieged Leningrad (a battlefield to which Ingria has devoted much attention).

The Immortal Regiment is a registered entity with its own charter and a Tomsk-based coordinating committee, although the structure is rather loose, and many a local organizer has little or no contact with Tomsk.[14] Its status is that of a noncommercial and nonpolitical organization. Its primary goal is to preserve the memory of the war generation in the private memory of every family.[15] As Gabowitsch points out, the insistence on being nonpolitical can be interpreted as a "strategic defence against both co-optation and repression by the state" and a way of emphasizing family connections and the private side of war commemoration.[16] The Tomsk organizers have been keen on keeping the commemorative march private—or at least semi-private, since it is public by default—and therefore have tried to avoid too much official involvement. However, their means to control it are very limited, and the regiment has now taken on a more formal character.[17]

Most important, the Immortal Regiment provides a framework for individualized and personalized commemoration. Through its copycat format, it has provided a "horizontal initiative that has given local organizers and participants a sense of agency. It forced the state to adapt official events to this new format, giving more airtime to the Immortal Regiment than to the traditional military parade."[18] In this way, it continues the dual character Victory Day always had—as an official as well as private holiday. In St. Petersburg, the regiment is clearly linked to the procession of veterans that used to march along Nevsky Prospect on May 9 as it uses the same route and timetable. Before the advent of the Immortal Regiment, the traditional veterans procession also occasionally featured photographs carried by relatives.

The subject of immortality connects war commemoration to mythical times. Claude Lévi-Strauss called myths "machines for the suppression of time" since they operate with temporal concepts quite different from worldly, mechanical time.[19] One aspect of myths closely connected to their religious dimension is mythic time, which connects past and present through eternity.[20]

The passing of the war generation helps turn the war into a myth. The timeless existence of mythic time approaches a liminal condition, described by Victor Turner as a "moment in and out of time."[21] Liminality also extends to unburied soldiers. As Danny Kaplan argued, "The missing are situated at a unique juncture between the living and the dead . . . missing soldiers oscillate between the horizontal ties of the living and the vertical ties formed between the living and the dead."[22] Proper burial is what transforms the living into the dead; the missing— their remains, that is—have not been through this transition. Moreover, their physical remains are separated from their social identity.

The Unknown Soldier

In his now famous discussion of the imagined community of the nation, Benedict Anderson points to the Tomb of the Unknown Soldier as its most striking symbol. A solemn tribute to those who died for the county, these memorials capture the soul of the nation in a generic symbol of "our" dead. The unknown bones of the memorial stand for all war dead—worshiped and removed from the battle sites. The Unknown Soldier allows anyone who has lost a loved one to imagine the body at the site.

The Unknown Soldier is a memorial based on liminality. As Laura Wittman suggested, the bones at its center can be seen as both dead and still alive, as an individual and an entire humanity, as a real body but also a symbol. The Unknown Soldier in this venerated form was born out of the mass death of the First World War. He became *the* image of the nation's losses in modern war. Although the origins of the idea of burying an unknown soldier are obscure, it apparently arose simultaneously in Italy, France, and Britain during the First World War.[23] The idea rapidly spread to other countries involved in the conflict. The Tomb of the Unknown Soldier came to function as a national shrine in a way that dispersed military cemeteries could not.[24] The very namelessness makes the buried remains stand for everyone in the (national) community.

Individual burial and commemoration became important during the First World War. The mass death of trench warfare gave the belligerent nations the monumental task of dealing with and properly burying the fallen. Proper burial is about being interred in a proper site accompanied with the proper ceremony, but it is also about reestablishing connection between a dead body and some sort of enduring identity, which is crucial to complete the transformation from "missing" to "fallen." In many cases, however, the dead bodies were decomposed and tangled with one another to the extent that they lost their individual integrity. The Tomb of the Unknown Soldier is a memorial that focuses on mortality as a shared experience; physical presence compensates for the loss of a name. Thus, embodiment and anonymity are the two most important features of this type of memorial.[25] It differs from other memorials to the unknown dead, such as cenotaphs or ossuaries, which typically compensate for physical loss by providing a list of names.

In Russia, the Tomb of the Unknown Soldier appeared much later than in Western Europe. In December 1966, as part of the twenty-fifth anniversary of the Battle of Moscow, the remains of an unknown soldier were moved from a common grave and ceremoniously reburied near the Kremlin wall. The monument was unveiled in May 1967. The eternal flame was lit by a torch from the Field of Mars in Leningrad, where the Soviet Union's first such flame was ignited to commemorate those fallen in the revolution.

Originating in the West, the Unknown Soldier now has a less ubiquitous presence. The evolution of science and warfare suggests that every (i.e., every Western) death can be accounted for and every lost soldier can be mourned individually.[26] For the Unknown Soldier to fill its role, the soldier must truly be unknown. Wittman describes the elaborate searches and ceremonies involved in choosing the representative Unknown Soldier in Britain, France, Italy, and the United States: "In each case, numerous bodies had to be dug up from each battlefield in order to come up with one body that would qualify at once as anonymous, yet clearly of a specific nation."[27] In Washington, DC, the Tomb of the Unknown Soldier from the Vietnam War was left empty for ten years due to the lack of unidentifiable remains. Even the remains that were eventually buried there in 1998 were later identified and the grave emptied.[28]

In Russia, however, the Unknown Soldier remains perpetually unknown. There is no shortage of unidentifiable remains. He even has his own holiday, December 3, introduced in 2014. As reasons for introducing the new holiday, the head of the Presidential Administration, Sergei Ivanov, pointed not only to the significance of the victory in the war, and the high price that was paid for this victory, but also to the many missing and still unknown. Ivanov argued that there is no other country in the world to which a Day of the Unknown Soldier is as important as to Russia since no other country had as many soldiers missing in action as the Soviet Union.[29]

According to Thomas W. Laqueur, "The common-denominator body of the Unknown Soldier is the opposite end of the same discursive strategy that is evident in the enumeration of names."[30] The name is an important part of war memorials that can be traced back to the First World War and the increasing emphasis on the common soldier during the nineteenth century. The way the British Empire commemorated their dead in the First World War made Laqueur conclude that January 1915 marked the beginning of a new era of commemoration where the common soldier's name was memorialized or very consciously left to oblivion.[31] What had earlier been just scattered bodies placed in common graves were now collected to be buried and marked individually.[32]

Names are an integral part of many war memorials. Many English, Australian, and French towns contain an obelisk listing those native sons who gave their lives during the First World War. At both St. Petersburg State University and the Polytechnic University, there are memorial plaques to the students and employees who did not return from the war. The German war cemetery in Sologubovka outside Mga features stone after stone with the names of those buried there. To be able to make such a monument, there must be a list with some claim to finality, whether in a local or larger context. The Vietnam War Memorial in Washington, DC, has the goal to list all the American soldiers who died in that war. The Australian War Memorial in Canberra lists all Australians who have died in all the wars in which Australia has been a part. The former Soviet archives are too un-reliable to establish such a list.[33] Besides, the number of lives lost is just stagger-ing, with military losses alone estimated at 8.7 million. In the words of poet Olga Bergholz, inscribed in stone on the Piskariovskoe memorial cemetery where the victims who died during the siege of Leningrad are buried: "Your names are too numerous to be mentioned here."

In Siniavino, as in the case of Unknown Soldier memorials, the bones are surrogates for names. However, the names that are found have a much wider significance. The unknown soldiers unearthed by the search movement share the same separation of name and body; instead of being venerated, these are merely dirty, messy remains. As was the case during the trench warfare of the First World War, the remains are often tangled and hard to separate. They will be re-buried that way; in each coffin the bones are arranged to create one fictional body out of the remains of many fallen.

This inseparability of the remains also points to the battlefield fraternity, to the bonds forged between soldiers in battle.[34] This fraternity, with its connota-tions of (male) friendship and kinship, links to Anderson's argument, accord-ing to which nationalism should not be understood as a political ideology but as having more in common with kinship or religion. Kinship in this context signals ties that are horizontal—that is, members of the nation are brothers—but also has temporal dimensions stressing intergenerational ties. Often this is tied to the idea of a single origin. Family and kinship are important images of the nation and the community it represents. A nation can be understood as a community that spans generations. This perception prescribes duties to the ancestors as the forebearers of the nation.[35]

Getting to Know Soldiers

The goal of the search movement is to give the fallen a proper burial. Whenever pos-sible, the remains should be identified. Central to that effort are the so-called death medallions (see previous discussion)—black ebonite capsules used in the Red Army in lieu of ID tags. Each capsule contained a piece of paper filled out with pencil. After seventy years—despite being protected by an ebonite capsule—this paper is hard to read, to say the least. Hence, even if found, a medallion is no guar-antee of successful identification. Very often, those fallen in battle were reported as missing in action. If a fellow soldier witnessed the death of his comrade, he might inform his superiors, who might or might not pass the tragic news to the next of kin. Besides, the soldiers themselves did not always know the names of the fallen. The losses were high, as was servicemen turnover.[36]

Finding a medallion is the highlight of a search and can be followed by cheers and cries of joy. The excitement of discovery often turns to disappointment if

Fig. 6.2. A soldier's death medallion, May 2015. Photo by Johanna Dahlin.

the medallion is empty or unreadable. If the capsule was not securely closed, the paper disintegrates quickly. It sometimes happens that there was never a paper inside in the first place. "Is it tightly shut?" is a typical question members of the search team ask each other before opening a medallion. There is also certain ceremony involved in the opening of a medallion. A designated member of the search party takes an educated guess as to the prospects of identification. Still, the medallion will not be opened until everyone is back in the camp.

Medallions were introduced in the Red Army in 1925. Initially made of tin, they bore an uncanny resemblance to Russian Orthodox icons carried as charms, into which a folded paper was placed beneath a small hatch. In 1940, this type of medallion was replaced with the ebonite one. The new medallions varied depending on place of manufacture. That so few soldiers actually carried a medallion is due in part to the fact that it was not universally in use until after the end of the war. For reasons that are unclear, it was abolished in 1942.[37] Hence, only servicemen who enlisted in 1941 or earlier carried it. Even then, not everyone was issued a medallion. Besides, many servicemen carried empty capsules. Private (*krasnoarmeyets*) Apolonov, mentioned earlier in this chapter, was mobilized into the army during the period when medallions were distributed. Not only did he receive the medallion, but he also took good care of it. Apolonov was nearly forty years old when he was killed. Ingria member Alexander claims the identified soldiers often were older and therefore had a greater sense of responsibility.

Many of them were family men and thus might be more conscious of their mortality than their younger comrades in arms. "The young ones were only good for dying," as Alexander puts it.

Establishing the name of the fallen soldier means more than just that. To be missing in action was a cruel destiny in the Soviet Union. According to Catherine Merridale, order no. 270 from August 1941 implied that those who went missing in action acquired the same status as deserters.[38] Signed by Stalin, the order targeted perceived traitors and cowards. The law proclaimed cowardice a crime punishable by death. Anyone who deserted from the front line or "gave himself prisoner" was to be considered an enemy of the people, which was followed by the arrest of his family members. In Stalin's Soviet Union, this was a familiar threat: having a family member sentenced during the Great Terror of 1937–38 imposed a stigma undermining a person's social status. Many a child of arrested parents avoided mentioning that fact in their biographies—say, to gain entry to higher education. What was radically new in order no. 270 was the threat of imprisonment.[39] The emphasis on moral deficiency (which is even more pronounced in order no. 227 of June 28, 1942, better known as "Not a Step Back!") can be seen as an attempt to cover up tangible shortcomings in the army. If there was no body, it could not be proven that the person in question had not been taken prisoner, and the stigma of a morally corrupt individual—a criminal, in fact—could not be lifted. The symbolism and moral redress invested in an identified soldier can thus be enormous.

The missing soldiers—neither dead nor alive—became trapped in a liminal state. Instead of heroically dying for their country, the fallen on the battlefields involuntarily put themselves in the same position as traitors. The consequences for the next of kin varied insofar as missing in action was not in itself a criminal offence, but pensions were not dispensed to the families of those missing in action, as opposed to the confirmed fallen. Many of the relatives with whom Ingria comes into contact have stories to tell of how their lives were affected by the "suspicious status" of a parent missing in action. The daughter of a soldier contacted by Ingria in September 2011 came for his funeral the following spring. When the search unit first contacted her, it was the first time since September 1941 that she had heard of her father. She repeated then and again—in her speech at the funeral, to journalists interviewing her, and in her interactions with Ingria—that her father did not just go missing but died with honor for his country. She kept asking why authorities entered "went missing" in his records when he was actually killed in battle. Although this was very common, Evgenii Ilin was at a loss to give her any good explanation as to *why*. While waiting for the funeral to begin, she shared with me how the nonpayment of pension made life very difficult for her mother and the family's three children. Thinking that perhaps her father had been taken prisoner, they used to meet the transports of released POWs that arrived for further internment in Kazakhstan (where the family lived at the time) to see if he was possibly among them.

The name is not just a keyword to search in the OBD database or in the memorial books (*knigi pamiati*), which list the names of the fallen. The name itself has great symbolic meaning. The name helps separate the identified soldiers from the rest. Several books list the names retrieved from medallions. Some of the monuments erected in the Siniavino Heights have names engraved on them; long lists of names constitute a centerpiece of the memorial at Maluksa (also in the Kirov district). These name lists do not claim any finality. They do not stand for everyone who died at that particular spot or even those who are buried by the memorial. The names are used to single out, not to unite. The name itself becomes a memorial the nameless cannot have. Vital information on many of the missing soldiers certainly exists in OBD or the memorial books, but the names and the remains are disconnected and will likely remain so.

The "sanitary burials" encountered by the search units are a far cry from the neat military cemeteries of the Western Front. Here, bodies were hastily dumped into a pit and covered by dirt, often by the Germans after they had conquered a given area. There is no good explanation for the Soviet indifference to dead bodies except the huge number of them. At the same time, the Germans also experienced heavy losses, albeit not as significant as the Soviets, and yet they managed to bury proportionally more of their fallen. This seeming indifference to dead bodies is a difficult question for the search movement. While the movement's point of departure is that the state has not done enough, it also operates within a patriotic framework established and managed by the very same state.[40]

In Russia, *patriotism* is a flexible concept. Generally accepted as inherently "good," it enjoys broad public support and gives legitimacy to a wide range of activities. In effect, patriotism is a vessel that can be filled with different content. In her discussion of so-called patriotic clubs in Russia (the search movement is included in this category), Marlene Laruelle pointed out significant differences in interpretation of patriotism by those groups and also between their interpretations and that of the Kremlin.[41] The concept of patriotism is thus quite elastic, with only vague ideological underpinning. This elasticity is important to keep in mind when discussing patriotism in relation to the search movement (e.g., true patriots can sometimes be critical of the state while always maintaining their loyalty to the country).

There is no shortage of unidentified or unidentifiable soldiers in the Siniavino Heights, yet those who matter the most are the ones who have been identified. The soldiers whose names have been established are commemorated in addition to the funeral. On the particular spot where they died and were found, the search unit erects a wooden post with a memorial plaque containing information from the medallion. Such a post was erected for Apolonov. During the 2010 summer expedition, a post was created from a cut-down birch tree onto which a memorial plaque was fastened. The plaque features Vasilii Apolonov's name, place of origin, date of birth and death, the date he was found, and the name of the search unit that unearthed his remains. Above the plaque is affixed a metal star. The post is carried into the forest to the exact spot—recorded on GPS but found by memory—where Alexander found Apolonov's remains and medallion. Quite unceremoniously, a hole is dug, and the post is erected. A Soviet helmet belonging to Apolonov, or any of his fallen comrades, is placed on top of the post. A group photograph is taken by the freshly erected memorial. All identified soldiers are marked in this way, with their own little memorial erected on the exact spot where they were found.

There seem to be such posts everywhere in the woods. It is never spelled out who exactly found the soldier, but everyone seems to know that information. The posts become markers, referred to by the soldier's last name or that of the finder. A designation may read "by Apolonov" or a site may be described as situated "near Olga's soldier." The posts represent consciously created sites of memory but also a part of the living memory of the group. They not only commemorate the soldiers but are also a collective memory of the group's own work. The search units, while carving out their own space in the memorial landscape, also project their unique interpretation of the war. While it is not in direct confrontation with the "official" interpretation, it qualifies the difficult road to victory. It emphasizes collective and individual suffering and the devaluation of the sacrifice through the mere fact of soldiers left neglected.

Participation in the Immortal Regiment is effectively an extension of the group's mission. The members of the search unit take up roles as vicarious relatives, carrying the portraits of individuals with whom they have established a special relationship. In this case, however, the soldiers already have relatives or there would not have been portraits available. Those commemorated by the Immortal Regiment march have all been identified. It is the great nameless mass, however, who "need" such vicarious relatives. Lacking name and shape beyond the actual remains, they are much harder to commemorate individually.

The Immortal Regiment

On the afternoon of May 9, 2015, the search unit Ingria gathers outside the Vladimir Cathedral in St. Petersburg to take part in the Immortal Regiment march. Ekaterina, who has been with the unit for nearly ten years, assembles the twenty-one placards the unit will now carry. The placards feature wartime photographs of soldiers the search unit found and identified. Ekaterina is helped by twelve-year-old Roma, the son of the unit's deputy leader, who hands out the placards to arriving members of the group. Looking through the portraits, they try to assign the group members "their own" soldiers whenever possible.

Fig. 6.3. Taking part in the Immortal Regiment, May 2015. Photo by Johanna Dahlin.

As the group gathers, leader Evgenii Ilin is interviewed by several media outlets. Group members are happy to see each other. When everyone has arrived, Ingria joins the crowd at Marat Street from where the march is supposed to start. And they wait, and wait, and wait before the march finally, and initially very slowly, takes off.

While the typical participant is someone with a portrait of a relative, Ingria are carrying photographs of people unrelated to them but with whom the group has established a specific bond. A soldier is "yours" if you were the one who found the remains. "I know that face," Vladimir says as he inspects the portrait of Konstantin Napadailov that I have been assigned. Next Vladimir tells me where Napadailov's remains were found and how he took Napadailov's elderly son out to the battlefields when the latter came to visit the search unit and see for himself where his father had died. All around me, I hear similar conversations as Ingria members inspect each other's placards and recount the stories of where, how, and by whom this or that particular soldier was found. As mentioned earlier, Ingria has been able to identify sixty-eight soldiers through the years. They acquired the twenty-seven portraits they carried in the march through their contact with the fallen soldiers' relatives.

This is the second year Ingria has taken part in the Immortal Regiment march. The twenty-one members carrying the portraits along Nevsky Prospect constitute a larger part of the group. Simultaneously, one of Ingria's three annual search expeditions is being held in the woods and bogs east of St. Petersburg, and many members of the group would rather be there and not waste hours on the road to and from the city.

While the march promises immortality, it signals the very real mortality of war veterans. On the afternoon of May 9, veterans used to march along Nevsky Prospect to cheers and shouts of hooray from the crowd. Now, vintage cars carrying the remaining few veterans are incorporated into the Immortal Regiment march. We cannot see the veterans, however; in fact, we cannot see anything at all as the procession hardly moves. Vladimir is happy he did not bring along his small daughter, and Nikita, who did bring his family, could not stay long as his youngest became too frightened seeing so many people. According to news reports, a lot of spectators came to cheer the march, but as our party finally starts moving and reaches Nevsky Prospect, the crowds have already dispersed. Still, there are cheers, shouts of hooray, and songs by those who partake in the march. The experience of being part of the march is quite different from watching it on TV.

As we reach Palace Square, Ingria gathers near the bridge. Egor, whose birthday is on Victory Day, distributes pieces of pie (*pirog*) to everyone. The placards are disassembled to be used again next year. Part of the group is preparing to take the train and head for the woods to join those who stayed behind in the camp. Others leave to join Victory Day celebrations with friends and families. A small group remains; I join them for the favorite St. Petersburg pastime of walking around (*guliat po gorodu*), taking in the city as day slowly turns to night, toasting the occasion with a bottle of cheap brandy and bitter chocolate, and later finding a good vantage point from which to catch the fireworks. I am particularly happy to catch up with Daniil—a chemist, university lecturer, and the very first person to join Ingria. "Victory Day is changing," he says later that evening as the smoke of the anniversary fireworks is fading and the crowds are dispersing. "I can count the number of veterans I've seen today on the fingers of one hand," he continues. "Earlier today we walked around with our flowers, looking for someone to salute. In five years' time, there will be no more veterans left. What will remain then? Just partying—no real memory." Another group member interjects, "But the veteran's children, they will be around." Daniil stands his ground: "You might not agree with me, but Victory Day is changing."

Conclusion

Daniil is right. Not just Victory Day, but the collective memory of the war is undergoing a change. It is disappearing from living memory. Over time, the personal connection to the war has grown weaker. The dual nature of private grief and official pomp might also vanish. There is little left to counter the official view of the war that emphasizes valor and heroism. At the same time, Victory Day is becoming of lesser relevance to many people—state-staged spectacles are not to everyone's taste. For those involved in the search movement, however, the war has a different meaning. They are having a firsthand experience—not of the war itself but of the very tangible traces of destruction and suffering it brought about.

The medallions—the black ebonite capsules—are the focal point of the search. Finding one, however, is not a goal in itself. It can cause disappointment (if empty or unreadable), or it can be a starting point for a new search: a search for the name and relatives of that particular individual.

Full closure is only possible when identified remains are properly buried and connected to a social context through the relatives of the dead soldiers. The process of identification is about giving the nameless a name. It also helps establish contact with the relatives of the missing soldiers. Finding relatives is in and of itself a slow and complicated process made all the more difficult by the fall of the Soviet Union, with relatives possibly living in a different country. Seven decades after the war's end, search units are occasionally met with indifference when they first tell relatives of their finds, particularly if the next of kin are no longer alive. More often, however, the message is highly appreciated. It can also be very emotional, especially for children of the missing soldiers who might have wondered for a lifetime what actually happened to their fathers. Sometimes it becomes a starting point for a long and lasting relationship. By locating and identifying the dead soldiers, Ingria's members become their vicarious relatives: they receive photographs and letters, which are stored in the group's "headquarters," exhibited in Ingria's small museum, and carried in the Immortal Regiment march.

The name is all that separates the identified solders from the mass of the nameless dead. They are handled separately, are buried in separate coffins, and have their name engraved on a memorial post erected in the woods. Effectively, they become concepts. Apolonov, Kharitonin, Gorbachov, and others are not just soldiers but part of Ingria's mental map of the Siniavino area. The identified soldiers give their names to the sites where their remains are found. The erected plaques serve as memorials to both the missing soldiers and the search movement. By means of the name and what it stands for, the search movement also reaches out to the wider society. Instead of the dead being represented by an Unknown Soldier, each and every reclaimed name represents all those who may remain nameless. The names and the unnamed bones are finally connected.

As a mirror image of the Tomb of the Unknown Soldier, the Immortal Regiment extends the promise of eternal youth and timeless existence—which is often extended to those who perished—to the ones who actually survived the war and grew old. As the veterans who participated in past celebrations are now increasingly replaced by portraits, the war acquires the quality of a myth existing in parallel time. Forever young, the veterans are reliving their past heroic deeds. And when they are no longer alive, the photographs symbolize a wartime persona disconnected from the feeble aging body.

The Tomb of the Unknown Soldier and the remains of the missing on the battlefields represent two sides of war commemoration in Russia—one central, one peripheral; one by the Kremlin in Moscow, one in the woods and bogs of the Kirov district. Both speak of great human losses experienced by the Soviet Union in the Second World War, but in different ways. Vasilii Apolonov, the "known" soldier profiled in this chapter, has a representational potential yet to be realized. He may be a symbol of collective heroism or neglected cannon fodder. He may stand for a mnemonic vehicle of history, an unduly prop in the agenda of the present Russian regime, or simply signify closure for the Apolonov family, should they ever be identified.

Notes

1. In sanitary burial, bodies were interred hastily and unceremoniously to prevent diseases from spreading.

2. Johanna Dahlin, *Kriget är inte över förrän den sista soldaten är begraven: Minnesarbete och gemenskap kring andra världskriget i S:t Petersburg med omnejd* (PhD thesis, University of Linköping, 2012), 108–9. OBD Memorial can be found online at https://www.obd-memorial.ru.

3. Figures (as of July 2017) are posted on the search unit's website, http://www.ingria-poisk.ru.

4. For a discussion on the Soviet war losses, see, for example, Mark Harrison, "Counting Soviet Deaths in the Great Patriotic War: Comment," *Europe-Asia Studies* 55, no. 6 (2003): 939–44.

5. Cf. Nina Tumarkin, *The Living and the Dead: The Rise and Fall of the Cult of World War II in Russia* (New York: Basic Books, 1994); Dahlin, *Kriget är inte över*.

6. When appearing on the program *Otkrytaia studiia* on the St. Petersburg TV5 channel on May 16, 2008, Yevgenii Ilin settled on the number of five million missing, although he stressed it was a rough estimate; "Poiskovye otriady," http://www.5-tv.ru /video/502331/.

7. See, for example, James V. Wertsch, *Voices of Collective Remembering* (Cambridge: Cambridge University Press, 2002).

8. Tumarkin, *The Living and the Dead*, 135. Among other things, Tumarkin relates how the original estimate of seven to eight million deaths was raised to seventeen million after the demise of Stalin before Nikita Khrushchev offered the figure twenty million in 1961.

9. For a detailed discussion, see Dahlin, *Kriget är inte över*.

10. Anna Krylova, "Dancing on the Graves of the Dead: Building a World War II Memorial in Post-Soviet Russia," in *Memory and the Impact of Political Transformation in Public Space*, ed. Daniel J. Walkowitz and Lisa M. Knauer (London: Duke University Press, 2004), 83–102.

11. As Mischa Gabowitsch points out, many of the entries on the Immortal Regiment website are based on information from the OBD Memorial database. OBD Memorial is run by the Russian Ministry of Defense and was the first portal to offer this type of information.

These two databases exemplify the intersection of public and private initiatives in Russian memory politics. See Mischa Gabowitsch, "Are Copycats Subversive? Strategy-31, the Russian Runs, the Immortal Regiment, and the Transformative Potential of Non-Hierarchical Movements," *Problems of Post-Communism* (2016): 1–18.

12. Gabowitsch, "Are Copycats Subversive?," 18.

13. "Kommentarii po organizatsii shestvia 9 maia ot koordinatorov," Bessmertnyi Polk, May 10, 2015, http://moypolk.ru/sankt-peterburg/news/kommentariy-po-organizacii -shestviya-9-maya-ot-koordinatorov.

14. Gabowitsch, "Are Copycats Subversive?," 12.

15. "Ustav polka," Bessmertnyi Polk, accessed January 21, 2021, http://moypolk.ru /ustav-polka.

16. Gabowitsch, "Are Copycats Subversive?," 12. See also Pål Kolstø, "Symbol of the War—But Which One? The St. George Ribbon in Russian Nation-Building," *Slavonic & East European Review* 94, no. 4 (2016): 660–701.

17. Gabowitsch, "Are Copycats Subversive?," 12; Kolstø, "Symbol of the War," 684.

18. Gabowitsch, "Are Copycats Subversive?," 12. Gabowitsch notes that "this regular state hijacking of commemorative initiatives is facilitated by the fact that they, in turn, have consistently drawn on a repertoire preformatted for them by the state."

19. Claude Lévi-Strauss, *Mythologiques I* (Paris: Plon, Cop., 1964), 24.

20. This appeal to mythic time—eternal and unchangeable, with characters frozen in time—is not unique to Russia, of course. In the "Ode of Remembrance" often recited at Australian Anzac memorial events, the following lines are incanted: "They shall grow not old, as we that are left grow old: Age shall not weary them, nor the years condemn. At the going down of the sun and in the morning, We will remember them." The "Ode of Remembrance" is taken from Laurence Binyon's poem "For the Fallen," which was first published in the *Times* in September 1914.

21. Cf. Victor Turner, *The Forest of Symbols: Aspects of Ndembu Ritual* (Ithaca, NY: Cornell University Press, 1967); Victor Turner, *The Ritual Process: Structure and Antistructure* (New York: Aldine de Gruyter, 1995).

22. Danny Kaplan, "Commemorating a Suspended Death: Missing Soldiers and National Solidarity in Israel," *American Ethnologist* 35, no. 3 (2008): 413–27.

23. Laura Wittman, *The Tomb of the Unknown Soldier, Modern Mourning and the Reinvention of the Mystical Body* (Toronto: University of Toronto Press, 2011).

24. George L. Mosse, *Fallen Soldiers: Reshaping the Memory of the World Wars* (New York: Oxford University Press, 1990), 94–95.

25. Wittman, *The Tomb of the Unknown Soldier*, 10, 12, 19.

26. Cf. Nataliya Danilova, *The Politics of War Commemoration in the UK and Russia* (London: Palgrave McMillan, 2015).

27. Wittman, *The Tomb of the Unknown Soldier*, 58.

28. Michael J. Allen, "'Sacrilege of a Strange, Contemporary Kind': The Unknown Soldier and the Imagined Community after the Vietnam War," *History & Memory* 23, no. 2 (2011): 90–131.

29. "Gosduma obiavila 3 dekabria Dnem Neizvestnogo Soldata," TASS, October 24, 2014, http://tass.ru/obschestvo/1530127.

30. Thomas W. Laqueur, "Memory and Naming in the Great War," in *Commemorations: The Politics of National Identity*, ed. John R. Gillis (Princeton, NJ: Princeton University Press, 1996), 163.

31. Laqueur, "Memory and Naming," 153.

32. Laqueur, "Memory and Naming," 153.

33. Cf. Catherine Merridale, *Ivan's War: Life and Death in the Red Army, 1939–1945* (London: Picador, 2005).

34. Kaplan, "Commemorating a Suspended Death," 413–27.

35. Janna Thompson, "Patriotism and the Obligations of History," in *Patriotism: Philosophical and Political Perspectives*, ed. Igor Primoratz and Aleksandar Pavkovic (London: Ashgate, 2008), 49. See also Johanna Dahlin, "'No One Is Forgotten, Nothing Is Forgotten': Duty, Patriotism and the Russian Search Movement," *Europe-Asia Studies* 69, no. 7 (2017): 1070–89.

36. See, for example, Isolda Ivanova, *Siniavino: Osennie boi 1941–1942 godov* (St. Petersburg: Politekhnika, 2008).

37. I can only speculate as to why medallions were abolished. The most cynical suggestion I have heard is that the state wanted to avoid paying pensions to the relatives of the fallen. One may also speculate that it reflects the authorities' desire to cover up huge military losses.

38. Merridale, *Ivan's War*, 98.

39. Merridale, *Ivan's War*, 98.

40. For a discussion of the tension between patriotism and state criticism, see Dahlin, "'No One Is Forgotten, Nothing Is Forgotten.'"

41. Marlene Laruelle, "Patriotic Youth Clubs in Russia: Professional Niches, Cultural Capital and Narratives of Social Engagement," *Europe-Asia Studies* 67, no. 1 (2015).

JOHANNA DAHLIN is Research Fellow at Linköping University. Her doctoral dissertation, "Until the Last Soldier is Buried" (2012), deals with the memory of the Second World War in contemporary Russia and specifically with the efforts to identify the remains of Soviet soldiers who died in combat.

7 Fighters of the Invisible Front: Reimaging the Aftermath of the Great Patriotic War in Recent Russian Television Series

Boris Noordenbos

Over the past decade, prime-time Russian television has been flooded with spy thrillers and police procedurals set in the aftermath of the Second World War. In the television series *Liquidation* (*Likvidatsia*, directed by Sergei Ursuliak, Inter/Rossiia, 2007), Odessa's criminal investigation department fights rampant gangs and former Nazi collaborators who plague the city in 1946; in *Black Cats* (*Chernye koshki*, Evgenii Lavrentiev, Channel One, 2013), crime fighters in Rostov-na-Donu uncover a US-Nazi conspiracy revolving around the production of a nuclear weapon; and in both *The Cry of the Owl* (*Krik sovy*, Oleg Pogodin, Channel One, 2013) and *Executioner* (*Palach*, Viacheslav Nikiforov, Channel One, 2015), murderous ex-collaborators, now posing as law-abiding citizens, cast a long shadow over postwar communities in provincial Russia.

While none of these television series are set during the war, the evil infiltrating the Soviet Union in their stories is invariably traced back to the Nazi occupation. These action-packed spy thrillers tell of a battle against the remnants of German fascism and the local and foreign sympathizers who affected scores of Soviet citizens and communities in the late 1940s and even in the Khrushchev and Brezhnev eras. In the aftermath of the war, these series suggest that the enemy went underground to continue undermining Soviet society through connivance rather than naked force. Heroic roles are reserved for talented Russian spies or no-nonsense inspectors—"fighters of the invisible front" (*boitsy nevidimogo fronta*), as the Soviet phrase had it—keen to root out sinister fascist subversion.

These television productions adhere to the norms of popular culture, providing entertainment that does not aspire to historiographic accuracy or rigor. Their portrayal of intrigues and conspiracies makes no claim to be truthful but rather allows for the building of suspense and the unexpected plot twists essential to retaining a television audience week after week. However, as cultural reimaginations of the past that are ideologically and historically rooted in the present, these series' fixation on the perennial struggle against foreign enemies and their local allies powerfully resonates with contemporary political and social concerns.

In proposing that the fight against German fascists and their sympathizers spilled over into the late 1940s, 1950s, or even 1960s, these series comply with the state-sponsored interpretation of the Great Patriotic War as the decisive event of the twentieth century. Moreover, the contemporary rediscovery of the spy thriller as a cinematic genre that flourished during the Cold War cannot be seen in isolation from Russia's escalated conflict with Ukraine or soured relations with the European Union and the United States.[1] This chapter argues that these contemporary spy and detective series, by forging intricate links and connecting disparate events, eras, and cultural narratives, engage in a form of cultural memory that leans heavily on the logic of myth.

The current mythologization of Soviet history, and specifically the Great Patriotic War, has received significant academic attention. Russian sociologists such as Dina Khapaeva, Boris Dubin, and Lev Gudkov have claimed that the state-backed memory projects of the Putin era have made the triumph over Nazism into one of present-day Russia's foundational myths. The emphasis on Russian war heroism, they argue, helps center the collective memory of the multifaceted Soviet experience on one congratulatory focal point, glossing over Stalinist crimes and cementing the new state-centered patriotism and nationalist consensus the Putin government has been cultivating.[2]

As Lev Gudkov observed in 2005, the Soviet victory over Nazi Germany has become a "symbol that functions, . . . for the entire [Russian] society, as the most important element of collective identification, [as] a yardstick offering a particular lens for evaluating the past and, in part, for understanding the present and future. The victory of 1945 . . . is the only positive pillar of national self-consciousness in post-Soviet society."[3] The mythologization of the Soviet victory over Nazism brings with it, according to these scholars, a self-righteous triumphalism and messianism (i.e., Russia as the only true victor that liberated Europe from Nazism) that are relentlessly held up to the countries of the former Socialist bloc that have less favorable memories of the Soviet era.[4]

Surprisingly, while *myth* is a recurrent reference point in academic discussions on remembrance in post-Soviet Russia, the term is hardly ever refined conceptually. For many, myths amount to forms of falsification or simplification that thwart fact-based historical investigation or nuanced analyses of Soviet history.[5] In addition, scholars have pointed out that war myths, ever since the late 1940s, have been instrumental in cementing political authority.[6] Valuable as these approaches are, they often overlook the particular presentation of historical time and collective belonging so characteristic of mythmaking. Later I will present my own analysis of myth, but for now it suffices to say that mythic stories tend to rely on schematic "scripts" that imaginatively bind together collective identities through their "powerful cohesive force."[7] Furthermore, as the following analysis suggests, the schematic quality of myths means they can readily be transposed from their original historical contexts. Myths often serve as recurring cultural narratives employed to understand disparate historical eras and diverse political events.[8]

Liquidating the Empire's Enemies

Sergei Ursuliak's *Liquidation* (*Likvidatsia*) from 2007 is perhaps the most acclaimed retro-style detective series of the Putin era. Attracting more than 40 percent of the television audience, the series proved wildly popular.[9] Set in 1946 Odessa, *Liquidation* offers a nostalgic picture of the city in desaturated colors. This romanticized Odessa brims with flamboyant characters, many of them Jewish, who employ local slang and speak in the region's melodiously intoned accent. Adding to the atmosphere are musical intermezzos set in bars, theaters, and a boarding school where a children's choir performs. Anachronistically, these musical scenes include a performance by Leonid Utesov of his famous 1951 song "At the Black Sea," which sings Odessa's praises.

Liquidation's plot documents the efforts of Odessa's criminal investigation department to control the gangs who murder, steal, and engage in smuggling with impunity amid the chaos of the postwar years. The main character is the department's head, lieutenant-colonel David Gotsman, a streetwise Odessa local. He repeatedly clashes with Marshal Georgy Zhukov, who has been sent to Odessa after his falling out with Stalin in the spring of 1946. Now heading the Odessa Military District, Zhukov takes a straightforward approach to the city's crime problem, aiming to "liquidate" Odessa's thieves by whatever means necessary. Gotsman, however, rightly intuits that the real danger does not come from petty pickpockets. Thanks to Gotsman, one of his own men gets exposed as an Abwehr-trained anti-Soviet intelligence agent who is running Odessa's underworld disguised as a police official.

The rivalry between Gotsman and Zhukov underscores the contrast between open warfare and the fascinating intricacies of the "invisible front" from which the series derives its suspense. While Zhukov embodies the military discipline and linearity that are vital in defeating the enemy on the battlefield, Gotsman is a man of wit and imagination—the qualities essential to fighting the insidious conspiratorial tactics of the Soviet empire's ideological foes. The Gotsman-Zhukov competition references the renowned multiepisode police procedural *The Meeting Place Cannot Be Changed* (*Mesto vstrechi izmenit nelzia*), directed by Stanislav Govorukhin and released in 1979. It is easy to see the similarities between the shrewd Gotsman and the Soviet series' crowd favorite: the detective Gleb Zheglov, played by Vladimir Vysotskii. Another cult Soviet production, the legendary spy series *Seventeen Moments of Spring* (to which I will return), featuring the melancholic, intelligent Otto von Stierlitz (played by Viacheslav Tikhonov), serves as a recurring point of reference, too. Channel One's comedy show *The Big Difference* (*Bolshaia raznitsa*), for instance, staged a parody of *Liquidation* shortly after its release, featuring a delicate Stierlitz endowed with Gotsman's bravura and tuneful Odessa accent. According to Stephen Norris, with *Liquidation* Ursuliak sought to create a "composite character, a retrofitted hero whose actions and beliefs can serve as a model for present-day viewers looking for cinematic heroes."[10]

While many rooted for Gotsman and adored the romanticized version of "Odessa-mama," not all viewers found the plot's intrigues convincing. The aims of the main villain, the Nazi-trained anti-Soviet saboteur, remain obscure. Is he fanatically pursuing his subversive activities even after the Abwehr ceased to exist? Or, as one blogger wondered, are his attempts to undermine the reestablishment of Soviet power also motivated by a nationalist (Ukrainian?) and separatist political agenda?[11] Another viewer felt that *Liquidation* hinted at the presence of "Bandera adepts in [1946] Odessa" but considered this suggestion utterly far-fetched and unconvincing.[12] While the central intrigue and the motivations behind it are never satisfyingly explained, the series paved the way for television productions showing an "invisible battle" against (former) Nazis and/or their local accomplices in fascinating detail.

The twelve-part *Black Cats* (2013) is widely seen as a loose remake of *Liquidation*. It is set not in Odessa but in Rostov-na-Donu, and the events take place one year later, in 1947. While *Liquidation*'s commentary on historical context was limited to a few voice-over remarks in the first episode, *Black Cats* goes to greater lengths to inform the audience about the era in which it is set. Each episode begins with period footage and a voice-over sketching the wider historical panorama of the (fictional) events. The voice-over's remarks—for example, on the nascent postwar rivalry between the Soviet Union and the United States—explain that the future of the Nazi atomic program became one of the key issues in early Cold War competition: "Fighters of the invisible front used all available means to obtain secret information [about the former German nuclear weapon project]." The rivalry between American imperialists (and their tenacious fascist stooges) and Soviet intelligence officials to acquire nuclear know-how is indeed the central premise of the series. *Liquidation* merely hints at ongoing fascist subversion while *Black Cats* mines the full potential of such a scenario.

Like *Liquidation*, *Black Cats* gestures profusely to the Soviet classic *The Meeting Place Cannot Be Changed*, in which the protagonists fought a gang of robbers called "The Black Cat." Its hero, a major in Rostov's criminal investigation department named Egor Dragun (Pavel Derevianko), shows striking similarities, in both his attire and behavior, to Captain Gleb Zheglov of *The Meeting Place*. The story, however, deviates from its Soviet precursor and is more closely aligned with that of *Liquidation*. Early on, Dragun's department is confronted with a series of brazen crimes, including the raiding of trucks, attacks on military men, and the plundering of food stores. According to Dragun, the sophistication of these actions points not to petty thugs but to military saboteurs or intelligence agents. Suspecting the involvement of (former) Nazis, Dragun confides to a subordinate, "That war of ours has not yet ended."

The higher-ups in the party and the Ministry of Internal Affairs, however, balk at the idea that there might still be German spies operating in Rostov. "These stories about fascists must stop!" fumes Prokhor Kuplenov, a regional party official. "They *are* not, and *cannot* be, among us!" Those in positions of power are more concerned with fighting ordinary criminals and preparing for the repatriation of German POWs from a camp in the Rostov region. The process of repatriation is supervised by the charming MGB colonel Pavel Burov (Pavel Trubiner), newly arrived from Moscow. He is to vet the German POWs prior to their release, ensuring that no war criminal goes back to Germany unpunished.

Meanwhile, Dragun and his men begin to suspect that the criminals terrorizing the city might be members of the so-called Brandenburg 800 subdivision, an Abwehr special forces unit (which actually existed) of men trained to infiltrate enemy territory. Dragun obtains top-secret film footage left by the Germans that sheds light on this unit's mission. After analyzing the footage (his Jewish friends' Yiddish helps translate from the German), Dragun concludes that the tactics of Rostov's enigmatic criminals resemble those of the Brandenburgers.

These Brandenburgers, it emerges, stayed behind in the Soviet Union and now seek to free the German atomic scientist Joost Hartl, who had managed to hide among the German POWs as a regular serviceman. When Colonel Burov identifies the scientist during his interrogations of the POWs, the pace of *Black Cats'* revelations accelerates and the story lines converge. Burov, it turns out, is himself a Brandenburger and a former SS Sturmbahnführer whose actual name is Karl Lange. He hopes to smuggle Hartl out of the country in an operation funded by the Americans, who want to recruit Hartl for their atomic program or at least keep him out of Soviet hands. Although Burov/Lange's ultimate loyalties (to American imperialism, German Nazism, or both) remain obscure, he persuades Hartl to cooperate by telling him that the former Nazi elite can "restore the Third Reich" to its previous glory through the development of an atomic weapon.

The subsequent plot developments are even more dramatic. In one of the city's underground bunkers, other Brandenburgers have hidden an atomic bomb's plutonium core, and Hartl's expertise has the capacity of turning it into a

Fig. 7.1. A still from *Black Cats*. In the underground bunker of the Brandenburger spies: MGB caps used for disguise have been lifted out of Abwehr store boxes.

superweapon. If Hartl and Lange escape with the device, the series suggests, the Soviet Union's fascist-imperialist enemies could achieve a triumphant *Endsieg*. Just in time, Dragun realizes that he had seen Burov in the film footage of the Brandenburg unit and grasps that the well-respected colonel is, in fact, the villainous mastermind behind the vast anti-Soviet conspiracy. In the series' final episodes, Dragun is assisted by well-meaning gangsters from the city's Jewish-run criminal underworld (who are eager to eliminate the fascist rogues). With their help, Dragun blocks Lange and Hartl's route to the Soviet border, although not before engaging in spectacular Hollywood-inspired shoot-outs and fistfights, parts of which are shown in slow motion.

Mythologizing the "Invisible Front"

In essence, *Black Cats* articulates the "invisible front" more forcefully than *Liquidation*. Here nobody is what he or she appears to be. Even the charming secretary of the regional Communist Party leader turns out to be a ruthless Nazi Obersturmbahnführer. This insistence on disguised identities and subterranean battles against fascist enemies has far-reaching implications. In 2007, critics of *Liquidation* had already commented that the series recycled Soviet myths about deceitful ideological saboteurs. Maria Galina, for instance, contended that *Liquidation* harked back to "the myth from the Stalinist era about 'enemies of the people,' operating under the guise of trustworthy Soviet citizens."[13] This repurposed Soviet narrative is taken to its extreme in *Black Cats*, where the threat posed by the "craftily camouflaged enemy" (*umelo zakonspirirovannyi vrag*), as one of the series' characters puts it, is omnipresent.

Black Cats is deeply anachronistic, not only in its identification of a Nazi threat in 1947 but also in its twenty-first-century recycling of Stalinist discourses and Brezhnev-era cinematic genres. Wrapping the Soviet myth of "fighters of the invisible front" in a Hollywood gloss, this production joins a much wider contemporary trend in which Soviet models and narratives have been adapted to the requirements of contemporary (postmodern) mass culture. The tendency was described at length by Mark Lipovetskii, who coined the term *post-sots* for such odd cultural hybrids.[14] Rehabilitating and adapting a socialist-realist aesthetics that revolves around self-sacrifice, heroism, and Manichaean oppositions between good and evil, the culture of *post-sots* presupposes an unproblematic durability of Soviet forms in the radically different cultural and ideological context of post-Soviet life and culture.

While Lipovetskii often refers to the persistence of Soviet "myths" in post-Soviet culture, he uses the term in a commonsensical way. The understanding of *post-sots* and its particular manifestations in the series discussed here benefits from closer scrutiny of its relation to myth. Building on work by Claude Lévi-Strauss, Georges Dumézil, Roland Barthes, and others, Bruce Lincoln argued that myth "packages a specific, contingent system of discrimination in a particularly attractive and memorable form," thereby guaranteeing its prolonged cultural life in variants that continually recalibrate the "sociotaxonomic order."[15] Creating simplified categorizations, myth shapes identities and legitimacies, presenting its structures and hierarchies as a fact of nature rather than an artifact of culture. In Lincoln's reading, the naturalizing and legitimizing effects of myth determine its status as "ideology in narrative form."[16] It is easy to see how the culture of *post-sots*, with its inclination toward schematic stories of good and evil and its tendency to recycle Soviet ideologemes as timeless truths rather than historically or ideologically determined narratives, relies on such a notion.

To better grasp the series' reformatting of history, we should keep in mind some interplay among myth, memory, and history. Of particular importance here are Mircea Eliade's remarks on the differences between modern conceptions of history and mythical efforts to make sense of time.[17] For Eliade, myth constitutes the "abolition of time through the imitation of archetypes and the repetition of paradigmatic gestures."[18] In the mythical worldview, events have no specific, contingent historical significance but derive their meaning from being a manifestation of a timeless scheme.[19]

This emphasis on myth as structured by reinstantiations of paradigmatic models has been further explored by Aleida Assmann, one of the key voices in memory studies since the 1990s. Building on work by the anthropologist Paul Connerton, Assmann sees repetition as an inherent part of memory that is institutionalized, for instance, through anniversaries and recurring commemorative rituals. Periodic commemorations, however, do not necessarily involve mythologization. Myth emerges only when remembrance tends to erase the difference between past and present and/or blend historical events. Assmann submits that myth collapses different time periods, a propensity that ultimately elevates mythologized events out of historical linearity altogether.[20]

The series analyzed here, I argue, demonstrate such a mythic detachment of events from their original historical origins. This is not to say that the series entirely abolish a connection to historical time and to the Second World War in particular. In both *Liquidation* and *Black Cats*, the war marks the historical moment when Nazis and their accomplices gained sway over law-abiding Soviet citizens. Yet these series rely on a mythic vision of history as structured by simple, repeatable scripts that shape identities in unquestionable ways: the heroic battle of Soviet/Russian patriots against dastardly fascists is still being played out, albeit in a subterranean variant, even after the war's end. As one critic cogently put it, the central premise of *Black Cats* is that "fascists/spies are always among us."[21] It is precisely this double reading of the fascist threat—as a historical reality linked to the war and as a persistent scenario open to novel manifestations in other periods—that explains these series' numerous, puzzling anachronisms.

Turning the struggle against fascism into a repeatable script is not the only thing these productions do. By rehabilitating the cinematic genre of the spy adventure, they sever its ties to the political and ideological context of the Cold War from which the genre sprouted. The historically and culturally specific myth of the "fighters of the invisible front" heroically combatting devious Nazi plotters and their supposed Western allies is uncritically transposed from the Soviet Union of the 1950s, 1960s, and 1970s to the post-Soviet media landscape, despite the obvious incommensurability.

One should pay close attention to the content of this recycling of Soviet discourses and, in particular, to the mythic categorization of enemies as a process inextricably bound with the construction of an imagined Soviet/Russian "we." *Black Cats*, *Liquidation*, and the other series analyzed here use *fascism* as a catch-all term for "the enemy" and as an antithesis of Soviet/Russian patriotism. Lev Gudkov traces this cultural mechanism back to the Soviet mantra of "anti-fascism," a vague Cold War notion that increasingly came to stand for the Soviet rejection of all things West, including capitalism and liberalism. Through a process of "negative identification," the "struggle against fascism" became essential to Soviet (and later Russian) notions of collective belonging and "social wholeness."[22]

Both *Liquidation* and *Black Cats* make use of this mechanism. They insistently counterbalance "fascist" hatred with multiethnic Soviet solidarity. Both series feature sympathetic Russians, Jews, Ukrainians, and Armenians—easily identifiable by their dress, accent, and music—who, within the framework of the

Soviet state, engage in friendly, tolerant, and harmonious relationships with one another. As a powerful antimodel, "fascism" helps cement a multiethnic "imagined community" that sometimes reminds the viewer of the Soviet notion of "fraternity of peoples."[23]

As a validation of Gudkov's analysis, the struggle against "fascism" in these series leaves the exact identity of the enemy open to interpretation. As the critic Andrei Arkhangelskii pointed out, the plot of *Black Cats* is indebted to the Soviet spy films of the Cold War decades that revolved around collusion between former fascists and Western intelligence services. According to Arkhangelskii, late Soviet cinema strove to provide a "genealogy of evil [by connecting] past evil (Nazism) to contemporary evil (America)."[24] Imperialist-fascist collusion is indeed repeatedly invoked in *Black Cats*—for instance, when Burov/Lange admits to Hartl that the Americans have promised him one million dollars if he delivers Hartl to them alive and 30 percent of that sum if he can prove that Hartl has been killed.

A brief detour illustrates the extent to which *Black Cats* and several other recent series dust off, in their categorization of enemies, the pet subjects of the Soviet espionage genre. A paradigmatic example is the twelve-part miniseries *Seventeen Moments of Spring* (*Semnadtsat mgnovenii vesny*) from 1973, a production that boosted the popularity of the spy thriller for generations to come and became a persistent cultural reference point during the Soviet and post-Soviet eras. Directed by Tatiana Lioznova and based on Iulian Semenov's novel of the same title, it was "one of the most important 'low' culture events of the Brezhnev period."[25] Over the decades, the series—shown every year in the run-up to Victory Day—became, according to Steven Lovell, the "biggest cult phenomenon in the history of Soviet (and indeed Russian) television."[26] Set during the last months of the Second World War, the film chronicles the adventures of a mole, the Soviet spy Maksim Isaev (Viacheslav Tikhonov), who has infiltrated the Nazi elite under the false identity of SS Standartenführer Otto von Stierlitz. His bosses in the GRU (Soviet military intelligence service) have tasked him with thwarting the secret plans for a peace treaty between the United States and Germany that, if realized, would treacherously cold-shoulder the Soviet Union.

Unlike his counterparts in series like *Black Cats* and *Liquidation*, Stierlitz is perhaps a more passive hero (an emblematic figure of the period of so-called stagnation under Brezhnev, according to Elena Prokhorova).[27] Furthermore, these contemporary productions represent a reversal of the Stierlitz model, featuring Nazi spies infiltrating Soviet institutions rather than the other way around. They share, however, *Seventeen Moments'* fascination with crafty agents who cunningly conceal their real identities and patriotic Soviet intelligence officers who almost single-handedly save the motherland from its enemies. Crucially, *Black Cats* borrows from cultural texts like *Seventeen Moments* a vision in which the hot war against German Nazis seamlessly merges into the cold war against capitalist adversaries.

In *Seventeen Moments*, secret rapprochement between German fascism and American imperialism dangerously harms the Soviet Union's interests.[28] Toward its finale we learn that Heinrich Müller and Martin Bormann aim to use the Nazi party's gold reserves to secure the future dissemination of Nazi propaganda. The cynical Müller explains to Stierlitz that the Nazis "must have storytellers who'll remold the message for those who'll live twenty years from now." The series thus anticipates the danger of a fascist-capitalist repackaging of Nazi ideology but also explains postwar, and Cold War, realities through the enemies' wartime intrigues.

While *Seventeen Moments* perfectly aligns with Arkhangelskii's remarks about a Soviet spy tradition that endeavored to provide a genealogy of evil, in *Black Cats* and *Liquidation*, the exact nature of the "enemy" is much vaguer. *Seventeen Moments* still keenly (although not always successfully) insisted on historical accuracy—including historical figures in its plot, meticulously reproducing the uniforms of various Nazi ranks, and relying profusely on documentary footage. In *Black Cats* and *Liquidation*, by contrast, adversaries are collapsed into one ill-defined category composed of American imperialists, Ukrainian separatists, Nazi spies, and SS Obersturmbahführers—all of whom engage in treacherous, loose alliances. In *Black Cats*, for example, the audience never gets to learn why defeated fascists would quixotically cling to the idea that the Third Reich could be restored. And while the Americans are said to be complicit in the nefarious scheme, the nature of their involvement remains unclear. In presenting a befogged revision of history, these series unmoor the narrative of an "invisible front" from its specific historical (Cold War) anchoring and reformat it as a mythic struggle against vaguely defined Western forces.

Extending the Myth into the Postwar Decades

Two other recent detective adventures, *The Cry of the Owl* (*Krik sovy*, Oleg Pogodin, 2013) and *Executioner* (*Palach*, Viacheslav Nikiforov, 2015), set the struggle against fascism much later than *Black Cats* and *Liquidation*—in 1957 and 1965, respectively. But the ingredients of the ten-part *Cry of the Owl*, dubbed "*Liquidation* lite [*sic*]" by the critic Dmitrii Cheremnov, are surprisingly similar to those of the productions discussed earlier.[29] Here, too, crime fighters in provincial Russia (the town of Ostrov near Pskov) suspect that aggressive thugs are involved in a fascist conspiracy.

The war veteran and police captain Iurii Sirotin (Evgenii Diatlov) ends up in the hospital after being shot and wounded in a confrontation with a criminal gang. The physician on duty hears his comatose patient mumbling in flawless

German, and the local KGB captain, Ivan Mitin (Sergei Puskepalis), is summoned to investigate the case. Mitin soon concludes that Sirotin was not the law-abiding war hero he pretended to be. In fact, he was involved in a secret operation to provide the region's leading gangsters with German passports. Mitin regularly clashes with the unpolished police major Andrei Balakhin (Andrei Merzlikin), who insists Sirotin is trustworthy and tries to convince Mitin that he is on the wrong track. Even greater resistance comes from Ostrov's inhabitants. After Khrushchev's condemnatory speech to the Twentieth Congress, respect for the intelligence services has reached a historical low. The KGB captain is feared and despised in the town, and even the town's children pelt him with stones and mud.

Sirotin, it turns out, is but one member of a well-connected spy ring active in the town. The main villain is Alexander Gorobets, the apparently sympathetic director of the local war museum who had been an infamously cruel executioner in the concentration camp Salaspils during the war. The museum, housed in the former Nazi headquarters, harbors an extensive German archive in its cellar. Gorobets now wants to trade the archive, which has attracted the interest of foreign intelligence services, for German passports for himself and other collaborators-cum-criminals, which will allow them to flee abroad.

The Cry of the Owl brims with citations from both *The Meeting Place Cannot Be Changed* (especially the duo Mitin-Balakhnin, which evokes the Sharapov-Zheglov relationship) and *Seventeen Moments*. The latter series resonates in various plot twists. In addition, the even-toned voice-over, which in *The Cry of the Owl* regularly articulates the thoughts of Mitin (whose character seems inspired by Stierlitz's contemplative traits), is obviously borrowed from the intrusive narrator's voice in *Seventeen Moments*.[30]

This alignment with the Soviet spy tradition comes with an outdated Cold War rhetoric. In compliance with the late Soviet obsession with fascist-Western collusion, the series emphasizes the foreign contacts of these ex-collaborators: they use a wartime radio transmitter from the museum, presumably to tip off their contacts abroad; their plan is to obtain German passports and cross the border; and the spy ring is apparently in touch with unspecified "Western intelligence services." On the other hand, the tone of *The Cry of the Owl* is not as triumphant as its compliance with the Soviet espionage tradition might suggest. The series lacks the typical celebration of the intelligence services. Instead, it directs attention to the long-lasting, detrimental social impact of the NKVD-orchestrated repression of the 1930s, during which Mitin's own mother was arrested and executed.

By the same token, Mitin ultimately abstains from adopting revanchist attitudes toward ex-collaborators. In Ostrov, it is emphasized, almost everyone worked for the Germans; the Nazi archive on which the story's intrigues hinge contains invaluable information on the local inhabitants' wartime activities.

Fig. 7.2. A still from *The Cry of the Owl*. "Hände hoch!" When KBG captain Mitin arrests the Nazi collaborator and "Western" spy Gorobets in 1957, he addresses him in German.

Mitin, however, decides not to pass the files to his KGB superiors, pretending that the archive has been lost through his mistake, even though this decision will irreparably damage his career. With the main villain behind bars, forgetfulness, the series suggests, is the only possible remedy against the shadow of fascism that looms large over the town. For one reviewer, this nuanced treatment of historical guilt (acknowledging both collaboration and Soviet repression) and its legacies made *The Cry of the Owl* the "most important Russian television series produced in the last twenty years."[31]

Executioner (*Palach*), aired on Channel One in January 2015, is a more recent example of the current emphasis on a prolonged battle against fascist elements. This police procedural was inspired by the story of Antonina Makarova, better known as Tonka the machine gunner. The actual Antonina had enlisted as a Soviet nurse. In the aftermath of a German attack in 1941 that decimated her unit, she ended up in the semi-autonomous Lokot region in Central Russia and was eventually hired as an executioner for the collaborationist police forces. In 1942 and 1943, Tonka reportedly machine-gunned hundreds of Soviet POWs, as well as Soviet partisans and their families (although the judge in her 1978 trial concluded that she had personally killed 160 people).[32]

Executioner revolves around Tonka's arrest, which it sets in 1965 rather than in the late 1970s, when the actual Tonka was arrested, convicted, and sentenced to death. In a village near Moscow, a number of brutal murders are committed, the first during the twentieth-anniversary celebrations of the Soviet victory in the

Fig. 7.3. A still from *Executioner*. The moment of disclosure: in one of the wartime scenes, Tonka the machine gunner finds a carnival mask she will later wear during the executions. The viewer here identifies Tonka as Raisa, the music teacher from the 1965 storyline.

Great Patriotic War. The victims are all killed in the same fashion: a gunshot to each of their eyes. The protagonist, police major Ivan Cherkassov (Andrei Smoliakov, who was also featured in the television series *Mosgaz* [2012] and *Spider* [*Pauk*, 2015]), begins to suspect the crimes are connected to the history of Tonka the machine gunner, who apparently killed injured POWs in this fashion. The series offers a succession of clues that culminate in the revelation that the village's sympathetic music teacher, Raisa, is actually Tonka.

At the war's end, she had cleverly tricked the arriving Soviet troops into believing she was a partisan fighter. The acts of murder she had committed in the postwar years, including that of her own stepson Petia on Victory Day, were supposed to prevent her true identity from being disclosed. As she later admits, Petia and several other young villagers had gone too far in ferreting out her past, and she wanted to protect her blood relatives from the shame and prosecution that would have followed had her secret been revealed. Raisa/Tonka's wartime activities are shown in flashbacks. However, since she is wearing a carnival mask during the executions—a liberty taken by the makers of the series—the viewer does not know for sure which of the postwar characters was the real Tonka.

Unlike *Liquidation*, *Black Cats*, and *The Cry of the Owl*, *Executioner* centers not on politically driven subversion but on an individual Soviet citizen whose crimes are mitigated by her status as a victim. Certainly, Tonka's past acts of treason are presented as despicable and her contemporary crimes as monstrous. Yet the flashback scenes, which begin when she gets separated from her unit during the German attack, vividly portray her suffering. While wandering through the forests of Briansk Oblast, Tonka meets another lost Soviet soldier, who rapes her. More suffering follows after she is captured by the Nazis. She is again raped, she is beaten for days on end, and she is thrown into a locked pit and deprived of food and water. Only after a failed suicide attempt, and after she is forcibly made to drink schnapps, does she consent to work as an executioner.

Instead of portraying Tonka as the opportunistic collaborator she may have been, these scenes point to her unfathomable suffering as an explanation for her treason. According to a reviewer in the journal *Iskusstvo kino*, the history of the *actual* Tonka is horrific precisely because it recalls the "banality of evil": the real Antonina Makarova never showed remorse and even explained to her KGB interrogators that her work as an executioner was "just a job"—and not a particularly demanding one, at that—because she "did not know" the people she had killed. The series, however, takes away this most unsettling part of Tonka's story (her unrepentant killing of innocent people) by casting her cruelties as an effect of wartime abuses, largely by the Nazis.[33]

Like *The Cry of the Owl*, *Executioner* is more concerned with the impact of fascism than with a continued battle against it. At the same time, the myth of the "invisible front," prominently featured in both series, blurs the distinction between the war and its insidious continuation. In *The Cry of the Owl*, Mitin remarks that it is as if the war "has ended only yesterday" in Ostrov, and in *Executioner* the cat-and-mouse game between inspector and villain is framed as an extension of the war itself: Raisa still uses her trademark method of shooting her victims in the eyes, the villagers are murdered with a German Walther gun, and Cherkassov understands that the recent shots (metaphorically) "come from the war." Furthermore, the opening scenes of *Executioner*, in which the villagers cheerfully celebrate the twentieth anniversary of the victory over Nazism, merely underscore that, even two decades later, the fascist threat has not entirely abated. The heroes do not celebrate their victory as professionals until the final episode, after the identity of Raisa/Tonka has been uncovered. First the inspectors are congratulated personally by Leonid Brezhnev, who toasts "to our victory." Later, Cherkassov, together with his son and colleague, celebrate their achievement by singing war-themed songs. These moments mark the men's decisive triumph "on the invisible front."

Even though *The Cry of the Owl* and *Executioner* both deal with the delicate issue of collaboration, their applications of the myth of the "invisible front" have different undertones. The former series clings to an idea of a fascist-Western conspiracy while acknowledging the cruel and arbitrary persecutions of the NKVD under Stalin and the collaboration of opportunistic Soviet citizens during the war. Collective guilt in the series functions as unmourned collective trauma, which explains the story's melancholy tone.[34] *Executioner*, however, while portraying atrocities carried out by Nazi collaborators in vivid color, is significantly more triumphant in its message. Tonka/Raisa's individual trauma (aesthetically highlighted in some scenes through her flashbacks to wartime brutalities) does not allow for a treatment of collaboration as a social problem.[35] In *The Cry of the Owl*, wartime collaboration raised questions about the social cohesion of a postwar community, but in *Executioner*, the myth of a struggle against fascist danger effectively solidifies the social harmony of a rural microcosm that allegorically signifies the Soviet community as a whole.

Conclusion

In this chapter I analyzed the myth of a subterranean war against insidious fascist aggression as it appears in contemporary Russian historical television series. In these popular-cultural revisions of history, the Soviet triumph over Nazism is elevated from its specific place in history and transposed, in real or symbolic form, to other moments in time: to 1946, when fascist-separatist subversion was rooted out by a devoted Soviet inspector in Odessa (*Liquidation*); to 1947, when the restoration of the Third Reich through the acquisition of nuclear weapons was decisively forestalled (*Black Cats*); or to 1965, when a rural Russian community was cleansed of its insidious fascist poison and victory could finally be celebrated (*Executioner*). Here I turn to examine the political utility of a mythologized cultural memory that takes the struggle against fascism and its supposed allies beyond the contingencies of space and time.

Much has been written about Russia's memory wars with Ukraine, which tend to pivot on the Second World War and, in particular, the role of Stepan Bandera's Ukrainian Liberation Army (which revolted against Soviet power and, at least for a short period, allied itself with the Nazis).[36] By way of conclusion, I discuss a recent media event that illuminates the political dimensions of the cultural obsession with the "invisible front" and its relevance to Russia's ongoing (memory) war with Ukraine.

Aired on Rossiia One in March 2015 on the first anniversary of Crimea's annexation, Andrei Kondrashov's documentary *Crimea: Homeward Bound* (*Krym: Put na rodinu*) attracted a vast audience.[37] In two and a half hours of epic storytelling and spectacular visualizations, the film presented testimonials of pro-Russian fighters, an interview with Vladimir Putin, and slick reconstructions of the heroic efforts of the Crimean People's Defense Forces to protect the peninsula from "Ukrainian nationalists." Earlier, Putin had denied the direct participation of Russian troops in the conflict, but now he openly boasted that the annexation of Crimea had been a well-executed special operation that involved Russian GRU troops, marines, and airborne forces and was personally overseen by the president himself.

The documentary emphasizes the strategic wit and personal involvement of the president, who is shown to be always one step ahead of the new government in Kiev. The image of the operation as a "triumph of security planning and execution, with Mr. Putin at its heart," taps into Putin's reputation as a former KGB officer.[38] As Stephen Norris pointed out, since the turn of the century, Putin's popularity has been boosted by his KGB career in Germany, which aligned him with the patriotic aura and exciting adventurism à la Stierlitz.[39] Thus, as Mark Lipovetskii wrote in 2005, "precisely the shadow of Stierlitz helped this faceless nobody to become the people's favorite. . . . Russian collective unconsciousness elected Stierlitz for President."[40]

Putin unwittingly gave further credence to the Cold War espionage myth when he stated in the interview with Kondrashov that the "real puppeteers" behind the Ukrainian regime change and subsequent events were "our American partners and friends." This notion is further elaborated in a scene that suggests that NATO-trained Ukrainian marines in Feodosia "were in touch with the US consulate-general in Kiev" and that "large sums of money were transferred to their commander's bank account." Many of these troops refused to surrender, and the film asserts that these marines later committed horrific crimes against the civilian population of the Donbass region, "as if that was precisely what they were trained to do."[41]

Notwithstanding the accusations of US intervention, President Putin's remarks in the interview were still fairly diplomatic, stressing the legal foundations for the Crimean referendum and the right of the peninsula's population to self-determination. Other interviewees—among them members of the Crimean defense forces, Russian Cossack volunteers, and Crimean citizens but also the prosecutor general of the new Crimean Republic—routinely cast the struggle for Crimean self-control as a fight against "fascists," "Bandera men" (*banderovtsy*), or "Nazis."

The alleged threat of "fascist" Ukrainian aggression (supposedly backed by Western money) is further dramatized through a scene about a "penal expedition" from Kiev. The film asserts that at the end of February 2014, Ukrainian troops, "hardened by Maidan" and "armed to the teeth," planned to come to Simferopol by train to crush the Crimean resistance. The reconstructions leading up to the train's arrival show volunteering blacksmiths forging shields for the Crimean resistance fighters. The images are accompanied by foreboding music and an ominous voice-over ("zero hour had arrived"), enforcing the impression of an imminent epic battle. In the subsequent reconstruction, a Crimean commander receives a text message from the leader of the Crimean resistance, Sergei Aksenov: "The train with Banderas [*poezd s Banderami*] is here." Notwithstanding the dramatic buildup, the scene is ultimately anticlimactic: the train is empty, as the troops from Kiev supposedly backed off when they learned what awaited them. As the local commander comments in an interview, on that day "we closed our ranks, so that the fascists could not enter our land."

History is omnipresent in Kondrashov's documentary. The aforementioned scene paints the recent conflict along the lines of Soviet narratives about the need to bar the advance of fascism; other episodes emphasize the heroic role of the Red Army and the Black Sea Fleet during the Siege of Sevastopol, and President Putin explains that some of the Ukrainian marines agreed to sign the resignation papers that would formalize their surrender to Russia only after he had personally sent in Russian veterans of the Second World War to talk to them. These references to the Great Patriotic War go beyond simple historical analogy and work to present the recent Russian success in Crimea as a new phase in a paradigmatic struggle against fascist Western encroachments.

In Kondrashov's documentary the war is acting itself out in the present. As Eliot Borenstein cogently formulates it in his commentary on the Russian media coverage of the war in Ukraine: "The fighting in Ukraine [is] recast as a long-delayed sequel to World War II, with crypto-fascists emerging from their bunkers after seven decades of presumably cryogenic suspension."[42] It is no coincidence that in one of the documentary's reconstructions, the commander of the Crimean Defense Forces is warned about a train full of Banderas, a term that blends the historical figure and his alleged contemporary supporters (Banderovites). In her work on historical mythologies in post-Soviet Russia, Liudmila Mazur argued that a key "feature of myth is its ability to revive the past, bring it closer to the present, and pose as a viable option for the future."[43] Kondrashov's documentary pushes this procedure to the point where the boundaries separating the past, the present, and an anticipated future fascist threat become blurry.

The film borrows from the myth of "the invisible front" an emphasis on furtive fascist-Western collusion, a celebration of the supposed strategic supremacy of (former) Soviet intelligence agents, and a cultivation of a timeless Soviet/Russian triumphalism that forms the basis of a shared Russian identity. In the documentary's finale, the mythologized victory over fascism (rather than the right to self-determination emphasized by Putin) is what legitimizes the annexation of Crimea. Presenting the conflict over Crimea as a manifestation of Russia's perpetual struggle against (largely invisible) fascist-imperialist encroachments, it incorporates the pro-Russian inhabitants of Crimea into a mythic narrative of shared belonging.

In a particularly crass manner, *Crimea: Homeward Bound* thus subscribes to the same *post-sots* logic as the television series discussed earlier. The culture of *post-sots*, according to Lipovetskii, integrates the "post-Soviet experience into a 'well-worn' and familiar Soviet 'frame.'"[44] One may add to this that in all the cases analyzed here—albeit to a different extent and with differing degrees of success—the ideological underpinning of *post-sots* resided precisely in its reliance on myth—that is, in its obfuscation of the incompatibility of Soviet cultural "frames" and incommensurable post-Soviet experiences.

Notes

1. The history of Soviet espionage cinema goes back to the late 1940s and includes such classics as *Secret Agent* (*Podvig razvedchika*, 1947), *The Shield and The Sword* (*Shchit i mech*, 1968), and *Seventeen Moments of Spring* (*Semnadtsat mgnovenii vesny*, 1973).

2. Boris Dubin, "Pamiat, voina, pamiat o voine: Konstruirovanie proshlogo v sotsialnoi praktike poslednikh desiatiletii," *Otechestvennye zapiski* 43, no. 4 (2008), http://www.strana -oz.ru/2008/4/pamyat-voyna-pamyat-o-voyne-konstruirovanie-proshlogo-v-socialnoy -praktike-poslednih-desyatiletiy; Dina Khapaeva, "Triumphant Memory of the Perpetrators: Putin's Politics of Re-Stalinization," *Communist and Post-Communist Studies* 49, no. 1 (2016): 65; Dina Khapaeva, "Historical Memory in Post-Soviet Gothic Society," *Social Research* 76, no. 1 (Spring 2009): 368; Lev Gudkov, "'Pamiat o voine i massovaia identichnost rossiian,'" *Neprikosnovennyi zapas* 40–41, nos. 2–3 (2005), https://magazines.gorky.media/nz/2005/2 /pamyat-o-vojne-i-massovaya-identichnost-rossiyan.html.

3. Gudkov, "'Pamiat o voine.'"

4. Khapaeva, "Triumphant Memory of the Perpetrators," 65; Gudkov, "'Pamiat o voine.'"

5. Cf. Aleksandr Kustarev, "Mifologiia sovetskogo proshlogo," *Neprikosnovennyi zapas* 89, no. 3 (2009), https://magazines.gorky.media/nz/2005/2/pamyat-o-vojne-i-massovaya -identichnost-rossiyan.html; Teddy J. Uldricks, "War, Politics and Memory: Russian Historians Reevaluate the Origins of World War II," *History & Memory* 21, no. 2 (2009): 60–82; see also Lisa Kirschenbaum, "Introduction: World War II in Soviet and Post-Soviet Memory," *Soviet and Post-Soviet Review* 38, no. 2 (2011): 97–103.

6. Cf. Nina Tumarkin, "The Great Patriotic War as Myth and Memory," *European Review* 11, no. 4 (2003): 595–611; Amir Weiner, "The Making of a Dominant Myth: The Second World War and the Construction of Political Identities within the Soviet Polity," *Russian Review* 55, no. 4 (October 1996): 638–60.

7. For a general discussion of the cohesive, identity-shaping force of myth, see Duncan Bell, "Mythscapes: Memory, Mythology, and National Identity," *British Journal of Sociology* 54, no. 1 (March 2003): 63–81.

8. Cf. Svetlana Boym, *The Future of Nostalgia* (New York: Basic Books, 2001), 54.

9. On the popular cinephile website Kinopoisk, users gave the series an 8.4 out of 10.

10. Stephen Norris, "A Kiss for the KGB: Putin as Cinematic Hero," in *Russia's New fin de siècle: Contemporary Culture Between Past and Present*, ed. Birgit Beumers (London: Intellect Books, 2013), 163.

11. Mikhail Magid, "Retsenziia na film 'Likvidatsiia': Odesskie povstantsy v abrikosovyx dzhungliakh," Live Journal, December 31, 2007, http://shraibman.livejournal.com/10126 .html?thread=80782.

12. Alexei Gorodetskii, "Slona ne zametili," Kinopoisk, December 25, 2015, https://www .kinopoisk.ru/user/6666134/comment/2336164/.

13. Mariia Galina, "Replika odessitki," Booknik, February 26, 2008, http://booknik.ru/today/all/replika-odessitki/.

14. Mark Lipovetskii, *Paralogii: Transformatsii (post)modernistskogo diskursa v kul'ture 1920–2000-kh godov* (Moscow: Novoe literaturnoe obozrenie, 2008), 720–34.

15. Bruce Lincoln, *Theorizing Myth: Narrative, Ideology, and Scholarship* (Chicago: University of Chicago Press, 1999), 147, 150.

16. Lincoln, *Theorizing Myth*, 147.

17. Eliade's work is controversial for its reduction of myth to a phenomenon of archaic or primitive cultures and their supposed affinity for the sacred, among other reasons. Regardless, his analysis has inspired the work of a new generation of students of mythography.

18. Mircea Eliade, *Myth of the Eternal Return: Cosmos and History* (Princeton, NJ: Princeton University Press, 1971), 35.

19. Eliade, *Myth*, 33–48.

20. Aleida Assmann, *Der lange Schatten der Vergangenheit: Erinnerungskultur und Geschichtspolitik* (Munich: C. H. Beck, 2014), 231–34. Cf. Roland Barthes's analysis of myth as a form of signification "constituted by the loss of the historical quality of things." Barthes further argues that "myth deprives the object of which it speaks of all History." Roland Barthes, *Mythologies* (London: Vintage Books), 169, 178.

21. Andrei Arkhangelskii, "Urka-patriotizm," *Kommersant*, March 10, 2014, https://www.kommersant.ru/doc/2422164.

22. Gudkov, "'Pamiat o voine'"; Lev Gudkov, *Negativnaia identichnost: Statii 1997–2002 godov* (Moscow: Novoe literaturnoe obozrenie, 2004).

23. Surprisingly, this aspect of *Liquidation* was enthusiastically welcomed by the journalist and writer Alexander Prokhanov, who has a controversial reputation for his antisemitic and neo-Stalinist views. Aleksandr Prokhanov, "Kartina maslom v imperskoi rame," *Zavtra* (blog), December 26, 2007, http://zavtra.ru/blogs/2007-12-2611.

24. Arkhangelskii, "Urka-patriotizm."

25. Catharine Nepomnyashchii, "The Blockbuster Miniseries on Russian TV: Isaev-Shtirlits, the Ambiguous Hero of *Seventeen Moments in Spring*," *Soviet and Post-Soviet Review* 29, no. 3 (2002): 257.

26. Stephen Lovell, "In Search of an Ending: *Seventeen Moments* and the Seventies," in *The Socialist Sixties: Crossing Borders in the Socialist World*, ed. Anne E. Gorsuch and Diane P. Koenker (Bloomington: Indiana University Press, 2013), 305.

27. Elena Prokhorova, "Fragmented Mythologies: Soviet TV Miniseries of the 1970s" (PhD diss., University of Pittsburgh, 2003), 811–22.

28. In its pre-détente view of Soviet-American relations, *Seventeen Moments* seems less aligned with the early 1970s than with the late 1960s.

29. Dmitrii Cheremnov, "Ia znaiu, chto vy delali v 1957-m," Gazeta.ru, November 7, 2013, https://www.gazeta.ru/culture/2013/11/07/a_5741193.shtml.

30. This voice, in the words of Elena Prokhorova, "often replace[d] characters' words, thoughts, and memories." See Prokhorova, "Fragmented Mythologies," 84.

31. Gektor, "Ostrov nevedeniia," Kinopoisk, November 12, 2013, https://www.kinopoisk.ru/user/53467/comment/1913109/.

32. Iurii Solovev, *Kratkii ocherk istorii sudoustroistva na brianskoi zemle* (Bryansk, Russia: Ladomir, 2014), 161.

33. Natalia Sirivlia, "Treugolnik Karpmana: 'Palach,' rezhisser Viacheslav Nikiforov," *Iskusstvo kino* 12 (December 2015), http://kinoart.ru/archive/2015/12/treugolnik-karpmana -palach-rezhisser-vyacheslav-nikiforov.

34. Cf. Dominick LaCapra, *Writing History, Writing Trauma* (Baltimore: Johns Hopkins University Press, 2001).

35. See Roger Luckhurst's remarks on the traumatic flashback in *The Trauma Question* (London: Routledge, 2008), 177–208.

36. See, for example, Iurii Ruban, "The 'Great Patriotic War' as a Weapon in the War against Ukraine," *Euromaidan Press*, April 22, 2015, http://euromaidanpress.com/2015/04/22 /the-great-patriotic-war-as-a-weapon-in-the-war-against-ukraine/; Sergei Medvedev, "Russkii resentiment," *Otechestvennye zapiski* 63, no. 6 (2014), http://magazines.russ.ru /oz/2014/6/3m.html; and Eliot Borenstein, "Undead Ukrainian Nazis (and the Americans Who Love Them)," Plots against Russia, May 16, 2017, http://plotsagainstrussia.org /eb7nyuedu/2017/5/16/undead-ukrainian-nazis-and-the-americans-who-love-them (site discontinued).

37. In Moscow alone, three million viewers tuned in to the film. Andrei Sinitsyn, "Vladimir Putin oboznachil novyi etap i uroven samoizoliatsii Rossii," *Vedomosti*, March 16, 2015.

38. Neil MacFarquhar, "Putins Says He Weighed Nuclear Alert over Crimea," *New York Times*, March 15, 2015.

39. Norris, "A Kiss for the KGB."

40. Mark Lipovetskii, "Iskusstvo alibi: 'Semnadtsat mgnovenii vesny' v svete nashego opyta," *Neprikosnovennyi zapas* 53, no. 3 (2007), http://magazines.russ.ru/nz/2007/3/li16 .html.

41. "Krym—Put na rodinu," Rossiia 24, March 18, 2015, video, 2:01:38, https://www .youtube.com/watch?v=N-ttlj-T2Uc&ab_channel=АндрейАкименко.

42. Borenstein, "Undead Ukrainian Nazis."

43. Liudmila Mazur, "Golden Age Mythology and the Nostalgia of Catastrophes in Post-Soviet Russia," *Canadian Slavonic Papers* 3–4 (2015): 232.

44. Lipovetskii, *Paralogii*, 725.

BORIS NOORDENBOS is Assistant Professor in Literary and Cultural Analysis at the University of Amsterdam. He is author of *Post-Soviet Literature and the Search for a Russian Identity* and editor (with Otto Boele and Ksenia Robbe) of *Post-Soviet Nostalgia: Confronting the Empire's Legacies.*

8 War, Cinema, and the Politics of Memory in Putin 2.0 Culture

Stephen M. Norris

THIS IS A story of three recent Russian films and their reception. This is also a tale of how cinema, politics, remembrance practices, and laws collide. Ultimately, this chapter is an examination of how movies help us understand the culture of the second Putin presidency, which we might call Putin 2.0.[1] This 2.0 culture has a minister of truth, Vladimir Medinskii, whose decisions have markedly shaped the cultural policies he oversees and the fates of the three films discussed here.

The films in question are Fedor Bondarchuk's blockbuster history, *Stalingrad*, which set box office records when it appeared in 2013; Khusein Erkenov's *Ordered to Forget* (*Prikazano zabyt'*), which ran into trouble with the Russian Ministry of Culture and received only one official screening; and Kim Druzhinin and Andrei Shaliopa's crowdsourced movie, *Panfilov's 28*, which drew on a Soviet-era heroic myth. All three films cover episodes from the Second World War that have acquired the quality of foundational moments for modern nationhood in Russia and Chechnya. That two of the films received extensive coverage in the national media and the other was effectively banned tells us a lot about the nature of Putin 2.0 culture and how the 2010s witnessed new forms of restrictions on the future of the Russian and Soviet pasts. *Panfilov's 28*, the third film to debut, helps clarify the political nature of the decision to promote Bondarchuk's film while effectively banning Erkenov's. As it turns out, the Putin 2.0 fixation on outlawing the "falsification of the past" is not so much a policy to identify histories that deny or distort events but rather a means to discredit contentious and problematic aspects of the past that the Russian state fears may get in the way of fostering patriotism. To get to that part of the story, however, a brief overview of Soviet memory and forgetting is due.

On Soviet Memory and Forgetting: Putin 1.0 Culture

The Soviet state and its officials constructed a specific memory culture associated with their attempts to remake society and its citizens. Tzvetan Todorov writes that totalitarian regimes "revealed the existence of a danger never before imagined: the blotting out of memory."[2] Through the takeover of information and communication, Todorov argues, a takeover of memory can also take place. Lies and inventions, distortions and half-truths—these are what dictatorships often offer in place of historical truth. "History is rewritten," Todorov continues, "with every change of those in power and encyclopedia readers are invited to cut out any pages which have become undesirable."[3] Todorov alerts us to the ways oppressive systems can manipulate the past and, with it, remembrance of things past; at the same time, he also warns us that an "important distinction needs to be made between the *recovery* of the past and its subsequent *use*."[4]

One of the case studies Todorov uses in order to demonstrate how totalitarian states blot out memory is that of Vasilii Grossman. His *Black Book*, compiled with Ilia Ehrenburg to document the massacre of Soviet Jews, including Grossman's mother, as well as his novel *Life and Fate*, which narrated the Soviet experience of the Second World War but also compared the Soviet system to the Nazis, "brought his disgrace."[5] Todorov uses Grossman as an example that provides meaning to otherwise empty phrases such as the "duty of memory" and "against forgetting," as well as a counterexample to the sacralization of the past.

Todorov's focus on Grossman fits within the broader paradigm outlined by Amir Weiner in his article "When Memory Counts." As Weiner explains, the Soviet state helped construct a specific memory culture after 1945 that focused on "ethnonational hierarchical heroism" and "universal suffering."[6] In order to construct a usable past out of the war as well as a narrative that fit the Stalinist state's totalizing aspirations, Soviet authorities stressed an interpretation that condensed the vast experiences of citizens to one in which all Soviet people suffered immensely but equally and where some national groups were more heroic than others: Russians were at the top, Chechens and other enemy nations at the bottom. Grossman figures in this study, too; according to Weiner, the author's writings threatened to reveal that Soviet Jews (and, by implication, other peoples) suffered more than others and that Soviet Jews (and again, by implication, other peoples) were just as heroic as their Russian comrades. In banning Grossman's works, Soviet authorities blotted out memories, as Todorov argued, and ensured the dominant narratives of heroism and suffering would be remembered, as Weiner argued.

Another possible case study—not mentioned by Todorov—is the fate of the "punished peoples," many from the Caucasus, who were deported during the Second World War under Stalin's orders for the "crime" of being Chechen, Crimean Tatar, Kalmyk, Balkar, Karachay, or Ingush.[7] NKVD head Lavrenty Beria issued a verbal order that any Chechen or Ingush who could not be transported should be liquidated. In the village of Khaibakh, NKVD officers locked more than seven hundred Chechens into a barn and burned it. Colonel Mikhail Gvishiani sent a message to Beria "only for your eyes" that stated, "In view of their

untransportability and with the goal of the strict and timely fulfillment of operation 'Gory' we were forced to liquidate more than 700 inhabitants in Khaibakh
settlement." Beria responded that Gvishiani had acted correctly and nominated
him for a medal and a promotion. The massacre has been shrouded in secrecy
and doubt ever since. Historian Jeffrey Burds stated that "limited documenta-
tion from Soviet archives confirms that more than 700 Chechens were killed in
Khaibakh, but the details of the massacre have not yet been released."[8] Because
of the memory parameters established after 1945 and outlined earlier, neither the
deportations nor the massacres that took place as a result could be officially remembered. Hence these events, much like Grossman's revelations, became the
source of subordinate memories.

These two case studies illustrate how hierarchical heroism and universal suffering functioned in Soviet memory and Soviet forgetting. Grossman's investigation into the murder of Soviet Jews threatened the official line. So, too, did the
events at Khaibakh and, more generally, the deportations of "punished peoples."
As a result, these two topics became taboo and subject to official forgetting. Instead, the Soviet state fostered remembrance practices around people, sites, and
events that illustrated the ways Soviet citizens sacrificed themselves to win the
war and collectively defended their motherland. The campaign to recognize
"Hero Cities," the Eternal Flames built as part of innumerable monuments, films
that illustrate sacrifice and heroism—these and other means of commemoration
helped consolidate hierarchical heroism and universal suffering as the key components of Soviet war remembrance. At the same time, these sites of memory
served to foster forgetting practices, especially concerning issues such as the
violence directed by Soviet officers at their own citizens or government policies
toward ethnic minorities.

Scholars have extensively demonstrated how the cult of the Great Patriotic
War functioned as the primary event that sustained the Soviet polity after 1945.[9]
Certain legends and sites helped generate official memories of the war in Soviet
culture. The Panfilov 28, a group of soldiers who died in the Battle of Moscow in
1941–42, and Pavlov's House, the site of intense fighting in Stalingrad, became
particularly important tales that captured the sort of patriotism, heroism, and
willingness to sacrifice oneself that Soviet leaders wanted to promote after the
war.[10] Red Army soldiers also drew inspiration from preexisting cultural mythologies, including *Chapaev, How the Steel Was Tempered*, and even the example set
by the Panfilov 28.[11] Pavlov's House was rebuilt in July 1943 and still serves as a
central site extolling the virtues on display there: the Soviet-era text still present
on the memorial lauds the heroic feats of arms and labor that came together in
the house. In Jochen Hellbeck's recent work on the Battle of Stalingrad, however,
Pavlov's House does not feature prominently in the memories of the city's defenders.[12] Rather, we should best understand the Panfilov 28 and the defenders

of the house as useful legends, or patriotic lessons, based on real events but used after the war to tell the right sort of war stories—what might be called "selective memories"—to Soviet citizens.[13]

In reference to Soviet-era memory cultures, Alexander Etkind argued that late-Soviet and post-Soviet culture produced "warped memory practices" and that Russia remains haunted by its pasts. According to Etkind, this situation arises in part from the lack of an external legal authority, an occupying force, or even a serious ethical debate in Russia to work through Soviet-era memory projects and collective guilt.[14] At the same time, through a comparison of German and Russian remembrance, Etkind sees "a modest hope for the future" and correctly notes that it took decades for Germany to work through the traumatic Nazi past.[15] Etkind believes that monuments, memorials, and museums (what he terms "hard memory") are more adequate forms of ensuring that remembrance takes place while novels, films, and debates (what he terms "soft memory") create endless cycles of uncertainty over the past. What is needed, at least in Etkind's view, are more "solid" forms of memory that address these haunted pasts.

Given that the Soviet state frequently built monuments to mythic events and people, I find Etkind's view not entirely convincing. As I explored in my book, *Blockbuster History in the New Russia*, the 2000s witnessed a host of films that mined the past in interesting, and sometimes profound, ways. Moreover, the patriotic culture that underpinned this cinematic remembrance project was not created exclusively by the state, even though Vladimir Putin certainly benefitted from it and frequently tapped into it: Putin gave a thumbs-up to Fedor Bondarchuk's Afghan War epic, *Ninth Company*. Russian officials did not set quotas for the number of foreign films shown, preferring to let Russian cinema stand on its own and compete openly. Neither did the Russian state prevent films from appearing: in the case of Aleksandr Atanesian's 2006 *Bastards* (*Svolochi*), which suggested the Soviet state used homeless children as cannon fodder in the Second World War, the Duma launched an investigation into its use of state funding, but the film still topped the box office.[16] In the 2000s, therefore, and especially in its "soft memory" products, Putin 1.0 culture provided some signs of guarded optimism for the future of the past.

A Socially Meaningful Blockbuster: Stalingrad

Set in the famous Pavlov's House and framed around the 2011 Japanese earthquake and tsunami, Fedor Bondarchuk's *Stalingrad* (2013) set box office records in Russia by making $51.8 million. It also did well in China, where nearly two million people saw it, helping raise its overall box office total to $68 million.[17] *Stalingrad* has two overlapping plotlines. The first is set in Pavlov's House and concerns the last remaining resident, nineteen-year-old Katia, who has refused to

Fig. 8.1. Mythic history: German troops attack Pavlov's House in Fedor Bondarchuk's *Stalingrad* (2013).

leave her apartment. She interacts with five soldiers defending the building: the voice-over tells us early on that Katia will have a child with one of these soldiers but that she considers all of them her son's "five fathers." The men embody different types who came to the city to defend it. Gromov, the captain, is a hero who has witnessed too much death already but is steadfast in preserving his honor as a professional soldier. Poliakov, nicknamed "Angel," is older than the captain and has preserved his religious beliefs. Sasha Nikiforov, the third, has been shaped by the war and desires nothing more than to kill the enemy. The two youngest are Chvanov, a villager who is also a sharpshooter-turned-sniper who witnessed the Germans murder his younger brother because his name was Vladimir Ilyich, and Sergei Astakhov (played by Bondarchuk's son), who is nicknamed "sissy" because he failed in an earlier mission. The plot includes some moving scenes and some sappy ones, particularly when the five celebrate Katia's birthday and when Gromov tells her that the others are not fighting for the motherland or Stalin, but for her. All five die, but not before impregnating their heroism into Katia and her son: the biological father, as the film eventually reveals, is Sergei. The son, according to the beginning and end scenes, volunteers to help victims of the 2011 Japanese earthquake, thus suggesting that the heroism of Stalingrad's defenders survived and was passed down to the next generation.

The second plotline concerns their German enemies, particularly Captain Peter Kahn (played by Thomas Kretschmann), who has been ruined by the war.

He has raped a Russian woman, Masha, but also protects her from other traumas. Kahn tells Masha that she—and, by extension, all Soviet citizens—has turned him into a beast while he claims to be "simply a soldier." Eventually the two fall in love with each other, and Kahn promises he will protect Masha once the battle is won; Chvanov ultimately kills her for being a collaborator. With the exception of a stereotypical colonel who is characterized as a timeless beast, most of the German soldiers are depicted as human counterparts to the Soviets, albeit less heroic. There is a mention, however passing, of the *Vernichtungskrieg* (the war of extermination) the Nazis waged: the sadistic Nazi officer orders a mother and daughter to be burned alive in a bombed-out bus because he suspects they are Jewish.

Stalingrad did not open up new avenues for exploring the Great Patriotic War and its legacies as much as it consolidated previous path-breaking explorations.[18] Its novelty, and partly the reason for its box-office success, is due to the fact that it is the first Russian film to be made in IMAX 3D.[19] Still, the film became a "socially meaningful blockbuster"—as Vladimir Medinskii, the minister of culture, described it—that combined high-quality effects with high levels of patriotism.[20]

The social meaningfulness came in spite of the "realities" of its plot, for Bondarchuk's film was based on Grossman's novel *Life and Fate*, which had several chapters dedicated to Pavlov's House, and Ilia Tilkin's short stories (Tilkin wrote the screenplay). The film certainly was big in every sense: Russian media outlets extensively covered its filming, its release, and its reception. Major newspapers and journals carried multiple reviews of the film, with critics divided in their assessment. Kinopoisk, a major website devoted to cinema—a Russian Rotten Tomatoes, of sorts—contained fifty-nine reviews from critics, 61 percent of them positive. The site also had more than 64,000 people rate it, averaging 5.7 out of 10, while 549 spectators posted reviews, 51 percent of them positive.[21]

Viktor Matizen, president of the Russian Film Critics Guild, did not like the film overall, citing its ponderous screenplay, distracting voice-over monologue, and unpersuasive plot elements. In his review, Matizen also cited the "Not One Step Back!" order and the humanity of some German soldiers in the film (although, he noted, not as humane as in Alexander Rogozhkin's *Cuckoo*, Dmitrii Meskhiev's *Ours*, and Alexei German Jr.'s *Last Train*) almost as afterthoughts: these formerly taboo topics Bondarchuk included in his film had already been explored on-screen. In the end, he praised the look of Stalingrad as Bondarchuk rendered it on-screen as an impressive achievement.[22]

The well-known film journalist Iurii Gladilshchikov proved more critical, calling the film "strange" (*strannyi*). He specifically mentioned the "Immaculate Conception" element to the plot, the "fairy tale" aspect to the military battle itself, its "ultra-contemporary" vision (3D, slo-mo) combined with its "old-fashioned" patriotic appeal, its excessive reliance on Orthodox imagery, and its overall mess-iness.[23] This is an interesting commentary as Russian Orthodoxy as the basis of patriotism—a taboo topic in the Soviet-era memory culture—had been incorpo-rated in Nikita Mikhalkov's bombastic *Burnt By the Sun 2* (2010) and earlier in Nikolai Dostal's popular 2005 television series, *Penal Battalion* (*Shtrafbat*).

Dmitrii Puchkov, a popular blogger and media commentator, did not like it, which should be no surprise to those familiar with his posts. He lamented that the film traded marketing and special effects for historical truth and insinuated that Bondarchuk had "equated the aggressor and defender, the killer and victim" by depicting German soldiers as humans.[24] The writer and journalist Dmitrii Bykov liked it, which might surprise a few.[25] Bykov proclaimed that Bondarchuk had "opened a new era in the understanding of the Second World War" and that "we" (i.e., the Soviet people) won by not focusing on Soviet-era myths (including the party, the evilness of Nazism, the superhuman heroism of Soviet soldiers, and so on). As Bykov argued, Bondarchuk got to the heart of the battle itself, even if in operatic format, to focus on the human factor in the ultimate victory over Hitler's Germany. Neither side, Bykov notes, is shown in caricatured fashion, but as humans.

Ordinary spectators who posted their reviews online evaluated the film along similar lines. Opinions diverged on whether the special effects helped or hindered spectators' grasp of the history of Stalingrad, whether the film's "new-ness" made it better or worse than Soviet-era films, and whether the love story or the depiction of Germans was justified. Two examples suffice: "Rebex" called the film "nano-realism" and blasted its "primitive set of myths," its wooden actors, its bland patriotism, and its overall falseness. He gave it a 2 out of 10. By contrast, "Tea Fairy" gave it a 9 out of 10, praising the effects that made you "stop eating your popcorn" and concluding, "I have not seen anything bigger, more spectacu-lar, and more plausible in our domestic film industry." It was not a masterpiece, she wrote, but a "milestone."[26]

Stalingrad, in other words, offers little new in terms of the way it approached the war, its causes, its violence, or even its exploration of formerly taboo topics. The only novel aspect is its format, IMAX 3D.[27] The film makes no new claims with regard to history or memory; it was formatted to appeal to a new generation and their concerns. Stalingrad on-screen is still an epic battle full of emotion, death, and destruction. At the same time, what was not new by 2013 standards would have caused some controversy before 1991, particularly in its humane de-piction of German soldiers and Masha's story.

The most notable aspect of the press coverage—and it was indeed extensive—was the kinds of questions Bondarchuk received about the film's plot, its use of history, and its funding. In *Izvestia*, the film journalist Larisa Iusipova queried the director about the extent of state support for the $30 million budget and whether or not it was warranted. Bondarchuk stated that he received 30 percent from the state cinema fund—the newspaper noted that films can receive upwards of 70 percent of funding from the state—and that the rest came from producers such as the television channel Rossiia and VTB Bank. The director said the film was shot under "transparent market conditions" and the production funds from Rossiia and VTB would be "normal elsewhere in the world." Just as revealing, Bondarchuk stated in the interview that once he had the script and knew he wanted to film in IMAX 3D (which necessitates a large budget), he "went to Vladimir Putin [*ia prishel k Vladimiru Putinu*]" and told him about his plans. He further explained that the visit was justified—"we planned to make a film on a theme sacred for our country, using the latest Hollywood technology"—and that he knew "how it might be received by conservative parts of our society." Bondarchuk said that Putin played a major role in the film by granting personal approval to various scenes from the beginning and end of the film and interviewing several Stalingrad veterans so their voices could be heard onscreen. He also noted that, at the time of his visit, Putin was "just" the prime minister and headed the newly revamped cinema fund; Bondarchuk opined that it was not clear at that time what the rules of the game would be and whether the state would support large projects like this one. Bondarchuk personally thanked Putin for smoothing these issues out.[28]

In some respects, Iusipova's article is stunning. Entitled "Thank You, Putin, for *Stalingrad*" and appearing in a major newspaper, the interview reveals the ways state support functions in the second Putin presidency and the ways Bondarchuk has curried favor. The rules of the game are those established during the 2000s, when patriotic historical blockbusters offered a smorgasbord of feel-good stories about the Russian past. These films, including Bondarchuk's *Ninth Company*, simultaneously filled in historical blank spots ignored and/or forgotten during the Soviet era and provided a source of pride in Russia's patriotic pasts. This cinematic culture might be termed Putin 1.0: *Stalingrad* captures it well and illustrates how it survives in Putin 2.0 culture.

In terms of how cinematic remembrance functions and how films can interpret history, *Stalingrad* serves up safe fare. No one doubts that the battle took place and that Pavlov's House was a part of it. Numerous documents, eyewitness accounts (including Grossman's), and other sources testify to Stalingrad's significance. Bondarchuk tells exactly this history. His film's only new memory claim is implying that the heroism on display in that city was genetic, passed down to the present as a part of contemporary Russian DNA that allows Sergei and Katia's son to perform selfless acts in Japan: the son, it bears mentioning, saves German tourists buried in the rubble after the earthquake. At the same time, the story told in *Stalingrad*, while providing a historical interpretation of actual events, is not a "history" that rests entirely on facts. While Pavlov's House did exist, Soviet soldiers did defend it, and the Soviet state helped turn the site into a myth after 1943, Katia and her child's five fathers are all fictional characters. In one scholarly analysis of the film, Anastasia Kostetskaya has persuasively argued that Bondarchuk valorizes memory over history and presents his story "through the folkloric oral narrative device of the storytelling."[29]

A Historical Event That Did Not Happen: *Ordered to Forget*

The year before Bondarchuk's blockbuster, a minor scandal broke out over a film set in the context of the war. Akhtem Seitablaev's *Khaitarma* is about Amet-Khan Sultan, a Crimean Tatar pilot twice named Hero of the Soviet Union for his exploits during the Great Patriotic War. The state allowed him to return to his family, and Sultan subsequently witnesses the May 1944 mass deportation of the Crimean Tatars (he barely escapes deportation and manages to save his parents but is unsuccessful in rescuing his girlfriend). The film depicts the war as a heroic, patriotic endeavor and the deportations ordered by Stalin as a betrayal of that heroism. *Khaitarma* had other significance. Billed as a national history, the film's title is the name of a Crimean Tatar folk dance that serves as a "symbol of the eternal movement of life, dedicated to the memories of grandfathers and great-grandfathers, fathers and mothers, all those, without whom there would be neither us, our children, our memories, nor our culture."[30] Seitablaev plays Sultan; the story is also a personal one, for he was born in Uzbekistan to parents who had been deported.

The scandal occurred because Vladimir Andreev, the general consul of the Russian Federation in Crimea at the time, declared it to be a "distortion of the truth about the Great Patriotic War."[31] Andreev had not seen the film, but this did not prevent him from rendering judgment (his claim cost him his job). It did, however, provide the impetus for film journalist Elena Ardabatskaia to write about the film for the widely read newspaper *Moskovskii komsomolets*. In her review, Ardabatskaia noted that it was the "first film made on the territory of the USSR, and within the former USSR, on the theme of the Stalinist genocide of nations."[32] "Stories of that terrible day," she writes, "are transmitted from generation to generation," ensuring that the tragedy endures. While the film blends fact with fiction, she notes, it rests firmly on the memories of those who survived and the true story of Sultan, whose fearlessness is a "fact of history."

Khaitarma is notable not only for its content and the minor scandal—it did not get a wide release, and only 1,553 people rated it on Kinopoisk—but also for its use after the Russian annexation of Crimea in March 2014.[33] Jamala, the Ukrainian singer of Crimean Tatar origin and 2016 Eurovision song contest winner, wrote her song "1944" in the wake of the film and used its scenes for the official video.[34] Its afterlife also helps explain, in part, the chillier reception that met Khusein Erkenov's 2014 film about the deportation of Chechens in 1944.

Ordered to Forget does not rely on uncontested facts of history to tell its story. Instead, Erkenov centers his film on the February 1944 massacre at Khaibakh (Haybakh), when NKVD troops rounded up and then burned alive seven hundred residents of that mountainous Chechen village. Originally scheduled for a Grozny premiere, the film debuted instead on June 20, 2014, at the Moscow International Film Festival. That screening remains the only official one in Russia; the film did not appear in the festival's program either.[35] The change of venue and the silence on the part of the festival's organizers were due to the Ministry of Culture's refusal to certify *Ordered to Forget* for public distribution because the film allegedly constituted "falsification of history" that could "give rise to interethnic hatred." According to the minister of culture, Medinskii, the archives of the former NKVD contain "no evidence that the atrocity ever took place."[36]

The story of the film and the decision not to certify it can be traced through media reports in Chechnya. This goes back to the Soviet era but heats up in 2012, when the Chechnya-based paper *Vesti respubliki* published a story about the press conference on the eve of Erkenov's film release. The report announced that Erkenov's movie was based on "the real facts of what happened" yet warned that it would "cause a stir." Erkenov and the chief producer, Sultan Zaurbekov, declared that their film, which was then known under the working title *Ashes* (*Pepel*), would not be just an artistic or historical film but a victory for "historical justice." Although they admitted that one film could not possibly overcome decades of official amnesia and the trauma that ensued, they described it as an "echo of those years and a symbol of the spiritual strength of a small nation" that could honor the memory of those who perished while resounding among a younger generation of Chechens.[37] Less than a month later, the paper published a short piece introducing readers to the only remaining survivor of the Khaibakh massacre: seventy-eight-year-old Mumadi Elgakaev, who was eight years old in 1944 when his uncle pushed him off the roof of the barn before it went down in flames. The report noted that he had kept the memory of the horror alive.[38]

With the parameters established and the survivors introduced, *Vesti respubliki* and later *Kavkazkskii uzel* began expanding on the Khaibakh story. The newspaper published the reminiscences of Salamat Gaev, who was born in that village and described the decades of forgetting as the "embodiment of pain," an "open wound," and a "blow to the soul." Gaev recounted the rounding up of villagers, the fire, the screams, the deaths—stories he heard from other survivors. He also noted that he lost nineteen family members in Khaibakh's barn and that the oldest villager burned alive was 110 and the youngest were twins born one day before the massacre. Gaev's story mentioned an earlier investigation of Khaibakh, a memory that later became the filmmaker's main defense against the "falsification" claim; between 1987 and 1990, with the last Chechens having arrived home from forced exile, the region's chief prosecutor and local journalists looked into the circumstances of the massacre. Using oral testimonies, historical records, and forensic expertise, Dziyaudin Malsagov published a book in 1990 on the massacre with Gaev as a coauthor.[39]

Malsagov was not just a historian. He witnessed the Khaibakh massacre, but not from a victim's perspective. An ethnic Chechen born in 1914, he joined the Communist Party in the belief that he could help transform his native land. Appointed a people's commissar of justice at twenty-eight, he was ordered to help identify any Chechen who resisted Soviet rule. On February 24, 1944, Malsagov traveled to Khaibakh to see what to do about villagers who had not been deported because of bad weather. There he witnessed NKVD officers under the command of Mikhail Gvishiani set fire to the barn and shoot any villagers who tried to escape. Disturbed, he sent reports up the chain of command only to be sent into exile in Kazakhstan. He remained in exile until 1957, when he was allowed to return home. By that time, Malsagov had spoken to Nikita Khrushchev, who in turn ordered a secret investigation of what had happened in Khaibakh. As for Malsagov, he spent decades trying to keep the memory of the massacre alive. As Thomas De Waal wrote, Malsagov "was a uniquely tragic case of bearing witness," for his remembrance was "by definition an act of self-incrimination, and also of expiation."[40]

Malsagov's book, which appeared in reprint in the summer of 2013, was launched at the Memorial Complex in Honor of Akhmat Kadyrov. "Rise from the ashes, smoke, and fire, Khaibakh's soul, and all the souls of the murdered saints," went a song sung at the release party. Gaev was present at the book launch, along with other dignitaries. The celebration, in a way, certified the late Soviet investigation as "historical truth." The chairman of the Spiritual Administration of Muslims in the Chechen Republic, Sultan Mirzaev, declared that the book's publication was of great significance as a "manifestation of patriotism," adding that "we need to know the history of our people [*narod*]." The victims at Khaibakh, he stated, were "heroes and patriots," and in recognizing them, "we must know this terrible tragedy and remember that a similar one can never happen again." Archivists, historians, and other officials present at the event stated that remembering Khaibakh in Soviet times was considered a criminal offense and that "even now some are denying this genocide." The ceremony was also attended by Ruslan Kokanev, one of the scriptwriters and coproducers of the forthcoming feature film.[41]

Less than a year after this public event, the film's Grozny premiere was canceled. The decision by the Russian Ministry of Culture, according to which the film "falsified history," caught the Chechen media by surprise. *Kavkazskii uzel* reported on May 21, 2014, about the cancellation and quoted Kokanev, who stated that the order came from the Ministry of Culture. Kokanev lamented that he could see nothing in the film that would incite ethnic hatred and instead argued that the film showed the pain of both those who were victimized by the order and those who had to follow it.[42] Two days later, *Vesti respubliki* ran a story about a recent commemorative visit to Khaibakh that involved the descendants of those who had died there. The story conveyed the significance of the village in Chechen collective memory: "As we know, 70 years ago during the deportation of the Chechen nation on 27 February 1944, the tragic events occurred when Beria's executioners murdered hundreds of local residents."[43] The newspaper article acted as a counterweight to the ministry's decision and therefore did not have to mention the film at all.

In a lengthy interview granted to another Chechen media outlet, Kokanev expanded on the ministry's decision. The film's producer cast doubt on the ministry's label of the film as false, noting both the Khrushchev-era inquiry and the 1990 inquiry. Kokanev suggested the question was one of "deliberate delay" (*zatiagivanie*).[44] He also noted that the filming had been transparent and official, the sound had been recorded at Mosfilm, and the film had been screened before the Ministry of Culture. Kokanev doubled down on his original statements, arguing that Khaibakh was an "interwoven human tragedy" before tackling the "falsification" label head on: "Let's start with the fact that there is a village called Khaibakh. In this village there are the remains of a barn where people were burned. There were witnesses who saw it all. Their relatives are still alive." He noted that the last living person who witnessed the massacre firsthand, Mumadi Elgakaev, participated in the filming and appeared on-screen—a testament to the tragedy.[45] Film director Erkenov did not mince words when talking about the scandal to Gazeta.ru: "In Chechnya there's no question about whether or not there was a tragedy in Khaibakh."[46]

Kokanev was responding to a *Kommersant* piece that reported on the ministry's decision and the label of a "fictional story that could incite ethnic hatred" attached to the film.[47] The article quoted Kokanev's earlier statements as well as Salamat Gaev's but cast some implicit doubt on them; the phrase "according to Kokanev" was used throughout. These stories established the basic "fact" of the ministry's decision: the officials argued that no archival documents existed to prove the Khaibakh massacre. One month into the scandal, *Rossiiskaia gazeta* published an article titled "The Deportation of Chechens and Ingush: Tragic Truths and Myths." Written by Ivan Uspenskii, an archivist at the Russian State Military Archives, the opening paragraph acknowledges that the article was in response to the film and unambiguously states that an "archival investigation demonstrates that we are dealing with falsification." More precisely, Uspenskii declared that the so-called Gvishiani document on Khaibakh never existed and that the text that appeared in various print and online publications "raises doubts as to its authenticity."[48] In spite of the fact that the Khaibakh massacre had been reported in Russian newspapers during the 2000s—the Putin 1.0 era—the *Rossiiskaia gazeta* story effectively closed the door on the Russian official side to the controversy: Khaibakh was no longer history but a story.[49] Neither the film nor Medinskii's decision appear on the ministry's official website.[50]

For their part, the journalists of *Vesti respubliki* in Chechnya continued to publish stories related to the film and the events at Khaibakh. On May 10, 2016, in an article titled "We Remember . . . ," Malika Abalaeva recounted the deportation, quoted from a few poems written about it, and then focused on Khaibakh and the campaign of forgetting that had been waged against it: "The whole world knows about the Katyn tragedy. Anyone can go and see its memorial complex and honor the memory of innocent victims in mournful silence. But the village of Khaibakh is not on any map of the world. Some even argue that it never happened, and that all the horrible stories about it, which have been transferred from mouth to mouth, are no more than scary tales [*skazki*]."[51] To reverse this tendency, Abalaeva reprinted the Gvishiani document in full, followed by the memories of witnesses and survivors.

The scandal over the film ensured that only a few people saw it; the press reports found larger audiences. Kinopoisk has an entry on *Ordered to Forget* but no statistics and no links to reviews. Out of 242 people who rated the film on Kinopoisk (giving it a 5.44/10), only one wrote a review.[52] The film itself is a straightforward account of the 1944 events and their long-lasting legacy. Erkenov, who was born to deported parents in Uzbekistan, begins his account in the present, with a young boy in Grozny who travels back with his father and grandmother, Seda, to their ancestral village. There they visit the grave of his grandfather, Daud, and the boy notices it bears two dates for his death. When he asks why, the film travels back to 1944, when Daud and Seda lived in Khaibakh. Their nemesis is a local NKVD officer, Kasim, who wants Seda. Kasim arrests Daud's father, and Daud flees into the mountains to escape the same fate. With his rival out of the way, Kasim harasses Seda's family in an effort to get them to turn their daughter over to him. Seda's father instead greets the NKVD officer with a gun, and Seda flees into the mountains to join Daud. Kasim, meanwhile, is replaced by a new NKVD colonel, Mikhail Gvishiani. The rotation is due to Stalin's (and Beria's) order to deport the Chechen population in the region, which Gvishiani is expected to carry out. The rest of the film follows the roundups, the NKVD tactics, and the final decision to herd the locals into a barn and burn them after the weather prevents a deportation by train. Dziyaudin Malsagov makes an appearance: he collaborates with the NKVD because he believes the residents would be sent into exile by peaceful means only to watch in horror as the barn burns. Daud and Seda arrive back in time to witness the massacre. Daud sees one boy escape the burning barn and shoots an NKVD officer before the latter could kill the boy (we later learn that Daud's tombstone contains the 1944 date because, as Seda explains, although he lived, "his soul died that day"). The boy turns out to be Mumadi Elgakaev, who appears at the end.[53]

Fig. 8.2. Forgotten history: Khaibakh's barn burning in Khusein Erkenov's *Ordered to Forget* (2014).

Essentially, *Ordered to Forget* calls attention to aspects of the war that have been forgotten or relegated to the margins. Simultaneously, it narrates an important story that constitutes a significant part of modern Chechen nationhood by making it accepted "history." *Ordered to Forget* ultimately attempts to take what some scholars have termed "deportation memory" and make it part of the historical record. Rebecca Gould defined deportation memory as one that has "characterized the Muslim peoples of the Caucasus for the past half-century" and that is "more accustomed to homelessness than to the continuity of steady, inhabited spaces."[54] As the deportation affected all of Chechnya and left few traces, and the Soviet government deliberately suppressed its memory, Chechens and other deported peoples had to rely on a certain form of remembrance, mostly oral testimonies and family stories passed from generation to generation.[55] When the Soviet Union collapsed, Chechens put up the first memorial to the deportation only to see it destroyed in the First Chechen War, rebuilt after the Second, and moved by Ramzan Kadyrov in 2014 to a complex that memorializes victims of terrorism. No wonder Khaibakh matters so much: it provides a place, a location that can serve as the focal point for deportation memory.

The decision to declare the film in violation of the law preventing "falsification" of history did more than just bring into relief the contrast between well-documented history and oral testimonies. It also ensured that the events of 1944 would safely remain as a Chechen "deportation memory" and not disturb the heroic memory of the war promoted in contemporary Russia. The Ministry of Culture's decision cast doubt on the veracity of Malsagov's testimony and Elgakaev's memories, the previous Soviet-era investigations into the Khaibakh massacre, and the Chechen remembrance of 1944 all at once. Vladimir Medinskii's declaration that the film "falsified history" effectively banned a story that rested on more evidence than Bondarchuk's *Stalingrad*.

Medinskii's 28: Stories, Histories, Myths

Khaibakh is not the last history battle the Russian Ministry of Culture chose to fight. In July 2015, Sergei Mironenko, the head of the State Archive of the Russian Federation, published archival documents that revealed the story of the twenty-eight "Panfilov guardsmen" said to have sacrificed themselves in the defense of Moscow in 1941 to be a partial fake. The story of the twenty-eight is widely known and remembered in Russia: monuments to the Panfilov soldiers exist throughout the former Soviet Union, including a massive memorial outside Moscow and a similar one in Almaty, Kazakhstan. The documents demonstrate that a Soviet journalist embellished the story (not all the defenders died, and not all of them acted heroically) and that a Soviet prosecutor named N. Afanasiev found out the truth and reported it to other higher-ups (including Andrei Zhdanov), who ultimately decided not to make the findings public. The documents first came to light in the Khrushchev era, as Mironenko noted, but were then locked up in the archives again.[56] Minister of Culture Medinskii responded by stating that Mironenko was "neither a writer nor a journalist, [and certainly] not a fighter against historical falsifications," and declared that "if he wants to change profession, we will understand that."[57] In March 2016, Medinskii's ominous warning took on new meaning when it was announced that Mironenko had been demoted as head of the archives.[58]

One of the reasons for Medinskii's ire, as several reports noted, was that he had announced first in November 2013 and again in June 2015 that the Ministry of Culture officially backed a "military-patriotic film" titled *Panfilov's 28*.[59] Released on November 24, 2016, the film effectively presented falsified history à la Medinskii.[60] During the ensuing debate regarding the myth and its exposé, Andrei Shaliopa, the codirector and scriptwriter, had to acknowledge the ways the story of Panfilov's 28 blurred the lines between history and myth. The film itself mostly relied on the Soviet-era story and Soviet-era cinematic narratives: it shows the Panfilov men training for battle, and the film then follows them as they head to the front and defend the motherland. Compared to other post-Soviet films about the war, this one is retro in every sense of the word. Although it substitutes the term *Russian* for *Soviet*, *Panfilov's 28* does not explore any taboo subjects about the war. Instead, it narrates the everyday heroism of the men who fought to defend Moscow. The film did not do as well as hoped at the box office, earning just over $6 million, but it did receive an enormous amount of press coverage,

Fig. 8.3. Mythic history: Defending Moscow in Kim Druzhinin and Andrei Shaliopa's *Panfilov's 28* (2016).

particularly for its crowdfunding (it was the first Russian movie to be mostly funded this way) and its claim therefore to be a "people's movie." On Kinopoisk's website, 36,000 people rated it 7.6/10, and 384 people wrote reviews—309 of them positive. Most, like Shaliopa, declared they did not care for the story, which in part rested on a Soviet-era myth.[61]

The central actor in these battles was, of course, Medinskii. He labeled *Stalingrad* a "socially useful blockbuster" and helped provide the state funding for that patriotic epic. He did the same for *Panfilov's 28*. Following the film's release, Medinskii stated, "Even if it was all made up and Panfilov never existed, it's a sacred legend that people should not touch," calling anyone who did so "washed-up scum."[62] He also led the charge against *Ordered to Forget* that labeled the film as one that "falsified history." Medinskii then sparred with Mironenko over the Panfilov 28 documents, suggesting that only the Ministry of Culture could employ the "falsification" label.

That Medinskii posed as the "minister of truth" in these battles should raise eyebrows. An "academic" whose work has focused on "exposing" centuries-long "slanders" against the Russian state by Westerners—his dissertation examined early modern travelers to Muscovy and claimed that their accounts represented "evil slander of the Russian state, its rulers, and its people"—Medinskii's "research" has been criticized by actual academics and has been caught up in the ongoing plagiarism scandals involving Russian officials.[63] Prior to his appointment as minister of culture, Medinskii served as a member of the Commission to Counter Attempts to Falsify History to the Detriment of Russian Interests.[64] Maria Lipman branded him "Putin's culture cop" and a "typical figure in Russian officialdom" whose "primary motive is to curry favor with the man at the top, Vladimir Putin."[65] This is an apt description, yet, as the aforementioned cases indicate, Medinskii's ministry may be closer to a Ministry of Truth in the Orwellian sense. *Ordered to Forget* has gone down a memory hole while *Panfilov's 28* and the five men and a baby-to-be from Pavlov's House are "true stories."

The politics of memory involving recent Russian films about the Second World War raise larger questions about legends, narratives, histories, stories, artistic truths, and historical truths. Putin 2.0 culture overseen by Medinskii, the minister of truth, is a variation on Soviet policies—not outright bans on films that threaten official memory projects but casting doubt on the veracity of histories. Yet the effect is the same: no contentious pasts, no problematic histories that get in the way of patriotic legends. The three films examined here illustrate a disturbing trend in the politics of memory after 2012, when Vladimir Putin returned as Russia's president. *Stalingrad* is safe history told through a storytelling-style fictional account of Pavlov's House. *Panfilov's 28* recast another Soviet myth that has been definitively exposed as myth. And *Ordered to Forget*, the most truthful tale of the three—and the one that rests on the most accurate evidence as well as decades of marginalized deportation memory—was labeled by the minister of culture as false history. If Alexander Etkind had once seen a glimmer of optimism in post-Soviet remembrance but worried that "it is not historical knowledge that is at issue but its interpretation," the decisions by Medinskii and his ministry indicate that the Russian state is increasingly in the business of influencing both historical knowledge and its interpretation. The future of the Soviet past under Putin 2.0 is no longer a source for guarded optimism.

Notes

1. Maria Lipman sees the second Putin presidency as one where crackdowns on dissent have grown more intense, labeling it Putin 2.0. See her "How Putin Silences Dissent: Inside the Kremlin's Crackdown," *Foreign Affairs* 95, no. 1 (May/June 2016): 38–46.

2. Tzvetan Todorov, "The Uses and Abuses of Memory," in *What Happens to History: The Renewal of Ethics in Contemporary Thought*, ed. Howard Marchitello (New York: Routledge, 2001), 11.

3. Todorov, "The Uses and Abuses of Memory."

4. Todorov, "The Uses and Abuses of Memory," 12 (emphasis in the original).

5. Todorov, "The Uses and Abuses of Memory," 20.

6. Amir Weiner, "When Memory Counts: War, Genocide, and Postwar Soviet Jewry," in *Landscaping the Human Garden: Twentieth-Century Population Management in a Comparative Framework*, ed. Amir Weiner (Stanford, CA: Stanford University Press, 2003), 179.

7. The term *punished peoples* originates in Alexander Nekrich's 1978 book with the same title. For context see Jeffrey Burds, "The Soviet War against 'Fifth Columnists': The Case of Chechnya, 1942–44," *Journal of Contemporary History* 42 no. 2 (April 2007): 267–314.

8. Burds, "The Soviet War against 'Fifth Columnists,'" 305. The Gvishiani report and Beria response are also quoted in Zaindi Shakhbiev, *Sud'ba checheno-ingushkogo naroda* (Moscow: Rossiia molodaia, 1996), 249–55.

9. Cf. Nina Tumarkin, *The Living and the Dead: The Rise and Fall of the Cult of World War II in Russia* (New York: Basic Books, 1995) and Amir Weiner, *Making Sense of War: The Second World War and the Fate of the Bolshevik Revolution* (Princeton, NJ: Princeton University Press, 2002).

10. The "house" was an apartment building in central Stalingrad that Red Army soldiers held during the battle. "Pavlov" refers to Sergeant Iakov Pavlov, who commanded the platoon defending the building. There is debate about whether he was in the building during the battle; regardless, this site has passed into memory bearing his name. Thirty-one soldiers defended the house, and twenty-four were identified afterward (three of whom had died). While the majority were Russian or Ukrainian, the defenders included Tatar, Kazakh, Tajik, Uzbek, Kalmyk, and Georgian soldiers, as well as one Jewish soldier, allowing the Soviet state to promote the heroic defense as a truly "Soviet" one.

11. See Jochen Hellbeck, *Stalingrad: The City That Defeated the Third Reich* (New York: Public Affairs, 2015), 63. Hellbeck refers to Lieutenant Colonel Afanasii Svirin, who recounted using the example of the Panfilov 28 to motivate his troops at Stalingrad.

12. In particular, see Hellbeck's account by Alexander Rodimtsev, who fought at Stalingrad and also was interviewed by Vasilii Grossman. Hellbeck writes that "Rodimtsev does not address the defense of the so-called Pavlov House," which years later was hyped as a "grand story of the spirit of Soviet internationalism" by Soviet officials. Cf. Hellbeck, *Stalingrad*, 293. This is the only reference to the house in Hellbeck's authoritative history.

13. On the function of "war stories" and "selective memory," see Robert Moeller, *War Stories: The Search for a Usable Past in the Federal Republic of Germany* (Berkeley: University of California Press, 2003). Although Moeller's focus is on postwar West Germany, the general concepts are applicable to the Soviet case too.

14. Cf. Alexander Etkind, *Warped Mourning: Stories of the Undead in the Land of the Unburied* (Stanford, CA: Stanford University Press, 2013).

15. Etkind, *Warped Mourning*, 206.

16. See Stephen M. Norris, *Blockbuster History in the New Russia: Movies, Memory, Patriotism* (Bloomington: Indiana University Press, 2012).

17. These stats are from Kinopoisk's website: http://www.kinopoisk.ru/film/468196/. The film made $8.65 million in its first weekend in China, making it the first non-Chinese and non-Hollywood film to do so.

18. See Stephen M. Norris, "Guiding Stars: The Comet-Like Rise of the War Film in Putin's Russia: Recent World War II Films and Historical Memories," *Studies in Russian and Soviet Cinema* 1, no. 2 (2007): 163–89, and Norris, *Blockbuster History*, esp. chapter 6. Films such as *Star* (2002), *The Cuckoo* (2002), *Under the Sign of Taurus* (2003), *The Last Train* (2003), *Our Own* (2004), and *Bastards* (2006), just to pick a handful of examples, explored a number of taboo topics from the war, including how the Stalinist state treated Soviet POWs, relationships between German soldiers and Soviet civilians, life under German occupation, and the use of Soviet citizens as cannon fodder in battles.

19. See Seth Graham, "Review of *Stalingrad*," *KinoKultura* 44 (2014).

20. Quoted in Andrew Roth, "Russia's 'Stalingrad' Is a Hit on Screen," *New York Times*, November 11, 2013.

21. See Kinopoisk's website: http://www.kinopoisk.ru/film/468196/. The stats are accurate as of May 17, 2017.

22. Viktor Matizen, "Dom bez fundamenta," *Novye Izvestia*, October 16, 2013.

23. Iurii Gladilshchikov, "Fedor Bondarchuk i voina mirov," *Moskovskie novosti*, October 15, 2013.

24. Dmitrii Puchkov, "'Stalingrad': Marketing i prochaia spekuliatsiia na nashem uvazhenii k istorii," *Odnako*, October 18, 2013. Puchkov called this depiction the "dream of liberal idiots" and mocked, "So what if the Germans attacked our country and murdered 27 million of our citizens?"

25. Dmitrii Bykov, "Idet voina antichnaia," *Profil*, October 5, 2013.

26. Both comments (and 531 others, as of October 5, 2016) appear on Kinopoisk's website.

27. In the first scholarly article to appear about the film, Anastasia Kostetskaya argues that Bondarchuk's 3D IMAX vision "presents the embattled city as a mythical chronotope" that invites viewers to immerse themselves in the city while also championing a "mythic World War II as a new genre." See Anastasia Kostetskaya, "Stalingrad Re-Imagined as a Mythical Chronotope: Fedor Bondarchuk's Stalingrad in 3D," *Studies in Russian and Soviet Cinema* 10, no. 1 (2016): 2.

28. Larisa Iusipova, "Spasibo Putinu za 'Stalingrad,'" *Izvestia*, October 28, 2013.

29. Kostetskaya, "Stalingrad Re-Imagined as a Mythic Chronotope," 4.

30. These words appear during the opening titles of the film; the translation is from Chip Crane's "Review of *Khaitarma*," *KinoKultura* 45 (2014).

31. Quoted in Crane, "Review of *Khaitarma*."

32. Elena Ardabatskaia, "'Khaitarma': Bol odnogo naroda?," *Moskovskii komsomolets*, June 18, 2013.

33. Cf. Kinopoisk's website at http://www.kinopoisk.ru/film/745096/.

34. The original video featuring scenes from the film can be viewed here: MrNesemi, "Jamala New Clip 1944," May 18, 2016, video, 3:11, https://www.youtube.com/watch?v=h7k-l8JlPug.

35. Oleg Sulkin, "V Moskve pokazali zapreshchenyi film pro deportatsiiu chechentsev," *Golos Ameriki*, June 23, 2014.

36. Liz Fuller, "Banned Chechen Movie Screened at Moscow Film Festival," Radio Free Europe/Radio Liberty, June 23, 2014.

37. Zamila Kashtarova, "Khaibakh—otgolosk ne zazhivshei rany," *Vesti respubliki*, October 30, 2012.

38. Zamila Kashtarova, "Poslednii svidetel Khaibakha," *Vesti respubliki*, November 22, 2012.

39. Umisha Idrisova, "Khaibakh—pechal i bol moia," *Vesti respubliki*, May 13, 2013.

40. Thomas De Waal, "The English House: A Story of Chechnya," in *Wild East: Stories from the Last Frontier*, ed. Boris Fishman (Boston: Justin, Charles, and Co., 2003), 244.

41. Malika Abalaeva, "Nepotukhshee plamia Khaibakh," *Vesti respubliki*, June 26, 2013.

42. "Kokanev: Minkultury zapretilo pokazyvat v RF film o deportatsii chechentsev i ingushei v 1944 godu," *Kavkazskii uzel*, May 21, 2014.

43. Khamzat Umkhaev, "Neizvestnaia Chechnia: Nashkha-2014," *Vesti respubliki*, May 23, 2014.

44. Badma Biurchiev, "Istoriia Khaibakha—eto spletenie chelovecheskikh tragedii," *Kavpolit*, May 27, 2014.

45. Biurchiev, "Istoriia Khaibakha."

46. Alexei Krizhevskii, "'V Chechne net voprosa—byla ili net tragediia v Khaibakhe,'" Gazeta.ru, June 25, 2014.

47. Musa Murdanov and Viacheslav Kozlov, "V kino usmotrel nedokazannyi epizod," *Kommersant*, May 23, 2014.

48. Ivan Uspenskii, "Tolko dlia vashikh glaz . . . ," *Rossiiskaia gazeta*, June 25, 2014.

49. Cf. "Soprotivlaemost organizma," *Izvestia*, March 17, 2004. The 2004 *Izvestia* article appeared on the sixtieth anniversary of the deportation and interviewed Doku Zavgaev, then first secretary of the Grozny regional committee and later Russia's ambassador to Slovenia. Zavgaev talked about Gvishani's actions in Khaibakh, his role in the 1990 special commission to investigate the crime, and the historical facts, including survivors' testimonies, that proved the event happened.

50. Cf. website of the Ministry of Culture of the Russian Federation, http://mkrf.ru/ (as of May 20, 2016).

51. Malika Abalaeva, "My pomnim . . . ," *Vesti respubliki*, May 10, 2016. The article ends with lavish praise of the two Kadyrovs, father and son.

52. Cf. Kinopoisk's website at http://www.kinopoisk.ru/film/820724/.

53. For an insightful English-language review, see Chip Crane, "Review of *Ordered to Forget*," *KinoKultura* 49 (2015).

54. Rebecca Gould, "Leaving the House of Memory: Post-Soviet Traces of Deportation Memory," *Mosaic* 45, no. 2 (2012): 151.

55. In this way, Chechen deportation memory developed and functioned similarly to that of the Crimean Tatar memory of deportation. See Greta Lynn Uehling, *Beyond Memory: The Crimean Tatars' Deportation and Return* (New York: Palgrave Macmillan, 2004).

56. The documents are posted on the website of the Russian State Archives, "Spravka-doklad glavnogo voennogo prokurora N. Afanasieva 'O 28 panfilovtsakh,'" http://www.statearchive.ru/607.

57. Quoted in Tom Balmforth, "Russian Archive Chief Out after Debunking Soviet WWII Legend," Radio Free Europe/Radio Liberty, March 17, 2016.

58. Balmforth, "Russian Archive Chief Out." See also Peter Hobson, "Battle in the Archives: Uncovering Russia's Secret Past," *Moscow Times*, March 24, 2016.

59. "Film '28 panfilovtsev,' na kotoryi sobirali dengi v internete, vyidet v prokat oseniu," TASS, June 3, 2015, https://tass.ru/kultura/2015368.

60. See my review of the film for *KinoKultura* 56 (2017).

61. Cf. Kinopoisk's website at http://www.kinopoisk.ru/film/764465/ (as of May 17, 2017). See also the recent Russian novel that takes up the myth, Vladimir Pershanin, *28 Panfilovtsev* (Moscow: Iauza, 2016) and the recent addition to the "Vsia Pravda o Voine" series by O. S. Smyslov, *28 Panfilovtsev: Legendy i realnost* (Moscow: Veche, 2016). Both works were published in response to the film and the debates it prompted.

62. Quoted in Ola Cichowlas, "To Be Great Again, Russia Resurrects Soviet Legends," *Moscow Times*, December 1, 2016, https://www.themoscowtimes.com/2016/12/01/to-be-great-again-russia-resurrects-soviet-legends-a56380.

63. See the details and links to Russian sources in Maria Lipman, "Meet the Second-Rate Academic Who Is Vladimir Putin's Culture Cop," *New Republic*, May 23, 2014.

64. Medinskii's official bio is available on his website at http://www.medinskiy.ru/.

65. Lipman, "Meet the Second Rate Academic."

STEPHEN M. NORRIS is Professor of Russian History and Director of the Havighurst Center for Russian and Post-Soviet Studies at Miami University. He is author of *Blockbuster History in the New Russia: Movies, Memory, Patriotism*. He is editor (with Willard Sunderland) of *Russia's People of Empire: Life Stories from Eurasia, 1500 to the Present*, (with Helena Goscilo) of *Preserving Petersburg: History, Memory, Nostalgia*, and (with Zara M. Torlone) of *Insiders and Outsiders in Russian Cinema*. He is currently working on a biography of the most prolific Soviet political caricaturist, Boris Efimov.

PART III
REMEMBERING AND FRAMING THE SOVIET PAST BEYOND RUSSIA'S BORDERS

9 The 2014 Russian Memory Law in European Context

Nikolay Koposov

THE RUSSIAN MEMORY law, also known as the Yarovaia Act, was adopted in the midst of the Ukraine crisis in May 2014.[1] The law added a new article (article 354.1, Rehabilitation of Nazism) to the penal code of the Russian Federation: "The denial of facts established by the Judgment of the International Military Tribunal for the trial and punishment of major war criminals of European countries of the Axis, the justification of crimes established by the above-mentioned Judgment, as well as dissemination of knowingly false information on the activities of the USSR during the Second World War, when expressed publicly, are punishable by a fine of up to three hundred thousand rubles . . . or by deprivation of liberty for up to three years."[2] The punishment is increased to up to five years of imprisonment if "the same deeds [have been] committed with the use of one's official position or through the mass media, as well as with fabrication of prosecution evidence"[3] (which arguably applies to historical research that is not in line with the official interpretation of the Second World War). The act also provides that "public distribution of information expressing manifest disrespect toward society regarding Russia's days of military glory and the commemorative dates associated with the defense of the Fatherland or public insults to the symbols of Russia's military glory are punishable by a fine of up to three hundred thousand rubles . . . or by correctional labor for up to one year."[4]

The Yarovaia Act was long in the making: its first draft was presented to the Russian parliament in May 2009, although the idea of passing some kind of "antifascist" bill harks back to the mid-1990s. In the context of Boris Yeltsin's democratic reforms and his struggle against the Communist and nationalist opposition, the first Russian memory law drafts were inspired by the 1990 French Gayssot Act, which had made Holocaust denial a criminal offense. Russian democrats tried to formulate their bills—all of which were rejected by the Communist-dominated parliament—in terms broad enough to cover the denial of Communist crimes, while Russian Communists proposed introducing administrative (not criminal) liability for "propaganda of fascism" and positive assessments of fascist regimes. They were clearly unwilling to cede the moral high ground of antifascism to democrats but at the same time were cautious not to break with their own nationalist allies. In a modified form, this ban was included in the 2001 administrative code and the 2002 law on extremism: displaying fascist symbols became an administrative offense while disseminating profascist literature became lawful grounds for labeling as extremist and prohibiting an organization or mass media outlet charged with such dissemination.[5]

With the emergence of Vladimir Putin's authoritarian regime, however, the politics of memory in Russia took a different turn.[6] Instead of blaming the Communist past and using the notion of Russia's cultural heritage to stimulate "cultural patriotism" and counterbalance the negative assessment of the Soviet system (the main components of Yeltsin's history politics), the new regime began promoting the cult of the Great Patriotic War as a foundational event in Russian history. This cult allowed for whitewashing Soviet history, including Stalin's mass crimes, the memory of which has been marginalized by the heroic war myth. The cult of the war includes, as one of its main components, the notion of the Yalta postwar political order, which legitimizes Putin's neoimperial ambitions and simultaneously makes a majority of Eastern European countries reject the "new Russian ideology." It would be a simplification, however, to explain the rise of nationalism in Eastern Europe by the threat increasingly posed by Russia, even though Putin's politics of history has significantly contributed to the outbreak of the memory wars in the region. The 2014 Russian memory law (as well as restrictions on certain statements about the past legislated in a number of Eastern European countries) came into being in the context of those wars.

The immediate prehistory of the Yarovaia Act goes back to the Russian-Estonian war of words that ensued after the relocation of the "Bronze soldier" (a memorial to Soviet "soldier-liberators") from downtown Tallinn to a war cemetery in 2007.[7] This episode emboldened Russian nationalists such as Natalia Narochnitskaia, who sought to introduce new legislation that would "ban insults to the significance of [Russia's] great Victory."[8] Criminalization of Holocaust denial in the West was routinely evoked as precedent. The 2008 armed conflict with Georgia and the subsequent confrontation with the West, as well as the Prague Declaration on European Conscience and Communism calling for "recognition that many crimes committed in the name of Communism should be assessed as crimes against humanity . . . , in the same way Nazi crimes [had been] assessed by the Nuremberg Tribunal," further contributed to the radicalization of Putin's politics of memory.[9] The rise of the democratic protest movement in December 2011 and its May 2012 suppression by force showed that the "Putin consensus" of the 2000s, based on a compromise between liberal values and neoimperial restoration, had outlived itself. The regime drastically changed its cultural policy, adopted an aggressive posture vis-à-vis the West in international relations, and passed several repressive laws that introduced censorship of the internet, restricted the freedom of meetings, and proscribed "insults to religious sentiments" and "the denial of traditional family values."[10] A law criminalizing countermemories of the war was a logical continuation of this policy. Although the government's experts remained critical of the draft law due to its vagueness, the bill was passed in the wake of the 2014 annexation of Crimea, suggesting that the war myth was an essential component of the propaganda campaign aimed at justifying Putin's aggression against Ukraine.

Members of the Russian Duma claim that this particular piece of legislation is no different from Western memory laws.[11] I argue, to the contrary, that the Yarovaia Act is an extreme case of the kind of statutes regarding history enacted in Eastern Europe—statutes that victimize the past for the purpose of promoting state-centered national narratives instead of developing a democratic culture of memory. In order to determine the place of the Russian statute among similar acts passed in Europe, I propose a memory law typology.

The Evolution of Memory Laws

The term *memory laws* (French: *lois mémorielles*) was coined in the 2000s in France to retrospectively designate a series of laws that criminalized Holocaust denial and recognized other cases of mass atrocities (such as the massacre of Armenians in the Ottoman Empire and the slave trade) as genocides, without penalizing their denial. The emergence of the new term clearly shows that these laws were perceived as a novelty that could not be accounted for within traditional categories. The very expression *lois mémorielles* is lexically connected with *phénomène mémoriel*, which is a common way to refer to the rise of memory (or memory boom) in the late twentieth century. The laws in question were by no means the first legal attempt to regulate collective representations of the past and commemorative practices. Indeed, the laws grew out of a century-long tradition of the state expressing an official position on historical events. To distinguish between enactments that criminalize enunciations about the past and statements that in one way or another regulate historical memory, I refer to the former as "memory laws" and to the latter as "memory laws in a broad sense." The interplay between the two meanings of the concept can be heuristically productive in that it emphasizes both the novelty of the "new" memory laws and their interconnection with previous legislation.[12]

Ad hoc statutes that prohibit certain enunciations about past events are a fairly recent phenomenon going back to the 1980s. The Soviet Union had no memory laws in the narrow sense—notwithstanding the importance of history to the Communist ideology—although "incorrect" historical statements could be punished on the basis of the penal code's articles 70 and 190–1 that forbade anti-Soviet propaganda. The emergence of memory laws signals an important change in modern historical consciousness and suggests that the past has become a more important tool for establishing political legitimacy in the "age of memory" than it was in the age of history-based political ideologies (e.g., Communism, liberalism, or social democracy). Even more telling is that all memory laws, without exception, prohibit "incorrect" interpretations of specific historical events, which indicates that Western historical consciousness has become less centered on "master narratives" and more on the fragments of the past that symbolically represent national, ethnic, religious, and other communities. Most of these events are tragedies and traumas that have become central to the ways particular communities represent themselves in a context informed by the new culture of victimhood typical of the late twentieth and early twenty-first centuries.[13]

At the time of writing, twenty-seven European countries have passed ad hoc statutes specifically forbidding certain historical claims: Germany (1985, amended in 1994), France (1990, 2016), Austria (1992), Switzerland (1993), Belgium (1995), Spain (1995, 2007, 2015), Luxembourg (1997, 2012), Poland (1998, 2018), Liechtenstein (1999), the Czech Republic (2000, 2009), Slovakia (2001, 2005), Romania (2002, 2015), Slovenia (2004, 2008), Macedonia (2004), Andorra (2005), Cyprus (2006, 2011), Portugal (2007), Albania (2008), Malta (2009), Latvia (2009, 2014), Hungary (January 2010/June 2010), Montenegro (2010), Lithuania (2010), Bulgaria (2011), Greece (2014), Russia (2014), and Italy (2016). In addition, several other countries, including Ukraine, Turkey, and the Netherlands, have laws that show some "family resemblance" to those acts and can be considered borderline cases within the same category.[14]

The genealogy of memory laws can be traced to the antifascist legislation of the immediate postwar period, which developed into much broader antiracist laws after the collapse of colonialism. In the 1960s and 1970s, most Western countries passed acts outlawing hate speech. Those enactments (e.g., article 130 of the West German Penal Code as amended in 1960)[15] could be, and occasionally were, used for punishing Holocaust denial, without aspiring to regulating historical memory generally. Still, they provided the legal framework within which the first memory laws in the narrow sense came into being and the prerequisite background to the recent "punitive trend" in Western legislation (e.g., bans on hate speech), the late twentieth-century memory boom, and the projection of the memory of the Holocaust into the center of Western historical consciousness. Presently, most memory laws are incorporated in the respective penal code articles that prohibit hate speech and/or abject behavior marked by allusion to race or nationality.

Although countering Holocaust denial was the initial motivation for introducing memory laws, the scope of this kind of legislation was soon expanded to include the denial of other genocides for the purpose of combating racism and xenophobia beyond antisemitism. Still, memory laws owe a debt to the Holocaust denial legislation by aiming to criminalize *denial* of historical facts. Typically, this legislation also bans *justification* of certain crimes against humanity. Nevertheless, the memory of the Holocaust is commonly viewed (by such authoritative bodies as the European Court of Human Rights and the French Constitutional Council) as a sui generis case that legitimizes an ad hoc legal regime to the exclusion of other traumatic memories.[16] Hence there remains a tension between the notion of the uniqueness of Holocaust denial and the "thematic" expansion of the legislation criminalizing statements about the past.

The first attempt to introduce an ad hoc ban on Holocaust denial was undertaken in West Germany in 1982. However, the bill that was finally passed in 1985 can be deemed only a partial success: it facilitated the use of already existing legal norms for prosecuting deniers (Holocaust denial had de facto become illegal in West Germany as early as the 1970s).[17] In 1986, Israel adopted a law designating Holocaust denial a crime.[18] The 1990 French *loi Gayssot* created an important precedent for ad hoc memory laws in Europe and simultaneously provided a model for several international agreements (e.g., the 2008 European Council Framework Decision that obliged party states to criminalize the denial of the Holocaust and/or other genocides) and national statutes. Thus, the Gayssot Act reads: "Whoever should have disputed . . . the existence of one or of many crimes against humanity, as defined in Article 6 of the Statute of the International Military Tribunal annexed to the London Agreement of 8 August 1945, . . . shall be punished with [one year of imprisonment and/or a fine of 45,000 euros]."[19]

One can distinguish two stages in the evolution of memory laws. During the initial period, which lasted roughly from 1985 to 1998, those acts were adopted almost exclusively in "old" continental democracies such as Germany, France, Austria, Switzerland, and Belgium, most of which had been directly implicated in the Holocaust. Unsurprisingly, then, the memory of Nazi crimes was their main focus. The second period began in the late 1990s. It was characterized by further "internationalization" of memorialization; the role of the European Union in promoting it; the extension of memory laws to new subjects (e.g., the Armenian genocide, Communist crimes, the slave trade); their expansion into Southern and Eastern Europe; and the growing opposition to the judicialization of the past. Some of these laws were passed under pressure from the European Council, whose goal was to create a common vision of the tragic European past that would be endorsed by all member states, while other legal acts took cues from country-specific history.

The expansion of memory laws has resulted in a gradual change of their character. Initially conceived as a means of maintaining peace, they tended to become a weapon of choice in the ensuing "memory wars" fought within and/or between many European countries, of which Eastern Europe (alongside France) is the most obvious example. The first memory laws were by no means an unproblematic tool of history politics (one scholar called them the "most controversial limitation on freedom of expression to have flourished over the past few decades").[20] Since the 2000s, they have been increasingly criticized as a source of political manipulation.[21] Indeed, there is a striking difference between the context in which memory laws first emerged in the 1980s and early 1990s and that in which they further developed in the 2000s and 2010s, when Eastern Europe became the main center of legislative activity regarding the past.

During the 1990s, international politics was largely determined by the fall of Communism and the ascent of liberal democracy, of which humanistic victim-centered culture of memory was an important aspect. In contrast, the beginning of the new century has been marked by the continuing rise of national populism and Far Right movements all across Europe and the formation of authoritarian regimes in Russia, Turkey, Hungary, and Poland. In the former Communist countries, the rise of nationalism can be attributed in part to the difficulties of the transition period, which have exacerbated both their ever-present complex of inferiority vis-à-vis the West and their historical grievances against their neighbors. Some of the memory laws that have been adopted since 1998 faithfully reflect the emergence of a culture of memory different from that prevalent in a genuinely democratic society (i.e., memory based on sympathy to traditionally victimized groups and the general acceptance that the state should be held accountable for past crimes committed in its name). Eastern European memory laws tend to use history for the sake of nationalist mobilization—the exact opposite of what memory laws were meant to achieve in Western Europe and what the European Union sought to ensure by promoting such legislation.

Eastern European Confrontation with Memory (Laws)

In Eastern Europe, statutes criminalizing certain enunciations about the past have grown out of the politics of de-Communization of the 1990s rather than antifascist and antiracist legislation. Naturally, one must be cautious not to present Eastern European historical memory as uniform and/or static. Stefan Troebst identified several "cultures of memory" typical of different clusters of Eastern European countries and dependent on general attitudes to the legacy of Communism.[22] Indeed, as I argue, Eastern European memory laws follow two distinct models.

The process of de-Communization began in the aftermath of the 1989 "revolutions." Different in form, it went the furthest in the Czech Republic, Poland, and Hungary. De-Communization is a well-researched topic, so here I mention just a few acts with a particularly strong element of memory politics, including the Czechoslovak Lustration Act (1991), the German Stasi Records Act (1991), the Czech Act on the Illegality of the Communist Regime (1993), the Polish law establishing the Institute of National Remembrance (1998), the Slovak Nation's Memory Act (2002), and the 2011 Hungarian Basic Law, whose preamble ("National Avowal") and article U (amended in 2013) read almost like a declarative memory law. De-Communization laws laid the groundwork for criminalizing certain utterances about the past in the same way as antifascist and antiracist legislation created a framework for bans on Holocaust denial in Western Europe.

During the Communist period, Soviet bloc countries cultivated their self-image as champions of antifascism and reversely accused the capitalist West of being inherently fascist. They were typically among the first to sign international humanitarian law treaties (e.g., the 1948 Convention on the Prevention and Punishment of the Crime of Genocide and the 1968 Convention on the Non-Applicability of Statutory Limitations to War Crimes and Crimes against Humanity) and incorporate them into domestic law. Communist subjects, however, often viewed official antiracism and antifascism as hypocrisy. Unsurprisingly, the victims of Communism came to be seen as the main, although not only, victims of history in the region. As a result, the culture of victimhood developed in Eastern Europe along different lines than it did in Western Europe and the United States. Victimization of the past for the sake of national communities rather than a nation's repentance for state-sponsored crimes became typical of Eastern European historical memory. It concerns, first and foremost, the participation of the local population in mass crimes committed either by fascist or Communist regimes.

The process of decolonization contributed to antiracism becoming prominent in the West. Antiracism, in its turn, helped propel the Holocaust to the forefront of Western collective memory in the 1960s and 1970s. In contrast, none of the Eastern European countries, with the exception of Russia, was ever a colonial power. Eastern Europeans, for the most part, consider their countries to be constituent parts of Europe and take comparison with third-world countries as an insult. The significance of the Holocaust as a potent symbol of racially motivated crime was always less in Eastern Europe than it was in the West.

The Eastern Europeans' experience in the Second World War is another important factor influencing the development of the adjudication of the past in the region. The "bloodlands," as Timothy Snyder chose to call the countries squeezed between Stalin's Russia and Hitler's Germany, bore the brunt of the violence unleashed by the two totalitarian regimes.[23] The suffering experienced by Eastern Europeans at the hands of the Nazis does not mask the fact that a segment of the local population participated in the "Final Solution of the Jewish Question." Post-Communist regimes did not emphasize the mass murder of the Jews and claimed that Nazism had been an extreme manifestation of militarism and capitalism rather than racism. Consequently, Jewish victims were categorized as nationals of their respective countries or even as Communists or antifascists. It should be mentioned that the Western Allies, too, initially interpreted Nazism as a form of militarism, focusing on the war of aggression rather than the crime of genocide carried out by the Nazis. Meanwhile the notion of Nazi mass crimes began changing in the West in the 1960s and 1970s in conjunction with the rise of the memory of the Holocaust and the emergence of victim-centered historical memory ("régime victimo-mémoriel," to quote Johann Michel).[24] This shift never occurred in Soviet-controlled Eastern Europe. The Holocaust-centered culture of memory entered Eastern Europe only after the fall of Communism, with the prospect of joining the European Union serving as a catalyst. Even then, it faced resistance due to the rise of nationalism and the persistence of inherited interpretations of the past. Consequently, the pan-European memory, with its notion of shared responsibility for the Holocaust, did not make significant inroads in the newly admitted EU member states.[25]

Remembering Nazism and/or Stalinism

The notion of the "Yalta betrayal" is central to Eastern European cultures of remembrance. It commonly translates into a strong resentment against the West for having let Stalin subjugate Eastern European countries, for not being willing to hear their stories about the Soviet occupation, and for promoting instead a "difficult" memory of the Holocaust, in light of which they can no longer be unambiguously categorized as victims of history. The Molotov-Ribbentrop Pact and Stalin's complicity in unleashing the war are also highly sensitive topics in Eastern European history politics that facilitate the portrayal of Communism and Nazism as comparable criminal systems. Indeed, what the Soviet war myth praised as the liberation of Eastern Europe is usually seen there as the beginning of another forcible occupation. Soviet rule, which lasted far longer than the German one and left an enduring imprint on collective memory, is often perceived in this part of Europe as the main issue history politics must face. It is true that the post-1989 de-Communization agenda was partly modeled after, and often presented as an extension of, the de-Nazification program, not least because putting Communism on an equal footing with Nazism further legitimized a radical break from it. All in all, de-Communization was by far more significant than antifascism in countries such as Poland, Hungary, the Czech Republic, and the Baltic states.

To be sure, endorsing an interpretation of the war that paints the Soviet Union as another aggressor alongside Nazi Germany remains unacceptable for a large segment of Western opinion.[26] Such an interpretation entails uncomfortable implications for the West, not least because it undermines the "good war consensus," which is often evoked for legitimizing European integration and the practice of humanitarian intervention.[27] This further explains why the European Council fosters the criminalization of Holocaust denial but condemns

Communist crimes without supporting the legal ban on their denial, hence refusing the collective memory as it had developed in Eastern Europe.[28] This is why some Eastern European countries followed Brussel's recommendations of relevance to history—for example, the 2003 Additional Protocol to the Convention on Cybercrime and the 2008 Framework Decision—while others passed bills that reflected their own historical concerns.[29]

Eastern European memory laws differ from their Western European prototypes in several respects. All such laws in the East and in the West typically ban the denial of Nazi crimes and/or other genocides and crimes against humanity. References to war crimes are more prevalent in Eastern Europe, with eight out of twelve countries (not counting Russia) criminalizing their denial.[30] In Western Europe, by contrast, war crimes are mentioned in only four out of fourteen memory laws.[31] The denial of crimes against peace is outlawed in one Western European and five Eastern European countries.[32] This fact alone shows that the Soviet tradition of viewing the Nazis' main crime as starting the war is still alive in the former Eastern Bloc countries. Yet the most important difference between Western and Eastern European memory laws is still the criminalization of the denial of Communist crimes.

There are two main types of memory laws in Eastern Europe. Albania, Bulgaria, Macedonia, Montenegro, Romania, Slovakia, and Slovenia have banned Holocaust denial and/or the denial of crimes against humanity, in accordance with the French/EU model, while Poland, Hungary, Lithuania, Latvia, and the Czech Republic outlaw the denial of both Nazi and Communist crimes. However, Hungary and Latvia first passed Western-style Holocaust denial laws (in January 2010 and May 2010, respectively) but later switched to the Polish model (Poland was the first country to criminalize the denial of both Nazi and Communist crimes, in 1998). In Hungary, this happened in June 2010, shortly after Viktor Orban came to power, and in Latvia, in May 2014, after the beginning of the Russian aggression against Ukraine.

The adoption of statutes of the former type gives an impression of compliance with the European Council's recommendations. Thus, Albania, Slovenia, and Macedonia adopted their memory laws in compliance with the 2003 Additional Protocol to the Convention on Cybercrime, while Bulgaria and Montenegro did so to satisfy the requirements formulated in the 2008 Framework Decision.

In contrast, laws of the latter type seem to reflect more accurately the peculiarities of Eastern European memory. By outlawing the denial of Nazi and Communist crimes, the lawmakers arguably intended to shift the blame for historical injustices entirely onto the USSR and Nazi Germany, respectively, and thus to whitewash their countries' national narratives. The 1998 Polish and 2010 Lithuanian statutes clearly demonstrate the tendency toward "deflective negationism" (as Michael Shafir termed it).[33]

In Poland, a ban on certain statements about the past was introduced by the 1998 law on the creation of the Institute of National Remembrance. Article 55 of the law stipulates that "anyone who publicly and contrary to the facts denies crimes referred to in art. 1, point 1 shall be subject to a fine or the penalty of imprisonment of up to three years." The punishable crimes are the following:

> a. Crimes perpetrated against ethnic Poles and Polish citizens of other ethnicity between September 1, 1939 and December 31, 1989: Nazi crimes, Communist crimes, and other crimes against peace and humanity, or war crimes, perpetrated against ethnic Poles or Polish citizens of other ethnicity between September 1, 1939 until July 31, 1990,
>
> b. other politically motivated reprisals carried out by the officers of the Polish law enforcement agencies, the judiciary, or persons acting on their orders.[34]

Obviously, the law views both Nazi and Communist crimes as belonging to the category of crimes against humanity. However, offenses committed by the law enforcement agencies of Communist Poland—conceivably perpetrated by individual functionaries rather than the Polish state or the Polish United Workers' Party—do not fall into this category. Hence, the lawmakers have done their utmost to minimize the Polish state's responsibility for the Communist terror "against the Polish nation." It is clearly not by chance that the law emphasizes the concept of crimes *against the Polish nation*. The law tacitly prohibits Holocaust denial by subsuming the extermination of the Jews under "crimes perpetrated . . . against Polish citizens of other ethnicity." The implicit reference to the Holocaust unwittingly continues the Soviet tradition of subsuming the genocide of the Jews among other Nazi crimes.

Similarly, the 2010 Lithuanian memory law, as spelled out in article 170.2 of the penal code, bans the denial of "crimes of genocide or other crimes against humanity or war crimes committed by the USSR or Nazi Germany in the territory of the Republic of Lithuania or against the inhabitants of the Republic of Lithuania."[35] This is yet another case of whitewashing the national past because many Lithuanians did, in fact, collaborate with the Soviet regime while some were also complicit in the mass murder of Jews.

In January 2018, the Polish right-wing government passed a new memory law that aims at "protecting the good name of the Polish Republic and the Polish nation." The law stipulates that "anyone who publicly and contrary to the facts ascribes to the Polish people or the Polish state responsibility or coresponsibility for Nazi crimes . . . , or for other offenses constituting crimes against peace, [crimes against] humanity or war crimes, or in any other way grossly diminishes the responsibility of the actual perpetrators of these crimes shall be subject to a fine or the penalty of imprisonment of up to three years."[36]

Indeed, Nazi crimes were committed by the Nazis, and Poles should not be blamed for those crimes. However, the mention of "other offenses," which may refer to the role the Poles themselves played in the extermination of Polish Jews during and in the aftermath of the Second World War, changes everything. By passing this enactment, Poland moved from shifting the blame for historical injustices onto others to openly protecting the memory of the perpetrators of crimes against humanity. This alone makes the 2018 Polish statute more similar to the 2014 Russian enactment than to other Eastern European de-Communization memory laws. However, in June 2018, Poland had to decriminalize the offense in response to international pressure.[37]

There are obvious differences between the clusters of Eastern European countries that have adopted different types of memory laws. The countries that have criminalized the denial of Communist crimes tend to be more developed economically than those that have not done so. They have been more successful in implementing market reforms and—to use Troebst's classification—have a less ambiguous attitude toward their Communist past. Many of the countries that have not prohibited the denial of Communist crimes were relatively more independent from Moscow during the Soviet period (Albania, Romania, and the former Yugoslavia, to which Slovenia, Montenegro, and Macedonia then belonged) while the countries that have banned it have a far stronger record of anti-Communist resistance (armed insurgency in Latvia and Lithuania in the late 1940s and early 1950s, the 1956 Hungarian revolution, the 1968 Prague Spring, and the Solidarność movement in Poland in the 1980s). In addition, most countries belonging to the latter group feel more vulnerable because of Putin's neoimperial ambitions and are involved in harsh disputes with Moscow about the past. Laws criminalizing the denial of Communist crimes are at the same time an effect of and an important instrument in the memory wars they fight with Russia.

The 2014 Russian memory law was a direct consequence of those memory wars. In a way, it was a reaction to Eastern European "de-Communization" memory laws, most of which had been adopted a while ago. Chronologically, Russia's opponents in memory wars were the first to develop a history politics infrastructure, including institutes of national remembrance, museums of occupations, and relevant amendment to criminal law. However, this does not mean the Kremlin is on the defensive in these conflicts, for its neoimperialist rhetoric and cultivation of the Stalinist myth of the causes and consequences of the Second World War have been crucial to the formation of the Eastern European "anti-Russian" politics of memory in the first place.

A Failed Attempt to "Civilize" the Russian War Myth

To better understand the meaning of the 2014 Russian statute, I compare it with several other Russian bills, the authors of which sought to find a middle ground between the Russian myth of the Second World War and Western memories of the Holocaust, with the obvious goal of making that myth more acceptable internationally. These bills were initiated by Boris Spiegel, a Russian "oligarch," politician, and prominent Russian Jewish activist. In June 2010, he created World without Nazism, an "international human rights movement" that set out to counter the resurgence of Nazi ideology and historical revisionism.

The memory of the Holocaust was almost nonexistent in Russia (as well as other Communist countries) during the Soviet period. In the late 1980s, however, awareness of the Holocaust rapidly developed in the context of Gorbachev's perestroika in response to the growing Far Right movement. It was promoted, in particular, by a group of Russian Jewish activists that included notable intellectuals, historians, and democratic politicians such as Mikhail Gefter, Alla Gerber, Evgenii Proshechkin, and Ilia Altman. That group established (with the support of Yeltsin's government and Moscow city authorities) the Russian Research and Educational Holocaust Center (1992), followed by the Interregional Holocaust Foundation (1997).[38] Their efforts notwithstanding, the memory of the Holocaust remained peripheral to Russian national memory.

The ascent of Putin's regime, which intensified memory wars between Russia and its former satellites as well as the general confrontation with the West, changed the status of the memory of the Holocaust in Russia. On the one hand, this memory, as well as the notion of human rights, gradually came to be seen as an ideological weapon wielded by the West in its "crusade" against Russia. On the other hand, Holocaust commemoration was promising insofar as the Nazis did indeed find collaborators in some Eastern European countries—a fact the politics of memory in those countries tended to obscure. The Kremlin entertained an idea of building a "coalition of memory" with the West against its Eastern European opponents. However, the traditional Stalinist war myth is of little use here. Unsurprisingly, several groups of pro-Kremlin politicians and historians—exemplified by the Historical Memory Foundation (created in 2008) and Spiegel's World without Nazism—began exploring ways of modernizing this myth by integrating the memory of the Holocaust.[39] It is worth noting that this particular history policy began taking shape during Dmitrii Medvedev's presidency, which was marked by hesitant attempts to modernize the government's ideological agenda.

In 2012, acting as a deputy chair of the Federation Council's Committee on Constitutional Legislation, Spiegel convinced the Interparliamentary Assembly of Member Nations of the Commonwealth of Independent States (CIS) to approve the framework law On the Inadmissibility of Actions Aimed at the Rehabilitation of Nazism and the Heroization of Nazi Criminals and Their Accomplices.[40] This bill proposed a complex strategy for promoting the Russian war myth, this time in combination with the memory of the Holocaust. In Spiegel's view, the CIS model law would play a role similar to that of the 2008 European

Council Framework Decision. In March 2013, Spiegel introduced two bills into the Duma, the first of which reproduced the CIS framework law while the second proposed expanding the list of offences enumerated in article 282 of the penal code by including the rehabilitation of Nazism and Holocaust denial.[41] Had Spiegel's proposal been accepted, article 282 would have criminalized "actions aiming at advocating hatred or enmity, rehabilitating Nazism, glorifying Nazi criminals and their accomplices, denying the Holocaust, disparaging the human dignity of a person or a group of persons on the basis of gender, race, nationality, language, origins, religion, or belonging to a social group, committed publicly or thorough the media."[42]

Spiegel's bill was similar to Western European Holocaust denial laws, which consider Nazi crimes to be offences of a racist nature. However, this approach encroached on the "purity" of the Russian war myth and was therefore rejected by the Duma. Spiegel had to resign from the Federation Council in March 2013, nominally because of a new law that forbade combining positions in the parliament with those in international NGOs (including World without Nazism).

His successor as deputy chair of the Committee on Constitutional Legislation, Konstantin Dobrynin (a young lawyer from St. Petersburg who is reportedly close to Prime Minister Medvedev), continued promoting Spiegel's drafts. In April 2014, when the Yarovaia law was about to be approved by the parliament, Dobrynin and his colleagues made a last-ditch effort to stop it by submitting new versions of their own bills, which reproduced Spiegel's drafts of 2013.[43] Notably, Holocaust denial had disappeared from the new drafts, which now proposed to criminalize only the "rehabilitation of Nazism and the heroization of Nazi criminals and their accomplices." Once Holocaust denial was removed from the list of criminal offences, however, Dobrynin's proposal ceased to be a meaningful alternative to the Yarovaia law and remained an expression of the institutional competition between the two houses of the Russian parliament (the Yarovaia Act was initiated by the Duma leadership).

Even under Medvedev, Russian authorities preferred to promote the memory of the Holocaust indirectly through an international NGO. After Putin's 2012 reelection as Russia's president, and especially after the 2014 Russian aggression against Ukraine, legitimizing the Stalinist war myth by incorporating it into the Holocaust-centered Western historical narrative ceased to be part of the Kremlin's agenda.

The Russian memory law can be regarded as an extreme case of the deplorable Eastern European tendency of using such legislation for the protection of national narratives because it openly endorses the memory of an oppressive regime against that of its victims. The only similar statute is article 301 of the Turkish penal code (as amended in 2005), which criminalizes insults to the Turkish state and is normally used against those who recognize the extermination of the

Armenians in the Ottoman Empire as genocide.[44] In a more moderate form, this tendency is manifest in those acts that shift the blame for historical injustices entirely to other nations (Nazi Germany or Stalin's USSR) and draw a veil over their own populations' participation in Nazi or Communist crimes, respectively.[45] In contrast, Western European (and some Eastern European) memory laws, notwithstanding their shortcomings, protect the memory of victims of state-sponsored crimes.

Notes

1. Irina Yarovaia, a State Duma deputy for the ruling United Russia Party, played a key role in passing the law.

2. Federal Law no. 128-FZ of May 5, 2014, O vnesenii izmenenii v otdelnye zakonodatelnye akty Rossiiskoi Federatsii.

3. Federal Law no. 128-FZ, article 1.2.

4. Federal Law no. 128-FZ, article 1.3.

5. Alexander Verkhovskii, *Politika gosudarstva po otnosheniyu k natsional-radikalnym obiedineniiam, 1991–2002* (Moscow: Tsentr "Sova," 2013), 84–129.

6. Nanci Adler, "The Future of the Soviet Past Remains Unpredictable: The Resurrection of Stalinist Symbols amidst the Exhumation of Mass Graves," *Europe-Asia Studies* 57, no. 8 (2005): 1093–119; Dina Khapaeva, "Historical Memory in Post-Soviet Gothic Society," *Social Research* 76, no. 1 (2009): 359–94.

7. Karsten Brüggemann and Andres Kasekamp, "The Politics of History and the 'War Monuments' in Estonia," *Nationalities Papers* 36, no. 3 (2008): 425–48; Maria Mälksoo, *The Politics of Becoming European: A Study of Polish and Baltic Post-Cold Security Imaginaries* (London: Routledge, 2010), 106–16; and Meike Wulf, *Shadowlands: Memory and History in Post-Soviet Estonia* (New York: Berghahn Books, 2016), 156–63.

8. Natalia Narochnitskaia, "Komu vygoden peresmotr itogov Vtoroi mirovoi?," *Rossiia segodniia*, May 8, 2007, http://pressmia.ru/pressclub/20070508/65130644.html.

9. Prague Declaration on European Conscience and Communism of June 3, 2008, available at http://www.praguedeclaration.eu.

10. Federal Law no. 136-FZ of June 29, 2013, O vnesenii izmenenii v statiu 148 Ugolovnogo kodeksa Rossiiskoi Federatsii i otdelnye zakonodatelnye akty Rossiiskoi Federatsii v tseliakh protivodeistviia oskorbleniiu religioznykh ubezhdenii i chuvstv grazhdan; and Federal Law no. 135-FZ of June 29, 2013, O vnesenii izmenenii v statiu 5 Federalnogo zakona "O zashchite detei ot informatsii, prichiniaiushchei vred ikh zdoroviu i razvitiiu i otdelnye zakonodatelnye akty Rossiiskoi Federatsii v tseliakh zashchity detei ot informatsii, propagandiruiushchei otritsanie traditsionnykh semeinykh tsennostei."

11. Cf. the rationale for the May 5, 2014, law outlined at the State Duma website, http://asozd2.duma.gov.ru/main.nsf/%28SpravkaNew%29?OpenAgent&RN=197582-5&02 (site discontinued); the draft law is filed as 197582–5.

12. On memory laws, see Uladzislau Belavusau and Aleksandra Gliszczynska-Grabias, eds., *Law and Memory: Towards Legal Governance of History* (Cambridge: Cambridge University Press, 2017); Marc Olivier Baruch, *Des lois indignes? Les Historiens, la politique*

et le droit (Paris: Talandier, 2013); Robert A. Kahn, *Holocaust Denial and the Law: A Comparative Study* (Basingstoke, UK: Palgrave Macmillan, 2004); Ivan Hare and James Weinstein, eds., *Extreme Speech and Democracy* (Oxford: Oxford University Press, 2009); Luigi Cajani, "Criminal Laws on History: The Case of the European Union," *Historein* 11 (2011): 19–48; Stiina Löytömäki, *Law and the Politics of Memory: Confronting the Past* (London: Routledge, 2014); Nikolay Koposov, *Memory Laws, Memory Wars: The Politics of the Past in Europe and Russia* (Cambridge: Cambridge University Press, 2017).

13. On the culture of victimhood, see Robert Elias, *The Politics of Victimization: Victims, Victimology, and Human Rights* (Oxford: Oxford University Press, 1986); Carolyn J. Dean, *Aversion and Erasure: The Fate of the Victim after the Holocaust* (Ithaca, NY: Cornell University Press, 2010); Alyson M. Cole, *The Cult of True Victimhood: From the War on Welfare to the War on Terror* (Stanford, CA: Stanford University Press, 2007).

14. Between January 2014 and April 2015, Ukraine had a law criminalizing the denial or justification of fascist crimes against humanity. Currently, Ukrainian legislation declares illegal, yet not punishable, the denial of the Holodomor as a genocide of the Ukrainian people (since 2006) and insults to the memory of "fighters for Ukraine's independence" (since April 2015). Turkey has no memory law per se; article 301 of its penal code, which criminalizes denigration of the Turkish nation, is widely used against those who declare the 1915 mass murder of the Armenians as genocide. Finally, the Netherlands has (since 1997) a Supreme Court ruling that Holocaust denial is an insult to the Jews and is punishable as a racially motivated defamation of a group of persons. Several Western countries consistently refuse to introduce such laws, which they view as an infringement on the freedom of expression. These are typically common law countries (such as the United States, Canada, and Great Britain) and the Nordic countries (Denmark, Sweden, Norway, and Finland), whose legal culture has been influenced by the common law tradition.

15. See article 130 of the German Criminal Code. See also Benedikt Rohrssen, *Von der "Anreizung zum Klassenkampf" zur "Volksverhetzung" (§ 130 StGB): Reformdiskussion und Gesetzgebung seit dem 19. Jahrhundert* (Berlin: De Gruyter Recht, 2009), 162–66.

16. Paolo Lobba, "The Fate of the Prohibition against Genocide Denial," *European Criminal Law Review* 4, no. 1 (2014): 59–78.

17. Eric Stein, "History against Free Speech: The New German Law against the 'Auschwitz'—and Other—'Lies,'" *Michigan Law Review* 85, no. 2 (1986): 303; Robert A. Kahn, "Informal Censorship of Holocaust Revisionism in the United States and Germany," *George Mason University Civil Rights Law Journal* 9, no. 1 (1998): 140.

18. Cf. Article 2 of Israel's Denial of Holocaust (Prohibition) Law 5746–1986 of July 8, 1986, at Israel Ministry of Foreign Affairs, https://mfa.gov.il/mfa/aboutisrael/history/holocaust /pages/denial%20of%20holocaust%20-prohibition-%20law-%205746-1986-.aspx.

19. Talia Naamat, Nina Osin, and Dina Porat, eds., *Legislating for Equality: A Multinational Collection of Non-Discrimination Norms*, vol. 1, *Europe* (Leiden, Neth.: Martinus Nijhoff, 2012), 156–57.

20. Erik Bleich, "The Rise of Hate Speech and Hate Crime Laws in Liberal Democracies," *Journal of Ethnic and Migration Studies* 37, no. 6 (2011): 920.

21. Thus, Timothy Garton Ash spoke ironically about the imaginary "horse-trading behind closed doors in Brussels (Polish official to French counterpart: 'OK, we'll give you the Armenian genocide if you give us the Ukrainian famine.') Pure Gogol." See his "The Freedom of Historical Debate Is Under Attack by the Memory Police," *Guardian*, October 16, 2008.

22. Stefan Troebst, "Halecki Revisited: Europe's Conflicting Cultures of Remembrance," in *A European Memory? Contested Histories and Politics of Remembrance*, ed. Małgorzata Pakier and Bo Stråth (New York: Berghahn Books, 2010), 58; Stefan Troebst, "Was für ein Teppich? Postkommunistische Erinnerungskulturen in Ost(mittel)europa," in *Der Kommunismus im Museum: Formen der Auseinandersetzung in Deutschland und Ostmitteleuropa*, ed. Volkhart Knigge and Ulrich Mälert (Cologne: Böhlau, 2005), 31–54.

23. Cf. Timothy Snyder, *Bloodlands: Europe between Hitler and Stalin* (New York: Basic Books, 2010).

24. Johann Michel, "L'institutionalisation du crime contre l'humanité et l'avènement du régime victimo-mémoriel en France," *Canadian Journal of Political Science* 43, no. 3 (2011): 663–84.

25. Michael Shafir, "Denying the Shoah in Post-Communist Eastern Europe," in *Holocaust Denial: The Politics of Perfidy*, ed. Robert S. Wistrich (Berlin: Walter de Gruyter, 2012), 27–65; Stephen E. Atkins, *Holocaust Denial as an International Movement* (Westport, CT: Praeger, 2009), 136–41.

26. Tony Judt, *Postwar: A History of Europe Since 1945* (New York: Penguin Books, 2005), 826.

27. Maja Zehfuss, *Wounds of Memory: The Politics of War in Germany* (Cambridge: Cambridge University Press, 2007), 7–13; Gavriel D. Rosenfeld, *Hi Hitler! How the Nazi Past Is Being Normalized in Contemporary Culture* (Cambridge: Cambridge University Press, 2015), 29–77.

28. European Parliament Resolution of 2 April 2009 on European Conscience and Totalitarianism.

29. Additional Protocol to the Convention on Cybercrime, Concerning the Criminalization of Acts of a Racist and Xenophobic Nature Committed through Computer Systems of January 28, 2003; European Council Framework Decision 2008/913/JHA of 28 November 2008 on Combating Certain Forms and Expressions of Racism and Xenophobia by Means of Criminal Law.

30. Macedonia, Slovakia, Slovenia, the Czech Republic, Latvia, Lithuania, Montenegro, and Romania.

31. In Luxembourg, Portugal, Malta, and Greece.

32. Portugal in the West and Poland, Slovakia, the Czech Republic, Latvia, and Bulgaria in the East.

33. Michael Shafir, "Between Denial and 'Comparative Trivialization': Holocaust Negationism in Post-Communist East Central Europe," in *The Treatment of the Holocaust in Hungary and Romania during the Post-Communist Era*, ed. Randolph L. Braham (New York: City University of New York and Social Sciences Monographs, 2004), 44.

34. Law no. 155 of December 18, 1998, O Instytucie Pamięci Narodowej—Komisji Ścigania Zbrodni przeciwko Narodowi Polskiemu.

35. Law no. VIII-1968 of September 26, 2000, on the Approval and Entry into Force of the Criminal Code.

36. Law of January 26, 2018, O zmianie ustawy o Instytucie Pamięci Narodowej—Komisji Ścigania Zbrodni przeciwko Narodowi Polskiemu . . . , article 6.

37. Law of June 27, 2018, O zmianie ustawy o Instytucie Pamięci Narodowej—Komisji Ścigania Zbrodni przeciwko Narodowi Polskiemu . . . , article 1.

38. Klas-Göran Karlsson, "The Reception of the Holocaust in Russia: Silence, Conspiracy, and Glimpses of Light," in *Bringing the Dark Past to Light: The Reception of the Holocaust in Postcommunist Europe*, ed. John-Paul Himka and Joanna Beata Michlic (Lincoln: University of Nebraska Press, 2013), 487–514; Tarik Cyril Amar, "A Disturbed Silence: Discourse on the Holocaust in the Soviet West as an Anti-Site of Memory," in *The Holocaust in the East: Local Perpetrators and Soviet Responses*, ed. Michael David-Fox, Peter Holquist, and Alexander M. Martin (Pittsburgh, PA: University of Pittsburgh Press, 2014), 158–84.

39. The Historical Memory Foundation deals extensively with collaboration with Nazi Germany in East Europe, specifically in Ukraine and the Baltic states. Cf. Alexander Diukov, *Vtorostepennyi vrag: OUN, UPA i reshenie "evreiskogo voprosa"* (Moscow: Regnum, 2008) and Alexander Diukov, *"The Soviet Story": Mekhanizmy lzhi* (Moscow: Regnum, 2008). Notably, both books were published by Regnum News Agency, which is run by Modest Kolerov, a well-known Russian nationalist.

40. Interparliamentary Assembly of Member Nations of the Community of Independent States, law of May 17, 2012, O nedopustimosti deistvii po reabilitatsii natsizma, geroizatsii natsistskikh prestupnikov i ikh posobnikov.

41. Draft Law no. 246071–6 of March 25, 2013, O nedopustimosti deistvii po reabilitatsii natsizma, geroizatsii natsistskikh prestupnikov i ikh posobnikov, otritsaniiu Holokosta.

42. Draft Law no. 246065–6 of March 25, 2013, O vnesenii izmenenii v statiiu 282 Ugolovnogo kodeksa Rossiiskoi Federatsii.

43. Draft Law no. 504872–6 of April 22, 2014, O protivodeistvii reabilitatsii natsizma, geroizatsii natsistskikh prestupnikov i ikh posobnikov; Draft Law no. 504840–6 of April 22, 2014, O vnesenii izmenenii v statiiu 1 Federalnogo zakona "O protivodeistvii ekstremistskoi deiatelnosti."

44. Naamat, Osin, and Porat, *Legislating for Equality*, 478.

45. The 1998 Polish law, the 2000 Czech law, the 2010 Lithuanian law, the June 2010 Hungarian law, and the 2014 Latvian law.

NIKOLAY KOPOSOV is Visiting Professor at Emory University. He was Founding Dean of Smolny College of Liberal Arts and Sciences, a joint venture of Saint-Petersburg State University and Bard College. He is author and/or editor of ten books, including *Memory Laws, Memory Wars: The Politics of the Past in Europe and Russia* and *De l'imagination historique*.

10 Tenacious Pasts: Geopolitics and the Polish-Russian Group on Difficult Matters

George Soroka

ANDREAS HUYSSEN ONCE asserted that "we seem to suffer from a hypertrophy of memory, not history."[1] Although it was published in 2003, Huyssen's diagnosis is as relevant today as it was then. Indeed, in recent years the world has witnessed the furious return of nationalized frames of remembering, a phenomenon especially pronounced in post-Communist Europe.[2] Emerging in the late 1980s and early 1990s but really coming into its own in the 2000s, this overall trend, which has raised the salience of historical interpretation and the politics surrounding it, merits systematic study.[3] However, while this chapter engages deductively with these broader currents, its empirical ambitions are more modest: it surveys Polish-Soviet, and later Polish-Russian, intergovernmental relations through the lens of a bilateral group charged with addressing what are euphemistically termed "blanks spots" in the shared histories of these two countries.

Its initial incarnation, known as the Joint Historical Commission, functioned from 1987 to 1989 before succumbing to the political upheavals of the day. However, the need for such an entity did not vanish with the fall of Communism, leading to the formation of the Polish-Russian Group on Difficult Matters in 2002. This first post-Soviet attempt to reestablish dialogue over problematic legacies, for reasons related to the group's composition and the broader geopolitical climate at the time, proved a failure. Yet in 2008, changing domestic and regional realities enabled it to be reconstituted with a new membership. In this iteration the group was active through late 2013, when the Ukrainian crisis intervened and deteriorating relations between Poland and Russia led to the cessation of its activities.

Currently, the future of this body remains unclear. Former Polish foreign minister Adam Daniel Rotfeld, who served as its cochair alongside his Russian counterpart, Anatolii Torkunov, resigned in December 2015. A little over a year later, in March 2017, Poland's then foreign minister, Witold Waszczykowski, announced that the Polish side of the group was being reconstituted. In response, the Russian Ministry of Foreign Affairs replied that it had "serious doubts" about reviving it in a bilateral format given the poor state of relations between the two countries, the blame for which it placed squarely on Warsaw.[4] Meanwhile, Torkunov, rector of Moscow's State Institute of International Relations (MGIMO), stated that he would not agree to stay on as cochair if the group were revitalized.[5] Further doubts about the ability of this entity to be resurrected anytime soon were raised in late 2018, when the Polish government shuttered the Lublin-based Institute of East-Central Europe (IEŚW). This led the newly appointed head of the Polish side, Mirosław Filipowicz (who was also the director of IEŚW), to resign in protest not long afterward. Consequently, as of early 2019, the Polish component of the group is also nonfunctional.[6]

Having existed in several iterations over a long time, this body represents an intriguing optic through which to observe the dynamics of Polish-Russian history politics. This is especially so given that it was composed primarily of academics meeting at the behest of their respective governments to look into contentious legacies overwhelmingly stemming from the Soviet period. That these legacies continued to affect bilateral relations long after the Soviet Union's collapse attests to the entrenched nature of the past in the foreign affairs of both countries.

This was not the only bilateral group that sought to improve Polish-Russian relations (e.g., the Polish-Russian Forum for Civic Dialogue and the Intergovernmental Commission on Economic Cooperation). Nor did it represent a lone attempt to elucidate the facts of history; other attempts included the official Russian investigation into the 1940 Katyn massacre (by far the most significant stumbling block in recent Polish-Russian relations) and the establishment of the Institute of National Remembrance (IPN) in Poland in 2000.[7] Neither was it unique insofar as the political use of history is concerned; a prime example of this trend was the establishment, while Dmitrii Medvedev was in office, of the Presidential Commission to Counter Attempts to Falsify History to the Detriment of Russia's Interests (2009–12). Finally, efforts to repair cross-border relations were never confined to the dyad of Poland-Russia; they also included bodies such as the Foundation for Polish-German Reconciliation, the Polish-Ukrainian Commission on History, and the Russian-Japanese Commission on Difficult Issues. However, what sets the Polish-Russian Group on Difficult Matters apart is the sheer extent to which historical factors have played a deleterious role in relations between Poland and Russia and the inability of the two sides, despite repeated attempts, to bridge the interpretive chasm that continues to exist between them.

Setting the Stage

"The historical facts are incontrovertible, but they may be interpreted in various ways," wrote Rotfeld and Torkunov in their introduction to the 2010 Polish-Russian edited volume that represents one of the main accomplishments of the group.[8] As revealed in this quote, the group's mandate was not so much to reach a common historical understanding (although it did involve an attempt to establish the scope and scale of less well-documented crimes) as to attenuate the discord resulting from divergent narratives concerning the past, with the road to reconciliation less about fostering interpretive convergence than deemphasizing the political salience of problematic legacies. Consequently, it is worth examining how the expectations of Polish-Russian historical dialogue changed over time and how shifting political perspectives came to affect this body.

Historical commissions such as the Polish-Russian initiative share many similarities with truth (and reconciliation) commissions. According to Priscilla Hayner, the latter seek to influence the "social understanding and acceptance of the country's past, not just to resolve specific facts."[9] Similarly, historical commissions have been set up "in a variety of contexts where 'difficult' and shameful historical episodes cast a long shadow over contemporary society and where debates over the past have become the subject of political wrangling."[10] Both entities also exhibit strong political undercurrents. As Alexander Karn observes regarding historical bodies convened to deal with the legacy of the Holocaust, they have typically "served as political troubleshooters for their governments, which were still largely guided by the logic of *realpolitik*."[11]

Yet there are important differences between truth and historical commissions. For one, historical commissions are more prone to transcend national boundaries, with bilateral organizations "now a fixture in Europe."[12] Their temporal remit is also broader in that they deal with "long-term memories of group animosity, including cases in which individual perpetrators and victims are no longer alive, yet their actions and suffering continue to haunt the national memory."[13] Moreover, while truth commissions are tasked with ascertaining the circumstances surrounding crimes against individuals or groups, historical commissions—although they may collect such evidence and even share it with prosecutors—are usually charged with gathering facts at a higher aggregative level (i.e., beyond that of the individual). Finally, historical commissions are dominated by academics, whereas the composition of truth commissions tends to be broader.

Despite its name and bilateral nature, the Polish-Soviet Joint Historical Commission operated much like a truth commission, albeit one hobbled by ideological considerations and limited archival access. Meanwhile, its successor, the Polish-Russian Group on Difficult Matters, functioned more like a standard historical commission in that it was primarily concerned with working through interpretations of known facts.

Poland versus Russia: Differences in Societal and Political Remembrance

Poles and Russians remember their shared pasts quite differently. For example, on the seventieth anniversary of the start of the Second World War, in 2009, 72 percent of Poles surveyed answered that Poland was the "most heroic" nation during this conflict. And when asked who suffered the most during the war, 63 percent answered Poles, 36 percent Jews, and only 3 percent Russians.[14] Faced with similar questions, Russian respondents would no doubt reply very differently.[15] Attesting to this, since the early 1990s, the majority of Russians have consistently held that the Soviet Union could have prevailed in the Second World War without the help of its allies.[16] Nonetheless, it is not the facts but rather the interpretations underpinning these perceptions that are typically contested.

The act of remembering proceeds at both societal and political levels, with the term *collective memory* frequently associated with mass-level discourses. This is, however, a notoriously imprecise concept, as individuals and even subnational groupings vary dramatically in their interpretations of the past, both within and across states. Nonetheless, the basic contours of nationalized ways of relating to history are discernible, in large part due to the influence of cultural inputs (e.g., music, literature, film) and the mnemonic shaping that occurs through educational institutions and official commemorative practices. Yet a society's collective memory, to the extent it actually exists, is not necessarily synonymous with the narratives propounded by its leaders.[17]

At the extreme, particularly traumatic or otherwise significant historical events may become so thoroughly interwoven into the fabric of national identity that they function as mnemonic touchstones capable of transcending themselves. For example, for Poles, the 1940 Katyn massacre has been rendered just such an "event out of time." Today, its recall not only encompasses the approximately twenty-two thousand Polish military reservists, officers, and border guards murdered by the Soviet NKVD but also the meanings that have subsequently been ascribed to this act, including reactions to the decades of deceit engendered by the Communist-era cover-up and the 2010 crash that claimed the life of President Lech Kaczyński and the ninety-five others flying with him to Smolensk to mark its seventieth anniversary. A similar dynamic has played out in relation to the Red Army's role in the Second World War, which has become particularly salient politically in post-Soviet Russia. Signaling this, in 2014 Russian parliamentarians adopted legislation making it a criminal offense to "spread intentionally false information about the Soviet Union's activities during World War II." It is interesting that this law not only seeks to protect the state rather than its victims from criticism but is also inherently reactive, coming as it did on the heels of increasingly vocal protestations from the former satellite states of the Soviet Union that the Red Army did not bring liberation in the Second World War so much as the exchange of one occupier for another.[18]

Consequently, it is not difficult to understand why history is so prone to politicization, especially as its interpretation frequently serves as a proxy and shorthand for identity. The inherently didactic character this grants historical politics goes a long way toward explaining why the past is so often invoked in interstate disputes.

1987–89: The Polish-Soviet Joint Historical Commission

The first systematic attempt to deal with contentious historical issues followed on the heels of the Declaration on Soviet-Polish Cooperation in the Fields of Ideology, Science, and Culture, signed during the visit of Poland's general secretary Wojciech Jaruzelski to Moscow on April 21, 1987.[19] Specifically, the declaration held that "the PZPR and KPSS attach great importance to the joint study of historical relations between our states, parties and nations" and consequently claimed "all episodes, including also the dramatic ones, should receive an objective and clear interpretation."[20] The Joint Historical Commission began meeting the following month, tasked with looking into the "blank spots" that existed between Poland and the Soviet Union.

As Elizabeth Valkenier observed, the commission "was composed of trusted historians picked by each Party, many of whom did not enjoy much confidence within the profession."[21] Chairing Poland's delegation was Jarema Maciszewski, head of the Academy of Social Sciences and a historian of seventeenth-century Polish-Russian relations, while the Soviet side was led by Georgii Smirnov, director of the Institute of Marxism-Leninism and reportedly Mikhail Gorbachev's advisor on ideological matters.[22]

The political dimensions of the commission were evident from the outset.[23] It was also very much a product of the unsettled regional politics of the 1980s: Gorbachev had just embarked on an audacious series of social and economic reforms in the Soviet Union while Jaruzelski was struggling to address the muscular challenge posed by the Solidarity movement in Poland. Indicative of this fraught situation, Poland's Public Opinion Research Center (CBOS) as early as 1985 had produced a list of historical episodes that were fomenting public unrest and breeding distrust of the authorities.[24] As a result, the Polish People's Republic (PRL) was especially in need of bolstering its legitimacy; growing political dissent not only contributed to societal demands to know the truth about specific historical events but also fundamentally threatened the stability of the Communist system. Moreover, Jaruzelski—who, along with his family, had been deported to Siberia by the Soviets during the Second World War—appeared genuinely interested in resolving the historical issues that existed between the PRL and the USSR.[25]

As a result, the commission had the dual purpose of reconciling Polish and Soviet citizens and propping up the respective regimes they lived under. This did not, however, mean the specific goals of the two sides were perfectly aligned: "While the Poles pushed for full truth and publicity about the blank spots and politically sensitive topics in Soviet-Polish relations, the Soviets resented being asked in effect to 'repent' and preferred to direct attention to the study of issues that united rather than divided the two nations—like their common struggle against the Nazis. Obviously the Polish side was struggling for its political life, hoping to buy public support by exposing Soviet misdeeds, and trying to mollify Polish nationalism. For the Soviet side the issues were not as pressing, either politically or emotionally."[26] Neither were the Polish and Soviet authorities equally insistent on maintaining direct control over the commission. Polish members of the commission enjoyed a considerable degree of autonomy compared to their Soviet colleagues, who were still "severely constrained by Party discipline and constantly had to consult with the political authorities."[27]

Given the greater societal and political salience of the commission to the Poles, it is unsurprising that they led the way in designating the historical topics it would cover. There were six key events for the Polish side, which Jaruzelski himself enumerated in a July 1987 article that examined why Poles distrusted the Soviet Union: (1) the Polish-Bolshevik War of 1919–21; (2) Stalin's purge of the Polish Communist Party in the 1930s; (3) the Soviet Union's 1939 incursion into Poland; (4) the Katyn massacre; (5) the deportation of Poles to the USSR; and (6) the role of the Soviet Army in the 1944 Warsaw Uprising.[28] However, these topics were not equally prominent in Poland's collective consciousness. As Maciszewski subsequently noted, the Polish side was primarily concerned with clarifying the circumstances surrounding Katyn.[29] Not far behind, however, were questions surrounding the Molotov-Ribbentrop Pact and the Soviet annexation of eastern Poland in September of 1939.

This is not to imply that these were the only historical issues of significance to Polish society. For obvious reasons, the commission could not broach some topics—for example, how Communist rule was imposed in Poland after 1945. The Soviets, too, had historical grievances they wanted to take up with the Poles, including the treatment of Red Army soldiers held in Polish prison camps during the Polish-Bolshevik War in 1919–21 and the paucity of monuments to Soviet soldiers who died while fighting German forces in Poland. However, the Polish side appeared unmoved by Soviet concerns.[30]

The Joint Historical Commission held its first plenary session in Moscow on May 18–20, 1987. Expectations were high given the societal openness beginning to flourish in the wake of Gorbachev's implementation of glasnost. So it was not surprising that there were indications the commission would have a salutary effect on interstate relations despite a lack of immediate progress. For instance, an otherwise formulaic and ideologically orthodox piece Smirnov published in September 1987 made two startling concessions. First, Smirnov admitted that the Second World War was, for Poland, "from the outset a defensive and just war" (contrary to the earlier class-based condemnation of "bourgeois" interwar Poland); second, he rebuked, in no uncertain terms, former Soviet foreign minister Vyacheslav Molotov, who, on October 31, 1939, delivered a "preposterous appraisal of the Polish state as 'an ugly product of the Versailles Treaty.'"[31]

The next meeting, initially planned for November 1987, instead took place in Warsaw between February 29 and March 3, 1988. Not a great deal was accomplished during this gathering either, with substantive progress on issues of importance to the Polish side hampered by deliberate stalling on the part of the Soviet authorities. Working independently, however, the Polish members of the commission nevertheless made headway. Consequently, in May 1988, they presented their Soviet colleagues with a report that contested the findings of the 1944 Soviet commission tasked with investigating the Katyn massacre.[32]

The Poles' conclusion—namely that the Soviets rather than the Germans were responsible for the killings—contradicted decades of official denials by the USSR (and the PRL). It also guaranteed that the commission's third plenary session, which took place in Moscow during November 29–December 1, 1988, would prove difficult.[33] The terse meeting summary released afterward simply noted that the members of the commission had examined the evidence "prepared by the Polish side on the basis of Western and Polish scholarly sources concerning the fate of the Polish officers interned in 1939 who died at Katyn, and decided that the question requires thorough additional study."[34]

Due to this Soviet intransigence, some Polish members of the commission threatened to resign, reflecting the fact that in Poland it was becoming increasingly possible to discuss Soviet-era political crimes. For example, according to a CBOS poll released in July 1988 (timed to coincide with Gorbachev's visit to Warsaw), among secondary school students who knew about the Katyn massacre, 68 percent blamed the USSR.[35] Still, Gorbachev did not admit Soviet responsibility during this trip. During a tense meeting with Polish intellectuals in Warsaw, he acknowledged that he was aware many Poles considered Katyn to be "the work of Stalin and Beria" but urged his audience to remember that this was not a foregone conclusion. He also emphasized that Katyn represented a "common tragedy," noting that there were two monuments next to the mass graves outside Smolensk—one dedicated to the Polish prisoners and the other to Red Army POWs "shot there by the fascists."[36] Further underscoring the emergence of severe historical differences between the two states, on March 7, 1989, Jerzy Urban, a spokesman for the Polish government, acknowledged that the Soviet NKVD was responsible for the killings.[37]

Riding this wave of political reforms, the commission's third session proved a linchpin for Polish collective memory in yet another regard. Prior to the meeting, commission members had prepared a joint report on the outbreak of the Second World War. The report was significant due to its confirmation of the existence of the secret protocol attached to the Molotov-Ribbentrop Pact, which enabled the Soviet annexation of eastern Poland. This served as an indication that the Soviet Foreign Ministry under Eduard Shevardnadze no longer felt the need to zealously protect Stalin's foreign policy record (although Włodzimierz Kowalski, a Polish member of the commission, had already published the relevant text in 1987).[38]

As Valkenier pointed out, the report was factually accurate and well-documented. The Soviet side, however, continued arguing that, due to geopolitics, the USSR had no choice but to sign a nonaggression pact with Germany. This proved a hard sell in Poland, which was less interested in "broader issues of international diplomacy."[39] Underscoring the politicized nature of the commission's work, this report was not made public until May 25, 1989. It was released shortly before the first semi-free elections in Poland since 1945 to show that the government led by the Polish United Workers' Party (PZPR) was not merely a Soviet puppet. Still, as the commentary accompanying its publication in *Trybuna Ludu* attests, it essentially amounted to a plea to the Polish electorate not to undermine Poland's alliance with the USSR.[40]

Planned for May–June 1989, a fourth plenary session never materialized. The commission was disbanded soon thereafter due to the collapse of the PZPR's hegemonic position in Poland, and in July 1990, the new Mazowiecki government dissolved the Polish Academy of Social Sciences and forced Maciszewski into retirement.[41]

In retrospect, the commission did little to reconcile the historical perspectives of the two states; this was mainly due to the ideological and political undercurrents that informed their respective positions, particularly on the Soviet side. It did, however, bring into sharp relief the interpretive divides between Poland and Russia, which provided the impetus for the Polish side to pursue a line of historical inquiry that would have been impossible just scant years before. In this respect, while initially convened to provide a "pressure valve" for intersocietal tensions and intended to bolster the legitimacy of the PRL and the USSR, the commission ultimately took on a life of its own.

In particular, it also established a precedent for later Polish-Russian discussions over shared history, although one wherein the expression of Polish grievances predominated. Given that twentieth-century geopolitics provided the Soviet Union with more opportunities to victimize Poles than the reverse, it is not surprising that the Polish side largely drove the agenda of the commission and repeatedly pressed for "truth concessions" from the Soviet side. As a result, the latter found itself consistently on the defensive, which ended up generating considerable resentment. Moreover, this resentment carried over into the post-Soviet period as the perception took root that the Polish side was acting unreasonably in asking Russia to admit responsibility for anything and everything associated with the Soviet regime.[42]

The Polish-Russian Group on Difficult Matters: A Failed New Beginning

Russian president Vladimir Putin's first visit to Poland in January 2002 came at a time of mounting tensions between the two neighbors. In a calculated move, Putin arrived on the eve of Liberation Day, the day Soviet forces finally wrested

control of Poland from the Nazis. Prior to the visit, the Polish media had speculated that Putin would offer an apology for Katyn; when this did not happen,
it provoked a negative public reaction. Meanwhile, the Russian political establishment was growing uneasy with the equivalence increasingly being drawn by
many in Poland between Nazism and Stalinism. Still, Putin's trip led to some
diplomatic progress, including an agreement to form the joint Polish-Russian
Group on Difficult Matters.

However, the inaugural version of this group only met twice (once in 2002
and again in 2005) and produced no tangible results. Unlike the Polish-Soviet
Joint Commission that came before it and the 2008 body that replaced it—both of
which were dominated by academics—this version was largely composed of politicians and diplomats. In a candid 2016 discussion, Adam Daniel Rotfeld (who
was appointed to head the Polish side) admitted that the group "was condemned
to fail from the very beginning" because it was composed of high-ranking officials who "could not resolve the problems that are non-negotiable."[43] This still-
born effort also fell victim to rapidly worsening political relations between the
two countries.[44] Among the contributing factors were the advent of Ukraine's
Orange Revolution and Russia's retaliatory embargo on Polish meat imports.[45]
These tensions resulted from, among other reasons, Polish president Aleksander
Kwaśniewski backing Viktor Yushchenko in his attempt to have the results of the
first (falsified) 2004 Ukrainian election nullified (Putin supported Yushchenko's
opponent, Viktor Yanukovych).

Relations were further damaged by the March 11, 2005, announcement that
Russia's chief military prosecutor was closing the more-than-decade-long investigation into the Katyn massacre. The decision was made on the dubious grounds
that those who perpetrated the killings were all dead. Not only did the Russian
side refuse to release the bulk of the documents pertaining to the massacre (out
of 183 volumes assembled, 116 remained sealed as state secrets), but it also refused
to formally exonerate the victims or recognize Katyn as either a war crime or
a case of genocide (categories not subject to the statute of limitations under international law). Adding insult to injury, the final report only confirmed 1,803
deaths out of the almost 15,000 officers held in the three main internment camps.
The fate of the approximately 7,000 additional Poles held in prisons across the
western Soviet borderlands was not mentioned.[46]

The final nail in the coffin of this initial post-Communist attempt at bilateral
historical dialogue came when the center-right and nationalistic Law and Order
Party (PiS) won both the presidential and parliamentary elections in 2005, ensuring the Polish government would pursue a more aggressively anti-Russian historical politics. Not coincidentally, the group was only revived on the joint initiative
of then Polish foreign minister Radosław Sikorski and his Russian counterpart,
Sergei Lavrov, after the center-left Citizen's Platform (PO) gained control of the

Polish legislature in 2007, removing Jarosław Kaczyński (PiS) from the post of prime minister and replacing him with Donald Tusk (PO).

2008–13: Progress Despite Impediments

The Polish architects of reanimating the Group on Difficult Matters clearly had the example of postwar reconciliation with Germany in mind. According to Sikorski, the body was an "attempt to at least establish the facts of common history" as "our experience with the Germans is that we were able to reconcile truly when the Germans owned up to the facts."[47] Moreover, the 1965 letter seeking reconciliation sent by Polish bishops to their German counterparts—widely seen as a turning point in relations between the two nations—gives an indication of why members of the group were eager to involve the Polish Catholic Church and the Russian Orthodox Church in their efforts.

However, they were not oblivious to the substantial differences between Polish-German (and Russian-German) and Polish-Russian reconciliation efforts. As Rotfeld observed, Polish-German relations improved over recent decades not only because of international agreements, new joint institutions, and individual efforts "but, most importantly, thanks to the emergence of a new *community of interests*."[48] But in the case of Polish-Russian rapprochement, it is not just institutional, legal, and cultural differences that pose difficulties; an exacerbating factor is the absence of shared strategic objectives. As Sławomir Dębski notes, in Franco-German reconciliation efforts, both states had similar political aims, but in the case of Poland and Russia, common objectives are not intuitively obvious.[49] Building bridges to Russia is also more difficult because the "Russian people have a deep sense of having been a victim rather than a perpetrator."[50]

Unsurprisingly, media reports on the early work of the group revealed an entrenched political and societal distrust between the two nations. For example, on the cusp of its first meeting, an incendiary article in the Polish newspaper *Dzennik* speculated that the Russian side would accuse Poland of causing or prolonging the Second World War.[51] Likewise, on the occasion of the group's November 2008 meeting in Moscow, the official *Parlamentskaia gazeta* wondered why the Poles were so worked up about Katyn, musing that it was perhaps so that the "world will once again . . . see in Russia a monster, with an historical tragedy crossing over and becoming an instrument of contemporary politics?"[52]

Despite all these potential difficulties, Sikorski and Lavrov reached an agreement to reestablish the group during their December 2007 summit in Brussels, after which the former phoned Rotfeld and asked him to once again cochair the Polish side.[53] Rotfeld and Torkunov, who were already acquainted, first met in their new capacities in February 2008, also in Brussels.[54] When it came to prospective group members, Rotfeld reported that Torkunov proposed a number of

distinguished candidates, all of whom had limited expertise in Polish-Russian relations.[55] This led Rotfeld to volunteer the names of seven Russians he felt would
be good additions to the group's roster. Torkunov's agreement to include them
convinced Rotfeld that his Russian counterpart was serious about the endeavor
and willing to engage individuals "who are decent, honest, and with whom one
can discuss [matters] in a very open way."[56] At the same time, while the reformed
body was "far from servile" to the foreign policy goals of either state, according
to Artem Malgin, a Russian member of the group, it lacked a specific mandate.[57]
Defining the group's mission and goals was therefore effectively relegated to the
cochairs and members.

According to Rotfeld, the biggest challenge facing the revived body was the
existence of "two different narratives about the same facts and events."[58] Consequently, during the first plenary session, he proposed that group members "not
negotiate" over interpretations since "history means to tell the truth, and the
truth cannot be the subject of negotiation." The group thus resolved to operate
according to two fundamental principles: members would express their views as
individuals rather than state representatives, and all discussions were to be depoliticized.[59] Rotfeld and Torkunov also decided not to broach issues the group
had "no authority or authorization" to deal with, especially questions related to
property restitution and other financial matters. Instead, it was agreed that the
body would engage in drawing up "principled and realistic" policy recommendations with the aim of removing "historical obstacles from the agenda of current
politics" and putting together a collection of essays on the entangled history of
the two countries "that would reach the widest possible audience."[60]

What emerged from these conversations was a list of fifteen historical problems the group agreed to address. The resultant edited volume would feature
parallel articles articulating the views of the Polish and Russian researchers
on each of the following topics: Polish-Soviet relations in 1917–21; the interwar
period; the causes of the Second World War; the Soviet incursion into Poland
in 1939–41; the 1940 Katyn massacre; the Second World War; the first postwar
decade, 1945–55; the Thaw/Twentieth Communist Party Congress; the dissident
movement; the Soviet Union and martial law in 1980–81; post-Communist
transformations in Poland and Russia; Polish-Soviet economic relations;
Polish-Russian relations since 1990; mutual perceptions of Poles and Russians;
and access to archives.

Many topics on the list were the same as those the Polish-Soviet Joint Historical Commission had considered previously. In particular, the matter of the
Katyn massacre once again assumed center stage for the Polish side, with Rotfeld
explaining that "without resolving this issue we will not be able to move forward."[61] Torkunov also sought closure regarding Katyn yet remarked that the
Russians were not going to just respond to Polish accusations. Instead, he invited

group members to "raise questions, especially regarding the general role of totalitarian regimes in Europe in the 1920s and 1930s, including in Poland."[62]

According to the 2015 English-language edition of *White Spots–Black Spots*, a total of twelve full meetings of the group took place between June 2008 and November 2013, alternating between Russia and Poland. A thirteenth meeting was scheduled to take place in Lublin in May–June 2014, but the Ukrainian crisis, and Russia's annexation of Crimea, caused it to be postponed indefinitely.[63]

Three takeaways stand out in connection with these sessions. First, the topics the group considered evolved significantly over time. Second, its members had sustained contact with representatives of both the Polish Catholic Church and the Russian Orthodox Church and tried to involve them in their work. Finally, group members—and the cochairs especially—interacted frequently with leading political figures in Poland and Russia.

Regarding the topics under consideration, earlier meetings generally focused on the interwar period and the Second World War. (It was not exclusively Polish concerns that drove the agenda; the Russian side also urged discussion of issues relevant to them, such as Red Army soldiers who died in Polish custody during the Polish-Bolshevik War.) However, following the publication of the edited volume in 2010, the group's deliberations expanded well beyond its original remit. For example, during the 2011 meeting in Riga, discussions centered on EU-Russia relations and an upcoming conference on Russia's Time of Troubles (1598–1613). Matters related to European security and cooperation also began to feature prominently in later meetings.

This broadening of the topics under consideration suggests that by 2011 or so, the group's members felt they had accomplished as much as they possibly could with respect to the Katyn massacre and the Molotov-Ribbentrop Pact. New challenges, however, soon arose in Polish-Russian relations. During its meeting in Gdansk in 2013, for instance, the group took up the refusal of the Russian government to return the wreckage of the Tu-154 that crashed outside Smolensk in 2010 (two Polish group members, Andrzej Kremer and Andrzej Przewoźnik, were among the victims).

Concerning the group's contact with the Polish Catholic Church and the Russian Orthodox Church, the cochairs met with Metropolitan Hilarion of Volokolamsk in Moscow on April 24, 2009, and group members met with Cardinal Stanisław Dziwisz during the 2009 Krakow plenary session. This laid the groundwork for Patriarch Kirill's visit to Poland in August 2012 (the first such visit in some thousand years).[64] This led the churches to issue a joint message concerning the need for forgiveness and reconciliation that echoed the 1965 Polish-German communication.

Meanwhile, the political importance attached to the work of the group manifested in frequent contacts between its members and top figures in both governments. For example, at the time of the first plenary session in Warsaw (June 12–14, 2008), the cochairs were received first by Polish president Lech Kaczyński and then by Sikorski and Tusk. They subsequently also met with Lavrov as part of the October 27–28, 2008, plenary session in Moscow.[65] Likewise, on April 7, 2010, Rotfeld and Torkunov sat down with Tusk and Putin (at the time Russia's prime minister) while they were in Smolensk to commemorate the seventieth anniversary of the Katyn massacre. Other political figures who took an interest in the group's work included Lech Wałęsa and then Polish president Bronisław Komorowski. In addition, the group also maintained regular contact with the Polish-Russian Civic Forum (chaired on the Polish side by the movie director Krzyztof Zanussi and on the Russian side by Leonid Drachevskii, former ambassador to Poland), which provided a "convenient channel through which to inform the general public about the work of the group."[66]

Judging the lasting legacy of the Polish-Russian Group on Difficult Matters is a complex endeavor. Torkunov once characterized the group's efforts as "academic diplomacy," noting that such bilateral bodies not only have to be professional, but also "influential within their own countries," to be effective. He went on to aver that political leadership is decisive in determining whether efforts at rapprochement and reconciliation succeed or fail, observing that many present-day problems involving history stem primarily from their politicization.[67] Consequently, assessing what this body did or did not manage to achieve must be considered with these caveats in mind. No matter how well group members got along (according to Rotfeld, squabbles more frequently arose within the ranks of Poles or Russians than across national divides) or what narratives about the past they agreed on, Polish-Russian relations in the realm of memory have always been contingent on geopolitics.[68]

Many of the projects proposed (these generally involved publications) during the group's tenure never came to fruition. But other initiatives did. For example, parallel Polish-Russian and Russian-Polish Centers for Dialogue and Understanding, the establishment of which was advocated in a June 22, 2009, letter signed by Rotfeld and Torkunov, were eventually created.[69] However, while both centers still exist under the aegis of their respective Ministry of Culture, in recent years they have increasingly worked at cross-purposes, without reciprocal cooperation.[70]

Similarly, the group seemingly played a role in bringing about the joint visit of Putin and Tusk to the Katyn Forest on April 7, 2010, to mark the anniversary of the massacre.[71] (However, this is not the only factor that made Moscow soften its policy line on Katyn; according to a leaked memorandum from February 2010, Russian officials had come to believe that Poland was using unresolved questions over the massacre to block progress on Russian-EU relations.)[72] Further rapprochement was evinced in the wake of the April 10, 2010, Smolensk disaster, when both sides again made a concerted effort to put the matter of Katyn behind them. As a result, on November 26 of that year, the Russian Duma passed its first resolution denouncing Stalin and condemning Katyn as a political crime.[73] And in November 2011, assurances were given by the then Russian ambassador to Poland, Alexander Alekseev, that a decision had already been made "at the highest levels" to formally rehabilitate the Poles killed in the massacre and release the remaining classified records pertaining to it. However, ultimately nothing came of this, and within a span of months, relations reverted to the previous status quo on historical matters.[74]

Similarly, the legacy of the 1919–21 Polish-Bolshevik War, specifically as it concerns the captured Red Army soldiers who perished while in Polish custody, has not been laid to rest despite the group's considerable attention to the matter. Since the early 1990s, this issue has served as a sort of moral "anti-Katyn" for Russian politicians, who have disputed not only the number of prisoners who died but also the conditions of their incarceration.[75] While mainstream historians (including the group's Russian members) agree that the deaths resulted from poor living conditions and contagious diseases rather than orchestrated attempts at extermination, this interpretation has not always been accepted in Russia. Although the 2010 publication provides estimates of the number of prisoners who perished that range from sixteen or seventeen thousand (according to Polish researchers) to twenty-five or twenty-eight thousand (according to the Russian account), this has not prevented Russian politicians and journalists from routinely citing figures several times higher.[76] Meanwhile, in February 2015, the Russian Ministry of Culture pledged that expanded museum complexes at Katyn and Mednoe (both burial sites associated with the 1940 massacre) would also address the fate of the Red Army soldiers held in Polish camps two decades earlier as a way of demonstrating Polish crimes against the Russian nation.[77]

Undoubtedly, however, the major impediment to the group's work was rapidly deteriorating Polish-Russian relations over Ukraine. Rising tensions not only resulted in a cessation of the group's activities but also led to the cancellation of the cross-cultural celebrations planned for 2015 (a Polish Year in Russia and a Russian Year in Poland). But bilateral relations had already been deteriorating for some time prior to the 2013–14 Maidan protests. In particular, Moscow became less conciliatory on issues related to history after Putin regained the presidency in 2012 (many Poles were supportive of the 2011–13 Bolotnaya protests in Moscow). Meanwhile, soon after the Smolensk tragedy, conspiracy theories surrounding the crash began to circulate in Poland. Promoted by prominent figures such as Jarosław Kaczyński and former foreign minister Ana Fotyga, they rejuvenated mistrust of Moscow's motives.[78] This trend has been further exacerbated since 2015, when PiS regained power. As Rotfeld observed in 2016, "neither Russians nor Poles are ready now to enter into dialogue . . . for the [sic] reasons of a very internal nature."[79]

2017 Redux: A Victim of History or Politics?

On March 9, 2017, then foreign minister Witold Waszczykowski announced that the Polish side was relaunching its half of the Group on Difficult Matters with a new membership. He emphasized that, despite the tensions that exist between them, "Russia and Poland are neighbors, and substantive dialogue that overcomes stereotypes lies in our mutual interest."[80] Historian Mirosław Filipowicz was announced as the new Polish cochair. During the inauguration ceremony, Filipowicz stressed that the gesture was meant to demonstrate Poland's willingness to maintain "non-political communication channels with the Russian side."[81] (Waszczykowski admitted in a 2017 interview that the only regular contacts the two sides still maintained were over Poland's UN Security Council status.)[82]

In a candid June 2018 interview with the author, Filipowicz revealed he was surprised that Deputy Foreign Minister Marek Ziółkowski had asked him to head the renewed group during a fall 2016 meeting in Warsaw, as he was not a "person connected to the new government."[83] According to Filipowicz, he was promised autonomy in constituting the Polish side of the group and selecting prospective topics.[84] However, he also agreed with the Foreign Ministry's suggestion to not raise difficult issues in talks with the Russian side in order to see if a more far-ranging breakthrough in bilateral relations could be achieved.

On the day of Waszczykowski's announcement, Filipowicz reports that he wrote a letter to Torkunov informing him that the Polish side was reconstituting the group and offering to meet in either Warsaw or Moscow. They eventually ended up meeting in Moscow at MGIMO, along with Alexander Chubarian (the head of the Institute of World History of the Russian Academy of Sciences, with whom Filipowicz had already been cooperating on a joint Polish-Russian textbook project) and Vladimir Grigoriev of the Federal Agency on Press and Media (Rospechat). During that meeting, Torkunov informed him that he was willing to be a member of the revived group but not its cochair. Filipowicz reported that it seemed as if everyone was waiting on the Russian Foreign Ministry to decide on whether to proceed.

As regards its broader vision, Filipowicz claims he saw no need for any new iteration of the group to return to the questions raised during Rotfeld's tenure. Instead, he stressed the need to seek nonconventional ways of breaking Polish-Russian stereotypes by highlighting "positive episodes" in Polish-Russian relations as an antidote to the political rhetoric swirling in Poland around the Smolensk crash and allegations that it had been an assassination. Filipowicz likewise observes that, from a scholarly standpoint, the matters of Katyn and the Polish-Bolshevik War POWs are closed. Thus, the fundamental issues remaining in Polish-Russian relations concern the need to break unfortunate mutual stereotypes and disagreements over how to characterize the 1939 Soviet annexation of eastern Poland.

In selecting the group's Polish members, Filipowicz (who consulted with Rotfeld on the matter) notes that he was guided by the following three criteria: his personal trust in the individuals in question, their practical usefulness, and the expertise they brought with them. He also wanted to demonstrate to the Russian side that he was willing to upend the status quo, a decision reflected in the appointment of a Polish Orthodox theologian, Fr. Prof. Henryk Paprocki, to the group. An additional interesting detail Filipowicz shared was that initially the Polish members of the group met regularly with Deputy Foreign Minister Bartosz Cichochki and other Polish officials to discuss matters related to Russia.

Ruminating on the stalled effort to reconstitute the group, Filipowicz opined that neither side had thought the process through. He speculated that either the Poles caught the Russians unaware with their announcement or the Russian side was deliberately trying to hamper Polish efforts. He also cited Poland's declining relevance for Russian geopolitics given its weakened position in the EU and increasingly problematic relations with the United States and Israel over its adoption of a contentious memory law in January 2018 (which was interpreted as an attempt to whitewash less-than-valorous behavior on the part of some Poles during the Second World War), all of which further reduced Russian motivations to cooperate.

Moreover, while Filipowicz agreed that Russian actions in Ukraine were not helping bilateral relations, he noted that neither were those of Ukrainian or Polish nationalists. As a result, he stated that "if we were to think only about intergovernmental contacts, I would be 100 percent pessimistic" about the group's chances of success. However, he did not rule out the possibility that, if the Foreign Ministry saw fit to change the scope of the group, it might be possible to cooperate with nongovernmental entities in Russia.

Russia, however, did not reciprocate the efforts of the Polish side, apparently desiring the normalization of diplomatic relations before resuming bilateral discussions over historical matters. Meanwhile, in late November 2018, the Polish government dissolved the IEŚW, replacing it with a government-backed think tank focused on Central European (i.e., not Russian) issues.[85] Filipowicz—who had made it clear that he would view the closure of IEŚW as a vote of no confidence in him personally—resigned from the leadership of the group soon afterward.

Conclusion

The deliberations of the Polish-Russian Group on Difficult Matters did not principally concern facts and events. The facts, in most cases, had been known for years. What was important was juxtaposing Polish and Russian perceptions and different historical interpretations of the same facts. Counterintuitively, the Polish and Russian academics had fairly convergent views on the most sensitive and difficult historical issues (e.g., the Katyn massacre, the Molotov-Ribbentrop Pact, the Red Army's invasion and incorporation of eastern Poland, etc.). However, it was much tougher to communicate a nuanced understanding of the historical evidence to millions of Poles and Russians. This proved beyond the group's abilities.[86]

In many respects, Poland and Russia are neighbors that do not really know one another. Despite sharing a border, high-level state visits are rare (the last visit of a Russian president to Poland occurred in December 2010; the previous took place in January 2002). All this has contributed to mutual distrust and an inability to resolve controversies over the past that continue to afflict Polish-Russian relations at the official level. It has also reinforced negative stereotypes on both sides, making it more difficult to accept alternate viewpoints at the societal level. As Marek Radziwon pointed out, while experts have examined episodes such as Katyn in great detail, that knowledge has not trickled down into mass consciousness, rendering the past a still-potent source of conflict.[87] So the question is not just how to reconcile historical narratives but how to attenuate the use of history for political purposes.

Answering this may prove a tall order. It is difficult to imagine how genuine dialogue about the past can occur in countries like Russia and Poland, which are increasingly turning away from liberalism and the pluralistic discourse it fosters. While the Russian side has, in the words of Sikorski, "reverted to an imperial use of history for the greater glory of the Russian state," Poland has also moved in a more nationalist direction in recent years.[88]

At the same time, the historical sources of political conflict between Poland and Russia have not changed all that much over the years. Many of them (along with their attendant rhetoric) trace back to the same issues that were fomenting discord during the time of the Polish-Soviet Joint Historical Commission. This speaks to the tendency of historical controversies to become politically entrenched and amplified, rather than defused, over time.

Ironically, in the end, a group established for the purpose of advancing bilateral relations became the victim of geopolitics. Saddled with the dual and arguably incompatible mandate of fulfilling both a political and a historiographical function, the members of the Polish-Russian Group on Difficult Matters were frequently able to reach consensus on the historical facts or at least accept divergent interpretations of those facts. This principle of compromise, however, did not translate into political or societal reconciliation. Historians may reach well-considered conclusions, but politics may make it impossible for those conclusions to ever resonate more widely.[89]

Notes

1. Andreas Huyssen, ed., *Present Pasts: Urban Palimpsests and the Politics of Memory,* (Stanford, CA: Stanford University Press, 2003), 3.

2. George Soroka and Félix Krawatzek, "Nationalism, Democracy, and Memory Laws," *Journal of Democracy* 30, no. 2 (April 2019): 157–71; and George Soroka, "Combative Pasts: The Politics of History in Post-Communist Europe," *New Eastern Europe* 25, no. 1 (2017): 108–15.

3. See Félix Krawatzek and George Soroka, "Bringing the Past into the Present: Towards a New Social Scientific Research Agenda," *Journal of Politics* 80, no. 4 (October 2018): e74–e79.

4. As cited in Ariadna Rokossovskaia, "V MID RF otvetili na zaiavleniia Polshi o dvustoronnem dialoge," *Rossiiskaia gazeta,* March 23, 2017. Earlier that year, however, the Polish press reported—citing former diplomat Witold Jurasz—that the Russian side was interested in resuming cooperation on this front (Paweł Wroński, "MSZ odnawia Polsko-Rosyjską Grupę ds. Trudnych: Ale nie wszyscy zaproszeni chcą współpracować," *Gazeta wyborcza,* February 2, 2017).

5. The Russian side was never formally disbanded. "A. Torkunow nie będzie współprzewodniczył Polsko-Rosyjskiej Grupie do Spraw Trudnych," Dzieje.pl, March 21, 2017, https://dzieje.pl/aktualnosci/anatolij-torkunow-nie-bedzie-wspolprzewodniczyl -polsko-rosyjskiej-grupie-do-spraw.

6. Tomasz Stępniewski, personal communication, February 21, 2019.

7. On Katyn, see Alexander Etkind et al., *Remembering Katyn* (Malden, MA: Polity, 2012); Anna Cienciala et al., eds., *Katyn: A Crime without Punishment* (New Haven, CT: Yale University Press, 2008); and George Sanford, *Katyn and the Soviet Massacre of 1940: Truth, Justice and Memory* (New York: Routledge, 2005).

8. Adam D. Rotfeld and Anatolii W. Torkunov, eds., *Białe plamy–Czarne plamy: Sprawy trudne w relacjach polsko-rosyjskich (1918–2008)* (Warsaw: PISM, 2010), 11. See also the Russian edition, *Belye piatna–Chernye piatna: Slozhnye voprosy v rossiisko-polskikh otnosheniiakh* (Moscow: Aspekt, 2010), and the later English edition, *White Spots–Black Spots: Difficult Matters in Polish-Russian Relations, 1918–2008* (Pittsburgh, PA: University of Pittsburgh Press, 2015).

9. Priscilla B. Hayner, *Unspeakable Truths: Transitional Justice and the Challenge of Truth Commissions* (New York: Routledge, 2011), 11.

10. Alexander Karn, "Impossible History? Holocaust Commissions as Narrators of Trauma," *Yod: revue des études hébraïques et juives* 21 (2018): 2.

11. Karn, "Impossible History?"

12. Elazar Barkan, "Introduction: Historians and Historical Reconciliation," *American Historical Review* 114, no. 4 (2009): 901.

13. Barkan, "Introduction: Historians and Historical Reconciliation," 903.

14. Note: more than one answer was possible. TNS OBOP, "Kolektywna pamięć i niezałatwione sprawy z II wojny światowej," August 2009, http://tnsglobal.pl/archiv_files /K.058-09_Kolektywna_pamiec_i_niezalatwione_sprawy_z_II_wojny_swiatowej _Oo8ao9.pdf.

15. "Bolshoi terror i repressii," Levada Center, September 7, 2017, http://www.levada .ru/2017/09/07/16561/.

16. "Velikaia Otechestvennaia voina," Levada Center, June 22, 2017, http://www.levada.ru/2017/06/22/velikaya-otechestvennaya-vojna-2/.

17. Thomas U. Berger, *War, Guilt, and World Politics after World War II* (New York: Cambridge University Press, 2012), 13.

18. See Nikolay Koposov, *Memory Laws, Memory Wars: The Politics of the Past in Europe and Russia* (New York: Cambridge University Press, 2017).

19. Although Jaruzelski and Soviet general secretary Mikhail Gorbachev had already broached the topic when they met on April 27, 1985. See Thomas S. Szayna, "Addressing 'Blank Spots' in Polish-Soviet Relations," *Problems of Communism* 37, no. 6 (1988): 38–39.

20. The text appeared on April 22, 1987, in *Trybuna Ludu*. Translation as appears in Elizabeth K. Valkenier, "Historiography and Liberalization in Polish-Soviet Relations," *Final Report to the National Council for Soviet and East European Research* (August 1989), 66n8.

21. Elizabeth Kridl Valkenier, "Glasnost and Filling in the 'Blank Spots' in the History of Polish-Soviet Relations, 1987–1990," *Polish Review* 36, no. 3 (1991): 247. See also Valkenier, "Historiography," 6–8, and Szayna, "Addressing 'Blank Spots,'" 37–61.

22. Valkenier, "Historiography," 7.

23. See Jarema Maciszewski, "Słowo wstępne," in *Zbrodnia Katynska: Z prac polskiej części wspólnej Komisji Partyjnych Historyków Polski i ZSRR* (Warsaw: Akademia Nauk Społecznych, 1990), 24, and Georgii Smirnov, *Uroki minuvshego* (Moscow: Rosspen, 1997), 205.

24. Piotr Kwiatkowski and Andrzej Szpociński, "Badania sociologiczne nad świadomością historyczną," *Edukacja Polityczna* 12 (1988): 161, as cited in Valkenier, "Historiography," 66n6.

25. Jaruzelski, who became the chief of staff of the Polish Armed Forces in 1964 and Poland's minister of defense in 1968, recounts raising questions about Katyn with contacts in the Soviet military as early as the 1960s and 1970s. See "Słowo wstępne," in Jarema Maciszewski, *Katyn: Wydrzeć prawdę* (Pultusk, Poland: Akademia Humanistyczna im. A. Gieysztora, 2010), 9–10. He also reportedly raised the issue with Gorbachev on more than one occasion during the 1980s.

26. Valkenier, "Historiography," viii–ix.

27. Valkenier, "Historiography," ix. For instance, the Soviet side did not want to publish certain documents related to the Polish-Bolshevik War, fearing that publicizing Lenin's desire to export revolution would jeopardize Gorbachev's foreign policy.

28. Jaruzelski, "Ku nowym horyzontom," *Nowe Drogi* 7, no. 458 (July 1987): 5–19, as cited in Valkenier, "Glasnost and Filling in the 'Blank Spots,'" 250. A Russian-language version of the article appeared in *Kommunist* 11 (1987): 59–73.

29. Maciszewski, "Słowo wstępne," in *Zbrodnia Katynska*, 3.

30. Valkenier, "Historiography," 16.

31. Georgi Smirnov, "Returning to the Lessons of the Past," *New Times* 35 (September 2, 1987): 20–21. Indicative of Polish sensitivities on the matter, Molotov's comment is often translated into Polish as the "bastard of the Versailles Treaty."

32. Headed by the prominent academician Nikolai Burdenko, this body was convened in January 1944 to counter accusations that the Soviet Union was responsible for the killings. After a rushed "investigation," the commission concluded that the Nazis were the actual culprits. The report also claimed that German troops executed some five hundred Soviet POWs in the Katyn Forest, making it a tragic place for both sides (although this assertion has not been corroborated and appears to be apocryphal).

33. Valkenier, "Historiography," 24.

34. "Sotrudnichestvo istorikov," *Pravda*, December 3, 1988; it was simultaneously published in the December 3–4, 1988, edition of *Trybuna Ludu*.

35. Valkenier, "Glasnost and Filling in the 'Blank Spots,'" 252–53.

36. Mikhail Gorbachev, *Inteligencja wobec nowych problemów socjalizmu: spotkanie Michaiła Gorbaczowa z przedstawicielami polskiej inteligencji* (Warsaw: KiW, 1988), 89.

37. Valkenier, "Glasnost and Filling in the 'Blank Spots,'" 253; "Historiography," 24. Valkenier cites excerpts from Urban's comments, which originally appeared in *Trybuna Ludu* on March 8, 1989.

38. Valkenier, "Glasnost and Filling in the 'Blank Spots,'" 254n14. Nonetheless, it was not until February 1990 that the Soviet Union acknowledged its existence.

39. Valkenier, "Glasnost and Filling in the 'Blank Spots,'" 254.

40. Valkenier, "Glasnost and Filling in the 'Blank Spots,'" 255–56. It simultaneously appeared in *Pravda* and *Trybuna Ludu* on May 25, 1989.

41. Reportedly, in the fall of 1990 Soviet academics unsuccessfully proposed that the commission be reconstituted (Valkenier, "Glasnost and Filling in the 'Blank Spots,'" 266–67).

42. See Georgii Smirnov, "O 'belykh piatnakh,'" *Pravda*, March 12, 1988.

43. Adam Daniel Rotfeld talk at IWM Vienna, "Poland, Ukraine, Russia: Difficult Past, Uncertain Future," October 10, 2016, http://www.iwm.at/events/event/russia-ukraine -poland-difficult-past-uncertain-future/.

44. Rotfeld and Torkunov, *White Spots–Black Spots*, 2.

45. Sławomir Dębski, "V poiskakh dialoga s Rossiei," *Novaia Polsha*, December 2011, https://www.novayapolsha.pl/pdf/2011/12.pdf.

46. V. K. Kondratov, "Otvet GVP GP RF na obrashchenie Obshchestva 'Memorial' po voprosu o Katynskom rassledovanii," Military Chief Prosecutor's Office, March 24, 2005. https://runivers.ru/doc/d2.php?SECTION_ID=6776&CENTER_ELEMENT _ID=147368&PORTAL_ID=7138.

47. Author's interview with Radosław Sikorski, April 18, 2018.

48. Adam Daniel Rotfeld, "Strategy for Reconciliation: Concept-Process-Experience" (keynote speech, OSCE workshop, Towards a Strategy for Reconciliation in the OSCE Area, Vienna, December 18, 2012). Emphasis in original.

49. Sławomir Dębski, "Historical Reconciliation—Lessons Learned and Best Practices" (OSCE workshop, Towards a Strategy for Reconciliation in the OSCE Area, Vienna, December 18, 2012).

50. Rotfeld, "Strategy for Reconciliation."

51. Marcin Wojciechowski, "Reaktywacja trudnych rozmów z Rosją," *Gazeta wyborcza*, June 14, 2008.

52. Nikolai Dorofeev, "Voprosy slozhnye: A otvety?," *Parlamentskaia gazeta*, November 11, 2008.

53. Rotfeld, "Poland, Ukraine, Russia."

54. Rotfeld and Torkunov, *White Spots–Black Spots*, appendix A.

55. Rotfeld, "Poland, Ukraine, Russia."

56. Rotfeld, "Poland, Ukraine, Russia."

57. Artem Malgin, "Ottolknutsia ot proshlogo i poiti vpered," *Ekspert*, April 12, 2010, 63.

58. As cited in Judy Dempsey, "Not Yet Buried: Polish-Russian Rapprochement," Carnegie Europe, August 25, 2014, http://carnegieeurope.eu/strategiceurope/56446.

59. Rotfeld, "Poland, Ukraine, Russia."

60. Rotfeld and Torkunov, *White Spots–Black Spots*, 4–5.

61. As cited in Valerii Masterov, "Tolko pravda," *Vremia novostei*, October 30, 2008.

62. Interfax interview conducted on June 15, 2008, by Peter Cheremushkin (personal correspondence with Cheremushkin, December 14, 2018).

63. "Polish-Russian Contact Group Postpones Meeting—Again," *Polish Express*, March 30, 2015, https://en.polishexpress.co.uk/polish-russian-contact-group-postpones-meeting.

64. Rotfeld, "Poland, Ukraine, Russia."

65. As cited in Wacław Radziwinowicz, "Komisja polsko-rosyjska: wyjaśnijmy Katyń," *Gazeta wyborcza*, October 28, 2008.

66. Rotfeld and Torkunov, *White Spots–Black Spots*, 7.

67. Anatolii Torkunov, "Reconciliation-Rapprochement-Distress/Detente: Synonymous Notions" (OSCE workshop, Towards a Strategy for Reconciliation in the OSCE Area, Vienna, December 18, 2012).

68. Rotfeld, "Poland, Ukraine, Russia."

69. Ariadna Rokossovskaia interview with Adam Daniel Rotfeld ("Na obshchem iazyke," *Rossiiskaia gazeta*, July 17, 2012); Valerii Masterov interview with Rotfeld ("Otnosheniia mezhdu Polshei i Rossiei otiagoshchalis tem, chto liuboi trudnyi vopros stanovilsia politicheskim," *Vremia novostei*, October 6, 2010).

70. Marek Radziwon, "Polish-Russian Conflicts and Efforts Aimed at Reconciliation," *Yearbook of the Institute of East-Central Europe* 16, no. 2 (2018): 137, 139. The respective websites are http://www.cprdip.pl/centrum,o_nas.html and http://www.rospolcentr.ru/.

71. In marked contrast to 2010, in 2015 (which was also the fifth anniversary of the Smolensk crash), the Katyn Forest memorial was only visited by low-level delegations from Poland and Russia.

72. Konstantin Gaaze and Mikhail Zygar, "Let the Sun Shine Again," *Russkiy Newsweek*, May 10–16, 2010, as reproduced in *Johnson's Russia List*, 96.

73. State Duma, "Zaiavlenie Gosudarstvennoi Dumy Federalnogo Sobraniia Rossiiskoi Federatsii o Katynskoi tragedii i ee zhertvakh," November 26, 2010, http://pravo.gov.ru /proxy/ips/?docbody=&link_id=0&nd=102143155&intelsearch=&firstDoc=1&lastDoc=1.

74. As cited in Marcin Wojciechowski, "Rosjanie rehabilitują Katyn," *Gazeta wyborcza*, November 2, 2011. This allegedly constituted a preemptive attempt by Russia to ward off the consequences of an impending ruling by the European Court of Human Rights regarding the massacre that was expected to be detrimental to Russian interests. In 2011, the court had agreed to hear a case brought by the relatives of twelve Katyn victims (*Janowiec and Others v. Russia*) who claimed their rights were violated by the Russian authorities, whom they accused of not carrying out a proper investigation. However, the court's final decision on October 21, 2013, was not especially favorable for the Polish side. See Ireneusz Kamiński, "The Katyn Massacres before the European Court of Human Rights: From Justice Delayed to Justice Permanently Denied," *East European Politics and Societies* 29, no. 4 (November 2015): 784–810.

75. See Wacław Radziwinowicz's interview with Boris Nosov, "Szukanie anty-Katynia," *Gazeta wyborcza*, August 12–13, 2000.

76. Anatolii Anisimov, for example, claimed that "up to 130 thousand Red Army soldiers found their way into Polish prisons, out of whom few returned home alive" ("Zadushim drug druga: V obiatiiakh," *Parlamentskaia gazeta*, November 22, 2013).

77. "Rosja rozbuduje muzea w Katyniu i Miednoje: Powstanie tam kontrowersyjna wystawa," PolskieRadio.pl, January 30, 2016, http://www.polskieradio.pl/5/3/Artykul /1577015,Rosja-rozbuduje-muzea-w-Katyniu-i-Miednoje-Powstanie-tam-kontrowersyjna -wystawa.

78. Between 2012 and 2015, the percentage of those surveyed who believed the crash was "definitely" or "more likely than not" deliberately caused ranged from 25 to 33 percent. This was significantly tied to party affiliation: while the overall figure stood at 31 percent in early 2015, 58 percent of PiS supporters agreed with this contention while only 10 percent of PO supporters felt likewise. "Przed piątą rocznicą katastrofy smoleńskiej," *CBOS Komunikat z badań NR 49/2015* (April 2015).

79. Rotfeld, "Poland, Ukraine, Russia."

80. Polish Ministry of Foreign Affairs, "Polish-Russian Group for Difficult Matters Resumes Its Activities," March 9, 2017, https://www.msz.gov.pl/en/news/polish_russian _group_for_difficult_matters_resumes_its_activities?channel=www (site discontinued).

81. "Poland Is Ready to Work with Russia despite Difficulties," Radio Poland, August 7, 2017, http://archiwum.thenews.pl/1/10/Artykul/319793,Poland-ready-to-work-with-Russia -despite-difficulties-FM.

82. Galina Dudina interview with Witold Waszczykowski, "'Vzaimnosti i gotovnosti k dialogu my ne vidim,'" *Kommersant*, August 7, 2017.

83. Author's interview with Mirosław Filipowicz, June 21, 2018. Unless otherwise noted, all subsequent quotes and paraphrases of Filipowicz are from this interview.

84. This promise was not kept, as Waszczykowski eventually insisted that Katarzyna Pełczyńska-Nałęcz, the former ambassador to Russia, be removed from the list of potential group members. Reportedly, this was because Pełczyńska-Nałęcz had made comments critical of the PiS government.

85. See Małgorzata Domagała, "PiS likwiduje Instytut Europy Środkowo-Wschodniej. PO: Chodzi o czystkę," *Gazeta wyborcza*, November 30, 2018.

86. Rokossovskaia interview with Rotfeld, "Na obshchem iazyke."

87. Radziwon, "Polish-Russian Conflicts," 129–41.

88. Interview with Sikorski.

89. See, for instance, "Polemika: O trudnych relacjach polsko-rosyjskich," *Gazeta wyborcza*, October 16, 2015.

GEORGE SOROKA is Lecturer on Government and Assistant Director of Undergraduate Studies in the Government Department of Harvard University. He has recently published in *East European Politics and Societies, Foreign Affairs, The Journal of Democracy*, and *Problems of Post-Communism*. He is currently working on a book that examines how history has influenced contemporary political processes in France, Russia, Spain, and Ukraine.

11 The 1968 Invasion of Czechoslovakia: Return to the Soviet Interpretation

Štěpán Černoušek

THIS CHAPTER EXPLORES how the Prague Spring and the invasion of Czechoslovakia that followed are portrayed in today's Russia. The documentary *The Warsaw Pact: Declassified Pages*, broadcast in May 2015 on Rossiia One TV channel, provides a focal point for my analysis of revisionist history. I situate this documentary in the context of an evolving Russian discourse on the Soviet past and discuss further revisionist perspectives on the 1968 Czechoslovakia invasion.

The Russian Federation is currently undergoing extraordinary times. The annexation of Crimea in March 2014 and the armed conflict in the eastern part of Ukraine served as a trigger mechanism for Russia's president, Vladimir Putin, who terminated cooperation with the West and effectively declared a new epoch in Russian history. Russia's occupation of Crimea contravened international treaties and effectively broke with the tradition of the past seventy years during which no European state had annexed the territory of a neighboring state against its will. During his speech in the Kremlin announcing the "reunification" of Crimea with Russia, Putin contrasted it to US policy: "The United States of America prefer not to be guided by international law in their practical policies, but by the rule of the gun. They have come to believe in their exclusivity and exceptionalism, that they can decide the destinies of the world, that only they can ever be right."[1] Putin effectively adopted Cold War vocabulary and, by extension, Soviet rhetoric. Russia is using such rhetoric with increased frequency—for instance, in relation to historical events such as the Warsaw Pact 1968 invasion of Czechoslovakia.

The invasion of August 1968 came in the wake of the so-called Prague Spring. The Prague Spring was a period of political liberalization in Czechoslovakia ushered in during January 1968 due to changes in the Communist Party leadership. Among other substantial changes, the new authorities stopped censoring the press, gradually replaced functionaries at all levels, and indirectly sparked an unprecedented outpouring of cultural creativity. The first secretary of the Communist Party, Alexander Dubček, who embodied the Prague Spring, enjoyed tremendous popular support in Czechoslovakia. Dubček and his associates launched a process of democratization that involved handing over certain decision-making powers to democratically elected social structures. These changes prompted the moniker "socialism with a human face."

The Soviet leadership, which had underestimated the extent of Dubček's reforms, decided to use military force to forestall any potentially contagious effect of the Prague Spring on the rest of the Communist bloc. In addition, the Kremlin could not tolerate questioning the leadership role of the Soviet Union.

During the night of August 20–21, five armies of the Warsaw Pact launched Operation Danube. The military invasion of Czechoslovakia was led by the Soviet Union with the participation of troops from Poland, Bulgaria, Hungary, and East Germany (the latter military contingent did not cross the border). Of the member states of the Warsaw Pact—a Communist bloc military alliance founded in 1955 on the basis of the Treaty of Friendship, Cooperation, and Mutual Assistance—only Albania and Romania did not participate in the invasion.

During the invasion, some 6,300 tanks and as many as 500,000 ground troops were deployed to Czechoslovakia. In spite of the massive unarmed protests by Czechoslovak citizens, the Soviet Union ultimately reached its objective of stopping the democratization process in Czechoslovakia.

The Warsaw Pact: Declassified Pages Documentary

A majority of the Russian population receive their news from state-controlled television and therefore are vulnerable to propaganda. The documentary *The Warsaw Pact: Declassified Pages*, which projects the Soviet position on the occupation of Czechoslovakia in August 1968, effectively falls into the category of propaganda.

The documentary was broadcast on the main state TV channel, Rossiia One, on March 23, 2015.[2] The script was developed by screenwriter Marina Petukhova and director Dmitrii Ushakov for the All-Russian State Television and Radio Broadcasting Company, VGTRK, which owns Rossiia One. It was produced as part of a documentary series marking the seventieth anniversary of the Soviet victory over Nazi Germany. The forty-four-minute film features a ten-minute segment on the invasion of Czechoslovakia in August 1968.

Based on the classification of documentary films developed by Bill Nichols, *The Warsaw Pact: Declassified Pages* is an example of the expository mode and a combination of the historical model (depicting what happened, affixing interpretation or point of view), the witness model (witnesses describing their personal experiences), and the case defense model (evidence and examples serving to encourage a particular opinion).[3] However, in the case of the Rossiia One documentary, the last of the three models is compromised as the evidence and specific examples are all made up. *The Warsaw Pact: Declassified Pages* substantiates

Nichols's thesis that documentary films usually interpret evidence and facts in an expressive, compelling manner and render them from a particular perspective in a voice that is usually personal and passionate.[4] The main problem with the Rossiia One production is that much of the evidence and facts it cites are fabricated, meaning it does not match the standards of a documentary. Based on false facts, it is essentially an example of manipulation and propaganda.

The documentary as a whole conveys the idea that the Warsaw Pact was a meaningful military treaty that safeguarded a peace whose collapse should be regarded as unfortunate. The beginning of the film portrays Vladimir Lobov, chief of staff of the joint armed forces of the Warsaw Pact in 1989–91, who recalls the June 1990 negotiations on dissolving what the voice-over calls "one of the most powerful organizations in the twentieth century." Alongside brief appearances by one-time French foreign minister Roland Dumas and Horst Teltschik, then advisor to German chancellor Helmut Kohl—who unsentimentally describe the end of the Cold War—far more space is given to former East German defense minister Theodor Hoffmann, who nostalgically recalls brotherhood in arms, vodka-filled evenings, and funny stories depicting the Warsaw Pact solely as a guarantor of peace.[5]

Voice-over plays a key role in the documentary. A captivating voice informs the viewers that "throughout its existence the Warsaw Pact had been accused of aggression; naturally that accusation was made by another military pact, NATO."[6] When NATO is mentioned, the screen shows Soviet caricatures depicting ruthless American capitalists with blood on their hands. Whenever the Warsaw Pact comes into the picture, however, the viewers see peace posters featuring doves and similar imagery. Indeed, a giant dove is featured in the film's logo, which appears on screen over dramatic music. The logo with the dove is also incorporated into the captions.

The voice-over let the viewers know that, immediately after the defeat of Nazi Germany, the United Kingdom and the United States began preparing for war against the Soviet Union and were about to start "arming fascists again."[7] This is confirmed by Nikita Khrushchev's son, Sergei Khrushchev, who comments on a number of sequences in the film. On one particular occasion, he speaks of Winston Churchill's apparent "anti-Soviet and anti-Russian" sentiment. Sergei Khrushchev also discusses US plans to drop nuclear bombs on Soviet cities and put millions of Soviet citizens to the sword in the name of democracy. The narrator explains that this was only prevented by the USSR's development of strategic bombers and its own atomic weapons.

Vladimir Bruz, referred to as a "researcher into the history of the Warsaw Pact organization," appears throughout the documentary. At one point he blames the start of the Cold War on the United States, which was allegedly striving for world domination. This claim is driven home by the voice-over, which explains that Washington wished to spark a war with the Soviet Union on foreign territory, with Europe fitting the bill perfectly. Therefore, it began turning the European countries that later founded NATO against the USSR. The creation of the Warsaw Pact in 1955 was, according to the documentary, merely a response to the creation of NATO. A quarter of the way through the documentary, an infographic and the narrator's persuasive voice emphasize that the Warsaw Pact had fewer soldiers in Europe than NATO did. Furthermore, the former's technology was predominantly defensive while the latter's was offensive. "Just any expert would interpret these figures as proving the aggressive posture of the NATO and the defensive of the Warsaw Pact. Naturally, this kind of information never appeared in the Western popular press," argues the narrator.[8]

Vladimir Bruz later adds that the Western press constantly referred to Warsaw Pact aggression—using Hungary in 1956 and Czechoslovakia in 1968 as examples. "They didn't present any other arguments," says Bruz.[9] "Is it possible at all to regard the events of 1956 in Hungary and 1968 in Czechoslovakia as acts aggression by the Warsaw Pact?" asks the voice-over forcefully, preparing the way for a detailed examination of those events. While the filmmakers devote a mere thirty seconds to the events in Hungary—with Sergei Khrushchev explaining that Hungary was Germany's closest ally in the war and hence the Soviet Army was duty bound to ensure law and order there—they spent an entire ten minutes discussing the invasion of Czechoslovakia.

A Segment of the Documentary on the 1968 Invasion of Czechoslovakia: "Saving Peace and Stability"

The section involving the invasion of Czechoslovakia is central to the documentary. The filmmakers use this particular example—in fact the only specific example in the entire documentary—to prove the defensive and peacekeeping function of the Warsaw Pact.

Over shots of contemporary Prague, the narrator states that the "events in Czechoslovakia in 1968 proved a major test for the Warsaw Pact joint military forces." Iurii Sinelshchikov, currently a Russian Duma member for the Communist Party and formerly a soldier who took part in the invasion, explains, "They shot at us from the top [of the buildings] with a machine gun."[10] A clip from the 1969 Soviet propaganda film *Czechoslovakia: A Trial Year* rationalizes the invasion as follows: "They shot at the sons of those who had liberated them in 1945, and yet they're calling themselves patriots." Subsequently, Sinelshchikov describes where Soviet tanks took position in Wenceslas Square and how Czech citizens set them on fire.

I now turn to the events that preceded the invasion. The alleged NATO military exercises held in West Germany next to the border with Czechoslovakia, which also received attention from the makers of *Czechoslovakia: A Trial Year*, serve as the main point of reference. Sinelshchikov asserts that the Prague police had been mobilized in the spring of 1968 with the creation of a "shock unit, Club 231, so called because many of its members had been previously convicted under article 213 of the Law on the Defense of the Republic, including many former fascists, SS men, and Nazi collaborators."[11] The voice-over then adds that many today attempt to present the organization "as a regular opposition group, but it had much more in common with mercenaries."[12] Another clip from *Czechoslovakia: A Trial Year* tells of Czechoslovak border guards removing barriers at the border with West Germany and 368,000 West Germans settled on Czechoslovak territory six months prior to the invasion.

Vladimir Bruz justifies the invasion by referring to Socialist states' mutual protection duty. The voice-over declares, over bells ringing in the background, that an armed coup was being prepared in Prague. Footage from *Czechoslovakia: A Trial Year* shows weapons caches allegedly discovered in Prague and throughout the country, "with the help of which rabid enemies of the Czechoslovak people wanted to bring about a situation of unrestrained terror."[13] In the relatively lengthy segment that follows, Sinelshchikov goes through the range of weapons allegedly discovered.

In the next segment, the voice-over claims that protests against the occupation took place at just a handful of locations in downtown Prague. On the outskirts of Prague and in the countryside, Czechoslovak citizens expressed support for the occupation forces. In September 1968, on the eve of their departure, members of the invasion force received invitations from neighboring villages. Over romantic music, Vladimir Lobov, chief of staff of the joint armed forces of the Warsaw Pact in 1989–91, recalls all-night visits with locals who kissed and hugged them and filled their vehicles with baskets of food.[14] "The situation that arose in Prague in 1968 posed a threat to the entire Socialist bloc. That's why we acted as one, except Albania," explains the voice-over, bringing the film segment on Czechoslovakia to a climax.

The following segment, which returns to the dissolution of the Warsaw Pact in June 1990, is also of significance to this analysis. Lobov recalls Václav Havel speaking at the meeting and reportedly saying, "Gentlemen, I propose that instead of the three issues meant to be addressed here today we deal with only one—the dissolution of the Warsaw Pact."[15] He pauses for dramatic effect, his voice trembling with anger, while melodramatic, unsettling music plays in the background. Havel thus becomes one of the main culprits in the destruction of a guarantor of peace and stability, the Warsaw Pact.

At Odds with the Facts

The Warsaw Pact: Declassified Pages can be safely described as a misrepresentation and distortion. It manipulates the facts, gives no room for alternative opinions, and in some cases puts forward claims that are utterly mendacious.

Everything seems to serve a singular objective: the rehabilitation of the Warsaw Pact as a guarantor of peace and stability in the eyes of the Russian public. Subordinate to this is the use of music, documentary footage, and infographics that stress the Warsaw Pact's peaceful aims on the one hand and the negative political developments in Czechoslovakia, including the Prague Spring and the resolve of Czechoslovak citizens to defend it, on the other.

The sense of objectivity is created through the use of interviews, including with select foreigners. Yet the documentary gives no space to even one voice from the Czech Republic and/or Slovakia, despite the fact that the film was shot in Prague. Not a single Czech/Slovak historian or eyewitness is interviewed. Neither are any of the Russian historians who have provided a critical assessment of the August 1968 invasion and its causes and consequences.[16] In the view of Ondřej Tůma, director of the Institute of Contemporary History at the Czech Academy of Sciences, the documentary signifies a return to the most offensive methods of Soviet propaganda, which Moscow used in 1968 to justify a military intervention that under international law was nothing short of unprovoked aggression against a sovereign state. In his words, "It rehashes many discarded claims of preparations for an armed coup and weapons caches discovered by Soviet soldiers (these were in fact people's militia arms depots), NATO preparations for an active intervention in Czechoslovakia (throughout the entire 'Czechoslovak crisis' the West behaved with utter passivity), resistance to the invasion being restricted to central Prague (in reality, the resistance by Czechs and Slovaks was nationwide, determined, and intense, and it was only discontinued following the capitulation of the Czechoslovak leadership in Moscow), and so on."[17]

The documentary also ignores the fact that protests against the invasion and occupation of Czechoslovakia also took place within the Soviet Union. These protests were not confined to the best-known demonstration, by the so-called Magnificent Eight, in Red Square on August 25, 1968; hundreds of isolated protests took place throughout the Soviet Union.[18] The claim that Club 231 was a band composed of former fascists, SS men, and Nazi collaborators cannot be corroborated. Furthermore, the documentary makes no mention of the 108 civilian victims of the military invasion of Czechoslovakia in 1968.[19]

The glorification of the Warsaw Pact legacy says a great deal about today's Russia and its relationship to the Soviet past, of which it is evidently proud. A broader objective is to foster nostalgia, nurture a national myth of the positive role the Soviet Union played in the world, and ultimately vindicate Putin's current policies, which "just" put matters back on the right old track. As Jan Jaroš wrote about the misuse of film for Nazi and Communist propaganda: "Every nation, or respective state institution, happily refers to the glorious past . . . and, if necessary, in the interest of adding even greater luster, does not hesitate to unequivocally distort, fabricate, and even bamboozle it."[20] Today's Russia may be inadvertently fulfilling

Jaroš's definition of a totalitarian regime that prescribes "what is to be accepted as a positive legacy of the past and what, by contrast, is preassigned the role of a despised enemy that should—under ideal circumstances—be completely destroyed."[21]

Responses to the Documentary

Within a few days of its airing on Rossiia One, *The Warsaw Pact: Declassified Pages* was picked up by the Czech and Slovak media, sparking a huge response and popular indignation. The Slovak Ministry of Foreign Affairs was the first to react. In a statement on May 31, 2015, it said that "rewriting history and falsifying historical truth can damage mutual relations between the two countries."[22]

The Czech minister of foreign affairs, Lubomír Zaorálek, informed the Russian ambassador to the Czech Republic, Sergei Kiselev, that "we cannot permit the truth about the events of 1968 in Czechoslovakia to be crudely disrespected in this way." According to the minister, the ambassador attempted to downplay the importance of the film and emphasized the continued validity of statements by Soviet president Mikhail Gorbachev and his Russian successors who acknowledged Russian moral responsibility for the 1968 invasion of Czechoslovakia.[23]

The Russian documentary was also condemned by Czech president Miloš Zeman, who is otherwise indulgent toward Russia: "It [the invasion] wasn't a mistake, it was a crime. Of course I insist on that view. It is clear that journalistic intelligence, in this case involving Russian television, has gone to the dogs, because there obviously wasn't any attempt at an armed coup."[24]

The entity behind the documentary, VGTRK, rejected the Czech objections. "The documentary film *The Warsaw Pact: Declassified Pages* conforms to all the principles of journalism and was produced in accordance with ethical norms," stated VGTRK's director of international relations, Piotr Fiodorov. He continued, "The film expresses the views of historians, witnesses, and participants in those events. Nowhere is it stated in the running commentary that it [those views] is true and accurate. That many of the facts featured in the film are not to the liking of today's Central Europe is a different matter."[25]

The incensed Czech response was also registered by the Russian media, which devoted a surprising amount of space to it. Many editorials expressed understanding of the Czech reaction and surprise at Rossiia One's production. Headlines such as "Scandal: The Czech Republic and Slovakia Demand Explanation from Russia over Film on Invasion of Czechoslovakia" were common.[26] A well-known commentator, Andrei Kolesnikov, rhetorically inquired about the purpose of the film, which explained away the military invasion as preempting an alleged coup supported by the West and hence damaged relations with the Czech Republic and Slovakia: "The film was meant to draw a parallel to Kiev's Maidan. It is not intended for external, but internal audiences. Here Czechoslovakia is used merely to build a bridge between events of half a century ago and today. Who would believe that the Czechs may take offense? Do we ever remember that the year 1968 represents a historical trauma to both the Czechs and the Slovaks?"[27]

The Russian Perspective on 1968

Kolesnikov is correct to pinpoint that the events of August 1968 remain a trauma to Czech society that has fundamentally affected their country for decades to come, but for ordinary Russians, it is just one episode in a series of Soviet and/or Russian military interventions: Finland in 1939, Hungary in 1956, Czechoslovakia in 1968, Afghanistan in 1979, Chechnya in 1994 and 1999, Georgia in 2008, and Ukraine in 2014.

What happened in Czechoslovakia in 1968 receives little, if any, space in contemporary Russian history textbooks. One of the widely used textbooks—*Istoriia Rossii, 1945–2007* (History of Russia) by Alexander Filippov, Alexander Danilov, and Anatolii Utkin—presents the Prague Spring as an internal struggle within the Czechoslovak Communist Party, where the "progressives," with Alexander Dubček at the top, enjoyed major public support. The textbook interprets the military invasion as a consequence of mistrust of Czechoslovakia by other Warsaw Pact member states and plays it down as "armed troops crossing the border." The section on 1968 Czechoslovakia is introduced by the statement that the "Soviet Union suffered a moral and political defeat in a socialist camp country."[28] This is, of course, a step forward compared to the following Soviet-era textbook interpretation: "Imperialistic reaction and its agents attempted to pull Czechoslovakia away from the socialist camp. In that critical moment the Soviet Union and other Warsaw Pact countries helped the fraternal nation of Czechoslovakia to thwart the threat of restoration of capitalism."[29]

Still, no unequivocally critical consensus of the 1968 invasion developed in Russia following the collapse of the Soviet Union. According to a 2013 opinion poll conducted by the independent Levada Center in Moscow, nearly half of the Russians surveyed had never heard of the 1968 invasion. Only 14 percent viewed it as violent interference into the internal affairs of another country or as proof of the incompatibility of socialism and democracy.[30] Public ignorance has contributed to allowing the events of August 1968 to become a subject of manipulation aimed at reviving the Soviet legacy and thus boosting Russians' national pride.

Return to the Soviet interpretation of the 1968 events in Czechoslovakia has become more pronounced in recent years. Two edited volumes dealing with the suppression of the Prague Spring appeared in Russia in 2010. The independent Alexander Yakovlev Foundation published a book of thematic essays and documents—*"Prazhskaia vesna" i mezhdunarodnyi krizis 1968 goda* (the Prague

Spring and the international crisis of 1968)—that examines the events in Czechoslovakia from a broader European perspective.[31] The Russian Ministry of the Interior put together a selection of KGB documents, *Chekhoslovatskie sobytiia 1968 goda glazami KGB i MVD SSSR* (Czechoslovak events of 1968 from the perspective of the KGB and the Ministry of the Interior of the USSR).[32] The summary of the latter book projects an unreconstructed Soviet view on the events of August 1968: "The collection meticulously explains the planned and coordinated expansion of Western secret services against Czechoslovakia, which they regarded as a weak link in the strategic paradigm of the Eastern Bloc."[33]

This kind of rhetoric is increasingly making inroads in Russia and is sanctioned at the top. Thus, the official publication of the Russian National Guard, *Na boevom postu*, printed an article in 2017 titled "According to the Danube Plan." The article falsely claims that Czechoslovakia in 1968 was on the verge of a civil war that was only prevented by the military invasion and the exemplary conduct of the Soviet Army.[34]

A similar piece was published during President Miloš Zeman's official visit to Moscow in November 2017. This, too, sparked a major international scandal. During the first day of Zeman's visit, the radio and television station of the Russian Army, TV Zvezda, published an article by Leonid Maslovskii titled "Czechoslovakia Must Be Grateful to the USSR for 1968: The History of the Prague Spring."[35] Making use of Soviet rhetoric and contradicting the facts, the author claimed the military invasion of Czechoslovakia prevented a coup d'état masterminded by the West, preserved peace in Czechoslovakia for twenty-odd years, and showed there was "no better nation in the world than the Russians." Due to the fact that the article was published under the aegis of the Russian Ministry of Defense, the Czech media took it as an official Russian position. President Zeman rejected the tenet of the article and demanded an apology during a meeting with the Russian prime minister, Dmitrii Medvedev. The latter immediately apologized and stated that the text did not reflect the official position of the Russian government. The article vanished from the website of TV Zvezda and was replaced by another titled "Prague, 1968: A Cross-Generational Perspective."[36] This piece reflected the Czechoslovak position, referred to the condemnation of the invasion by the Soviet leadership in 1989, and, if coincidentally, highlighted the alleged heroism of Miloš Zeman during August 1968. Some in the Czech Republic even speculated that the entire issue had been jointly manufactured to alleviate the deep-seated suspicion that Zeman is openly pro-Russian.[37]

The Russian Ministry of Foreign Affairs, for its part, referred to the official Russian position on the 1968 invasion supposedly expressed in the 1993 Treaty on Cordial Relations and Cooperation between the Russian Federation and the Czech Republic.[38] The treaty's preamble speaks of a desire to draw a line under the totalitarian past and refers to the unacceptable use of force against Czechoslovakia in 1968 and the subsequent unlawful presence of Soviet troops on Czechoslovak territory.

The whole affair raises the essential question of the Russian Federation's official position on historical watershed events like 1968 Czechoslovakia. One may ask what takes priority: old treaties whose wording is not popularly known or contemporary publications by various Russian ministries. If the Russian government genuinely pays heed to the bilateral treaty with the Czech Republic, the article on the TV Zvezda website is in direct contravention of the position stated in the former document. However, the real issue lies elsewhere—namely, whether the Russian leadership takes notice of formal statements it made in the past in its current politics. Hence the discrepancy. The Russian state exercises nearly full control over media and yet permits the state channel, Rossiia One, to broadcast such documentaries as the 2015 *The Warsaw Pact: Declassified Pages*, which describes the 1968 invasion as safeguarding world peace and the Prague Spring as Western aggression. It is this televised interpretation that reaches millions of ordinary Russians, not the wording of a treaty from 1993. Coincidentally, in the very same 1993 treaty, Russia acknowledged the inviolability of European borders, yet twenty years later, in violation of that treaty, it unlawfully annexed part of Ukrainian territory. As has been proven then and again, the Russian state pays little attention to official documents, including bilateral treaties.

The Hungarian Uprising of 1956 as Another Example of Historical Revisionism in Russia

Almost identical mechanisms can be observed in the Russian state's view on the bloody suppression of the Hungarian Revolution. Between October 23 and November 10, 1956, a nationwide uprising against the Stalinist dictatorship and Soviet occupation took place in Hungary. The Soviet army was deployed against civilian protesters, who responded with armed resistance. As a result of the military crackdown, several tens of thousands of Hungarians (according to Hungarian sources) were killed.

While this is regarded as one of the most important events in twentieth century history in Hungary, 57 percent of Russians say they know nothing about it, and 28 percent perceive it as a counterrevolution and provocation by the West. Only 7 percent of Russians think of the events of 1956 as an uprising.[39] Alongside serious academic studies on the 1956 Hungarian uprising available in Russian, the official Russian publications smack of Soviet rhetoric. In 2009, the Russian Ministry of the Interior published a collection of documents (in Russian)—*The Hungarian Uprising in 1956 from a Perspective of the KGB and the Ministry of Interior of the USSR*—in which the anonymous editors argue that "Hungarian events were one of the first 'color' revolutions in history organized by US intelligent services."[40]

In the case of the Hungarian Uprising, this interpretation has been promoted on television. On the occasion of the sixtieth anniversary of the uprising—on October 23, 2016—one of the most watched Russian television propagandists, Dmitrii Kiselev, declared on his program *Vesti Nedeli* on the Rossiia Channel that the "anti-Soviet sentiment of the Hungarians were backed by Western intelligence officers who already then were developing a technology of transforming initially peaceful protests into bloody chaos, a pogrom. Essentially, the first ever color revolution, the 'orange revolution,' in a country [we consider] friendly to us took place in Hungary."[41]

The Hungarian government formally objected to such an interpretation by stating that "Hungary will not tolerate anyone speaking in a humiliating manner about the revolution and its heroes." The Russian Foreign Ministry subsequently declared that the official position of the Russian Federation on the events of 1956 had not changed and remained the same as President Vladimir Putin had previously stated.[42] During Putin's visit to Hungary in February 2006, he laid flowers on the memorial to the victims of the revolution and quoted Boris Yeltsin, who in 1992 condemned the Soviet leadership's decision to invade Hungary: "Today's Russia is not the Soviet Union, but I must openly say that we all have a sense of moral responsibility for these events."[43]

As in the case of the invasion of Czechoslovakia in 1968, the crucial issue here is that the vast majority of Russians are not aware of the formal government statements; the highly watched programs of Russian state television have a much greater impact. The executive director of Memorial, Elena Zhemkova, observed a tendency to shape the official position on events such as the Soviet intervention of Hungary in 1956 and Czechoslovakia in 1968 in accordance with the standard Soviet interpretation. Documentary films and positions put forward by a new generation of Russian propagandists serve as a testing ground for neo-Soviet rhetoric.[44]

Conclusion

Russian authorities did not hesitate to blatantly distort historical facts in recent years, cherry-picking Russian/Soviet achievements with a view to reinforce patriotism and cultivate an image of the Soviet Union as a progressive country whose "great" legacy is continued by today's Russia. This leads to a schizophrenic interpretation of history that fosters disregard for historical facts. In the case of the distorted view of the Warsaw Pact invasion of Czechoslovakia in 1968, the Russian government essentially holds a dual position. The dominant position—advanced through tendentious documentaries and articles in the Russian state-controlled media—is in line with the Soviet interpretation of "fraternal assistance" and is intended primarily for domestic audiences. However, when such an interpretation sparked indignation in the Czech Republic and Slovakia, as happened twice within the past few years, the Russian leadership dusted off lesser-known official documents condemning the invasion.

One of the problems is the lack of adequately publicized, state-supported information available to ordinary Russians. There has never been nationwide consensus in Russia on the need to condemn the Soviet regime as such. The same goes for individual, reprehensible acts by that regime, whether the military invasion of a foreign state or the exercise of political repression. While Czechs and Slovaks regard the military invasion of August 1968 as one of the most tragic events in the twentieth century, in Russia it is considered merely one of many historical episodes. Half the Russian population does not even know about it, while among those who do, only 14 percent evaluate it negatively. Cultivated ignorance makes the events of August 1968 in Czechoslovakia an attractive subject for Russian domestic propaganda to boost patriotic sentiment. The unfortunate tendency in today's Russia to uncritically reflect on the past may have grave consequences for the future.

Notes

1. See Vladimir Putin, "Obrashchenie Prezidenta Rossiiskoi Federatsii," March 18, 2014, http://kremlin.ru/events/president/news/20603.

2. See documentary at "Varshavskii Dogovor: Rassekrechennye stranitsy," Rossiia One, April 27, 2016, video, 44:00, https://www.youtube.com/watch?v=p6V-oD1T070&ab&ab_channel=ДмитрийУшаков.

3. Bill Nichols, *Úvod do dokumentárního filmu* (Prague: AMU, 2010), 164–67.

4. Nichols, *Úvod do dokumentárního filmu*, 162–63.

5. *The Warsaw Pact: Declassified Pages.*

6. *The Warsaw Pact: Declassified Pages.*

7. *The Warsaw Pact: Declassified Pages.*

8. *The Warsaw Pact: Declassified Pages.*

9. *The Warsaw Pact: Declassified Pages.*

10. *The Warsaw Pact: Declassified Pages.*

11. *The Warsaw Pact: Declassified Pages.*

12. *The Warsaw Pact: Declassified Pages.*

13. *The Warsaw Pact: Declassified Pages.*

14. *The Warsaw Pact: Declassified Pages.* The Soviet Army did not formally leave Czechoslovakia until 1991.

15. *The Warsaw Pact: Declassified Pages.*

16. See, for example, Nikita Petrov, "The KGB and the Czechoslovak Crisis in 1968," in *Invaze 1968: Ruský pohled*, ed. Josef Pazderka (Prague: Institute for the Study of Totalitarian Regimes, Torst, 2011), 130–46; Natalia Tomilina et al., *"Prazhskaia vesna" i mezhdunarodnyi krizis 1968 goda* (Moscow: Mezhdunarodnyi fond "Demokratiia," 2010).

17. Ondřej Tůma's statement broadcast by the Czech News Agency, May 29, 2015, http://www.usd.cas.cz/wp-content/uploads/2015/05/vyjadreni_pro_CTK.pdf.

18. A research project of the Institute for the Study of Totalitarian Regimes in Prague examined protests against the occupation of Czechoslovakia within the USSR. Cf. "Protesty proti okupaci československa v roce 1968 v zemích varšavské smlouvy," 2008, http://www.ustrcr.cz/cs/protesty-proti-okupaci-ceskoslovenska-v-roce-1968. The eight individuals who staged the public protest in Moscow were Larisa Bogoraz, Konstantin Babitskii, Vadim Delaunai, Vladimir Dremliuga, Pavel Litvinov, Natalia Gorbanevskaia, Viktor Fainberg, and Tatiana Baeva.

19. Milan Bárta et al., *Victims of the Occupation* (Prague: Institute for the Study of Totalitarian Regimes, 2008).

20. Jan Jaroš, "Film ve službách hnědé i rudé totality," in *Film a dějiny 2: Adolf Hitler a ti druzí—filmové obrazy zla*, ed. Petr Kopal (Prague: Institute for the Study of Totalitarian Regimes, 2009), 45.

21. Jaroš, "Film ve službách hnědé," 47.

22. "Slovenské ministerstvo zahraničí: Ruská reportáž o invazi v roce 1968 poškozuje vzájemné vztahy," *Hospodářské noviny*, May 31, 2015.

23. "Zaorálek se sešel s ruským velvyslancem, zkritizoval seznam," Aktuálně, June 1, 2015, http://zpravy.aktualne.cz/domaci/zaoralek-pozval-velvyslance-ruska-chce-resit-seznam-a-film/r~33e39448084f11e5b5ba0025900fea04/.

24. "Zeman obsoudil lži v dokumentu ruské televize o okupaci Československa v srpnu 1968," irozhlas, June 3, 2015, http://www.rozhlas.cz/zpravy/politika/_zprava/zeman-odsoudil-lzi-v-dokumentu-ruske-televize-o-okupaci-ceskoslovenska-v-srpnu-1968--1497638.

25. "VGTRK otvergla pretenzii Chekhii i Slovakii k filmu Varshavskiy dogovor," RBC, June 2, 2015, http://top.rbc.ru/politics/02/06/2015/556d96c59a7947fc27b5bd3d.

26. "Skandal: Chekhia i Slovakia trebuiut obiasnenii ot Rossii iz-za filma o vtorzhenii v Chekhoslovakiiu," Top News, June 2, 2015, http://www.topnews.ru/news_id_78379.html.

27. Andrei Kolesnikov, "Tanki snova v Prage," Gazeta.ru, June 2, 2015, http://www.gazeta.ru/comments/column/kolesnikov/6742545.shtml.

28. Alexander Filippov, Alexander Danilov, and Anatolii Utkin, *Istoriia Rossii, 1945–2007* (Moscow: Prosveshchenie, 2008), 164.

29. Maxim Kim, *Istoriia SSSR (1938–1978 gg.)*, history textbook for the tenth grade, quoted in Ksenia Donskaia, "Ideologiia dlia shkolnikov: Kak v 90-e menialis uchebniki istorii," Teorii i praktiki, accessed January 13, 2020, https://special.theoryandpractice.ru/history-books.

30. "Godovshchina vvoda voisk v Chekhoslovakiiu," Levada, August 22, 2013, https://www.levada.ru/2013/08/22/godovshhina-vvoda-vojsk-v-chehoslovakiyu/.

31. Tomilina et al., *"Prazhskaya vesna."*

32. Alexander Zdanovich et al., *Chekhoslovatskie sobytiia 1968 goda glazami KGB i MVD SSSR* (Moscow: Obedinennaia redaktsiia MVD Rossii, 2010).

33. Zdanovich et al., *Chekhoslovatskie sobytiia 1968*, 2.

34. Igor Sofronov and Timur Makoev, "Po planu Dunai," *Na boevom postu* 11, no. 8 (August 2017): 54–57.

35. Leonid Maslovskii, "Chechoslovakia dolzna byt blagodarna SSSR za 1968 god: Istoria prazhkoi vesny,'" TV Zvezda, November 21, 2017, https://web.archive.org/web/20171121211212/https://tvzvezda.ru/news/qhistory/content/201711210834-qi97.htm.

36. Dmitrii Sergeev, "Praga-1968: vzgliad cherez pokoleniia," TV Zvezda, November 22, 2017, https://tvzvezda.ru/news/qhistory/content/201711221454-sil9.htm.

37. See, for example, Marek Švehla, "Chtějí nám namluvit, že Zeman postavil do latě Medveděva?," Respekt, November 23, 2017, https://www.respekt.cz/komentare/jak-zeman -postavil-do-late-medvedeva.

38. Ministry of Foreign Affairs of the Russian Federation, Dogovor o druzhestvennykh otnosheniiakh i sotrudnichestve mezhdu Rossiiskoi Federatsiei i Cheshkoi Respublikoi, August 26, 1993, http://www.mid.ru/foreign_policy/international_contracts/2_contract /-/storage-viewer/bilateral/page-320/48307.

39. "Vengerskoe vosstanie 1956 goda," Levada, October 20, 2016, https://www.levada .ru/2016/10/20/vengerskoe-vosstanie-1956-goda/.

40. Russian Ministry of the Interior, *Vengerskie sobytiia 1956 goda glazami KGB i MVD SSSR: Sbornik dokumentov* (Moscow: Obiedinennaia redaktsiia MVD Rossii, 2009).

41. "Interventsiia SSSR v Vengriu v 1956 godu pokhozha na nyneshniuiu agressiiu putinskoi Rossii v Ukrainu," Fakty i kommentarii, October 28, 2016, http://fakty.ua/224639 -intervenciya-ssso-v-vengriyu-v-1956-godu-pohozha-na-nyneshnyuyu-agressiyu-putinskoj -rossii-v-ukrainu.

42. "MID Rossii otkrestilsia ot slov Kiseleva o sobytiiakh v Vengrii v 1956 godu," *Snob*, October 26, 2016, https://snob.ru/selected/entry/115568.

43. President of Russia, "Zaiavlenie dlia pressy posle peregovorov s Prezidentom Vengrii Laslo Shoiomom," February 28, 2006, http://kremlin.ru/events/president/transcripts/23457.

44. Personal communication from Elena Zhemkova, May 18, 2018.

ŠTĚPÁN ČERNOUŠEK is Chairman of the Gulag.cz Association and cofounder of the Virtual Museum of the Gulag (http://www.gulag.online). He is also a board member of Memorial: An International Historical, Educational, Charitable and Human Rights Society. He is currently working on the two projects: "Czechoslovak Citizens in the Gulag" and "Protests against Occupation of Czechoslovakia in 1968 in the Warsaw Pact Countries."

Index

Lightning Source UK Ltd.
Milton Keynes UK
UKHW011947240322
400569UK00001B/62